PORK AND NOODLE SALAD
Recipe on page 123

If you're like me, when you see the food pages of *Better Homes and Gardens*® magazine for the first time each month, you get inspired to get into the kitchen and cook. Everything always looks so delicious—and when I take the recipes home to try them, they always taste delicious too.

I first see them when they come across my desk—for you, it may be when they arrive in your mailbox, but the effect they have is the same. Yummy, comforting Chicken-Butternut Squash Soup from the February issue was just the thing to warm up a cold winter night. Our fabulous twist on an Italian classic—Strawberry-Goat Cheese Bruschetta—motivated me to try something new with the sweet, ripe berries in peak season in May.

The inspiring effect of our recipes is one of the reasons we produce our wonderful recipe annuals. We know that throughout the year, you see recipes you want to try, and we want you to be able to put your finger right on them—all in one handy place.

We know the last year has been challenging for so many people. When the going gets tough, it's wise to cook smart and eat well. That's why we kept this year's food simple, accessible, and budget-conscious—and every bit as delicious and inspirational as previous years' recipes.

In April, we serve up main dishes featuring budget-friendly and healthful main dishes featuring vegetables. In September, "On Top of Spaghetti" features nine fresh ways with everyone's favorite noodle—from elegant Shrimp, Chickpea, and Feta Cheese Nests to fun and kid-friendly Mac and Cheese Spaghetti.

In every issue, the "Everyday Easy" section provides fresh ideas for getting dinner on the table on time (30 minutes or less) and on budget (less than $4 per serving), and we get to try cream-of-the-crop winning recipes from readers all over the country in the ever-popular Prize Tested Recipes® contest.

Also this year, award-winning Chef Scott Peacock joined us for our American Classics series, in which he presents the very best of the basics—buttermilk biscuits, meat loaf, chicken and dumplings, and pound cake among them. (Everyone here who has tried the buttermilk biscuit recipe at home agrees—they are the best we've ever made!)

Whether our recipes come from professional chefs, readers, or one of our food editors, each one has been tested and approved by the pros in the Better Homes and Gardens® Test Kitchen, so you can be assured that it will turn out perfectly every time you make it.

From our kitchen to yours—enjoy!

Gayle

Gayle Goodson Butler, Editor in Chief
Better Homes and Gardens® magazine

Our seal assures you that every recipe in *Better Homes and Gardens® Annual Recipes 2009* has been tested in the Better Homes and Gardens® Test Kitchen. This means that each recipe is practical and reliable, and meets our high standards of taste appeal. We guarantee your satisfaction with this book for as long as you own it.

All of us at Meredith Consumer Marketing are dedicated to providing you with information and ideas to enhance your home. We welcome your comments and suggestions. Write to us at: Meredith Consumer Marketing, 1716 Locust St., Des Moines, IA 50309-3023.

Pictured on front cover: Chocolate-Cherry Stack Cake, page 33

Better Homes and Gardens.
ANNUAL
Recipes
2009

MEREDITH CORPORATION CONSUMER MARKETING
Vice President, Consumer Marketing: David Ball
Consumer Product Marketing Director: Steve Swanson
Consumer Product Marketing Manager: Wendy Merical
Business Manager: Todd Voss
Associate Director, Production: Douglas M. Johnston

WATERBURY PUBLICATIONS, INC.
Editorial Director: Lisa Kingsley
Associate Editor: Tricia Laning
Creative Director: Ken Carlson
Associate Design Director: Doug Samuelson
Contributing Art Director: Jill Budden
Contributing Copy Editor: Margaret Smith
Contributing Proofreaders: Terri Fredrickson, Gretchen Kauffman
Contributing Indexer: Elizabeth T. Parson

BETTER HOMES AND GARDENS® MAGAZINE
Editor in Chief: Gayle Goodson Butler
Art Director: Michael D. Belknap
Dupty Editor, Food and Entertaining: Nancy Wall Hopkins
Senior Food Editor: Richard Swearinger
Associate Food Editor: Erin Simpson
Editorial Assistant: Renee Irey

MEREDITH PUBLISHING GROUP
President: Jack Griffin
Executive Vice President: Andy Sareyan
Vice President, Manufacturing: Bruce Heston

MEREDITH CORPORATION
Chairman of the Board: William T. Kerr
President and Chief Executive Officer: Stephen M. Lacy

In Memoriam: E.T. Meredith III (1933–2003)

What is the best way to remove the seeds from a pomegranate without making a mess? Will someone please give me some fresh ideas for cooking and freezing big batch recipes for a busy weeknight? How do I cook with pie pumpkin? What are the different types of ginger? And how do I make light-as-a-feather biscuits?

No matter how seasoned you are in the kitchen, chances are you have questions now and then. Page after page of this book offers the answers and inspiration you seek to put great meals on your table. You'll find recipes, tips, solutions, and ideas for making your cooking better, easier, more healthful, and more creative.

LOOK FOR:

- **Our Monthly Feature:** Each chapter kicks off with seasonally inspired recipes. Easy-to-fix vegetable-rich soups and bisques are the perfect solution for winter dinners. Lovely brunch recipes for celebrating the spring holidays. Fresh salads, tangy sauces, and succulent sliders are on the menu for a feed-a-crowd summer barbecue bash. When the temperatures fall in autumn, you'll warm up to comforting stews, breads, and pies. And as the holidays approach, we have you covered with recipes and ideas brimming with great taste and good cheer.

- **What's Cooking:** Here we offer a closer look at a seasonal technique, cooking style, or recipe category—ways to help your cooking become better, fresher, and easier throughout the year. In February we feature Valentine-worthy decadent, delicious treats. Looking for mouthwatering recipes for your bounty of strawberries? Take a look at "What's Cooking" in May for recipes both savory and sweet. October features recipes for pumpkins that go beyond pie.

- **Everyday Easy:** Sure, cooking for gatherings and special occasions is a joy, but we also know your daily dilemma is "what's for dinner tonight?" Each month brings an answer for each weeknight—offering fresh and simple recipes meant to be filling, fast, easy on the budget, and easy on you.

- **Good and Healthy:** Supernutritious salads, healthful sandwiches, lightened-up dips and snacks—here are doable ideas and up-to-date information to bring good nutrition to your daily routine.

- **American Classics:** Chef Scott Peacock is an award-winning Southern food expert. Each month he shares a delicious recipe emphasizing fresh and seasonal ingredients and how-to techniques.

- **Prize Tested Recipes:** Starting on page 272, you'll find the entire year's winners in our monthly recipe contest, along with Honor Roll recipes—those that didn't make it into the magazine but were too delectable to omit from this book.

- **Recipe Icons:** Many recipes are marked with icons that tell you if they're Fast (under 30 minutes), Kid-Friendly, or Low Fat (for the nutrition guidelines, see page 335).

25

126

239

256

contents 2009

115

192

65

163

105

january

Inspired casual meals and desserts—from America's most popular pan—plus cook-and-freeze recipes.

SPANISH-STYLE RICE WITH
WINTER VEGETABLES
Recipe on page 11

SKILLET BEEF
TENDERLOIN

Skillet Sessions

Six scrumptious recipes for the skillet

MARIO BATALI'S
SPANISH-STYLE RICE WITH WINTER VEGETABLES

Mario's Spanish-style rice is cooked like risotto. This is a hands-on method that yields a flavorful, creamy dish for a crowd.

PREP: 25 MIN. COOK: 30 MIN.

1	to 2 tsp. saffron threads (½ gram) or Spanish paprika
7	to 8 cups vegetable broth (two 32-oz. boxes)
2	cups Arborio or short-grain rice
1	medium carrot, coarsely chopped
1	medium red sweet pepper, coarsely chopped
1	small turnip, peeled and chopped
½	small acorn squash, peeled, seeded, and cubed
4	green onions, thinly sliced
1	cup cremini mushrooms, quartered
½	medium zucchini, chopped
5	to 6 Tbsp. olive oil
	Fresh thyme leaves

1. In small saucepan combine saffron and 1 cup *water*; bring to boiling. Remove from heat. In large saucepan bring broth to boiling; reduce heat. Cover and keep warm.
2. In 12-inch skillet combine saffron mixture and rice; bring to boiling over high heat. Simmer, stirring frequently, until most liquid is absorbed. Add carrot, sweet pepper, turnip, squash, and 1 cup hot broth; bring to boiling; reduce heat to medium. Simmer and stir until most liquid is absorbed. Continue adding broth, 1 cup at a time, stirring constantly until liquid is absorbed and rice is just tender (about 20 minutes, adding 5 cups broth total).
3. Add green onions, mushrooms, zucchini, and 1 cup broth. Cook and stir until liquid is absorbed. Add remaining 1 to 2 cups broth. Cook and stir until vegetables are tender and rice is tender yet slightly firm in the center (about 10 minutes, adding 2 to 3 cups broth total).
4. Remove from heat; stir in 4 tablespoons of the olive oil. To serve, drizzle with remaining olive oil and sprinkle with thyme.
MAKES 8 SERVINGS.

EACH SERVING *263 cal, 9 g fat (1 g sat. fat), 0 mg chol, 840 mg sodium, 43 g carbo, 2 g fiber, 4 g pro. Daily Values: 47% vit. A, 46% vit. C, 2% calcium, 13% iron.*

FAST
BOB RAE'S
SKILLET BEEF TENDERLOIN

START TO FINISH: 30 MIN.

4	6-oz. beef tenderloin steaks (½ to ¾ inch thick)
1	Tbsp. butter
1	tsp. cooking oil or olive oil
4	shallots, halved if large, or ½ medium red onion cut in wedges
2	Tbsp. cognac, brandy, or dry red wine
½	cup beef broth
1	Tbsp. butter, softened
	Snipped Italian (flat-leaf) parsley
	Crushed pink peppercorns (optional)
1	recipe Braised Swiss Chard

1. Sprinkle steaks with *salt* and *pepper*. In 12-inch skillet heat 1 tablespoon butter and the oil over high heat. Cook steaks 1 to 2 minutes, until browned on underside. Reduce heat to medium. Turn steaks; cook 6 minutes more or until desired doneness (145°F for medium-rare). Remove steaks; keep warm.
2. Add shallots to skillet. Cook 5 minutes or until crisp-tender. Remove skillet from heat. Add cognac; return to medium heat. Cook 2 minutes, stirring to scrape up browned bits from pan. Add broth. Reduce heat to medium-low. Whisk in 1 tablespoon softened butter until smooth. Return steaks to skillet. Heat, spooning sauce over steaks. Top with parsley and peppercorns. Serve with Braised Swiss Chard.
MAKES 4 SERVINGS.

BRAISED SWISS CHARD Trim stems from 1 pound Swiss chard; rinse and dry. In Dutch oven heat 2 tablespoons cooking oil over medium heat. Add chard, cover; cook 2 minutes, stirring occasionally. Season with salt and pepper.
EACH SERVING *434 cal, 25 g fat (9 g sat. fat), 129 mg chol, 763 mg sodium, 7 g carbo, 2 g fiber, 40 g pro. Daily Values: 138% vit. A, 57% vit. C, 11% calcium, 27% iron.*

meet the cooks

We looked to these skillet fans to create recipes for the 12-inch pan of their choice, whether it's their own design or a classic standby.

PAULA DEEN is a TV chef, restaurateur, and cookbook author. Her most recent book is *Paula Deen's Kitchen Wisdom and Recipe Journal* (Simon & Schuster, $18.95).

MARIO BATALI takes his love for food to Spain in his new PBS series and accompanying book with Gwyneth Paltrow, *Spain: A Culinary Road Trip* (Harper Collins, $34.95).

NANCY WALL HOPKINS is deputy food editor of *Better Homes and Gardens* magazine. The 12-inch cast-iron skillet that she purchased just out of college is still a favorite tool of hers.

BOB RAE is president of Meyer Corporation, which includes BonJour Gourmet. He designed its clad metal line of pans, including the 12-inch skillet in this story.

DEBBIE SHORE finds her 12-inch skillet just the right size to bring dinner to the table for her daughter, Sofia, and herself.

NANCY WALL HOPKINS' CHOCOLATE GINGERBREAD WITH SIMMERED ORANGES

PREP: 35 MIN. BAKE: 40 MIN. OVEN: 350°F

2¾	cups all-purpose flour
1	Tbsp. ground ginger
1	tsp. baking soda
1	tsp. baking powder
1	tsp. ground black pepper (optional)
½	tsp. salt
¼	tsp. ground cloves
1	cup full-flavor molasses
2	Tbsp. butter, melted
2	Tbsp. butter
¼	cup fresh peeled ginger, cut in slivers
½	cup butter, softened
1	cup sugar
2	eggs
1	cup chopped bittersweet chocolate
	Whipped cream
1	recipe Simmered Oranges
	Chopped crystallized ginger (optional)

1. Heat oven to 350°F. In bowl combine flour, ground ginger, baking soda, baking powder, pepper, salt, and cloves; set aside. In small bowl combine molasses, 1 cup *water*, and 2 tablespoons melted butter; set aside.

2. In 12-inch oven-going skillet cook and stir 2 tablespoons butter and slivered ginger over medium heat just until butter is melted. Remove from heat; set aside.

3. In mixing bowl beat the ½ cup softened butter on medium speed for 30 seconds. Add sugar; beat until combined. Add eggs, one at a time, beating 1 minute after each. Alternately beat in flour mixture and molasses mixture, beating on low speed after each addition until combined. Stir in chocolate. Pour batter over butter-ginger mixture in hot skillet.

4. Bake 40 to 45 minutes or until a wooden toothpick inserted in center comes out clean. Cool in skillet on rack 30 minutes (center may dip slightly). Serve warm topped with whipped cream, Simmered Oranges, and crystallized ginger.

MAKES 12 TO 16 SERVINGS.

SIMMERED ORANGES Slice 4 oranges crosswise about ¼ inch thick. Discard seeds. In 12-inch skillet over medium heat bring 1½ cups sugar, and ¼ cup *each* water, orange juice, and lemon juice to boiling, stirring to dissolve sugar; reduce heat. Simmer, uncovered, 10 minutes or until syrupy. Add orange slices. Return to boiling; reduce heat. Simmer, uncovered, 3 minutes or just until oranges are tender, turning occasionally. Transfer to serving bowl. Cool.

EACH SERVING WITH ORANGES *559 cal, 18 g fat (11 g sat. fat), 66 mg chol, 328 mg sodium, 99 g carbo, 3 g fiber, 5 g pro. Daily Values: 12% vit. A, 22% vit. C, 94% calcium, 22% iron.*

CHOCOLATE GINGERBREAD
WITH SIMMERED ORANGES

PEPPER-AVOCADO
OMELET

DEBBIE SHORE'S
PEPPER-AVOCADO OMELET

For impromptu guacamole, mash the remaining avocado half with prepared salsa.

PREP: 15 MIN. COOK: 13 MIN. STAND: 10 MIN.

1	medium poblano or green sweet pepper, roasted,* seeded, and chopped
2	Tbsp. butter
2	eggs, lightly beaten
½	medium avocado, peeled, seeded, and coarsely chopped
¼	jalapeño pepper, thinly sliced (optional)
¼	cup Manchego cheese, shredded (1 oz.)
	Crushed red pepper
1	recipe Fresh Tomato Compote
	Toast

1. Roast poblano pepper; set aside. In 12-inch nonstick skillet heat butter over medium-high heat. Add eggs; gently swirl to spread eggs to edge of skillet.
2. When eggs begin to bubble, sprinkle with poblano, avocado, and jalapeño.
3. When omelet is very lightly brown at edges, add cheese. With spatula, loosen egg from sides; fold half the omelet over filling. Season with *black pepper* and crushed red pepper. Serve with Fresh Tomato Compote and toast. **MAKES 2 SERVINGS.**

FRESH TOMATO COMPOTE In medium skillet heat 1 tablespoon olive oil. Add ½ cup thinly sliced onion; cook 5 minutes or until tender. Add 1 cup halved cherry tomatoes, 1 tablespoon snipped fresh parsley, and ⅛ teaspoon *each* salt and ground black pepper. Heat through; serve with omelet.
*TO ROAST PEPPER Heat oven to 425°F. Halve pepper lengthwise; remove stems and seeds. Place halves, cut sides down, on foil-lined baking sheet. Roast 20 to 25 minutes. Wrap pepper in foil; let stand 10 minutes. Gently pull off skin in strips, using a sharp knife to help loosen.

EACH SERVING *509 cal, 37 g fat (15 g sat. fat), 262 mg chol, 703 mg sodium, 35 g carbo, 7 g fiber, 16 g pro. Daily Values: 39% vit. A, 276% vit. C, 29% calcium, 32% iron.*

KID-FRIENDLY

PAULA DEEN'S
HERB-FRIED CHICKEN

Paula buys a whole chicken and cuts it up herself. If you prefer, you may substitute all white or all dark meat.

PREP: 30 MIN. CHILL: 2 HR. COOK: 14 MIN.

1	3-lb. chicken, washed and cut in 8 serving pieces
2	cups all-purpose flour
½	cup snipped fresh sage or parsley
1	tsp. cracked black pepper
3	eggs
½	cup milk
	Peanut oil for frying
	Small fresh sage leaves
	Lemon wedges

1. Sprinkle chicken pieces with *salt* and *pepper*. Refrigerate, covered, 2 to 4 hours.
2. In bowl combine flour, the ½ cup herbs, and pepper; set aside. In shallow dish whisk together eggs and milk. Dip chicken in egg mixture, then coat with flour mixture. Repeat.
3. In deep 12-inch skillet add oil to depth of 1 inch (oil will rise as chicken is added). Heat oil to 350°F over medium-high heat.
4. Gently lower four chicken pieces at a time into hot oil (oil may spatter). Cook 14 to 16 minutes, turning after 8 minutes, or until brown and crisp and chicken is no longer pink (170°F for breasts, 180°F for thighs). Oil temperature will drop when chicken is added; adjust heat as needed to maintain oil temperature at 325°F. Drain chicken on wire rack or paper towels. Place in preheated 300°F oven while frying remaining chicken. To serve, top with sage leaves and lemon wedges. **MAKES 6 SERVINGS.**
EACH SERVING *694 cal, 45 g fat (11 g sat. fat), 223 mg chol, 544 mg sodium, 35 g carbo, 2 g fiber, 37 g pro. Daily Values: 18% vit. A, 30% vit. C, 8% calcium, 24% iron.*

What's Cooking

Cook-and-freeze big batch recipes

1 LOW FAT
Cook and Freeze
SPICE-RUBBED CHICKEN

Save yourself a trip to the grocery store by buying several meals' worth of chicken breasts at once. Coat in this sweet-spicy rub and cook. Freeze individually wrapped so you can pull and thaw as many or few as you need for a quick lunch or dinner.

PREP: 15 MIN. BAKE: 18 MIN. COOL: 30 MIN.
OVEN: 400°F

¼	cup packed brown sugar
2	Tbsp. paprika
2	tsp. salt
2	tsp. ground coriander
1	tsp. ground black pepper
1	tsp. garlic powder
½	tsp. cayenne pepper
16	skinless, boneless chicken breast halves (about 5 lb.)
2	Tbsp. cooking oil

1. For spice rub, in small bowl combine brown sugar, paprika, salt, coriander, black pepper, garlic powder, and cayenne pepper. Brush chicken with oil. Sprinkle chicken with spice rub on both sides. With fingers, gently rub in spice mixture. Arrange on two 15×10×1-inch baking pans. Refrigerate chicken for 15 minutes. Heat oven to 400°F.
2. Bake chicken breasts, one pan at a time, uncovered, for 18 to 20 minutes or until no longer pink (170°F). (Refrigerate second pan of chicken, covered, while baking the first pan.)
3. Let chicken stand 30 minutes to cool. Individually wrap chicken breasts in waxed paper. Divide wrapped chicken among two large freezer bags, removing as much air as possible from bags. Label and freeze up to 4 months. Thaw and use for Chicken-Noodle Toss with Greens, *right,* or other recipes. **MAKES 16 CHICKEN BREASTS.**

EACH CHICKEN BREAST *202 cal, 4 g fat (1 g sat. fat), 82 mg chol, 373 mg sodium, 5 g carbo, 1 g fiber, 34 g pro. Daily Values: 29% vit. A, 1% vit. C, 3% calcium, 9% iron.*

QUICK THAW Thaw in microwave oven at 30% power (medium-low) for 4 to 5 minutes for one chicken breast, turning once. Increase time by 3 to 4 minutes for each additional chicken breast.

2 FAST LOW FAT
Thaw and Remake
CHICKEN-NOODLE TOSS WITH GREENS

START TO FINISH: 20 MIN.

4	cups water
6	oz. medium rice sticks (noodles)
1	Tbsp. olive oil
2	Spice-Rubbed Chicken breast halves, thawed and sliced
2	Tbsp. lime juice
2	Tbsp. soy sauce
1	medium green onion, sliced
1	cup arugula leaves
½	cup packed basil leaves
¼	cup lightly packed cilantro leaves
	Crushed red pepper (optional)

1. Bring water to boiling. Place noodles in large heatproof bowl. Add boiling water. Let stand 10 minutes or until tender. Drain and transfer to large bowl.
2. In large skillet heat oil over medium-high heat. Add chicken. Reduce heat to medium. Cook and stir for 2 minutes or until heated through. Remove from heat. Stir in lime juice, soy sauce, and green onion. Transfer to noodles in bowl. Add arugula, basil, and cilantro to noodles. Toss to combine. Sprinkle crushed red pepper.
MAKES 4 SERVINGS.

EACH SERVING *297 cal, 6 g fat (1 g sat. fat), 41 mg chol, 727 mg sodium, 39 g carbo, 2 g fiber, 20 g pro. Daily Values: 25% vit. A, 9% vit. C, 5% calcium, 9% iron.*

the essentials

SAVE MONEY by stocking up during grocery sales. Use within time guidelines below.

- Cooked chicken breasts: 4 months
- Cooked meat dishes: 3 months
- Uncooked poultry: 1 year
- Uncooked beef roasts/steaks: 1 year
- Uncooked pork roasts/chops: 6 months
- Uncooked ground beef: 4 months
- Frozen vegetables and fruits: 1 year
- Bread and tortillas: 3 to 6 months
- Butter: 6 months

1

LOW FAT

Cook and Freeze
COWBOY CHUCK ROAST WITH ONION GRAVY

Dividing and freezing this roast in four 2-serving portions makes for quicker thawing. You'll need to thaw two 2-serving portions to make Ranchero Beef Hash, right.

PREP: 25 MIN. COOK: 1½ HR.

1	2½- to 3-lb. boneless beef chuck pot roast
1	tsp. salt
½	tsp. ground black pepper
1	Tbsp. cooking oil
2	medium onions, cut in wedges
3	cloves garlic, minced
1	cup brewed coffee
1	14.5-oz. can diced tomatoes
¼	cup bottled mole sauce

1. Trim fat from beef. Season beef on all sides with salt and pepper. In 5-quart Dutch oven brown beef on all sides in hot oil. Remove beef from Dutch oven and set aside.

2. In same Dutch oven cook onions over medium heat 4 to 5 minutes or just until edges begin to brown. Stir in garlic; cook 1 to 2 minutes or until fragrant. Place beef on onion mixture. Add coffee, undrained tomatoes, and mole sauce. Bring to boiling. Reduce heat and simmer, covered, 1½ to 2 hours or until beef is tender.

3. Divide cooked beef and sauce into 4 portions in airtight freezer containers. Let cool 30 minutes before covering. Freeze up to 3 months. Thaw and use to make Ranchero Beef Hash, *right*, or other recipes. **MAKES FOUR 2-SERVING PORTIONS.**

EACH SERVING *255 cal, 9 g fat (2 g sat. fat), 62 mg chol, 729 mg sodium, 9 g carbo, 2 g fiber, 33 g pro. Daily Values: 33% vit. A, 10% vit. C, 5% calcium, 18% iron.*

QUICK THAW Thaw in microwave oven at 30% power (medium-low) for 12 to 14 minutes, stirring and breaking up meat halfway through.

well contained

2 FAST
Thaw and Remake
RANCHERO BEEF HASH

START TO FINISH: 20 MIN.

1	lb. small red potatoes, chopped
2	Tbsp. cooking oil
1	medium carrot, shredded
½	recipe Cowboy Chuck Roast with Onion Gravy (2 portions), thawed Salt and ground black pepper
1	Tbsp. butter
4	eggs Fresh or refrigerated salsa
1	recipe Tortilla Strips (optional)

1. For hash, place potatoes in a 1½-quart microwave-safe casserole. Add 2 tablespoons water. Cover and cook on 100% power (high) for 5 to 7 minutes or just until tender, stirring once. Drain potatoes.

2. In large skillet heat oil over medium-high heat. Add potatoes. Cook, stirring occasionally, until potatoes are lightly browned and tender. Stir in carrot; cook and stir 2 minutes. Add roast and gravy, using a spoon to break beef in bite-size pieces; heat through. Season to taste with salt and pepper. Keep warm.

3. In extra-large skillet melt butter over medium heat. Break eggs in skillet; season with salt and pepper. Reduce heat to low; cook eggs 3 to 4 minutes, until whites are set and yolks begin to thicken. (For more doneness, turn eggs and continue cooking 30 seconds.)

4. Divide hash among plates. Top with one egg and salsa. Serve with tortilla strips.

MAKES 4 SERVINGS.

TORTILLA STRIPS Preheat oven to 425°F. Brush both sides of 4 corn tortillas with 2 teaspoons olive oil. Cut tortillas in thin strips; place on a 15×10×1-inch baking pan. Bake, uncovered, 5 minutes. Stir strips; bake 5 to 7 minutes more or until strips are lightly browned and crisp; cool.

EACH SERVING *507 cal, 24 g fat (7 g sat. fat), 282 mg chol, 1,029 mg sodium, 31 g carbo, 5 g fiber, 42 g pro. Daily Values: 93% vit. A, 29% vit. C, 10% calcium, 29% iron.*

FREEZE FAST Quick and even freezing preserves the taste and texture of foods. Divide large amounts of food into 1- to 2-serving portions; let cool at room temperature for 30 minutes. (If cooling longer, refrigerate.) Once cool, seal containers and freeze. If freezing several items at once, allow enough space around them so cold air can circulate and freeze the food evenly.

SMART STORAGE Make freezer bags easy to stack and to thaw by laying the sealed bags in a wide metal pan to freeze flat. Once frozen, remove bags from pan and stack. Place items to be stored the longest in the coldest part of the freezer at the back. Use the door for items to be used soonest.

USE IT Attach an index card to the fridge to keep track of what's in the freezer and the date it went in. Before grocery shopping, check the list to see what you have on hand in the freezer.

LOW FAT

1 Cook and Freeze
BASIC BEEF BOLOGNESE

PREP: 15 MIN. COOK: 45 MIN.

2	lb. lean ground beef
3	medium onions, chopped
2	medium carrots, chopped
1	stalk celery, chopped
4	cloves garlic, minced
2	28-oz. cans crushed tomatoes
1	6-oz. can tomato paste
½	cup dark beer or beef broth
1	Tbsp. Italian seasoning, crushed
1	tsp. sugar
½	tsp. crushed red pepper
¼	cup chopped fresh basil

1. In 4- to 5-quart Dutch oven cook beef, onions, carrots, celery, and garlic over medium heat for 10 minutes or until browned. Drain off fat.

2. Stir in undrained tomatoes, tomato paste, beer, Italian seasoning, sugar, ½ teaspoon *salt*, and red pepper. Bring to boiling over medium-high heat; reduce heat. Simmer, covered, 30 minutes. Stir in fresh basil and cook, uncovered, 5 minutes more, stirring often. Season to taste with *salt* and *black pepper*.

3. Divide sauce into 1-cup or 2-cup portions in airtight freezer containers. Let cool 30 minutes before covering. Freeze up to 6 months. Thaw and use to make Smoky Calzones, *right*, or other tomato sauce recipes. **MAKES ABOUT 10 CUPS.**

EACH 1 CUP SERVING *238 cal, 9 g fat (3 g sat. fat), 57 mg chol, 535 mg sodium, 20 g carbo, 5 g fiber, 20 g pro. Daily Values: 70% vit. A, 37% vit. C, 9% calcium, 25% iron.*

QUICK THAW Thaw in microwave oven at 30% power (medium-low) for 5 to 6 minutes for 1-cup portion or 10 to 12 minutes for 2-cup portion, stirring halfway through.

2 KID-FRIENDLY
Thaw and Remake
SMOKY CALZONE

STAND: 15 MIN. PREP: 25 MIN. BAKE: 35 MIN.
COOL: 10 MIN. OVEN: 375°F

1	1-lb. frozen pizza dough, thawed (one-third of a 3-lb. pkg.) Cornmeal
2	Tbsp. snipped fresh oregano or 2 tsp. dried oregano, crushed
1	2-cup portion Basic Beef Bolognese sauce, thawed
2	cups shredded smoked Gouda or cheddar cheese (8 oz.)
⅓	cup shredded Parmesan cheese (1 oz.) Snipped fresh oregano (optional) Crushed red pepper (optional)
1	1-cup portion Basic Beef Bolognese sauce, thawed (optional)

1. Let dough stand at room temperature 15 minutes. Preheat oven to 375°F. Sprinkle a large baking sheet with cornmeal; set aside.

2. On lightly floured surface roll dough to 15×12-inch oval. If dough is difficult to roll, let it rest a few minutes once or twice during rolling. Transfer to prepared baking sheet. Lightly brush dough with *olive oil*; sprinkle with oregano.

3. Spread the 2 cups Bolognese sauce on half the dough to within 2½ inches of edges. Top with Gouda cheese. Fold dough over filling; press edges together. Seal edges by pressing with fork tines. With sharp knife, cut several holes in top crust. Brush top with *olive oil*. Sprinkle with Parmesan cheese.

4. Bake 35 to 40 minutes or until golden and crisp. Sprinkle oregano and crushed red pepper. Cool on wire rack 10 minutes before cutting. Heat the 1 cup Bolognese sauce in microwave on 100% power (high) for 1 to 2 minutes or until heated through. Pass for dipping. **MAKES 4 SERVINGS.**

EACH SERVING *684 cal, 32 g fat (15 g sat. fat), 92 mg chol, 1,216 mg sodium, 64 g carbo, 4 g fiber, 33 g pro. Daily Values: 47% vit. A, 20% vit. C, 52% calcium, 114% iron.*

february

Warm up late-winter days with beautiful soup, perfect buttermilk biscuits, and ginger-infused food and drink.

26

36

44

CHOCOLATE-CHERRY
STACK CAKE
Recipe on page 33

SMOKY TOMATO-SALMON
CHOWDER

Lovin' Spoonfuls

Vegetable-rich soups—the perfect solution for winter dinners.

LOW FAT

SMOKY TOMATO-SALMON CHOWDER

When only skin-on salmon is available, bake as directed, skin sides down. Once cooked, use a large spatula to lift the fillets from the skin; discard skin. Proceed as directed.

START TO FINISH: 45 MIN. OVEN: 425°F

3	6-oz. fresh or frozen skinless salmon fillets
1	to 2 tsp. chili powder
2	medium red sweet peppers, halved lengthwise and seeded
1	medium sweet onion, cut in ½-inch slices
1	jalapeño pepper,* halved lengthwise and seeded
2	14-oz. cans chicken broth
1	14.5-oz. can fire-roasted diced tomatoes
1	large tomato, chopped (about ¾ cup)
2	Tbsp. coarsely chopped fresh Italian (flat-leaf) parsley
1	medium avocado, peeled, pitted, and sliced
	Chili powder

1. Thaw salmon, if frozen. Pat dry with paper towels. Sprinkle with chili powder and ½ teaspoon *salt*. Cover and refrigerate while roasting vegetables.

2. Heat oven to 425°F. Place sweet peppers, onion, and jalapeño pepper, cut sides down, on foil-lined baking sheet. Roast 15 to 20 minutes. Loosely wrap vegetables in foil; let stand 15 minutes.

3. Meanwhile, place salmon in a shallow greased baking pan; fold under thin edges. Bake 4 to 6 minutes per ½-inch thickness or until salmon flakes easily when tested with a fork; keep warm.

4. With sharp knife loosen and peel off skins from peppers; discard skins. Coarsely chop peppers and onion; transfer to large saucepan. Add broth and undrained tomatoes. Bring to boiling, stirring occasionally. Remove from heat. Season with *salt* and *black pepper*. Fold in chopped tomato and parsley.

5. To serve, ladle chowder into shallow bowls. Break salmon in pieces and divide among bowls. Top with avocado slices and sprinkle with chili powder.

MAKES 6 MAIN-DISH SERVINGS.

*NOTE Hot chile peppers, such as jalapeños, contain oils that may burn the skin and eyes. Wear plastic gloves when working with hot peppers or thoroughly wash bare hands with soap and water after handling them.

EACH SERVING *218 cal, 9 g fat (1 g sat. fat), 48 mg chol, 976 mg sodium, 14 g carbo, 3 g fiber, 20 g pro. Daily Values: 40% vit. A, 115% vit. C, 4% calcium, 10% iron.*

FAST

PUMPKIN SOUP WITH SPICED CROUTONS

In just half an hour this soup and buttery croutons can be ready to warm you.

START TO FINISH: 30 MIN.

2	medium carrots, sliced
2	Tbsp. butter
1	medium onion, finely chopped
1	stalk celery, finely chopped
1	clove garlic, minced
2	15-oz. cans pumpkin
1	32-oz. box reduced-sodium chicken broth
½	cup half-and-half or light cream
½	cup water
3	Tbsp. maple syrup
1	tsp. pumpkin pie spice
1	recipe Spiced Croutons
	Celery leaves (optional)

1. In large saucepan cook carrots in hot butter over medium heat for 2 minutes; add onion, celery, and garlic. Cook 8 to 10 minutes or until vegetables are tender. **2.** Stir in pumpkin, broth, half-and-half, water, maple syrup, and pumpkin pie spice. Heat through. Season with *salt* and *pepper*. **3.** To serve, top soup with Spiced Croutons and celery leaves.

MAKES 8 SIDE-DISH SERVINGS.

SPICED CROUTONS In bowl toss 3 cups of 1-inch bread cubes with 2 teaspoons pumpkin pie spice. In a large skillet cook bread cubes in 2 tablespoons hot butter for 8 minutes or until toasted, turning occasionally.

EACH SERVING WITH SPICED CROUTONS
200 cal, 9 g fat (5 g sat. fat), 21 mg chol, 590 mg sodium, 28 g carbo, 4 g fiber, 5 g pro. Daily Values: 387% vit. A, 12% vit. C, 9% calcium, 14% iron.

ITALIAN SPINACH SOUP

Each bowl of this brothy soup holds a healthful portion of greens. In the produce aisle look for peppery watercress with small dark green leaves. If unavailable, use arugula.

START TO FINISH: 35 MIN.

1	medium onion, chopped
4	cloves garlic, minced
2	tsp. dried Italian seasoning, crushed
2	Tbsp. butter
2	Tbsp. dry sherry (optional)
2	14-oz. cans chicken broth
1	large potato, peeled and chopped
2	9-oz. pkgs. fresh spinach or 1¼ lb. fresh spinach, washed and trimmed
2	cups watercress, tough stems removed
2	oz. Parmesan cheese, shaved
2	small tomatoes, quartered, seeded, and thinly sliced

1. In 4-quart Dutch oven cook onion, garlic, and Italian seasoning in hot butter over medium heat for 5 minutes or until onion is tender, stirring occasionally. **2.** If using sherry, remove Dutch oven from heat; slowly pour in sherry. Return to heat; cook and stir 1 minute. Add broth and potato. Bring to boiling. Simmer, covered, 10 minutes or until potato is tender. Remove from heat. **3.** Set aside 2 cups of the spinach. Stir remaining spinach, half at a time, into soup just until wilted. Cool about 5 minutes. **4.** Transfer soup, half at a time, to food processor or blender; cover and process or blend until smooth. Return to Dutch oven; heat through. Season with *salt*. **5.** To serve, top with reserved spinach, watercress, Parmesan, and tomatoes.

MAKES 6 SIDE-DISH SERVINGS.

EACH SERVING *151 cal, 7 g fat (4 g sat. fat), 18 mg chol, 881 mg sodium, 16 g carbo, 4 g fiber, 8 g pro. Daily Values: 177% vit. A, 65% vit. C, 23% calcium, 16% iron.*

ITALIAN SPINACH SOUP

ALL-AMERICAN CHEESEBURGER SOUP

For the full cheeseburger experience, serve this dish with toasted buns, burger toppings, and potato wedges.

START TO FINISH: 40 MIN.

1	lb. ground beef
1	medium onion, chopped
1	stalk celery, chopped
2	cloves garlic, minced
2	Tbsp. all-purpose flour
2	14-oz. cans lower-sodium beef broth
2	medium potatoes, scrubbed and coarsely chopped
1	14½-oz. can diced tomatoes, drained
1	8-oz. pkg. shredded cheddar and American cheese blend (2 cups)
1	6-oz. can tomato paste
¼	cup ketchup
2	Tbsp. Dijon-style mustard
1	cup whole milk
	Toasted buns or rolls
	Cheeseburger toppings, such as pickles, onions, lettuce, mustard, and/or ketchup (optional)

1. In 4-quart Dutch oven cook beef, onion, celery, and garlic over medium heat until meat is browned and vegetables are tender; drain off fat. Sprinkle flour on beef mixture; cook and stir 2 minutes. Stir in broth and potatoes. Bring to boiling, stirring occasionally. Reduce heat. Simmer, covered, 10 minutes or until potatoes are tender.

2. Stir in tomatoes, cheese, tomato paste, ketchup, and mustard. Cook and stir until cheese is melted and smooth and soup just comes to gentle boiling. Stir in milk; heat through. Serve with toasted buns and cheeseburger toppings.

MAKES 6 MAIN-DISH SERVINGS.

EACH SERVING *477 cal, 27 g fat (13 g sat. fat), 93 mg chol, 1,309 mg sodium, 28 g carbo, 4 g fiber, 29 g pro. Daily Values: 25% vit. A, 44% vit. C, 34% calcium, 20% iron.*

ALL-AMERICAN
CHEESEBURGER SOUP

LOW FAT

TWO-PEA SOUP

Green peas, parsley, and lemon juice make this a bright, fresh pea soup. Dry split peas and pork make it thick and hearty.

START TO FINISH: 1 HR. 30 MIN. OVEN: 425°F

1	large onion, cut in wedges
2	medium carrots, cut in 1-inch pieces
2	stalks celery, cut in 1-inch pieces
3	cloves garlic, peeled
1	Tbsp. olive oil
1	cup dry split peas, rinsed and drained
2	lb. meaty smoked pork hocks
½	tsp. dried summer savory or marjoram, crushed
¼	tsp. ground black pepper
1	16-oz. pkg. frozen green peas
⅓	cup packed fresh Italian (flat-leaf) parsley leaves
2	Tbsp. lemon juice

1. Heat oven to 425°F. In shallow baking pan toss onion, carrots, celery, and garlic in olive oil to coat. Roast, uncovered, 15 to 20 minutes or until vegetables are lightly browned on the edges, stirring once.

2. In 4-quart Dutch oven combine roasted vegetables, 6 cups *water*, dry peas, pork hocks, savory, and pepper. Bring to boiling; reduce heat. Simmer, covered, 45 minutes, stirring occasionally. Remove pork; set aside.

3. Stir frozen peas and parsley into soup. Cool about 5 minutes. Transfer soup, half at a time, to food processor or blender. Cover; process or blend until nearly smooth. Return to Dutch oven. Stir in lemon juice.

4. When cool, cut pork off bones. Chop pork, discard bones. Set aside ½ cup pork to top soup; add remaining to puréed soup. Heat through. Season with *salt* and *pepper*. To serve, top with the reserved chopped pork. **MAKES 6 MAIN-DISH SERVINGS.**

EACH SERVING *267 cal, 5 g fat (1 g sat. fat), 25 mg chol, 663 mg sodium, 35 g carbo, 13 g fiber, 21 g pro. Daily Values: 107% vit. A, 42% vit. C, 7% calcium, 18% iron.*

Slow Cooker Two-Pea Soup

Thaw frozen peas; set aside. Finely chop onion, carrots, celery, and garlic (do not roast vegetables). In 4- to 5-quart slow cooker combine the chopped vegetables, dry split peas, savory, pepper, and 4½ cups water. Add pork hocks; cover. Cook on low for 9 to 10 hours or on high for 4½ to 5 hours. Remove pork hocks. Place thawed peas and parsley in a blender. Add about 1 cup of the soup; process until smooth. Stir into soup in slow cooker. Carefully cut pork off bones; chop and add to soup. Season to taste with salt and pepper. Just before serving, stir in lemon juice.

TWO-PEA SOUP

CHICKEN-BUTTERNUT SQUASH SOUP

If your family prefers small pieces of chicken, remove meat from bone, chop in bite-size chunks, and stir into the soup.

START TO FINISH: 45 MIN. OVEN: 425°F/350°F

- 1¼ lb. butternut squash, peeled, seeded, and cut in ¾-inch pieces (4 cups)
- 1 small red onion, cut in ½-inch wedges
- 1 Tbsp. curry powder
- 1 Tbsp. olive oil
- 3 14-oz. cans reduced-sodium chicken broth
- 1 15- to 16-oz. can garbanzo beans (chickpeas), rinsed and drained
- ⅓ cup dried apricots, snipped
- ½ cup chopped walnuts
- 1 tsp. olive oil
- ¼ tsp. freshly grated or ground nutmeg
- 1 deli-roasted chicken, cut up
  Fresh cilantro leaves

1. Heat oven to 425°F. In shallow roasting pan toss squash and onion with curry powder and the 1 tablespoon oil. Roast, uncovered, 20 minutes or until tender. Reduce oven temperature to 350°F.
2. In 4-quart Dutch oven combine roasted vegetables, broth, beans, and apricots. Bring to boiling; reduce heat. Simmer, covered, 10 minutes. Cool about 5 minutes. Transfer half the soup to food processor or blender. Cover; process or blend until smooth. Return to Dutch oven; heat through.
3. Meanwhile, in a bowl toss walnuts with 1 teaspoon oil and the nutmeg. Spread nuts on baking sheet. Bake 7 minutes or until golden and toasted. Reheat chicken according to package directions, if needed.
4. To serve, top soup with nuts, chicken, and cilantro. **MAKES 6 MAIN-DISH SERVINGS.**

EACH SERVING *577 cal, 35 g fat (9 g sat. fat), 167 mg chol, 1,905 mg sodium, 30 g carbo, 6 g fiber, 44 g pro. Daily Values: 176% vit. A, 32% vit. C, 7% calcium, 25% iron.*

BEET AND APPLE SOUP WITH HORSERADISH CREAM

Combining fresh beets and apple creates a mellow, slightly sweet soup. Puréeing in a food processor or with an immersion blender makes it smooth and luscious. A standard blender will leave it slightly chunky.

START TO FINISH: 50 MIN.

- 10 medium beets (about 2½ pounds)
- 1 medium sweet onion, chopped
- 1 medium potato, peeled and chopped
- 1 small cooking apple, such as Granny Smith or Gala, peeled, cored, and chopped
- 3 14-oz. cans reduced-sodium chicken broth
- 2 Tbsp. dry sherry or white balsamic vinegar
- 1 8-oz. carton sour cream
- 2 Tbsp. prepared horseradish
- ¼ tsp. cayenne pepper
- 1 recipe Skillet Beets (optional)

1. Peel eight of the beets* and cut each in 1-inch pieces. (Reserve remaining two beets to make Skillet Beets.) In 4-quart Dutch oven combine the chopped beets, onion, potato, apple, and broth; bring to boiling. Reduce heat. Simmer, covered, 25 to 30 minutes or until tender. Cool about 5 minutes.
2. Transfer soup, half at a time, to food processor. Cover; process until smooth. (Or blend with immersion blender.) Return to Dutch oven. Stir in sherry. Season to taste with *salt* and *black pepper*. Heat through.
3. For Horseradish Cream, in small bowl combine sour cream, horseradish, and cayenne pepper; stir about ½ cup cream mixture into hot soup. Set remaining aside.
4. To serve, top soup with a dollop of Horseradish Cream and the Skillet Beets. **MAKES 6 TO 8 SIDE-DISH SERVINGS.**

SKILLET BEETS Trim tops from the two reserved beets to leave 1 inch of stem. Peel and thinly slice beets, from top to bottom. In large skillet cook beet slices in 2 tablespoons hot oil over medium heat 8 minutes or until tender, turning once.
*NOTE Peel beets with a sharp vegetable peeler or paring knife. To avoid staining your hands, wear gloves.

EACH SERVING *222 cal, 9 g fat (5 g sat. fat), 17 mg chol, 729 mg sodium, 31 g carbo, 6 g fiber, 7 g pro. Daily Values: 21% vit. A, 29% vit. C, 9% calcium, 9% iron.*

CHICKEN-BUTTERNUT SQUASH SOUP

BEET AND APPLE SOUP WITH
HORSERADISH CREAM

Make it kid-friendly

When serving soup to children, let them play dress-up
with their bowls by offering fun toppers. Serve an
assortment of bite-size crackers in shapes and colors.
Or, for a hands-on approach, let kids cut bread slices,
puff pastry, or pie pastry with small cookie cutters.
Bake until crisp and golden. For a healthful topper for
Beet and Apple Soup, slice apples crosswise to reveal
the star-shape core (be sure to remove the seeds).
Crumbled bacon, grated cheese, sliced pickles,
sunflower seeds, or fried tortilla or wonton wrapper
strips add variety. Ladle up the kids' bowls first so the
soup can cool. Serve with small spoons for them to
scoop up every bite.

What's Cooking
Sweet Comebacks

VERY RASPBERRY FRAPPÉS

The ratio of fruit to milk to gelato is balanced to make a drink that's too thick for a straw but perfect for a spoon. Substitute your favorite fruits if you like.

START TO FINISH: 15 MIN.

1½	cups frozen or fresh raspberries
3	Tbsp. raspberry liqueur or milk
1	Tbsp. seedless raspberry jam
2	cups raspberry or other berry gelato or ice cream
¼	cup milk
⅓	cup chopped chocolate bars, crushed shortbread cookies, or chocolate wafer cookies
	To top drink: Chocolate bars, shortbread cookies, or chocolate wafer cookies

1. Thaw raspberries, if frozen. Place 1 cup of the berries in blender or food processor. Cover and blend or process until smooth. Press puréed berries through fine-mesh sieve into bowl. Discard seeds. Add liqueur and jam to puréed berries; whisk until smooth.

2. For frappé, in blender or processor combine berry mixture, gelato, and milk. Cover and blend or process just until combined, stopping blender to scrape down sides as needed. Stir in chopped chocolate or crushed cookies.

3. Divide the remaining berries and frappé between two chilled glasses. Top with chocolate or cookies. Serve with long-handled spoons. **MAKES 2 SERVINGS.**

EACH SERVING *574 cal, 10 g fat (6 g sat. fat), 9 mg chol, 46 mg sodium, 109 g carbo, 7 g fiber, 5 g pro. Daily Values: 3% vit. A, 52% vit. C, 13% calcium, 5% iron.*

CHOCOLATE-CHERRY STACK CAKE

PREP: 40 MIN. BAKE: 22 MIN.

COOL: 10 MIN. OVEN: 350°F

¾	cup plus 1 tsp. all-purpose flour
⅓	cup plus 1 tsp. unsweetened cocoa powder
1	tsp. baking powder
½	tsp. baking soda
½	tsp. ground cinnamon
¼	tsp. salt
⅓	cup unsalted butter, softened
¾	cup sugar
2	eggs
1	tsp. vanilla
½	cup sour cream
1	recipe Cherry or Chocolate Frosting
1	recipe Chocolate-Dipped Cherries (optional)

1. Heat oven to 350°F. Grease two 6×2-inch round cake pans or springform pans. Mix 1 teaspoon *each* flour and cocoa powder; dust pans. Set pans aside.

2. In bowl combine ¾ cup flour, ⅓ cup cocoa powder, baking powder, baking soda, cinnamon, and salt; set aside.

3. In large mixing bowl with electric mixer beat butter on medium to high speed for 30 seconds. Add sugar; beat until smooth and fluffy. Beat in eggs and vanilla until smooth. Beat in sour cream and flour mixture. Pour batter in pans; spread evenly.

4. Bake 22 to 26 minutes or until tops spring back when lightly touched and edges begin to pull away from sides of pans. Cool in pans on wire rack 10 minutes. Remove from pans; cool on rack.

5. Use serrated knife to horizontally cut cakes in half to make 4 layers total. Place bottom layer on plate; spread with ⅔ cup frosting. Repeat with two more layers. Place top layer on cake. Heap remaining frosting, swirling in peaks. Refrigerate. To serve, top with Chocolate-Dipped Cherries.

MAKES 8 SERVINGS.

ALPHABET CUPCAKES

CHERRY FROSTING In large mixing bowl combine one 8-ounce carton sour cream, 1 cup whipping cream, 1½ cups powdered sugar, and 2 tablespoons maraschino cherry juice. Beat on medium-high until fluffy.

CHOCOLATE FROSTING In large mixing bowl combine one 8-ounce carton sour cream, 1 cup whipping cream, 1½ cups powdered sugar, and ¼ cup sifted unsweetened cocoa powder. Beat on medium-high speed until fluffy.

CHOCOLATE-DIPPED CHERRIES Drain 16 maraschino cherries with stems; pat dry with paper towels. In small microwave-safe bowl combine ½ cup semisweet chocolate pieces and 1 teaspoon shortening. Cook on 50% power (medium) 1½ to 2 minutes or until melted, stirring once. Dip cherries in chocolate; place on waxed paper until set. Store, covered, up to 24 hours.

ALPHABET CUPCAKES Preheat oven to 350°F. Prepare Chocolate-Cherry Stack Cake batter, *left.* Line sixteen 2½-inch muffin cups with paper bake cups. Fill each cup with two slightly rounded tablespoons of cake batter. Bake 18 minutes or until tops spring back. Cool completely on wire rack. To assemble, top each cupcake with Cherry or Chocolate Frosting (some frosting will be left over). Top with Alphabet Cookies.

ALPHABET COOKIES On a lightly floured surface knead ⅓ cup all-purpose flour into half of a 16.5-ounce package of refrigerated sugar cookie dough. Roll dough ¼ inch thick. Brush lightly with water; sprinkle with coarse red sugar. Cut 16 small cookies for cupcakes; cut remainder in other shapes. Bake small cookies in a preheated 375°F oven for 6 minutes; bake large cookies 7 to 8 minutes. Cool on wire racks. Use to decorate cupcakes.

EACH SERVING (1 SLICE) CAKE *492 cal, 29 g total fat (18 g sat. fat), 132 mg chol, 250 mg sodium, 56 g carbo, 2 g fiber, 6 g pro. Daily Values: 20% vit. A, 1% vit. C, 13% calcium, 8% iron.*

KID-FRIENDLY

CHOCOLATE-MALTED MOUSSE

PREP: 30 MIN. COOL: 30 MIN. CHILL: 1 TO 24 HR.

2	oz. malted milk balls (about ⅔ cup)
4	oz. milk chocolate, coarsely chopped
3	oz. bittersweet chocolate, coarsely chopped
3	cups whipping cream
⅓	cup chocolate malted milk powder
2	Tbsp. chocolate liqueur, almond liqueur, or milk
½	tsp. vanilla
1	Tbsp. sugar
2	tsp. unsweetened cocoa powder
	Malted milk balls (optional)

1. Place the 2 ounces malted milk balls in large resealable plastic bag; finely crush with rolling pin. Set aside.

2. For mousse, in small saucepan heat milk chocolate and bittersweet chocolate with ¼ cup of the whipping cream over low heat until smooth, stirring constantly. Stir in malted milk powder, liqueur, and vanilla. Cool to room temperature.

3. In large chilled mixing bowl with chilled beaters beat 1¾ cups whipping cream to stiff peaks (tips stand straight). Stir about ½ cup of the whipped cream into melted chocolate mixture; fold chocolate mixture into remaining whipped cream. Fold in crushed malted milk balls. Spoon into 1½- to 2-quart dish or 8 to 10 small bowls or glasses. Cover and refrigerate 1 to 24 hours.

4. In medium chilled bowl combine remaining 1 cup whipping cream, sugar, and cocoa powder; beat to soft peaks. Spoon on mousse. Top with malted milk balls.

MAKES 8 TO 10 SERVINGS.

EACH SERVING 520 cal, 43 g fat (27 g sat. fat), 127 mg chol, 90 mg sodium, 31 g carbo, 2 g fiber, 4 g pro. Daily Values: 27% vit. A, 2% vit. C, 12% calcium, 6% iron.

BITTERSWEET CHOCOLATE-WALNUT MERINGUE KISSES

PREP: 25 MIN. BAKE: 1½ HR. STAND: 30 MIN.
OVEN: 300°F/200°F

2	egg whites
¼	tsp. cream of tartar
½	cup superfine or regular granulated sugar
2	oz. bittersweet chocolate, coarsely chopped
⅓	cup chopped walnuts, toasted

1. Let egg whites stand in large bowl at room temperature 30 minutes. Heat oven to 300°F. Line cookie sheet with parchment paper or lightly greased foil.

2. Beat egg whites and cream of tartar on medium to high speed until soft peaks form (tips curl). Gradually add sugar, about 1 tablespoon at a time, beating until glossy and stiff peaks form (tips stand straight). Fold in ¼ cup of the chocolate and ¼ cup of the nuts.

3. Drop meringue in six mounds 2 inches apart on prepared sheet. Using back of spoon, swirl the top of each meringue into a high tip that curls.

4. Place meringues in oven; immediately decrease oven temperature to 200°F. Bake 1½ hours or until crisp and dry on outsides. Cool completely on sheet on wire rack. Gently peel cooled meringues off parchment or foil. To serve, sprinkle with remaining chocolate and nuts.

5. Store meringues in an airtight container at room temperature up to 24 hours.

MAKES 6 MERINGUES.

EACH SERVING 160 cal, 8 g fat (3 g sat. fat), 0 mg chol, 19 mg sodium, 23 g carbo, 1 g fiber, 3 g pro. Daily Values: 1% calcium, 5% iron.

CHOCOLATE-MALTED MOUSSE

meringue made easy

USE THE RIGHT BOWL. A metal, glass, or stoneware bowl is best for making meringue. Grease will prevent whites from incorporating air, so avoid plastic—which can be hard to get completely grease-free.

TELLTALE SIGNS If you've never made meringue, or it's been a while, the key to success is to watch the "look" of the egg whites. When they have a satin sheen, it's time to add more sugar. If they become lumpy or grainy, the eggs have been beaten too long. Toss them and start over.

Everyday Easy

Winter Warm-Ups

FAST | LOW FAT

TURKEY STEAKS WITH SPINACH, PEARS, AND BLUE CHEESE

START TO FINISH: 20 MIN.
BUDGET $2.85 PER SERVING

2	turkey breast tenderloins (1 to 1¼ lb.)
1	tsp. dried sage, crushed
	Salt and freshly ground black pepper
2	Tbsp. butter
1	6-oz. pkg. fresh baby spinach
1	large pear, cored and thinly sliced
¼	cup crumbled blue cheese

1. Horizontally split tenderloins to make four ½-inch-thick steaks. Rub turkey with sage; sprinkle with salt and pepper. In extra-large skillet cook steaks in 1 tablespoon of the butter over medium-high heat for 14 to 16 minutes or until no longer pink (170°F), turning once. (Reduce heat to medium if turkey browns too quickly.) Remove from skillet. Add spinach to skillet. Cook and stir just until wilted.

2. Meanwhile, in small skillet cook pear slices in remaining 1 tablespoon butter over medium to medium-high heat, stirring occasionally, for 5 minutes or until tender and lightly browned.

3. Serve steaks with spinach and pears. Top with blue cheese. **MAKES 4 SERVINGS.**
EACH SERVING *240 cal, 9 g fat (5 g sat. fat), 92 mg chol, 380 mg sodium, 8 g carbo, 2 g fiber, 31 g pro. Daily Values: 85% vit. A, 23% vit. C, 11% calcium, 14% iron.*

FAST

MINI MEAT LOAVES WITH GREEN BEANS

START TO FINISH: 22 MIN.
BUDGET: $3.25 PER SERVING

1	egg, lightly beaten
1	cup purchased pasta sauce
½	cup fine dry bread crumbs
¼	cup fresh basil leaves, coarsely chopped if large
1	lb. lean ground beef
1	cup shredded mozzarella cheese (4 oz.)
1	12-oz. pkg. fresh green beans, trimmed
1	Tbsp. olive oil
	Crushed red pepper (optional)

1. Heat oven to 450°F. Bring a medium saucepan of salted water to boiling.

2. Meanwhile, in a large bowl combine egg, ½ cup of the pasta sauce, bread crumbs, 2 tablespoons of the basil, and ¼ teaspoon *salt*. Add beef and ½ cup of the cheese; mix well. Divide beef mixture in four equal portions. Shape each portion in a 5½×2-inch oval. Place on 15×10×1-inch baking pan. Spoon on remaining pasta sauce and sprinkle with remaining cheese. Bake 15 minutes or until internal temperature registers 160°F.

3. Meanwhile, cook green beans in boiling salted water for 10 minutes. Drain; toss with 1 tablespoon olive oil and red pepper. Serve with meat loaves. Sprinkle all with remaining basil leaves. **MAKES 4 SERVINGS.**
EACH SERVING *496 cal, 29 g fat (12 g sat. fat), 145 mg chol, 742 mg. sodium, 25 g carbo, 5 g fiber, 34 g pro. Daily Values: 29% vit. A, 26% vit. C, 30% calcium, 27% iron.*

TURKEY STEAKS WITH SPINACH, PEARS, AND BLUE CHEESE

MINI MEAT LOAVES
WITH GREEN BEANS

FISH TOSTADAS WITH
CHILI-LIME CREAM

FAST

FISH TOSTADAS WITH CHILI-LIME CREAM

START TO FINISH: 20 MIN.
BUDGET $2.08 PER SERVING

1	lb. fresh tilapia or cod fillets
½	tsp. chili powder
1	lime, halved
½	cup sour cream
½	tsp. garlic powder
8	6-inch tostada shells
2	cups shredded cabbage mix
1	avocado, halved, seeded, peeled, and sliced (optional)
1	cup cherry tomatoes, quartered (optional)
	Bottled hot pepper sauce (optional)

1. Preheat broiler. Sprinkle fish with ¼ teaspoon of the chili powder and ¼ teaspoon *salt*. For chili-lime cream, in bowl squeeze 2 teaspoons juice from half the lime. Stir in sour cream, garlic powder, and remaining chili powder; set aside. Cut remaining lime half in wedges for serving.
2. Place fish on unheated greased broiler rack; tuck under thin edges. Place shells on baking sheet on lowest rack. Broil fish 4 inches from heat 4 to 6 minutes per ½-inch thickness, until fish flakes with fork. Break in chunks. Serve tostadas with cabbage, chili-lime cream, avocado, tomatoes, lime, and pepper sauce.
MAKES 4 SERVINGS.
EACH SERVING *278 cal, 14 g fat (5 g sat. fat), 67 mg chol, 303 mg sodium, 17 g carbo, 2 g fiber, 25 g pro. Daily Values: 6% vit. A, 25% vit. C, 7% calcium, 6% iron.*

SMOKY MUSHROOM STROGANOFF

HERBED CHICKEN, ORZO, AND ZUCCHINNI

FAST | **LOW FAT**

SMOKY MUSHROOM STROGANOFF

START TO FINISH: 18 MIN.
BUDGET $3.28 PER SERVING

1	8.8-oz. pkg. dried pappardelle (wide egg noodles)
1½	lb. pkg. sliced mushrooms, such as button, cremini, and/or shiitake
2	cloves garlic, minced (1 tsp.)
1	Tbsp. olive oil
1	8-oz. carton light sour cream
2	Tbsp. all-purpose flour
1½	tsp. smoked paprika
1	cup vegetable broth
	Snipped fresh Italian (flat-leaf) parsley (optional)

1. Cook noodles according to package directions. Drain; keep warm.
2. In extra-large skillet cook mushrooms and garlic in hot oil over medium-high heat 5 to 8 minutes or until tender, stirring occasionally. (Reduce heat if mushrooms brown quickly.) Remove with slotted spoon; cover to keep warm.
3. For sauce, in bowl combine sour cream, flour, paprika, and ¼ teaspoon *pepper*. Stir in broth until smooth. Add to skillet. Cook and stir until thickened and bubbly; cook and stir 1 minute more. Serve mushroom mixture and sauce over noodles. Sprinkle parsley. **MAKES 4 SERVINGS.**
EACH SERVING *407 cal, 13 g fat (5 g sat. fat), 72 mg chol, 443 mg sodium, 59 g carbo, 4 g fiber, 17 g pro. Daily Values: 15% vit. A, 9% vit. C, 11% calcium, 22% iron.*

FAST | **LOW FAT**

HERBED CHICKEN, ORZO, AND ZUCCHINI

START TO FINISH: 20 MIN.
BUDGET $3.12 PER SERVING

1	cup dried orzo
4	small skinless, boneless chicken breast halves (1 to 1¼ lb.)
1	tsp. dried basil
3	Tbsp. olive oil
2	medium zucchini, sliced
2	Tbsp. red wine vinegar
1	Tbsp. snipped fresh dill
	Lemon wedges (optional)
	Snipped fresh dill (optional)

1. Prepare orzo according to package directions; drain. Cover and keep warm.
2. Meanwhile, sprinkle chicken with the basil; season with *salt* and *ground black pepper*. In large skillet heat 1 tablespoon of the olive oil. Add chicken and cook 12 minutes or until no longer pink (170°F), turning once. Remove from skillet. Add zucchini to skillet; cook for 3 minutes or until crisp-tender.
3. In bowl whisk together vinegar, the remaining olive oil, and the 1 tablespoon fresh dill. Add orzo; toss. Season with *salt* and *pepper*. Serve chicken with orzo, zucchini, and fresh lemon wedges; sprinkle dill. **MAKES 4 SERVINGS.**
EACH SERVING *390 cal, 12 g fat (2 g sat. fat), 66 mg chol, 233 mg sodium, 35 g carbo, 3 g fiber, 33 g pro. Daily Values: 5% vit. A, 31% vit. C, 5% calcium, 16% iron.*

Good and Healthy

The Power of Ginger

Often called gingerroot, ginger is actually a knobby horizontal stem—known as a rhizome—that grows underground and has a warm, spicy, slightly citrus flavor. It has been used for centuries in China, the Mediterranean, and the West Indies for its culinary and medicinal properties. Traditionally, Western cuisines have used ginger primarily in desserts. Thanks to the growing attention to its healthful properties, ginger has made its way onto breakfast, lunch, and dinner tables across the country.

FAST | LOW FAT

STEAMED COD WITH GINGERY MUSHROOMS

PREP: 15 MIN. COOK: 8 MIN. PLUS 4 TO 6 MIN. PER ½-INCH THICKNESS OF FISH

1	lb. fresh or frozen skinless Alaska or gray cod, or tilapia fillets
½	tsp. ground ginger
1	Tbsp. finely chopped fresh ginger
2	tsp. canola oil
8	oz. fresh shiitake mushrooms, stemmed and halved
1	large red sweet pepper, seeded and cut in rings
½	cup sliced green onions
¼	cup dry white wine or reduced-sodium chicken broth
⅔	cup reduced-sodium chicken broth
	Thin strips green onions (optional)
	Thin slices fresh ginger (optional)

1. Thaw fish, if frozen. In a bowl combine the ½ teaspoon ground ginger, ¼ teaspoon *salt*, and ¼ teaspoon *black pepper*. Sprinkle on fish; set aside.

2. In skillet cook the 1 tablespoon fresh ginger in hot oil over medium-high heat for 15 seconds. Add mushrooms, pepper, and the ½ cup onions. Cook 5 minutes or until mushrooms are tender, stirring occasionally. Remove skillet from heat; add wine. Return to heat. Cook and stir until wine is almost evaporated. Add broth; bring to boiling.

3. Place fish on vegetables in skillet. Reduce heat; maintain gentle boiling. Cook, covered, 4 to 6 minutes for each ½-inch thickness of fish or until fish flakes easily when tested with fork. Serve fish and vegetables topped with onion strips and fresh ginger. Spoon cooking liquid over all. **MAKES 4 SERVINGS.**

EACH SERVING *155 cal, 3 g fat (0 g sat. fat), 48 mg chol, 308 mg sodium, 6 g carbo, 2 g fiber, 23 g pro. Daily Values: 22% vit. A, 71% vit. C, 3% calcium, 6% iron.*

types of ginger

1. GINGERROOT
WHAT Fresh ginger, native to southeast Asia.

FLAVOR The feistiest form; hot, spicy flavor.

FIND IT In the produce section. It's affordable —these recipes use about a quarter's worth each. A 4-inch piece yields 4 tablespoons, chopped.

USE IT Asian foods; in coleslaw and salads.

2. PICKLED GINGER
WHAT Slices of ginger briefly cooked and pickled in a vinegar-sugar brine.

FLAVOR Tangy, slightly hot, and refreshing.

FIND IT In jars in the Asian section of larger supermarkets.

USE IT Serve with sushi. Finely chop and add to rice, tuna salad, or sautéed broccoli.

3. CANDIED GINGER
WHAT Chunks of ginger cooked in sugar syrup.

FLAVOR Sweet with a touch of heat.

FIND IT Spice aisle or cookware stores.

USE IT Add to trail mix or chop and scatter on vegetables or desserts. Especially good with dark chocolate desserts.

4. GROUND GINGER
WHAT Dried, ground ginger— the most familiar form of the spice.

FLAVOR Mildly hot with assertive ginger flavor.

FIND IT Spice aisle.

USE IT Baking and spice rubs. To substitute for fresh ginger, use ¼ teaspoon for every 1 teaspoon fresh.

STEAMED COD WITH
GINGERY MUSHROOMS

why ginger is good for you

SOOTHES TROUBLED TUMMIES
Research backs up some grandmothers' claims that a cup of ginger tea can reduce nausea during pregnancy. Ginger wards off motion sickness too. Studies show medication is more effective for serious seasickness, but for mild discomfort, ginger may do the trick.

FIGHTS INFLAMMATION
High levels of inflammation have been linked to cancer, heart disease, asthma, and more, says nutritionist Monica Reinagel. Ginger appears to be an anti-inflammatory food. Reinagel says ¼ to ½ teaspoon of powdered or chopped fresh ginger worked into the diet may help reduce inflammation if consumed daily.

PROVIDES ANTIOXIDANTS
Ginger is ranked one of the top 50 foods because of these disease-fighting qualities. While you can't eat ginger in the same quantity as other antioxidant-rich foods, such as berries, it can still be a valuable addition to your diet.

GINGER
TEA

FAST | LOW FAT

DOUBLE-GINGERED ORANGE CARROTS

Use a sharp vegetable peeler to slice ginger in long, thin shavings.

PREP: 10 MIN. COOK: 20 MIN.

- 1½ lb. baby carrots with tops, trimmed, or 1 lb. small to medium carrots
- 2 tsp. olive oil
- ¼ cup orange juice
- 1 1-inch piece fresh ginger, peeled and shaved or cut in very thin slices
- 2 Tbsp. chopped, toasted hazelnuts
- 1 Tbsp. chopped crystallized ginger

1. Halve baby carrots lengthwise. Quarter small carrots lengthwise; cut crosswise in 3-inch pieces.
2. In nonstick skillet cook carrots in hot olive oil over medium heat 10 minutes, stirring once. Add orange juice, fresh ginger, and ¼ teaspoon *salt*; toss to coat. Cook, covered, 6 to 8 minutes or until carrots are tender. Uncover; cook 2 minutes or until liquid is reduced by half.
3. To serve, sprinkle with nuts and crystallized ginger. **MAKES 4 SERVINGS.**
EACH SERVING *109 cal, 5 g fat (1 g sat. fat), 0 mg chol, 224 mg sodium, 16 g carbo, 4 g fiber, 2 g pro. Daily Values: 380% vit. A, 15% vit. C, 4% calcium, 4% iron.*

FAST | LOW FAT

GINGER TEA

Soothing and healthful, this tea is good hot, iced, and as the sparkling fizz, above right.

PREP: 5 MIN. STAND: 5 MIN.

- 1 cup boiling water
- 4 ⅛-inch slices fresh ginger
- 1 small sprig fresh rosemary or fresh mint, or 2 strips lemon peel*
- ½ tsp. honey

1. Pour water in cup. Add fresh ginger, rosemary, and honey. Stir to dissolve honey. Steep 5 minutes. Remove ginger and rosemary or, for intense ginger and rosemary flavor, leave in ginger and rosemary while sipping. **MAKES 1 SERVING.**
ICED GINGER TEA Prepare Ginger Tea; remove ginger and rosemary. Refrigerate, covered, 2 hours. Serve over ice.

SPARKLING GINGER FIZZ Prepare Iced Ginger Tea using six ⅛-inch slices of fresh ginger. Pour tea in tall ice-filled glass. Pour in calorie-free ginger ale, carbonated water, or sparkling white wine.
***NOTE** Use only yellow peel; avoid the white pith of the lemon.
EACH SERVING HOT OR ICED TEA *11 cal, 0 g fat, 0 mg chol, 47 mg sodium, 3 g carbo, 0 g fiber, 0 g pro. Daily Values: 1% calcium.*

LOW FAT

GINGER-BEEF LETTUCE WRAPS

PREP: 20 MIN. FREEZE: 30 MIN.
MARINATE: 4 HR. COOK: 7 MIN.

- 1 lb. beef flank steak or boneless beef top round steak
- 1 medium yellow or green sweet pepper, seeded, cut in bite-size strips
- 1 small zucchini, trimmed and cut in thin bite-size strips
- ½ medium red onion, cut in thin wedges
- ⅓ cup ginger beer or ginger ale
- 3 Tbsp. reduced-sodium soy sauce
- 2 cloves garlic, minced
- ½ tsp. cornstarch
- 2 tsp. canola oil
- 2 Tbsp. finely chopped fresh ginger
- 12 Bibb or leaf lettuce leaves (about 2 heads)
- ¼ cup fresh cilantro leaves

1. Trim fat from beef. For easy slicing, wrap and freeze beef 30 to 45 minutes or until firm. Thinly slice beef across grain; place slices in self-sealing plastic bag. In a second self-sealing plastic bag combine sweet pepper, zucchini, and onion.
2. For marinade, in bowl combine ginger beer, soy sauce, and garlic. Divide marinade between beef and vegetables. Seal bags; turn to coat each. Refrigerate 4 to 6 hours, turning bags occasionally. Drain marinades into bowl. Stir in cornstarch; set aside.
3. Heat oil in large nonstick wok or extra-large nonstick skillet over medium-high heat. Add ginger; stir-fry 15 seconds. Add vegetables; stir-fry 3 to 5 minutes or until crisp-tender. Remove vegetables. Add half the beef to wok. Stir-fry 2 to 3 minutes or until beef is slightly pink in center. Remove beef. Repeat with remaining beef. Return all to wok, away from center. Stir marinade mixture; add to center of wok. Cook until bubbly. Toss beef and vegetables to coat. Remove from heat.
4. To serve, divide beef and vegetables among lettuce leaves, top with cilantro, and roll up. **MAKES 12 WRAPS (4 SERVINGS).**
EACH SERVING *258 cal, 11 g fat (4 g sat. fat), 46 mg chol, 517 mg sodium, 12 g carbo, 2 g fiber, 27 g pro. Daily Values: 64% vit. A, 168% vit. C, 6% calcium, 21% iron.*

GINGER-BEEF
LETTUCE WRAPS

American Classics
from Chef Scott Peacock
The Perfect Biscuit

FAST

CLASSIC BUTTERMILK BISCUITS

PREP: 10 MIN. BAKE: 8 TO 12 MIN.
OVEN: 500°F

5	cups sifted unbleached all-purpose flour (measured after sifting)
1	Tbsp. plus 1½ tsp. Homemade Baking Powder
1	Tbsp. kosher salt
½	cup plus 2 Tbsp. packed lard or butter, chilled
2	cups chilled buttermilk
3	Tbsp. unsalted butter, melted

1. Preheat oven to 500°F. In large bowl whisk together flour, Homemade Baking Powder, and kosher salt. Add lard, coating in flour. Working quickly, rub lard between fingertips until roughly half the lard is coarsely blended and half remains in large pieces, about ¾ inch.

2. Make a well in center of flour mixture. Add buttermilk all at once. With a large spoon stir mixture quickly, just until it is blended and begins to mass and form a sticky dough. (If dough appears dry, add 1 to 2 tablespoons additional buttermilk.)

3. Immediately turn dough onto generously floured surface. Using floured hands, knead briskly 8 to 10 times until cohesive ball of dough forms. Gently flatten dough with hands to even thickness. Using floured rolling pin, lightly roll dough to ¾ inch thickness.

4. Using a dinner fork dipped in flour, pierce dough completely through at ½-inch intervals. Flour a 2½- or 3-inch biscuit cutter. Stamp out rounds and arrange on heavy parchment-lined baking sheet. Add dough pieces, as is, to baking sheet (do not reroll dough).

5. Place on rack in upper third of oven. Bake 8 to 12 minutes, until crusty and golden brown. Remove. Brush with melted butter. Serve hot. **MAKES 12 TO 16 BISCUITS.**

HOMEMADE BAKING POWDER Sift together three times the following: ¼ cup cream of tartar and 2 tablespoons baking soda. Store in a clean, dry, tight-sealing jar at room temperature, away from direct sunlight, for up to 4 weeks.

EACH BISCUIT *231 cal, 12 g fat (3 g sat. fat), 8 mg chol, 200 mg sodium, 26 g carbo, 2 g fiber, 6 g pro. Daily Values: 8% vit. A, 18% vit. C, 7% calcium, 7% iron.*

CHOOSE YOUR FLOUR AND SIFT, SIFT, SIFT
Use any good unbleached all-purpose flour—unbleached flour contains more protein than bleached flour and makes a slightly sturdier biscuit. I prefer organic unbleached flour. Whichever flour you use, always sift the flour first and measure after sifting. Sifting the flour produces lighter biscuits.

"Working the lard in properly is the secret to success," says Scott. "First coat the lard in the flour mixture and rub between your fingertips until roughly half the lard is coarsely blended and the other half remains in large pieces, about ¾ inch in size."

STIR WITH A PURPOSE
When mixing the dough, stir just until the batter is well moistened and begins to cling together. Overworking can lead to tough, dry, and heavy biscuits; underworking can result in biscuits that are crumbly and leaden.

GO EASY ON ROLLING
Dust your rolling pin with flour and roll from center toward edges. Avoid pressing too firmly. If dough sticks to rolling pin, dust the pin, not the dough.

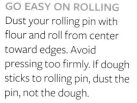

HANDLE WITH CARE
Go for a light touch when kneading. Knead gently but quickly and avoid pressing too firmly. Lift and fold the dough gently onto itself, giving it a quarter turn after each knead.

LET STEAM ESCAPE
Pricking the dough with a fork before baking allows steam to be released during baking and helps the biscuits rise more evenly.

DON'T TWIST
Cut biscuits out as close together as possible to get the maximum yield. Press down firmly, but do not twist the cutter. Twisting seals the sides, preventing biscuits from rising as nicely.

KEEP IT GENTLE
Slightly shake the filled cutter to free the biscuit. Don't overhandle. Arrange biscuits as close together as you can so they barely touch.

march

Celebrate spring with shared recipes from the Barefoot Contessa—and top prizewinners from our readers.

55

56

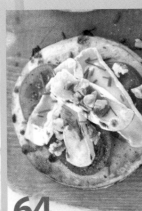
64

FRESH PEA SOUP
Recipe on page 49

SALAD WITH WARM
GOAT CHEESE

Ina Garten

Garden-Inspired Recipes

SALAD WITH WARM GOAT CHEESE

If you cannot find crottins, use a log of fresh goat cheese and cut vertically in slices. Copyright 2004, Barefoot in Paris, Clarkson/ Potter Publishers, all rights reserved.

PREP: 10 MIN. BAKE: 8 MIN. OVEN: 450°F

3	or 4 fresh small goat cheeses (crottins)
8	slices country white bread
	Good olive oil
	Salad greens for 4 salads
	Green Salad Vinaigrette, *right*
	Kosher salt
	Freshly ground black pepper

1. Heat oven to 450°F.

2. Cut each goat cheese round horizontally into 2 or 3 half-inch slices. Place bread on a baking sheet, brush lightly with olive oil, and place a slice of goat cheese on each piece. Bake for 8 to 10 minutes, until bread is toasted and cheese is warm.

3. Meanwhile, place salad greens in a large bowl and toss with enough Green Salad Vinaigrette to moisten. Divide the salad among 4 lunch plates. Place 2 slices of toasted bread on each salad, sprinkle with salt and pepper, and serve.

MAKES 4 SERVINGS.

EACH SERVING *565 cal, 45 g fat (11 g sat.fat), 75 mg chol, 998 mg sodium, 29 g carbo, 2 g fiber, 12 g pro. Daily Values: 25% vit. A, 9% vit. C, 20% calcium, 18% iron.*

GREEN SALAD VINAIGRETTE

Copyright 2004, Barefoot in Paris, Clarkson/ Potter Publishers, all rights reserved.

PREP: 15 MIN.

3	Tbsp. champagne vinegar or white wine vinegar
½	tsp. Dijon mustard
½	tsp. minced fresh garlic
1	extra-large egg yolk, at room temperature
¾	tsp. kosher salt
¼	tsp. freshly ground black pepper
½	cup good olive oil

1. In a small bowl, whisk together the vinegar, mustard, garlic, egg yolk, salt, and pepper. While whisking, slowly add the olive oil until the vinaigrette is emulsified.

MAKES 6 TO 8 SERVINGS.

FRESH PEA SOUP

Whether the peas are from the garden or the freezer, this flavorful soup is a taste of spring. Copyright 2006, Barefoot Contessa at Home, Clarkson/Potter Publishers, all rights reserved.

PREP: 25 MIN. COOK: 8 MIN.

2	Tbsp. unsalted butter
2	cups chopped leeks, white and light green parts (2 leeks)
1	cup chopped yellow onion
4	cups chicken stock, preferably homemade
5	cups freshly shelled peas or 2 (10-oz.) pkg. frozen peas
⅔	cup chopped fresh mint leaves, loosely packed
2	tsp. kosher salt
½	tsp. freshly ground black pepper
½	cup crème fraîche
½	cup chopped fresh chives
	Garlic croutons, for serving

1. Heat butter in a large saucepan, add the leeks and onion, and cook over medium-low heat for 5 to 10 minutes, until onion is tender. Add the chicken stock, increase heat to high, and bring to a boil. Add the peas and cook for 3 to 5 minutes, until peas are tender. (Frozen peas will take only 3 minutes.) Remove from heat; add the mint, salt, and pepper.

2. Purée soup in batches. Place 1 cup of soup in a blender, place lid on top, and purée on low speed. With blender still running, open the vent hole in the lid and slowly add more soup until blender is three-quarters full. Pour puréed soup into a large bowl and repeat until all the soup is puréed. Whisk in the crème fraîche and chives and taste for seasoning. Serve hot with garlic croutons.

MAKES 6 SERVINGS.

EACH SERVING *298 cal, 14 g fat (8 g sat. fat), 42 mg chol, 913 mg sodium, 32 g carbo, 8 g fiber, 12 g pro. Daily Values: 53% vit. A, 96% vit. C, 9% calcium, 23% iron.*

egg swap

INA MAKES HER GREEN SALAD VINAIGRETTE with a fresh raw egg yolk for a wonderfully creamy dressing. If you are concerned about the safety of using a raw egg yolk, use 2 tablespoons refrigerated or frozen egg product, thawed, in place of the yolk. The yolk can be omitted altogether, but the dressing will be less rich and creamy.

meet Ina

When Ina Garten, aka the Barefoot Contessa, prepares food on camera, her calm demeanor and love of fresh ingredients make throwing a dinner party look downright relaxing. She's also the author of six beautiful and inspiring cookbooks, beginning with *Barefoot Contessa Cookbook* in 1999. Ina has since cooked and written her way through *Barefoot Contessa Parties!* (2001), *Barefoot Contessa Family Style* (2002), *Barefoot in Paris* (2004), and *Barefoot Contessa at Home* (2006). Her new book, *Barefoot Contessa Back to Basics* (Clarkson/Potter, 2008; $35), shows home cooks how to turn ordinary ingredients into extraordinary meals.

Her royal moniker comes from a specialty food store she once owned in the Hamptons. Ina bought the business with its name, The Barefoot Contessa, which was taken from the 1954 movie starring Ava Gardner. Ina now sells a line of food products, Barefoot Contessa Pantry.

Ina films her Food Network show, *Barefoot Contessa*, at home—in her barn, a new building on her property that's complete with a gorgeous kitchen. It's here that she whips up meals for her husband Jeffery, her friends, and her viewers. Her kitchen/barn offers ample dining space—and opens up into her garden, where she serves cocktails (or s'mores) around a massive fire pit.

RACK OF LAMB

Copyright 2001, Barefoot Contessa Parties!, *Clarkson/Potter Publishers, all rights reserved.*

PREP: 15 MIN. ROAST: 20 MIN. MARINATE: 1 HR.

1½	Tbsp. kosher salt
2	Tbsp. minced fresh rosemary
3	garlic cloves, minced
½	cup Dijon mustard
1	Tbsp. balsamic vinegar
2	racks of lamb, "frenched"

1. In bowl of a food processor fitted with a steel blade, process the salt, rosemary, and garlic until they're as finely minced as possible. Add the mustard and balsamic vinegar and process for 1 minute.
2. Place the lamb in a roasting pan with the ribs curving down and coat the tops with the mustard mixture. Allow to stand for 1 hour at room temperature.
3. Preheat oven to 450°F.
4. Roast lamb for exactly 20 minutes for rare or 25 minutes for medium-rare. Remove from oven and cover with aluminum foil. Allow to sit for 15 minutes, then cut into individual ribs and serve. **MAKES 6 SERVINGS.**
EACH SERVING *386 cal, 33 g fat (17 g sat. fat), 84 mg chol, 1,969 mg sodium, 1 g carbo, 0 g fiber, 16 g pro. Daily Values: 1% vit. C, 2% calcium, 9% iron.*

FAST

GREEN GREEN SPRING VEGETABLES

Copyright 2002, Barefoot Contessa Family Style, *Clarkson/Potter Publishers, all rights reserved.*

START TO FINISH: 25 MIN.

¼	lb. French string beans (haricot vert), ends removed
	Kosher salt
¼	lb. sugar snap peas, ends and strings removed
¼	lb. asparagus, ends removed
½	lb. Broccolini™, ends removed
2	Tbsp. unsalted butter
1	Tbsp. good olive oil
3	large shallots, sliced
½	tsp. freshly ground black pepper

1. Blanch the string beans in a large pot of boiling salted water for 1 minute only. Lift beans from water with a slotted spoon or sieve and immerse them in a bowl of ice water. Add the snap peas to the same boiling water and cook for 1 minute, until al dente, adding them to the ice water and beans. Cut asparagus in 2-inch lengths diagonally and cook in the boiling water for 2 minutes, and add to ice water. Cut broccolini in half, boil for 1 minute, and add to ice water. When all the vegetables in the water are cold, drain well.
2. When ready to serve, heat the butter and oil in a very large sauté pan or large pot. Sauté the shallots over medium heat for 5 minutes, tossing occasionally, until lightly browned. Add drained vegetables to shallots with ½ teaspoon salt and the pepper; toss. Cook just until vegetables are heated through. Serve hot. **MAKES 4 TO 6 SERVINGS.**
EACH SERVING *126 cal, 9 g fat (4 g sat. fat), 15 mg chol, 147 mg sodium, 9 g carbo, 3 g fiber, 4 g pro. Daily Values: 14% vit. A, 32% vit. C, 10% calcium, 12% iron.*

GREEN GREEN
SPRING
VEGETABLES

PARMESAN CHICKEN
WITH LEMON
VINAIGRETTE

PARMESAN CHICKEN

*Copyright 2002, Barefoot Contessa
Family Style, Clarkson/Potter Publishers,
all rights reserved.*

PREP: 30 MIN. COOK: 4 MIN.

6	skinless, boneless chicken breasts
1	cup all-purpose flour
1	tsp. kosher salt
½	tsp. freshly ground black pepper
2	extra-large eggs
1¼	cups seasoned dry bread crumbs
½	cup freshly grated Parmesan cheese, plus extra for serving
	Unsalted butter
	Good olive oil
	Salad greens for 6, washed and spun dry
	Lemon Vinaigrette

1. Pound chicken breasts until they are
¼ inch thick. You can use either a meat
mallet or a rolling pin.
2. Combine the flour, salt, and pepper
on a dinner plate. On a second plate, beat
the eggs with 1 tablespoon water. On a third
plate, combine the bread crumbs
and ½ cup grated Parmesan cheese. Coat
chicken breasts on both sides with flour
mixture, then dip both sides into egg
mixture and dredge both sides in bread
crumb mixture, pressing lightly.
3. Heat 1 tablespoon of butter and
1 tablespoon of olive oil in a large sauté
pan and cook 2 or 3 chicken breasts on
medium-low heat for 2 to 3 minutes on each
side, until cooked through. Add more butter
and oil and cook the rest of the chicken
breasts. Toss the salad greens with Lemon
Vinaigrette. Place a mound of salad on each
hot chicken breast. Serve with extra grated
Parmesan. **MAKES 6 SERVINGS.**

*EACH SERVING 638 cal, 34 g fat (8 g sat. fat),
174 mg chol, 1,158 mg sodium, 37 g carbo,
3 g fiber, 46 g pro. Daily Values: 22% vit. A,
21% vit. C, 18% calcium, 24% iron.*

LEMON VINAIGRETTE

¼	cup freshly squeezed lemon juice (2 lemons)
½	cup good olive oil
½	tsp. kosher salt
¼	tsp. freshly ground black pepper

1. In a small bowl, whisk together the
lemon juice, olive oil, salt, and pepper.

ORZO WITH
ROASTED
VEGETABLES

ORZO WITH ROASTED VEGETABLES

*Copyright 2001, Barefoot Contessa Parties!,
Clarkson/Potter Publishers, all rights reserved.*

START TO FINISH: 1 HR. OVEN: 425°F

1	small eggplant, peeled and ¾-inch diced
1	red bell pepper, 1-inch diced
1	yellow bell pepper, 1-inch diced
1	red onion, peeled and 1-inch diced
2	garlic cloves, minced
⅓	cup good olive oil
1½	tsp. kosher salt
½	tsp. freshly ground black pepper
½	lb. orzo

For the dressing:

⅓	cup freshly squeezed lemon juice (2 lemons)
⅓	cup good olive oil
1	tsp. kosher salt
½	tsp. freshly ground black pepper

To assemble:

4	scallions, minced (white and green parts)
¼	cup pignolis (pine nuts), toasted
¾	lb. good feta, ½-inch diced (not crumbled)
15	fresh basil leaves, cut into thin strips

1. Preheat oven to 425°F. Toss the eggplant,
bell peppers, onion, and garlic with the olive
oil, salt, and pepper on a large baking sheet.
Roast for 40 minutes, until browned,
turning once with a spatula.
2. Meanwhile, cook the orzo in boiling salted
water for 7 to 9 minutes, until tender. Drain
and transfer to a large serving bowl.
3. Add roasted vegetables to the orzo,
scraping all the liquid and seasonings from
the roasting pan into the pasta bowl.
4. For dressing, combine lemon juice, olive
oil, salt, and pepper and pour on orzo and
vegetables. Cool to room temperature. Add
the scallions, pignolis, feta, and basil. Check
seasonings; serve at room temperature.
MAKES 6 SERVINGS.

*EACH SERVING 587 cal, 41 g fat (12 g sat. fat),
50 mg chol, 1,445 mg sodium, 42 g carbo,
5 g fiber, 15 g pro. Daily Values: 23% vit. A,
156% vit. C, 32% calcium, 16% iron.*

small-pot stock

This variation reduces Ina's recipe by a third and easily fits in a 5- to 6-quart stockpot. Makes 2 quarts.

Halve or cut up a 5-pound roasting chicken (halve or cut so that it fits in the pot and is submerged when water is added) or use two small broiler/fryer chickens. In a 5- to 6-quart stockpot combine the chicken; 1 large yellow onion, unpeeled and quartered; 2 carrots, unpeeled and halved; 2 small celery stalks with leaves, cut in thirds; 2 small parsnips, unpeeled and halved; 6 sprigs fresh Italian (flat-leaf) parsley; 5 sprigs fresh thyme; 5 sprigs fresh dill; 3 cloves garlic, unpeeled and cut in half crosswise; 2 teaspoons kosher salt; and ½ teaspoon whole black peppercorns. Add 10 cups water. Simmer as in main recipe.

KITCHEN NOTE: The chicken meat will be dry after simmering for several hours but can be reserved and used for soups or casseroles.

LOW FAT
CHICKEN STOCK

Stock is similar to broth but is typically richer and more concentrated. It gels when chilled, but will liquefy again when heated. If you do not have a pot large enough to make 6 quarts as Ina does, see "Small-Pot Stock," left. Copyright 2006, Barefoot Contessa at Home, *Clarkson/Potter Publishers, all rights reserved.*

PREP: 1 HR. COOK: 4 HR.

3	5-lb. whole roasting chickens
3	large yellow onions, unpeeled and quartered
6	carrots, unpeeled, halved
4	celery stalks with leaves, cut in thirds
4	parsnips, unpeeled, cut in half (optional)
20	sprigs fresh flat-leaf parsley
15	sprigs fresh thyme
20	sprigs fresh dill
1	head garlic, unpeeled, cut in half crosswise
2	Tbsp. kosher salt
2	tsp. whole black peppercorns

1. Place chickens, onions, carrots, celery, parsnips (if using), parsley, thyme, dill, garlic, salt, and peppercorns in a 16- to 20-quart stockpot. Add 7 quarts water and bring to a boil. Simmer uncovered for

SPRING GREEN RISOTTO

4 hours. Strain the entire contents of the pot through a colander and discard the solids. Pack in quart containers and chill overnight. Refrigerate for up to 5 days or freeze for up to 6 months. **MAKES 6 QUARTS.**

EACH 1-CUP PORTION *19 cal, 2 g fat (1 g sat. fat), 2 mg chol, 490 mg sodium, 0 g carbo, 0 g fiber, 0 g pro. Daily Values: 1% calcium.*

SPRING GREEN RISOTTO

Copyright 2008, Barefoot Contessa Back to Basics, Clarkson/Potter Publishers, all rights reserved.

START TO FINISH: 55 MIN.

1½	Tbsp. good olive oil
1½	Tbsp. unsalted butter
3	cups chopped leeks, white and light green parts (2 leeks)
1	cup chopped fennel
1½	cups Arborio rice
⅔	cup dry white wine
4	to 5 cups simmering chicken stock, preferably homemade
1	lb. thin asparagus
10	oz. frozen peas, defrosted, or 1½ cups shelled fresh peas
1	Tbsp. freshly grated lemon zest (2 lemons) Kosher salt and freshly ground black pepper
2	Tbsp. freshly squeezed lemon juice
⅓	cup mascarpone cheese, preferably Italian
½	cup freshly grated Parmesan cheese, plus extra for serving

1. Heat olive oil and butter in a medium saucepan over medium heat. Add the leeks and fennel and sauté for 5 to 7 minutes, until tender. Add the rice and stir for a minute to coat with the oil, butter, and vegetables. Add the white wine and simmer over low heat, stirring constantly, until most of the wine has been absorbed. Add the chicken stock, 2 ladles at a time, stirring almost constantly and waiting for the stock to be absorbed before adding more. This process should take 25 to 30 minutes.

2. Meanwhile, cut asparagus diagonally in 1½-inch lengths and discard tough ends. Blanch in boiling salted water for 4 to 5 minutes, until al dente. Drain and cool immediately in ice water. (If using fresh peas, blanch them in the boiling salted water for a few minutes until the starchiness is gone.)

3. When risotto has cooked for 15 minutes, drain the asparagus and add to the risotto with the peas, lemon zest, 2 teaspoons salt, and 1 teaspoon pepper. Continue cooking and adding stock, stirring almost constantly, until rice is tender but still firm.

CARROT CAKE CUPCAKES

4. Whisk the lemon juice and mascarpone together in a small bowl. When the risotto is done, turn off heat and stir in the mascarpone mixture plus the Parmesan cheese and chives. Set aside off the heat for a few minutes, sprinkle with salt and pepper, and serve hot with a sprinkling of chives and more Parmesan cheese.

MAKES 4 DINNER/6 APPETIZER SERVINGS.

EACH DINNER SERVING *670 cal, 24 g fat (11 g sat. fat), 51 mg chol, 735 mg sodium, 88 g carbo, 7 g fiber, 25 g pro. Daily Values: 67% vit. A, 57% vit. C, 21% calcium, 38% iron.*

CARROT CAKE CUPCAKES

Copyright 2001, Barefoot Contessa Parties!, Clarkson/Potter Publishers, all rights reserved.

PREP: 45 MIN. BAKE: 45 MIN. OVEN: 400°F/350°F

2	cups granulated sugar
1⅓	cups vegetable oil
3	extra-large eggs, at room temperature
1	tsp. pure vanilla extract
2	cups all-purpose flour plus 1 Tbsp.
2	tsp. ground cinnamon
2	tsp. baking soda
1½	tsp. kosher salt
1	lb. carrots, grated
1	cup raisins
1	cup chopped walnuts

For the frosting:

¾	lb. cream cheese, at room temperature
½	lb. unsalted butter, at room temperature
1	tsp. pure vanilla extract
1	lb. confectioner's sugar, sieved

For the decoration:

2	Tbsp. unsalted butter
1	cup shaved or grated carrots
3	Tbsp. good maple syrup

1. Preheat oven to 400°F. Line muffin pans with paper liners.

2. Beat the sugar, oil, and eggs together in bowl of electric mixer fitted with paddle attachment until light yellow. Add vanilla. In another bowl sift together 2 cups flour, the cinnamon, baking soda, and salt.

3. Add dry ingredients to the wet ingredients. Toss the carrots, raisins, and walnuts with 1 tablespoon flour. Add to the batter and mix well (I use my hands—they work best!).

4. Scoop batter into muffin cups until each is almost full. Bake for 10 minutes, then lower the oven to 350°F and bake for 35 minutes, or until a toothpick comes out clean. Let cool on a wire rack.

5. For frosting, mix cream cheese, butter, and vanilla in bowl of electric mixer fitted with paddle attachment until combined. Add confectioner's sugar; mix until smooth.

6. For the decoration, melt the butter in a skillet over medium heat; add the carrots and maple syrup and sauté for 2 to 3 minutes, until carrots are tender. Spread them on a paper towel to cool.

7. When cupcakes are cool, frost them generously and garnish with big pinches of sautéed carrots. **MAKES 22 CUPCAKES.**

EACH SERVING *532 cal, 32 g fat (11 g sat. fat), 76 mg chol, 323 mg sodium, 59 g carbo, 2 g fiber, 5 g pro. Daily Values: 98% vit. A, 3% vit. C, 4% calcium, 7% iron.*

What's Cooking
Readers' Winning Recipes

SWEET POTATO HASH
WITH SPICY HOLLANDAISE

SWEET POTATO HASH WITH SPICY HOLLANDAISE

PREP: 30 MIN. COOK: 10 MIN.

8	slices thick-sliced bacon
3	medium sweet potatoes, cut in ½-inch pieces
1	medium onion, chopped
	Salt and ground black pepper
2	to 4 Tbsp. pure maple syrup
2	Tbsp. cider vinegar
8	eggs
1	cup milk
¼	cup butter
1	0.9-oz. envelope hollandaise sauce mix
1	Tbsp. chopped canned chipotle peppers in adobo sauce
	Fresh chives

1. In 12-inch skillet cook bacon until crisp; drain on paper towels. Crumble half the bacon. Drain all but 3 tablespoons drippings from skillet. Meanwhile, cook sweet potatoes in boiling salted water for 3 minutes or just until tender; drain.

2. In skillet cook onion in hot drippings until tender. Add sweet potatoes and cook until potatoes begin to crisp and brown. Season to taste with salt and pepper; transfer to bowl. Stir in crumbled bacon and maple syrup; keep warm.

3. Rinse skillet and fill half full of water. Add vinegar to water; bring to boiling. Reduce heat to simmer (bubbles should barely break the surface of the water). Break one egg into measuring cup. Holding the lip of the cup as close to the water as possible, slide egg slowly into water. Repeat with remaining eggs, allowing each egg an equal amount of space. Simmer eggs, uncovered, for 3 to 5 minutes or until the whites are completely set and yolks begin to thicken but are not hard. Remove eggs with slotted spoon and place them in large pan of warm water to keep them warm.

4. In small saucepan combine milk, butter, and hollandaise sauce mix. Whisk and heat over medium heat until thickened and bubbly. Stir in peppers.

5. To serve, transfer sweet potato hash to serving plate, top with two poached eggs, and cover eggs with hollandaise sauce. Top with bacon strips and chives.

MAKES 4 SERVINGS.

EACH SERVING *599 cal, 39 g fat (17 g sat. fat), 485 mg chol, 1,054 mg sodium, 38 g carbo, 4 g fiber, 23 g pro. Daily Values: 297% vit. A, 8% vit. C, 17% calcium, 16% iron.*

CHICKEN-BERRY SALAD

CHICKEN-BERRY SALAD

PREP: 30 MIN. MARINATE: 1 HR.

½	cup fresh orange juice
¼	cup fresh lime juice
¼	cup fresh lemon juice
1	Tbsp. extra virgin olive oil
1	tsp. chopped fresh basil
¾	tsp. salt
½	tsp. ground black pepper
4	medium skinless, boneless chicken breast halves (1 ¼ to 1 ½ lb. total)
3	cups fresh blackberries
¼	cup red wine vinegar
3	Tbsp. sugar
1	tsp. Dijon-style mustard
¼	tsp. dried oregano, crushed
½	cup extra virgin olive oil
1	8-oz. pkg. Mediterranean mixed salad greens
2	medium pears, cored and thinly sliced
¾	cup crumbled feta cheese (3 oz.)

1. In small bowl stir together orange, lime, and lemon juices; 1 tablespoon oil; basil; ½ teaspoon of the salt; and ¼ teaspoon pepper. Place chicken in resealable plastic bag set in large bowl. Pour juice mixture over chicken; seal bag. Refrigerate 1 to 4 hours, turning bag occasionally.

2. For dressing, in blender combine 1 cup of the blackberries, vinegar, sugar, mustard, oregano, ¼ teaspoon salt, and ¼ teaspoon pepper. Cover and blend until smooth. With blender running, slowly add ½ cup oil in thin steady stream until well combined. Transfer to serving container. Cover and refrigerate until serving time.

3. Drain chicken, discarding marinade. For charcoal grill, place chicken on the rack of an uncovered grill directly over medium coals. Grill for 12 to 15 minutes or until done (170°F), turning once. (For gas grill, preheat grill. Reduce heat to medium. Add chicken to grill rack. Cover and grill as above.)

4. Slice chicken. Divide greens among 4 serving plates. Top with chicken, pears, and remaining 2 cups berries. Top each with some of the dressing and feta cheese. Pass remaining dressing. **MAKES 4 SERVINGS.**

EACH SERVING *603 cal, 35 g fat (7 g sat. fat), 101 mg chol, 427 mg sodium, 36 g carbo, 9 g fiber, 38 g pro. Daily Values: 22% vit. A, 60% vit. C, 19% calcium, 15% iron.*

FAST

WINTER SQUASH AND SAGE SAUSAGE CHILI

START TO FINISH: 20 MIN.

- 1 lb. bulk sage sausage or other sausage
- 1 15-oz. can cannellini beans, drained
- 1 12-oz. pkg. frozen winter squash purée, thawed
- 1 cup chunky-style chipotle salsa or other salsa
- 1½ cups water
- 1 3.5-oz. pkg. herb-flavored goat cheese, crumbled
  Fresh sage (optional)

1. In large saucepan cook sausage over medium heat until brown and no pink remains, stirring to break up; drain fat. Stir in beans, squash, salsa, and water. Bring to boiling; reduce heat. Simmer, uncovered, 10 minutes, stirring occasionally. Serve in bowls; sprinkle goat cheese and fresh sage. **MAKES 4 SERVINGS.**

EACH SERVING *385 cal, 14 g fat (7 g sat. fat), 119 mg chol, 1,466 mg sodium, 34 g carbo, 7 g fiber, 39 g pro. Daily Values: 99% vit. A, 19% vit. C, 32% calcium, 23% iron.*

LEMON-GRILLED SALMON WITH CORN SALAD

START TO FINISH: 35 MIN.

1½	cups cooked and cooled fresh or frozen yellow corn kernels
⅓	cup chopped red sweet pepper
¼	cup snipped fresh chives or thinly sliced green onions
3	Tbsp. thinly sliced fresh basil
2	Tbsp. pure maple syrup
2	Tbsp. lemon juice
¼	tsp. salt
1½	cups fresh blueberries
2	tsp. finely shredded lemon peel
1	tsp. ground cumin
½	tsp. salt
¼	tsp. ground black pepper
4	4- to 5-oz. fresh skinless salmon fillets
	Nonstick cooking spray
	Lemon slices and/or fresh basil sprigs (optional)

1. For corn salad, in bowl combine corn, sweet pepper, chives, basil, maple syrup, lemon juice, and the ¼ teaspoon salt. Add blueberries; toss gently to combine.

2. In small bowl combine lemon peel, cumin, the ½ teaspoon salt, and the black pepper. Sprinkle mixture on salmon fillets.

Lightly coat both sides of salmon fillets with nonstick spray.

3. For charcoal grill, grill salmon fillets on the rack of an uncovered grill directly over medium coals for 8 to 12 minutes or until fish flakes easily when tested with a fork, carefully turning once halfway through grilling. (For gas grill, preheat grill. Reduce heat to medium. Place salmon fillets on grill rack over heat. Cover and grill as above.)

4. Serve grilled salmon with corn salad. Garnish with lemon slices and/or fresh basil sprigs. **MAKES 4 SERVINGS.**

EACH SERVING *342 cal, 13 g fat (3 g sat. fat), 67 mg chol, 507 mg sodium, 32 g carbo, 4 g fiber, 25 g pro. Daily Values: 18% vit. A, 60% vit. C, 4% calcium, 6% iron.*

SANTA'S SPICY GINGERSNAPPERS

PREP: 45 MIN. BAKE: 12 MIN. PER BATCH
COOL: 2 MIN. PER BATCH OVEN: 350°F

1	cup raisins
1	cup unsalted butter, softened
2	cups packed brown sugar
2	eggs
1	Tbsp. chopped crystallized ginger
1	tsp. finely shredded orange peel
1	tsp. vanilla
3⅔	cups all-purpose flour
½	cup chopped pecans
1½	tsp. ground cinnamon
1	tsp. baking soda
½	tsp. baking powder
½	tsp. ground nutmeg
¼	tsp. ground ginger
¼	tsp. salt
1	recipe Pecan Topping
1	recipe Orange Glaze

1. Heat oven to 350°F. Place raisins and butter in food processor; process until raisins are chopped and combined with butter. Transfer mixture to extra-large mixing bowl. With electric mixer beat in brown sugar, eggs, crystallized ginger, orange peel, and vanilla until creamy.
2. In medium bowl combine flour, pecans, cinnamon, baking soda, baking powder, nutmeg, ginger, and salt. Gradually beat flour mixture into butter mixture. Mix until well combined.
3. With a 2-tablespoon cookie scoop, drop dough 4 inches apart on an ungreased cookie sheet. Flatten tops lightly. Spoon 1 teaspoon Pecan Topping on the center of each unbaked cookie.
4. Bake 12 to 13 minutes or just until edges are set. Cool on sheet for 2 minutes; transfer cookies to cooling rack. Cool completely.
5. Drizzle cooled cookies with Orange Glaze. **MAKES 3 DOZEN LARGE COOKIES.**
PECAN TOPPING In small bowl combine ½ cup chopped raisins, ½ cup chopped pecans, 3 tablespoons sour cream, and 2 tablespoons caramel topping. Cover and chill until ready to use.
ORANGE GLAZE In small bowl combine 1½ cups powdered sugar and 2 tablespoons orange juice.
EACH COOKIE *210 cal, 8 g fat (4 g sat. fat), 26 mg chol, 70 mg sodium, 34 g carbo, 1 g fiber, 2 g pro. Daily Values: 4% vit. A, 2% vit. C, 3% calcium, 6% iron.*

CARROT CHEESECAKE

PREP: 40 MIN. BAKE: 1 ½ HR. PLUS 8 MIN.
COOL: 45 MIN. CHILL: 4 HR. OVEN: 325°F

- 1 pkg. 2-layer-size carrot cake mix
- 1 cup water
- ½ cup cooking oil
- 6 eggs
- ½ cup raisins
- 3 8-oz. pkg. cream cheese, softened
- 1½ cups granulated sugar
- 2 tsp. vanilla
  Nonstick cooking spray
- 2 Tbsp. powdered sugar
- 1 Tbsp. water
- 1 tsp. ground cinnamon
- ½ cup coarsely chopped walnuts
- 1 cup powdered sugar
- 3 to 4 tsp. milk

1. Preheat oven to 325°F. Grease and flour 10-inch springform pan; set aside. In large bowl combine carrot cake mix, the 1 cup water, oil, and 3 of the eggs. Beat with electric mixer on low speed for 30 seconds, scraping sides of bowl constantly. Beat on medium speed for 3 minutes. Fold in raisins. Pour into pan.

2. In another large mixing bowl beat cream cheese with electric mixer on medium speed until smooth. Beat in granulated sugar and vanilla until smooth. Beat in remaining 3 eggs just until combined. Slowly pour over carrot cake layer. Place cheesecake pan on baking sheet.

3. Bake for 1½ to 1¾ hours or until center is set (top will be uneven and center may fall slightly as it cools). Cool in pan on wire rack for 15 minutes. Using small sharp knife, loosen cake from the sides of the pan. Cool 30 minutes. Remove sides of pan; cool completely. Refrigerate at least 4 hours before serving.

4. Preheat oven to 325° F. Line a small baking pan with foil; lightly coat foil with cooking spray. In bowl combine the 2 tablespoons powdered sugar, 1 tablespoon water, and cinnamon. Stir in walnuts. Spread nuts in even layer in prepared baking pan. Bake 8 minutes or until nuts are lightly toasted, stirring once. Cool.

5. In medium bowl combine 1 cup powdered sugar and enough milk to make of drizzling consistency. Cut cheesecake in wedges and place each wedge on serving plate. Drizzle each serving with some of the powdered sugar icing. Break up walnuts and place on cheesecake wedges.

MAKES 16 SERVINGS.

EACH SERVING *506 cal, 28 g fat (12 g sat. fat), 126 mg chol, 373 mg sodium, 59 g carbo, 0 g fiber, 8 g pro. Daily Values: 13% vit. A, 12% calcium, 8% iron.*

Everyday Easy
Speedy Suppers

SPINACH TORTELLINI WITH BEANS AND FETA

START TO FINISH: 20 MINUTES
BUDGET $3.22 PER SERVING

1	9-oz. pkg. refrigerated cheese-filled spinach tortellini
1	15-oz. can cannellini (white kidney) beans, rinsed and drained
¾	cup crumbled garlic-and-herb-flavored feta cheese (3 oz.)
2	Tbsp. olive oil
1	large tomato, chopped
	Ground black pepper
4	cups baby spinach

1. Cook tortellini according to package directions. Drain and return to saucepan.
2. Add drained beans, feta cheese, and olive oil to tortellini in saucepan. Cook over medium heat until beans are hot and cheese begins to melt, gently stirring occasionally. Add tomato; cook 1 minute more. Sprinkle black pepper.
3. Divide spinach among 4 dinner plates or shallow salad bowls. Top with tortellini mixture. **MAKES 4 SERVINGS.**
EACH SERVING *448 cal, 18 g fat (7 g sat. fat), 61 mg chol, 858 mg sodium, 55 g carbo, 9 g fiber, 24 g pro. Daily Values: 69% vit. A, 221% vit. C, 28% calcium, 19% iron.*

CITRUS SALSA SALMON

START TO FINISH: 20 MINUTES
BUDGET $3.58 PER SERVING

4	4- to 5-oz. skinless salmon fillets (¾ to 1 inch thick)
	Salt and ground black pepper
⅓	cup red jalapeño jelly
3	medium oranges, peeled, seeded, and coarsely chopped
1	medium grapefruit, peeled and sectioned
1	cup grape or cherry tomatoes, halved

1. Heat broiler. Lightly sprinkle salmon with salt and pepper. In small saucepan over low heat melt the jelly. Brush 2 tablespoons of the melted jelly on the salmon; reserve remaining jelly. Place salmon on unheated rack of broiler pan. Broil 4 inches from heat for 8 to 10 minutes or until salmon flakes when tested with a fork.
2. Meanwhile, for fresh citrus salsa, in medium bowl combine chopped oranges, grapefruit sections, halved tomatoes, and remaining jelly. Season with salt and pepper. Serve salmon with citrus salsa.
MAKES 4 SERVINGS.
EACH SERVING *362 cal, 13 g fat (3 g sat. fat), 67 mg chol, 223 mg sodium, 40 g carbo, 4 g fiber, 24 g pro. Daily Values: 27% vit. A, 136% vit. C, 7% calcium, 4% iron.*

SPINACH TORTELLINI WITH BEANS AND FETA

CITRUS SALSA
SALMON

FOCACCIA-CAMEMBERT
PIZZAS

BEEF AND TAPENADE
OPEN-FACE
SANDWICHES

GREEK CHICKEN
SALAD

FAST

FOCACCIA-CAMEMBERT PIZZAS

START TO FINISH: 20 MINUTES
BUDGET $3.67 PER SERVING

4   6-inch Italian flatbreads (focaccia)
2   large tomatoes, sliced
    Salt and ground black pepper
1   8-oz. round Camembert cheese,
    chilled
⅓   cup chopped walnuts
2   Tbsp. snipped fresh chives

1. Heat broiler. Place flatbreads on the
unheated rack of a broiler pan. Top with
tomato slices; sprinkle with salt and pepper.
Cut cheese in thin slices. Place cheese slices
on tomato slices.
2. Broil 4 to 5 inches from heat about
2 minutes or until cheese begins to melt.
Sprinkle with walnuts; broil 1 minute more.
Sprinkle with fresh chives.
MAKES 4 SERVINGS.
EACH SERVING *449 cal, 24 g fat (11 g sat. fat),
41 mg chol, 1,027 mg sodium, 41 g carbo,
6 g fiber, 21 g pro. Daily Values: 24% vit. A,
19% vit. C, 28% calcium, 8% iron.*

FAST

GREEK CHICKEN SALAD

START TO FINISH: 20 MINUTES
BUDGET $3.82 PER SERVING

1   2¼- to 2½-lb. deli-roasted chicken
1   5-oz. pkg. spring mix salad greens
2   small cucumbers, cut in spears
2   medium tomatoes, cut in wedges
⅔   cup bottled Greek salad dressing
    with feta cheese
    Cracked black pepper (optional)

1. Remove chicken from bones. Coarsely
chop chicken; cover and set aside.
2. Divide salad greens, cucumber spears,
and tomato wedges among 4 dinner plates
or salad bowls. Arrange chicken on
vegetables. Drizzle salad dressing. Sprinkle
with cracked black pepper.
MAKES 4 SERVINGS.
EACH SERVING *473 cal, 27 g fat (6 g sat. fat),
136 mg chol, 433 mg sodium, 9 g carbo, 9 g fiber,
46 g pro. Daily Values: 23% vit. A, 23% vit. C,
6% calcium, 14% iron.*

FAST

BEEF AND TAPENADE
OPEN-FACE SANDWICHES

START TO FINISH: 10 MINUTES
BUDGET $3.78 PER SERVING

⅓   cup light mayonnaise or salad dressing
1   tsp. Dijon-style or yellow mustard
4   slices crusty Italian country or
    sourdough bread
¼   cup olive tapenade
12   oz. thinly sliced deli roast beef
2   small tomatoes, thinly sliced
1   cup fresh baby spinach

1. In small bowl combine mayonnaise and
mustard. Lightly spread on one side of each
bread slice. Spread with tapenade. Top with
roast beef, tomato slices, and spinach.
MAKES 4 SERVINGS.
EACH SERVING *362 cal, 19 g fat (4 g sat. fat),
46 mg chol, 1,681 mg sodium, 21 g carbo,
2 g fiber, 21 g pro. Daily Values: 25% vit. A,
17% vit. C, 6% calcium, 15% iron.*

American Classics
from Chef Scott Peacock

Meat Loaf

CLASSIC MEAT LOAF

PREP: 40 MIN. BAKE: 60 MIN. OVEN: 350°F

2	Tbsp. unsalted butter
1¼	cups onions, finely diced
1¼	cups portobello or other mushrooms, finely chopped
½	cup celery, finely diced
½	tsp. dried thyme
1	tsp. finely chopped garlic
½	cup grated carrot
1	cup fresh bread crumbs
½	cup half-and-half or milk
2	eggs
1½	lb. ground chuck
½	lb. ground pork
4	slices bacon, finely chopped
1¾	tsp. kosher salt
½	tsp. freshly ground black pepper
½	cup ketchup
2	Tbsp. brown sugar
2	tsp. cider vinegar

1. Heat oven to 350°F. In large skillet heat butter until melted and foaming. Add onions, mushrooms, and celery. Season to taste with *kosher salt* and *black pepper*. Cook 3 minutes; do not brown.

2. Sprinkle thyme over onion mixture. Rub garlic and a pinch of salt into a paste. Add garlic paste to mushrom mixture in skillet. Cook and stir until onions are tender and translucent. Stir in grated carrot; remove from heat. Cool completely. Meanwhile, soak bread crumbs in half-and-half. Lightly beat eggs.

3. In large mixing bowl combine ground meats, bacon, cooled vegetables, and bread crumb mixture. Sprinkle the 1¾ teaspoons salt and the pepper. Using hands, mix until well blended.

4. Turn meat into rectangular baking dish. Using hands, shape in a 9×5-inch loaf. Make shallow indention around sides.

5. For ketchup topping, combine ketchup, brown sugar, and vinegar. Spoon on meat loaf. Bake on middle rack for 1 hour or until meat thermometer reaches 155°F. Let rest 10 minutes before slicing.

MAKES 4 SERVINGS.

EACH SERVING *518 cal, 38 g fat (15 g sat. fat), 160 mg chol, 1,013 mg sodium, 19 g carbo, .5 g fiber, 26 g pro. Daily Values: 32% vit. A, 10% vit. C, 8% calcium, 17% iron.*

GRATE FOR SUCCESS

"Grating the carrots ensures they soften during cooking and don't provide too much texture or crunch. The technique also distributes their sweetness throughout the meat loaf."

THE FINER THE BETTER

"Rubbing the garlic into a fine paste helps transfer its flavor throughout the loaf. Finely chop the cloves first, add a pinch of kosher salt, then use the side of the knife to mash and pull the garlic pieces into a paste."

CHOOSE SMALL PIECES

"Sautéing the onions, mushrooms, and celery in a bit of butter softens them and develops their flavor. Chop all vegetables in ¼-inch pieces."

GO LIGHT ON FILLER

"Meat loaf filler—bread crumbs or cubes—lightens the texture. Hand-cut pieces of white bread and soak them with half-and-half, which adds richness and evenly mixes the bread and meat together."

"Baking the meat loaf in a dish that is larger than the loaf improves browning and lets excess fat escape," says Scott. "A shallow indention along the edges keeps the delicious glaze on top."

MIXING BY HAND IS A MUST

"Using your hands to mix the meats is the most effective and efficient method. Fingers aerate as they blend, rather than mash."

ADD A PROVEN TOPPER

"A ketchup-based sauce caramelizes and intensifies during baking. And meat loaf would not be meat loaf without a sweet, tangy finish."

Holiday
from author Judy Bart Kancigor
Sweets for Passover

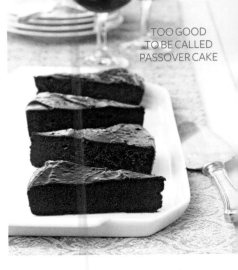

TOO GOOD
TO BE CALLED
PASSOVER CAKE

CHOCOLATE MACAROONS

PREP: 25 MIN. BAKE: 10 MIN. PER BATCH
OVEN: 350°F

2	cups semisweet or bittersweet chocolate chips
4	large egg whites
1	cup sugar
2	tsp. vanilla
½	tsp. fresh lemon juice
1½	cup sweetened flaked or shredded coconut

1. Melt chocolate in double boiler set over simmering water. Remove pan from heat; set aside to cool.
2. Move oven rack to center position. Heat oven to 350°F. Line baking sheet with parchment paper or grease lightly.
3. With electric mixer on medium-high speed beat egg whites until foamy, about 30 seconds. Add a pinch of *salt* and beat until soft peaks form. Add sugar, 1 tablespoon at a time, beating for 10 seconds after each addition, until stiff peaks form, about 6 minutes total. Beat in vanilla and lemon juice. Fold in the coconut and melted chocolate.
4. Drop batter by the teaspoon, 1 inch apart, on prepared baking sheet (batter will stiffen as it stands). Bake until macaroons puff, 10 to 13 minutes. (Do not allow the edges to brown.) Cool on baking sheet on wire rack, 1 to 2 minutes. Transfer macaroons to rack to cool completely.
5. Repeat with remaining macaroon batter. Serve immediately.
EACH MACAROON *56 cal, 3 g fat (2 g sat. fat), 0 g chol, 15 mg sodium, 8 g carbo, 1 g fiber, 1 g pro. Daily Values: 1% iron.*

TOO GOOD TO BE CALLED PASSOVER CAKE

"Some people think 'Passover' and they think 'boring and restrictive—can't be good,'" Judy says. "This cake will change their minds."

PREP: 25 MIN. BAKE: 25 MIN. COOL: 10 MIN.
OVEN: 350°F

8	oz. unsweetened chocolate, coarsely chopped
4	oz. semisweet chocolate, coarsely chopped
1⅓	cup sugar
1	cup kosher for Passover margarine or unsalted butter
5	eggs

1. Heat oven to 350°F. Butter a 9-inch round cake pan. Line bottom with round of parchment paper and butter the paper.
2. In food processor combine chopped chocolates. Process until finely chopped.
3. In saucepan bring sugar and ½ cup water to boiling. Stir to dissolve sugar.
4. With food processor running, add boiling sugar syrup to chocolate through feed tube. Add margarine, 2 tablespoons at a time. Add eggs. Process only until smooth.
5. Pour chocolate mixture into prepared pan. Place pan in roasting pan on rack in center of oven. Pour enough hot water into roasting pan to reach halfway up sides of pan. Bake 25 to 30 minutes, until knife

CHOCOLATE
MACAROONS

inserted in center comes out with just a few specks of chocolate clinging to it and cake begins to pull away from edges of pan. Transfer cake pan to a wire rack. Cool for 10 minutes.

6. Using a small sharp knife, loosen cake from pan sides. Cover cake surface with plastic wrap and invert onto baking sheet. Lift off pan; remove parchment. Invert a cake plate over cake; turn plate and baking sheet so cake is right side up. Remove plastic wrap. Serve warm or cold.

MAKES 16 SERVINGS.

EACH 1-SLICE SERVING *293 cal, 22 g fat (8 g sat. fat), 66 g chol, 159 mg sodium, 26 g carbo, 3 g fiber, 4 g pro. Daily Values: 12% vit. A, 3% calcium, 17% iron.*

PASSOVER APRICOT SQUARES

An "in-law of an in-law" created this Passover version of crumb cake. The results are more like a cookie than cake.

PREP: 20 MIN. BAKE: 50 MIN. OVEN: 325°F

1	cup kosher for Passover margarine or unsalted butter
1	cup sugar
2	large egg yolks
2	tsp. grated lemon peel
1	tsp. vanilla
¼	tsp. salt
2	cups matzo cake meal
1	12-oz. jar apricot preserves
¾	cup chopped walnuts

1. Heat oven to 325°F. Grease a 13×9×2-inch glass baking pan.

2. With an electric mixer beat margarine and sugar on medium speed until light and fluffy, about 2 minutes. Add egg yolks and continue beating until well combined, scraping bowl as necessary. Add lemon peel, vanilla, and salt. Reduce speed to medium-low and add matzo meal, beating just until combined.

3. Press about two-thirds of the mixture on the bottom of prepared pan and bake on the center rack for 20 minutes. Remove from oven and spread preserves evenly on crust. Sprinkle walnuts on preserves and crumble remaining matzo meal mixture on top. Bake until topping feels set and begins to turn golden, 30 to 35 minutes. Cool in pan on wire rack. Cut in squares to serve. **MAKES 12 TO 16 BARS.**

EACH BAR *414 cal, 21 g fat (10 g sat. fat), 76 mg chol, 63 mg sodium, 55 g carbo, 1 g fiber, 4 g pro. Daily Values: 11% vit. A, 5% vit. C, 2% calcium, 1% iron.*

observing Passover

JUDY BART KANCIGOR is the daughter of a cantor and has written a book on Jewish cooking, but she doesn't claim to be an expert on Passover. "I definitely would not be that last word," she says. She advises observant people to check with their local kosher experts for questions on recipes or ingredients.

april

Get fresh with healthful vegetable-based main dishes and a lovely brunch for celebrating the spring holidays.

77   78   82

TENDER-CRISP
SPRING BRAISE
Recipe on page 73

GOLDEN GREEN
PAELLA

Vegetable Plates

Main-dishes with lively flavor and good-for-you ingredients.

GOLDEN GREEN PAELLA

Paella is traditionally made with saffron, an expensive spice that imparts a yellow-orange tint. This dish gets its golden color and earthy kick from turmeric, a brightly hued spice related to ginger.

PREP: 30 MIN. COOK: 15 MIN.

2	Tbsp. extra virgin olive oil
8	oz. peeled and deveined medium shrimp, coarsely chopped
½	tsp. salt
¼	tsp. black pepper
1	large onion, chopped
3	cloves garlic, minced
1	cup instant brown rice
½	tsp. dried oregano, crushed
¼	tsp. ground turmeric
1	14-oz. can reduced-sodium chicken broth
8	oz. fresh sugar snap pea pods (2⅓ cups)
1	large green sweet pepper, cut in ½-inch pieces
2	green onions, diagonally sliced
2	Tbsp. chopped fresh Italian (flat-leaf) parsley

1. In large nonstick skillet heat 1 tablespoon of the oil over medium-high heat. Add shrimp; sprinkle with half the salt and pepper. Cook about 2 minutes or until shrimp are opaque, stirring occasionally. Remove from skillet; set aside.

2. Add remaining oil to skillet. Cook onion until almost tender. Add garlic; cook 1 minute. Stir in rice, oregano, and turmeric; cook and stir 1 minute. Add broth and remaining salt and pepper. Bring to boiling; reduce heat. Simmer, covered, 5 minutes or until most of the liquid is absorbed and rice is tender. Stir in peas and green pepper; cook 3 minutes. Stir in shrimp and sweet onions. Sprinkle with parsley. **MAKES 4 SERVINGS.**

EACH SERVING *239 cal, 8 g fat (1 g sat. fat), 86 mg chol, 620 mg sodium, 25 g carbo, 4 g fiber, 17 g pro. Daily Values: 21% vit. A, 111% vit. C, 8% calcium, 18% iron.*

TENDER-CRISP SPRING BRAISE

Not quite meatless, this dish gets its rich flavor from only a couple of chicken thighs.

START TO FINISH: 50 MIN.

3	Tbsp. olive oil
8	oz. new potatoes, cut in ½-inch slices
4	small carrots with tops, trimmed and diagonally cut in 1-inch pieces
4	cups mushrooms, halved (12 oz.)
1	large onion, cut in thin wedges
3	cloves garlic, peeled and sliced
1	lb. asparagus, trimmed and cut in 1½-inch pieces
2	skinless, boneless chicken thighs, cut in strips
½	tsp. salt
¼	tsp. pepper
¾	cup reduced-sodium chicken broth
1	Tbsp. snipped fresh tarragon

1. In 12-inch nonstick skillet heat 2 tablespoons oil over medium-high heat. Evenly layer potatoes and carrots in skillet. Cook, uncovered, 5 minutes, until potatoes are golden, turning once. Add mushrooms and onions. Cook 5 to 6 minutes, until vegetables are crisp-tender, stirring often. Add garlic and asparagus; cook 3 minutes. Transfer vegetables to bowl; set aside.

2. In same skillet heat remaining oil. Sprinkle chicken with half the salt and pepper. Cook chicken in hot oil about 3 minutes, until lightly browned, stirring occasionally. Add broth; bring to boiling. Reduce heat. Simmer, covered, about 3 minutes or until no pink remains. Increase heat to medium-high. Stir in cooked vegetables; heat through. Stir in snipped tarragon and remaining salt and pepper.

MAKES 4 SERVINGS.

EACH SERVING *266 cal, 12 g fat (2 g sat. fat), 29 mg chol, 483 mg sodium, 28 g carbo, 7 g fiber, 15 g pro. Daily Values: 223% vit. A, 47% vit. C, 8% calcium, 23% iron.*

green glossary

Terms to know as you shop for vegetables at grocery stores and farmers' markets.

SUSTAINABLE The aim of sustainable agriculture is to be profitable and meet human consumption needs while being environmentally sound. Sustainable agriculture also addresses the quality of life for farm workers and communities.

ORGANIC The USDA defines organic as food produced using sustainable agricultural practices with no synthetic fertilizers, conventional pesticides, or bioengineering. Organic animal products come from animals given no antibiotics or growth hormones. Look for the USDA's "Certified Organic" seal, which indicates the item is made with at least 95% organic ingredients.

NATURAL The FDA has not established a formal definition for the term "natural," but it does not object to the use of the term on product labels as long as the product contains no added color, artificial flavors, or synthetic substances. It says little about how the ingredients used to make the item should be grown or produced.

LOCAL This loose, unregulated term indicates an item was grown within a specific radius (typically no more than 100 miles). Buying locally produced foods supports local economies and the food tends to be fresh. Local does not always mean greener, however, because food shipped short distances may use less fuel-efficient means than items shipped long distances.

ORZO-STUFFED PEPPERS WITH FETA AND MINT

Skip washing an extra pot—and conserve water—by using the same Dutch oven to cook the orzo and the stuffed peppers.

PREP: 35 MIN. COOK: 20 MIN.

- ¾ cup dried orzo
- 4 oz. bulk Italian hot or mild (sweet) sausage
- 1 large onion, chopped
- 2 stalks celery, chopped
- 3 cloves garlic, minced
- 2 cups crumbled feta cheese (8 oz.)
- ¼ cup snipped fresh mint
- ¼ tsp. ground black pepper
- 6 medium-size red, orange, and/or yellow sweet peppers
- 1½ cups carrot or tomato juice
- ½ tsp. salt
  Fresh mint leaves

1. In 4- to-5 quart Dutch oven cook orzo according to package directions; drain. Set aside. Wipe Dutch oven dry; set aside.

2. In large nonstick skillet cook sausage, onion, celery, and garlic until sausage is browned and onion is tender. Remove from heat; drain fat. Stir in cooked orzo, cheese, mint, and black pepper.

3. Cut tops from peppers; remove seeds and ribs. Slightly trim bottoms of peppers to stand upright. Spoon orzo mixture into peppers and replace tops; set aside. In Dutch oven stir together carrot juice and salt. Stand

ORZO-STUFFED PEPPERS WITH FETA AND MINT

peppers upright in Dutch oven. Bring to boiling; reduce heat. Simmer, covered, 20 to 25 minutes or until peppers are tender.

4. Serve peppers on rimmed plates. Spoon over any remaining cooking juices. Sprinkle additional mint. **MAKES 6 SERVINGS.**

EACH SERVING *321 cal, 15 g fat (8 g sat. fat), 48 mg chol, 791 mg sodium, 34 g carbo, 5 g fiber, 13 g pro. Daily Values: 305% vit. A, 268% vit. C, 24% calcium, 15% iron.*

LOW FAT

VEGETABLES, BEEF, AND COUSCOUS

PREP: 25 MIN. COOK: 30 MIN.

1	tsp. ground cumin
½	tsp. ground cinnamon
¼	tsp. ground ginger
8	oz. beef chuck roast, cut in ½-inch cubes
2	Tbsp. olive oil
2	large onions, coarsely chopped
3	cloves garlic, minced
½	cup dried apricots, halved
½	cup dried tart cherries
2	bay leaves
8	to 12 mini sweet peppers, halved, or 4 small sweet peppers, quartered (seeds removed)
⅓	cup pitted kalamata olives
1½	cups Israeli-style couscous
	Fresh parsley, lemon peel, and/or seasoned olives (optional)

1. In bowl combine the cumin, ½ teaspoon *salt*, the cinnamon, ginger, and ¼ teaspoon *black pepper*. Add beef cubes; toss to coat.

2. In large skillet heat 1 tablespoon olive oil over medium-high heat. Add beef. Cook 4 minutes, until browned. Transfer to bowl.

3. Heat remaining olive oil in skillet; add onions. Cook until nearly tender. Add garlic; cook 1 minute. Return beef and juices to skillet with 1 cup *water*, apricots, half the cherries, and bay leaves. Bring to boiling; reduce heat. Simmer, covered, 20 minutes or until beef is tender. Increase heat to medium-high; add peppers. Cook 5 minutes, uncovered, until peppers are tender, stirring often. Stir in olives. Meanwhile, cook couscous with remaining cherries and ¼ teaspoon *salt* according to couscous package directions.

4. Remove and discard bay leaves from vegetable mixture. Serve vegetables with couscous, parsley, lemon peel, and olives. Drizzle pan juices. **MAKES 4 SERVINGS.**

EACH SERVING *511 cal, 11 g fat (2 g sat. fat), 25 mg chol, 616 mg sodium, 81 g carbo, 9 g fiber, 21 g pro. Daily Values: 96% vit. A, 265% vit. C, 6% calcium, 21% iron.*

VEGETABLES, BEEF, AND COUSCOUS

Israeli Couscous

Israeli-style couscous (also called pearl couscous), *bottom photo*, is a large flame-toasted variety, requiring longer cooking than common fine-grain couscous, *top photo*. Find Israeli couscous among specialty grains in supermarkets, or substitute regular couscous.

POTATO, ZUCCHINI, AND
CARROT PANCAKES

POTATO, ZUCCHINI, AND CARROT PANCAKES

PREP: 30 MIN. COOK: 8 MIN. PER BATCH
BAKE: 10 MIN. OVEN: 425°F

	Nonstick cooking spray
1	medium zucchini, shredded (about 1¼ cups)
1½	lb. baking potatoes, peeled and shredded (about 4 cups)
1	large carrot, shredded (about 1 cup)
¼	cup all-purpose flour
5	large eggs
2	tsp. chopped fresh thyme or ½ tsp. dried thyme, crushed
½	tsp. salt
¼	tsp. ground black pepper
1	Tbsp. canola oil
1	recipe Spring Greens Mixed peppercorns, crushed (optional)

1. Heat oven to 425°F. Lightly coat two small baking sheets with nonstick cooking spray; set aside.

2. Drain zucchini in a colander; press to squeeze out excess liquid. In large bowl combine zucchini, potatoes, carrot, flour, 1 of the eggs, thyme, salt, and pepper.

3. In a 12-inch large nonstick skillet heat half the oil over medium heat. To make a pancake, spoon about a 1-cup portion of potato mixture into skillet; evenly press and round edges with back of spatula to form a pancake. Cook two pancakes at a time, 4 to 5 minutes each side or until golden brown, turning once. Transfer to prepared baking sheet. Repeat with remaining oil and potato mixture.

4. With the back of a wooden spoon or a ¼-cup measure, gently press each pancake, slightly off-center, to make a 3-inch-diameter depression, deep enough to hold an egg (See "Pancake Nests," *right*.) Pour one egg in each nest. Place pancakes with eggs in oven, being careful not to tilt baking sheet. Bake, uncovered, 10 to 12 minutes or until eggs are cooked through. Transfer pancakes to serving plates. Serve with Spring Greens. Sprinkle with crushed peppercorns. **MAKES 4 SERVINGS.**

SPRING GREENS In large bowl combine 3 cups watercress and 1 small carrot, peeled and cut in long strips with vegetable peeler. For dressing, in bowl combine 2 teaspoons white wine vinegar, 1 teaspoon Dijon-style mustard, ¼ teaspoon salt, and dash of black pepper. Slowly whisk in 3 tablespoons olive oil. Toss with watercress and carrot strips.

EACH SERVING *362 cal, 20 g fat (4 g sat. fat), 264 mg chol, 599 mg sodium, 34 g carbo, 4 g fiber, 13 g pro. Daily Values: 126% vit. A, 76% vit. C, 10% calcium, 17% iron.*

pancake nests

To create pancake nests for the eggs, place cooked pancakes on two small baking sheets. Use the back of a spoon to make a well—slightly off-center and large enough to hold an egg—in each pancake. Crack an egg into a cup, then slip the egg into a nest. Bake as directed and serve hot.

What's Cooking
Spring Brunch

BREAD PUDDING QUICHE WITH BERRIES AND BACON

With flavors of French toast, this quiche has a cinnamon bread crumb crust. Bake the crust the day before and store at room temperature.

**PREP: 40 MIN. BAKE: 64 MIN. COOL: 15 MIN.
OVEN: 300°F/375°F/325°F**

7	to 8 slices cinnamon swirl bread cut in ½-inch cubes (about 5 cups)
⅓	cup butter, melted
5	eggs
1½	cups milk
1½	cups finely shredded Gruyère cheese (6 oz.)
2	tsp. all-purpose flour
¾	cup chopped cooked ham
½	cup chopped green onions
2	cups assorted fresh berries
4	slices bacon, crisp-cooked, drained, and broken in large pieces

picture-perfect

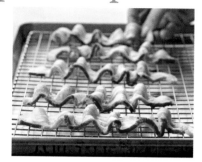

TO GET RIPPLED SLICES OF BACON to top the quiche, lay bacon in wavelike fashion on a wire rack set on a baking pan. Bake at 400°F 15 to 18 minutes or until bacon is crisp; cool.

FAST
HERB SALAD WITH CREAMY LEMON DRESSING

START TO FINISH: 20 MIN.

	Finely shredded peel and juice from 2 medium lemons
3	cloves garlic, minced
2	tsp. Dijon-style mustard
½	cup olive oil
½	cup sour cream
2	to 3 medium heads butterhead lettuce, torn, or 6 to 8 cups mixed baby salad greens
1½	cups assorted fresh herbs, such as chives, basil, parsley, or mint, torn
12	to 16 radishes, thinly sliced

1. For dressing, in bowl combine lemon peel and juice, garlic, mustard, and ¼ teaspoon each *salt* and *pepper*. Slowly whisk in oil until thickened. Whisk in sour cream.
2. Toss together lettuce and herbs; transfer to serving platter. Top with sliced radishes; pass dressing. **MAKES 6 TO 8 SERVINGS.**
EACH SERVING (WITH 3 TBSP. DRESSING)
215 cal, 22 g fat (5 g sat. fat), 7 mg chol, 161 mg sodium, 5 g carbo, 1 g fiber, 2 g pro. Daily Values: 64% vit. A, 51% vit. C, 7% calcium, 10% iron.

1. Heat oven to 300°F. Spread bread cubes in single layer on large ungreased baking sheet. Bake 10 to 15 minutes or until dry. Set aside 1 cup of the cubes.
2. For crust, place remaining bread cubes in food processor. Cover and process until reduced to fine crumbs. With food processor running, pour in melted butter until combined (mixture will be crumbly).
3. Increase oven to 375°F. Press crumb mixture on bottom and 1½ inches up sides of ungreased 9-inch springform pan or on bottom and up sides of 10-inch quiche dish. Bake 4 to 5 minutes or until lightly browned; cool. Reduce oven to 325°F.
4. In medium bowl whisk together eggs and milk. In small bowl toss together cheese, flour, and ¼ teaspoon each *salt* and *pepper*. Add to egg mixture. Fold in reserved bread cubes, ham, and green onions. Pour into prepared crust.
5. Bake 50 to 60 minutes or until knife inserted near center comes out clean. If necessary, after 30 minutes tent with foil to prevent overbrowning. Cool on wire rack 15 minutes. Remove sides of springform pan; loosen sides with a knife if necessary.
6. To serve, top with mixed berries and bacon. **MAKES 8 SERVINGS.**
EACH SERVING *366 cal, 23 g fat (12 g sat. fat), 191 mg chol, 725 mg sodium, 23 g carbo, 3 g fiber, 18 g pro. Daily Values: 16% vit. A, 16% vit. C, 35% calcium, 13% iron.*

HERB SALAD WITH CREAMY LEMON DRESSSING

CRISP CORNMEAL SCONES

These nibble-size scones are easy to mix. Instead of cutting in the butter, just shred it on a grater and toss it in.

PREP: 15 MIN. **BAKE:** 12 MIN. **OVEN:** 425°F

2	cups all-purpose flour
1	cup yellow cornmeal
2	Tbsp. granulated sugar
1½	tsp. baking powder
½	tsp. salt
½	cup cold butter, coarsely shredded or cubed
1	cup buttermilk
	Buttermilk
	Coarse sugar

1. Heat oven to 425°F. In large bowl whisk together flour, cornmeal, granulated sugar, baking powder, and salt.

2. Add shredded butter to flour mixture; toss to distribute. (Or cut cubed butter into flour mixture with pastry blender to resemble coarse crumbs.) Make well in center of flour-butter mixture. Add 1 cup buttermilk; stir with spoon until moistened. Do not overmix. (If dough appears dry, add 1 to 2 tablespoons additional buttermilk.)

3. Turn dough out onto floured surface. Gently knead by lifting and folding dough, 4 or 5 times, giving a quarter turn after each knead. Roll in 8-inch square, ¾ inch thick. Cut in 1½- to 2-inch squares. Place squares 1 inch apart on ungreased baking sheet. Brush with buttermilk; sprinkle coarse sugar. Bake 12 to 15 minutes or until lightly browned; cool scones on rack. Serve warm.

MAKES 16 TO 25 SCONES.

EACH SCONE *155 cal, 6 g fat (4 g sat. fat), 16 mg chol, 165 mg sodium, 24 g carbo, 1 g fiber, 3 g pro. Daily Values: 4% vit. A, 5% calcium, 6% iron.*

CRISP CORNMEAL SCONES

SWEET TOMATO JAM

Sharp tomatoes, cooked down with sugar and a hint of spices, soften to a sweet spreadable jam.

PREP: 10 MIN. COOK: 35 MIN. COOL: 1 HR.

- 1 lb. plum tomatoes, coarsely chopped (3 cups)
- ½ lb. red and/or yellow cherry or grape tomatoes, halved (1¾ cups)
- ½ cup sugar
- ½ tsp. ground cinnamon
- ¼ tsp. crushed red pepper (optional)

1. In saucepan combine tomatoes, sugar, cinnamon, and crushed red pepper. Bring to boiling, stirring often. Reduce heat; cook, uncovered, over medium-low heat for 35 minutes or until thickened, stirring occasionally. Remove from heat. Transfer to a bowl; cool. Serve or cover and refrigerate up to 3 days. **MAKES EIGHT ¼-CUP SERVINGS.**

EACH SERVING *64 cal, 0 g fat, 0 mg chol, 4 mg sodium, 16 g carbo, 1 g fiber, 1 g pro. Daily Values: 13% vit. A, 18% vit. C, 1% calcium, 1% iron.*

no-fuss ham

A quick stir-together glaze that's easy to customize gives ham a flavorful finish.

CHUTNEY GLAZED HAM Roast a 3- to 4-lb. boneless cooked ham in a 325°F oven for 1½ hours. For glaze, stir together a 9-oz. jar of mango chutney (snip any large pieces of fruit with scissors), 2 tablespoons honey, and 1 tablespoon coarse-ground mustard. Spoon some glaze on ham. Return to oven for 15 minutes (ham should reach 140°F). Serve with remaining glaze and roasted asparagus.

GLAZE ADD-INS Add chopped fresh mint, horseradish, crushed peppercorns, grated ginger, ground cloves, drained and chopped chipotle peppers, or shredded citrus peel.

SWEET TOMATO JAM

Everyday Easy
Weeknight Winners

FAST

COCONUT-LIME CHICKEN SOUP

START TO FINISH: 25 MINUTES
BUDGET $2.45 PER SERVING

1	2- to 2½-lb. deli-roasted chicken
1	15-oz. can unsweetened coconut milk
2	cups water
¼	cup lime juice (2 medium limes)
3	medium carrots, thin-sliced diagonally (about 1½ cups)
1	Tbsp. soy sauce
2	tsp. Thai seasoning blend
¼	tsp. salt
	Thai seasoning blend (optional)
	Fresh cilantro (optional)
	Lime wedges (optional)

1. Remove and discard skin and bones from chicken. Shred chicken. In large saucepan combine shredded chicken with coconut milk, water, lime juice, sliced carrots, soy sauce, the 2 teaspoons Thai seasoning, and salt. Bring to boiling; reduce heat and simmer, covered, 8 minutes or until carrots are crisp-tender.

2. To serve, sprinkle bowls of soup with additional Thai seasoning and cilantro. Pass lime wedges. **MAKES 4 SERVINGS.**
EACH SERVING *487 cal, 38 g fat (24 g sat. fat), 125 mg chol, 1,437 mg sodium, 11 g carbo, 1 g fiber, 29 g pro. Daily Values: 153% vit. A, 12% vit. C, 2% calcium, 17% iron.*

FAST

PECAN-CRUSTED SLIDERS

START TO FINISH: 25 MINUTES
BUDGET $2.08 PER SERVING

12	oz. pork tenderloin, sliced crosswise in 8 pieces
1	egg
2	Tbsp. honey
1	cup finely chopped pecans
1	small green apple
1½	cups shredded broccoli (broccoli slaw)
¼	cup mayonnaise
8	small buns or dinner rolls, split
	Dijon-style mustard (optional)

1. With palm of hand flatten pork slices to ¼ inch thickness. In a shallow dish whisk together egg and 1 tablespoon of the honey. In another shallow dish combine chopped nuts, 1 teaspoon *salt*, and ½ teaspoon *ground black pepper*. Dip pork in egg mixture, then nut mixture, pressing to coat.

2. In a 12-inch skillet heat *oil* over medium-high heat. Cook pork in hot oil 2 to 3 minutes per side or until golden and slightly pink in centers.

3. Meanwhile, for slaw, quarter apple; remove core and seeds; thinly slice. In bowl combine apple, shredded broccoli, mayonnaise, and 1 tablespoon honey. Season with *salt* and *pepper*. For sliders, place pork on buns or rolls; top with slaw. Pass mustard. **MAKES 4 (2-SLIDER) SERVINGS.**
EACH SERVING *694 cal, 44 g fat (6 g sat. fat), 115 mg chol, 1,029 mg sodium, 49 g carbo, 5 g fiber, 29 g pro. Daily Values: 21% vit. A, 49% vit. C, 15% calcium, 23% iron.*

COCONUT-LIME CHICKEN SOUP

PECAN-CRUSTED
SLIDERS

MEDITERRANEAN-
STYLE SNAPPER

FAST | **LOW FAT**

MEDITERRANEAN-STYLE SNAPPER

START TO FINISH: 15 MINUTES
BUDGET $3.71 PER SERVING

8	small cloves garlic
½	a 6.5-oz. jar oil-packed dried tomato halves with herbs (⅓ cup)
½	cup pitted mixed green olives
4	5- to 6-oz. red snapper fillets or other firm-flesh white fish
¼	cup crumbled feta cheese
	Fresh oregano leaves (optional)
	Pepperoncini (optional)

1. Peel garlic cloves. With side of wide knife smash garlic. For cooking oil, drain 1 tablespoon oil from dried tomatoes; heat the oil in 12-inch skillet. Add tomatoes, olives, and garlic to hot oil. Cook 2 to 3 minutes, until garlic is golden. Use slotted spoon to remove tomato-olive mixture. Reserve oil in skillet to cook fish. Set aside tomato-olive mixture.

2. Rinse and pat dry fish. Season with *salt* and *pepper*. Cook fish, skin sides down, in hot oil 4 to 6 minutes for each ½-inch thickness of fish or until skin is golden and crisp and fish flakes easily when tested with a fork, turning once halfway through cooking. Remove skin, if desired.

3. To serve, top fish with tomato-olive mixture, cheese, fresh oregano, and pepperoncini. **MAKES 4 SERVINGS.**

EACH SERVING *245 cal, 9 g fat (3 g sat. fat), 61 mg chol, 808 mg sodium, 8 g carbo, 1 g fiber, 32 g pro. Daily Values: 11% vit. A, 47% vit. C, 13% calcium, 7% iron.*

RAVIOLI-VEGETABLE STACKS

BLACK BEAN CAKES WITH SALSA

FAST

BLACK BEAN CAKES WITH SALSA

START TO FINISH: 25 MINUTES
BUDGET $1.60 PER SERVING

1½	cups prepared salsa
1	jalapeño pepper (see note, *page 25*)
2	15-oz. cans black beans, rinsed and drained
1	8.5-oz. pkg. corn muffin mix
1	Tbsp. chili powder
2	Tbsp. olive oil
½	cup sour cream
½	tsp. chili powder

1. In colander drain ½ cup of the salsa. Seed and finely chop half the jalapeño; thinly slice remaining half. In large bowl mash beans with vegetable masher or fork. Stir in muffin mix, drained salsa, 2½ teaspoons chili powder, and chopped jalapeño.

2. In 12-inch skillet heat 1 tablespoon oil over medium-high heat. Add four ½-cup mounds bean mixture to skillet. Flatten mounds with spatula to 3½-inch round cakes. Cook 3 minutes each side until browned. Remove from skillet. Repeat with remaining oil and bean mixture.

3. In bowl combine sour cream and ½ teaspoon chili powder. Top cakes with remaining salsa, sliced jalapeño, and seasoned sour cream.

MAKES 4 (2-CAKE) SERVINGS.

EACH SERVING *519 cal, 19 g fat (4 g sat. fat), 11 mg chol, 1,553 mg sodium, 79 g carbo, 12 g fiber, 20 g pro. Daily Values: 21% vit. A, 8% vit. C, 13% calcium, 24% iron.*

FAST

RAVIOLI VEGETABLE STACKS

START TO FINISH: 25 MINUTES
BUDGET $3.92 PER SERVING

1	lb. frozen sausage- or meat-filled ravioli
2	small zucchini
4	plum tomatoes, thinly sliced
3	Tbsp. olive oil
½	cup small fresh basil leaves
1	8-oz. pkg. shredded Italian-blend cheese (2 cups)
	Fresh basil (optional)

1. Heat oven to 425°F. Cook ravioli according to package directions. Trim and lengthwise slice zucchini. Add zucchini to ravioli during the last 3 minutes of cooking time. Drain, but do not rinse.

2. Thinly slice tomatoes. In 2-quart square baking dish layer half the tomato slices. Drizzle 1 tablespoon of the oil. Sprinkle half the basil. Using tongs, layer half the ravioli and sprinkle half the cheese. Layer zucchini slices; drizzle 1 tablespoon oil. Layer remaining ravioli, basil, cheese, and tomatoes; drizzle remaining oil. Season with *salt* and *ground black pepper*.

3. Bake, uncovered, 9 to 10 minutes or until cheese is melted and begins to brown. To serve, cut in squares; sprinkle with fresh basil. **MAKES 4 SERVINGS.**

EACH SERVING *571 cal, 33 g fat (12 g sat. fat), 114 mg chol, 1,258 mg sodium, 48 g carbo, 8 g fiber, 29 g pro. Daily Values: 34% vit. A, 53% vit. C, 49% calcium, 18% iron.*

American Classics
from Chef Scott Peacock
Chicken and Dumplings

CLASSIC CHICKEN AND DUMPLINGS
PREP: 50 MIN. CHILL: 2 HR. COOK: 65 MIN.

1	egg
3	Tbsp. cold water
2	Tbsp. peanut oil
½	tsp. kosher salt
1	cup all-purpose flour
1	4- to 4½-lb. broiler-fryer chicken, quartered
1	tsp. kosher salt
5	cups chicken stock or broth
2	cups water
2	stalks celery halved crosswise
1	medium onion, peeled and sliced in half
3	hard-cooked eggs, sliced
2	Tbsp. cold butter, cut in ¼-inch cubes
¼	cup whipping cream
	Ground black pepper

1. For dumplings, in medium bowl whisk together egg, cold water, oil, and the ½ teaspoon salt. Stir in flour. Mix until well blended and elastic. Cover. Refrigerate for 2 hours.

2. Season chicken, including back and neck, with the 1 teaspoon salt. Set aside. In 6-quart Dutch oven combine chicken stock, water, celery, onion, and pinch of kosher salt. Bring to boiling. Add chicken pieces, placing leg quarters and backbone first. Place breast, skin side down, on top. Reduce heat to just below simmer. Cover, leaving half-inch opening.

3. Cook 30 to 45 minutes or until breasts are done; remove. Continue cooking leg quarters 30 to 40 minutes until tender; remove chicken and vegetables. Set broth in pot aside. Discard vegetables. Set chicken aside. Cool. Remove skin. Pull meat from bones, tearing into large pieces. Set aside. Discard bones.

4. For dumplings, turn dough onto well-floured surface. Roll very thin, about ¹⁄₁₆ inch; cut in 1½- by 2½-inch pieces. Return broth to boiling. Season well with additional *kosher salt.* Add dumplings to broth, shaking pot occasionally. Do not stir. Cook 3 to 5 minutes. Add reserved chicken and egg. Reduce to simmer. Add butter, cream, and few grindings of pepper. Cook 2 minutes. Remove from heat; cover. Let stand 10 minutes. **MAKES 8 SERVINGS.**

EACH SERVING *655 cal, 35 g fat (12 g sat. fat), 309 mg chol, 955 mg sodium, 26 g carbo, 1 g fiber, 56 g pro. Daily Values: 10% vit. A, 4% vit. C, 7% calcium, 22% iron.*

POACH FOR SUCCESS

Poaching the chicken in broth makes for a rich, intensely flavored final dish. "Onion and a bit of celery enhance and contribute to the flavor of the chicken without covering up and diluting the taste."

the ideal chicken and dumplings

... ARE THE ESSENCE OF rich chicken flavor. Gentle poaching ensures a silken and tender texture.

... HAVE ULTRA-THIN dumplings that easily fold and drape around the meaty chicken pieces.

... HAVE BROTH that is intensely flavored, barely thickened, and is well seasoned with salt and pepper.

RELY ON FLOUR

Generously flour the surface for rolling dumplings. "Roll the dough with a quick, light touch, flouring as needed, until less than 1/16 of an inch.

GLOPPY CAN BE GOOD

"The dough looks unpromising at first—sticky and elastic—and should be allowed to rest at least a half hour before rolling." Use all-purpose flour to make the dumplings. Unbleached flour yields less-tender dumplings.

CUT QUICKLY

A pastry wheel or pizza cutter makes quick work of cutting the dumplings in equal sizes.

Roll it right: "When you roll the dough thin enough, you should be able to almost see through the dumplings," says Scott. "Don't shake off any excess flour—it thickens the broth and gives the dish body."

SHAKE, DON'T STIR

"To avoid sticking, shake the pot side to side from time to time. Stirring can break the dumplings."

may

Turn a bounty of strawberries into dishes both sweet and savory, and add fresh tastes to spring meals.

99 | 105 | 109

FRESH STRAWBERRY BARS
Recipe on page 91

STRAWBERRY-GOAT CHEESE
BRUSCHETTA

Strawberries

They go beyond shortcake.

FRESH STRAWBERRY BARS

The rich peanut butter base can be made ahead and frozen. For individual servings, cut the base in portions and freeze. Pull a portion from the freezer, thaw, and top with jam and berries for a last-minute dessert.

PREP: 25 MIN. BAKE: 25 MIN. OVEN: 350°F

¾	cup butter, softened
¾	cup peanut butter
1	cup packed brown sugar
½	cup granulated sugar
2	tsp. baking powder
¼	tsp. salt
2	eggs
1	tsp. vanilla
2¼	cups all-purpose flour
½	cup strawberry jam
4	cups small whole strawberries, halved or quartered

1. Heat oven to 350°F. Line 13×9×2-inch baking pan with foil, extending foil beyond edges. Set aside.

2. In large mixing bowl beat butter and peanut butter on medium to high for 30 seconds. Beat in sugars, baking powder, and salt until combined. Add eggs and vanilla; beat until combined. Beat in as much flour as you can with mixer. Stir in remaining flour.

3. Spread dough in prepared pan. Bake 25 minutes or until top is lightly browned and toothpick inserted near center comes out clean.

4. Cool completely on rack. Remove from pan by lifting foil. Spread jam and top with berries. Cut into bars. Serve at once or refrigerate up to 6 hours. **MAKES 24 BARS.**

MAKE AHEAD Wrap the peanut butter base in foil; store at room temperature up to 24 hours. Before serving, top with jam and berries. Or freeze the peanut butter base in a freezer container up to 3 months.

EACH BAR *225 cal, 10 g fat (5 g sat. fat), 33 mg chol, 143 mg sodium, 30 g carbo, 1 g fiber, 4 g pro. Daily Values: 4% vit. A, 24% vit. C, 5% calcium, 6% iron.*

STRAWBERRY-GOAT CHEESE BRUSCHETTA

PREP: 15 MIN. BROIL: 4 MIN.

1	8-oz. baguette
1	Tbsp. olive oil
1	4-oz. log goat cheese (chèvre)
1½	cups sliced strawberries
½	cup arugula
	Olive oil
	Sea salt or coarse salt
	Freshly ground black pepper
	Snipped fresh herbs

1. Heat broiler. Halve baguette crosswise, then lengthwise. Place, cut sides up, on large baking sheet. Brush with the 1 tablespoon oil. Broil, 3 to 4 inches from heat, for 1½ to 2 minutes or until lightly toasted.

2. Slice and divide cheese among toasts. Top with sliced berries. Broil 2 to 3 minutes or until cheese and berries soften. Remove from broiler; top with arugula. Drizzle additional oil. Sprinkle salt, pepper, and herbs. **MAKES 4 SERVINGS.**

EACH SERVING *346 cal, 16 g fat (7 g sat. fat), 22 mg chol, 616 mg sodium, 37 g carbo, 2 g fiber, 13 g pro. Daily Values: 10% vit. A, 55% vit. C, 13% calcium, 16% iron.*

strawberry picking

Savor the season. Follow these tips to select and store fresh strawberries.

SELECT plump, ripe, shiny red berries with green caps and leaves intact. Because strawberries do not ripen after picking, avoid those that are white or green at the stem end or have hard tips—signs of being unripe. Avoid those that are mushy, missing green caps, or have signs of mold. When picking berries at a patch, leave the caps on.

FRESH BERRIES are highly perishable. Plan to use them soon after picking or buying. Refrigerate them in a single layer, loosely covered. Wash and stem them right before using. Strawberries deteriorate rapidly after being washed.

TO FREEZE BERRIES, wash and stem them. Place in a single layer on a freezer-safe dish and freeze until hard. Transfer them to a freezer bag or container. Freeze for 8 to 10 months. Frozen strawberries do not have the same consistency as fresh, and they may be slightly mushy when thawed.

FAST

LAYERED SPINACH AND POT STICKER SALAD

Pot stickers are small dumplings made of wonton skins filled with meat. Also try the strawberry vinaigrette drizzled over grilled chicken or vegetables.

START TO FINISH: 30 MIN.

- 2　13-oz. pkg. frozen chicken pot stickers or two 16- to 19-oz. pkg. frozen cheese-filled tortellini
- 3½　cups fresh whole strawberries, hulled
- ½　cup red wine vinegar
- ⅓　cup strawberry jam
- ⅓　cup olive oil
- ½　tsp. ground ginger
- ¼　tsp. cayenne pepper
- 1　5-oz. pkg. baby spinach (8 cups)
- 1　recipe Spiced Chips

1. In 4- to 5-quart Dutch oven cook pot stickers or tortellini according to package directions; drain. Rinse gently in cold water; drain well and set aside.

2. Meanwhile, for vinaigrette, place 1½ cups berries in large trifle bowl. Crush with masher; whisk in vinegar, jam, oil, ginger, and pepper. Layer pot stickers and spinach. Quarter or slice remaining berries; layer on spinach. Refrigerate, covered, up to 1 hour. To serve, top with Spiced Chips*. **MAKES 12 SIDE-DISH OR 6 MAIN-DISH SERVINGS.**

SPICED CHIPS Heat oven to 350°F. In small bowl combine 1½ teaspoons chili powder and 1½ teaspoons brown sugar; set aside. Bake 4 cups ridged potato chips in shallow baking pan 5 minutes. Remove; sprinkle spice mixture.

---

*KITCHEN TIP If desired, invert salad into larger bowl to toss ingredients together.

EACH SIDE-DISH SERVING *248 cal, 10 g fat (2 g sat. fat), 9 mg chol, 358 mg sodium, 31 g carbo, 2 g fiber, 6 g pro. Daily Values: 24% vit. A, 52% vit. C, 3% calcium, 6% iron.*

FAST | LOW FAT

PULLED PORK WITH STRAWBERRY BBQ SAUCE

PREP: 30 MIN. COOK: 2 HR. STAND: 10 MIN.

- 1　2½- to 3-lb. boneless pork sirloin, shoulder, or butt roast
- 1　tsp. salt
- ½　tsp. ground black pepper
- 1　Tbsp. cooking oil
- 4　cups strawberries, halved or quartered
- ½　cup ketchup
- ¼　cup cider vinegar
- 4　cloves garlic, minced
- 1　tsp. dried rosemary, crushed
　　Bottled hot pepper sauce (optional)
- 8　rolls or buns, split
　　Fresh parsley leaves (optional)
　　Green tomato wedges (optional)

1. Trim fat from pork. Sprinkle pork with salt and pepper. In large Dutch oven over medium heat brown pork in hot oil on all sides. Add half the strawberries, the ketchup, vinegar, garlic, rosemary, and several dashes hot pepper sauce. Bring to boiling; reduce heat. Simmer, covered, 2 hours or until pork is tender. Remove pork from Dutch oven; loosely cover with foil. Let stand 10 minutes.

2. For strawberry BBQ sauce, skim fat from cooking liquid. Return liquid to Dutch oven; bring to boiling. Reduce heat. Simmer, uncovered, 8 minutes or until reduced to about 2 cups.

3. Using two forks, shred pork; discard fat. Stir 1 cup strawberry BBQ sauce into pork. Stir remaining strawberries into BBQ sauce.

4. Serve pork on buns. Top with additional sauce and parsley. Pass remaining sauce. Serve with tomato wedges.

MAKES 8 SANDWICHES.

EACH SANDWICH *359 cal, 10 g fat (3 g sat. fat), 89 mg chol, 738 mg sodium, 31 g carbo, 3 g fiber, 35 g pro. Daily Values: 3% vit. A, 77% vit. C, 10% calcium, 18% iron.*

LAYERED SPINACH AND POT STICKER SALAD

PULLED PORK
WITH STRAWBERRY
BBQ SAUCE

PARMESAN-STUFFED
CHICKEN AND MELTED
STRAWBERRIES

LOW FAT

PARMESAN-STUFFED CHICKEN AND MELTED STRAWBERRIES

PREP: 30 MIN. BAKE: 15 MIN. OVEN: 400°F

3	cups fresh strawberries (halve or quarter large berries)
2	Tbsp. white balsamic vinegar or white wine vinegar
¼	cup strawberry jam
	Sea salt or salt and black pepper
6	skinless, boneless chicken breast halves (about 3 lb.)
3	oz. Parmesan or white cheddar cheese
6	large fresh basil leaves
1	Tbsp. olive oil
2	cloves garlic, minced
	Snipped fresh basil

1. Heat oven to 400°F. In 3-quart baking dish combine strawberries, vinegar, and jam. Sprinkle salt and pepper; set aside.
2. Cut a horizontal pocket in each chicken breast half by cutting from one side almost, but not through, to the other side. Cut Parmesan cheese in six 3×½-inch pieces. Wrap a basil leaf around each piece of cheese; stuff into chicken breast pocket. Secure pockets closed with wooden toothpicks or skewers. Sprinkle with salt and pepper.
3. In 12-inch oven-safe skillet cook garlic in oil over medium heat for 30 seconds. Add chicken and cook 5 minutes or until golden brown, turning once. Transfer to oven. Bake, uncovered, 5 minutes. Place baking dish with the strawberry-jam mixture in oven. Bake 10 to 13 minutes or until chicken is no longer pink (170°F) and the berries are softened and jam mixture has thickened. Serve chicken with melted strawberries. Sprinkle with basil. **MAKES 6 SERVINGS.**

EACH SERVING *395 cal, 9 g fat (4 g sat. fat), 142 mg chol, 461 mg sodium, 17 g carbo, 2 g fiber, 58 g pro. Daily Values: 4% vit. A, 78% vit. C, 22% calcium, 13% iron.*

EASY STRAWBERRY JAM

LOW FAT

EASY STRAWBERRY JAM

PREP: 30 MIN. STAND: 10 MIN. + 24 HR.

4	cups fresh strawberries, hulled
4	cups sugar
1	1¾-oz. pkg. unflavored powdered fruit pectin
¾	cup water
2	Tbsp. fresh lemon juice
1	small lemon, thinly sliced

1. In large bowl crush berries with masher. Stir in sugar. Let stand 10 minutes, stirring occasionally.
2. In small saucepan combine pectin and water. Bring to boiling; boil 1 minute, stirring constantly. Remove from heat. Pour into berry mixture. Add lemon juice and stir 3 minutes or until sugar is dissolved and mixture is smooth. Stir in lemon slices.
3. Ladle jam into clean half-pint jars or freezer containers, leaving a ½-inch headspace. Seal and label. Let stand at room temperature 24 hours or until set.* Refrigerate up to 3 weeks or freeze up to 1 year. **MAKES ABOUT 5 HALF PINTS.**

***NOTE** Freezer jam does not set as firmly as cooked jam.*
EACH 2-TBSP. SERVING *87 cal, 0 g fat, 0 mg chol, 3 mg sodium, 23 g carbo, 0 g fiber, 0 g pro. Daily Values: 17% vit. C, 1% iron.*

SPARKLING JAM Prepare Easy Strawberry Jam except omit lemon juice and slices. Stir ¼ cup champagne or white wine and 1 to 2 tablespoons raspberry liqueur into berry mixture with pectin mixture.
BANANA-BERRY Prepare East Strawberry Jam except use 3 cups strawberries, 1 cup chopped banana (about two), and omit lemon juice and slices. Stir 2 tablespoons creme de banana (or lemon juice) into berry mixture with pectin. Stir 5 minutes, until sugar is dissolved (jam will set soft).

FAST

STRAWBERRY FRITTERS

START TO FINISH: 30 MIN.

- 16 medium strawberries (about 1 pint)
- 16 4-inch bamboo or wooden skewers
- ¼ cup honey mustard
- ¼ cup slivered almonds, toasted and chopped
- ¼ cup crushed saltine crackers (about 7 crackers)
  Cooking oil for deep-fat frying

1. Wash strawberries and thoroughly dry. Insert a skewer through top of each berry; set aside.

2. Place honey mustard in a small bowl. Combine almonds and crackers in another small bowl. Dip or spread bottom ⅔ of each berry with honey mustard; roll in almond mixture.

3. In a deep-fat fryer heat 2 inches cooking oil to 365°F. Fry strawberries, 2 at a time, for 15 seconds. Carefully remove with tongs, using the skewer or the uncoated portion of the berry. Drain on paper towels. Serve within 30 minutes of frying.

MAKES 16 APPETIZER SERVINGS.

EACH SERVING *85 cal, 8 g fat (1 g sat. fat), 0 mg chol, 37 mg sodium, 3 g carbo, 1 g fiber, 1 g pro. Daily Values: 18% vit. C, 1% calcium, 1% iron.*

STRAWBERRY MERINGUE PIE

Berries practically tumble out of this pie. To easily cut through the meringue, use a sharp serrated knife.

PREP: 45 MIN. BAKE: 45 MIN. STAND: 30 MIN.
CHILL: 30 MIN. OVEN: 450°F/300°F

- 1 rolled refrigerated unbaked piecrust (½ a 15-oz. pkg.)
- 3 egg whites
- ½ tsp. vanilla
- ¼ tsp. cream of tartar
- ½ cup sugar
- 7 Tbsp. lemon curd
- 5 cups fresh strawberries (halve large berries)
  Snipped fresh mint

1. Let unbaked crust stand at room temperature according to package directions. Heat oven to 450°F. Unroll crust; line 9-inch pie plate with crust. Flute edge, if desired. Prick bottom and sides of crust with fork. Bake 10 to 12 minutes or until golden brown. Remove from oven; cool on rack. Reduce oven temperature to 300°F.

2. Meanwhile, for meringue layer, in large mixing bowl let egg whites stand at room temperature 30 minutes. Add vanilla and cream of tartar. Beat on medium until soft peaks form. Gradually add sugar. Beat on high until stiff peaks form and sugar is almost dissolved. Spread in baked piecrust, building up meringue along edges. Bake 35 minutes. Cool on rack. Meringue will fall slightly.

3. In large micrwave-safe bowl heat lemon curd in microwave on 50% power (medium) 15 to 20 seconds. Spread 4 tablespoons warm curd on meringue. Add berries to remaining lemon curd; lightly stir to coat. Spoon into pie shell. Refrigerate 30 to 60 minutes. To serve, top with fresh mint. Cut with serrated knife. **MAKES 8 SERVINGS.**

EACH SERVING *262 cal, 8 g fat (3 g sat. fat), 16 mg chol, 143 mg sodium, 46 g carbo, 4 g fiber, 2 g pro. Daily Values: 89% vit. C, 2% calcium, 3% iron.*

STRAWBERRY FRITTERS

STRAWBERRY
MERINGUE PIE

What's Cooking
Break the dinnertime routine

BACON AND EGG
PASTA

BACON AND EGG PASTA

START TO FINISH: 35 MIN.

12	oz. dried linguine or thin spaghetti
5	pieces thick-sliced bacon, chopped
¼	cup dry white wine
3	cloves garlic, minced
¼	tsp. crushed red pepper
1	cup finely chopped red sweet pepper
4	eggs, lightly beaten
¾	cup half-and-half or light cream
1	cup fresh baby spinach
½	cup Asiago cheese, shredded (2 oz.)
¼	cup chopped fresh Italian (flat-leaf) parsley or basil
1	hard-cooked egg, peeled and chopped Shredded Asiago cheese (optional) Freshly ground black pepper

1. Cook pasta according to package directions. Drain, reserving 1 cup cooking liquid. Return pasta to pan; keep warm. Meanwhile, in large skillet cook bacon until crisp; remove bacon with slotted spoon and drain on paper towels. Reserve 1 tablespoon drippings in skillet; discard remaining drippings. Add wine, garlic, and crushed red pepper to drippings in skillet. Bring to boiling. Reduce heat; boil gently, uncovered, 3 minutes or until most of the liquid has evaporated. Stir in red sweet pepper; cook and stir 1 minute. Reduce heat to low.
2. In medium bowl whisk together eggs and half-and-half. Add egg mixture to skillet and cook, stirring constantly, 1 to 2 minutes or until egg mixture coats a metal spoon (160°F). Do not scramble.
3. Add egg mixture to pasta along with bacon, spinach, the ½ cup Asiago, and parsley. Cook over medium heat 1 minute just to heat through, tossing with tongs to combine. Add reserved pasta cooking liquid to pasta mixture as needed to make creamy. Top with hard-cooked egg, additional Asiago, and black pepper. Serve immediately. **MAKES 4 TO 6 SERVINGS.**

EACH SERVING *564 cal, 17 g fat (8 g sat. fat), 92 mg chol, 618 mg sodium, 71 g carbo, 4 g fiber, 28 g pro. Daily Values: 66% vit. A, 93% vit. C, 22% calcium, 26% iron.*

PORK AND POTATO STACK

PREP: 45 MIN. CHILL: 2 HR. OVEN: 425°F

1	lb. pork tenderloin
1	lb. Yukon gold potatoes
1	cup frozen shelled sweet soybeans (edamame)
1	medium zucchini or yellow squash
1	recipe Creamy Walnut-Garlic Vinaigrette
1	cup frozen whole kernel corn, thawed
½	cup sliced green onions (about 4) Shaved carrot (optional) Fresh tarragon and thyme (optional)

1. Heat oven to 425°F. Place pork on rack in roasting pan; sprinkle with *salt* and *black pepper*. Roast 35 minutes or until pork reaches 155°F on meat thermometer. Cover; let stand 5 minutes. Cut pork in bite-size pieces.
2. Meanwhile, using the ¼-inch slicing blade of food processor, slice potatoes (or slice with knife). In large saucepan cook potatoes and soybeans in lightly salted boiling water, covered, for 5 to 8 minutes or until potatoes are tender; drain.
3. Cut zucchini in 1½- to 2-inch lengths. Slice lengthwise in food processor (or slice with knife). Make Creamy Walnut-Garlic Vinaigrette in food processor.

4. In lightly greased 2-quart rectangular baking dish, layer half the potato-soybean mixture. Drizzle ⅓ cup vinaigrette. Evenly layer zucchini; drizzle ⅓ cup vinaigrette. Evenly arrange pork and remaining potato-soybean mixture; drizzle ⅓ cup vinaigrette. In small bowl combine corn, green onions, and remaining vinaigrette; spoon on salad.
5. Refrigerate, covered, 2 to 24 hours for flavors to meld. Top with carrots. Sprinkle tarragon and thyme. **MAKES 6 SERVINGS.**
CREAMY WALNUT-GARLIC VINAIGRETTE
In food processor combine ¼ cup refrigerated or frozen egg product, thawed; ¼ cup white wine vinegar; 1 teaspoon Dijon-style mustard; 1 teaspoon salt; 1 teaspoon snipped fresh tarragon or thyme (or ¼ teaspoon dried); ¼ teaspoon black pepper; and 3 cloves garlic, coarsely chopped. With food processor running, gradually add ⅓ cup olive oil. Process until thickened. Stir in ⅓ cup finely chopped toasted walnuts.

EACH SERVING *355 cal, 19 g fat (3 g sat. fat), 49 mg chol, 576 mg sodium, 24 g carbo, 4 g fiber, 23 g pro. Daily Values: 7% vit. A, 44% vit. C, 5% calcium, 15% iron.*

SHRIMP AND BEAN PACKETS

PREP: 15 MIN. BAKE: 20 MIN. OVEN: 350°F

1¼	lb. medium fresh or frozen shrimp
1	15-oz. can cannellini beans, rinsed and drained
1	large fresh tomato, thinly sliced
¼	cup sliced green onions (about 2)
¼	cup chicken broth
1	tsp. finely shredded lemon peel
1	Tbsp. lemon juice
1	tsp. olive oil
1	tsp. Old Bay or seafood seasoning
4	slices country-style bread, toasted Fresh basil and/or shredded Parmesan cheese (optional)

1. Thaw shrimp, if frozen. Peel and devein shrimp; set aside. Heat oven to 350°F. Fold four 24×18-inch sheets of heavy-duty foil in half. On center of foil, evenly divide beans, tomatoes, shrimp, and onions. Drizzle with broth, juice, and oil. Sprinkle seasoning, lemon peel, and *black pepper*.

2. Allowing room for steam to build, fold together narrow ends of foil; seal with double-fold. Place packets on baking sheet. Bake 20 minutes or until shrimp are opaque. Carefully open packets. Serve with bread. Top with basil and Parmesan.

MAKES 4 SERVINGS.

EACH SERVING *335 cal, 5 g fat (1 g sat. fat), 216 mg chol, 891 mg sodium, 35 g carbo, 6 g fiber, 39 g pro. Daily Values: 14% vit. A, 20% vit. C, 16% calcium, 33% iron.*

LOW FAT | KID-FRIENDLY
EASY CHICKEN AND RICE
PREP: 15 MIN. COOK: 20 MIN.

- 4 skinless, boneless chicken breast halves
- ¼ cup Spiced Tomato-Mushroom Blend, *right*
- 2 Tbsp. olive oil
- 1 cup long grain rice
- 1½ cups fresh sugar snap pea pods
  Fresh parsley (optional)
  Lemon wedges (optional)

1. Lightly coat chicken with 1 tablespoon of the spiced blend.
2. In large skillet cook chicken in hot olive oil over medium heat for 2 minutes on each side; remove from skillet. Stir remaining spiced blend and rice into skillet; cook 1 minute. Add 2½ cups *water*; return chicken to skillet. Bring to boiling. Reduce heat. Simmer, covered, 15 minutes.
3. Add pea pods to skillet. Cover. Cook 5 minutes more or until rice is tender. Serve with parsley and lemon wedges.
MAKES 4 SERVINGS.
EACH SERVING *428 cal, 9 g fat (2 g sat. fat), 82 mg chol, 625 mg sodium, 46 g carbo, 3 g fiber, 38 g pro. Daily Values: 1% vit. A, 10% vit. C, 8% calcium, 22% iron.*

SPICED TOMATO- MUSHROOM BLEND
START TO FINISH: 30 MIN.

- 1 cup dried tomatoes (not oil-packed)
- 1 oz. dried mushrooms (shiitake or morel)*
- ¼ cup dried minced onion
- 2 Tbsp. salt
- 1 Tbsp. dried thyme
- 1 Tbsp. cumin seed
- 2 tsp. crushed red pepper
- 1 tsp. garlic powder
- 1 tsp. ground cinnamon
- 1 tsp. ground cumin
- 1 tsp. ground cardamom
- ½ tsp. ground black pepper

1. In large bowl combine all ingredients. Place the mixture, one-fourth at a time, in blender. Cover and blend 30 seconds or until tomatoes are finely chopped. Transfer to storage container. Refrigerate; use seasoning blend within 1 month.
MAKES 8 (¼-CUP) PORTIONS.
*TEST KITCHEN TIP To remove grit from dried mushrooms, place in sieve and rinse under cold running water. Drain and pat dry. Place on baking sheet. Bake at 350°F. for 10 minutes or until dry and crisp.

make-a-dish ideas

A scoop of Spiced Tomato-Mushroom Blend is all the flavor needed to turn chicken, ground meat, grains, and pasta into dinner.

EASY CHILI Brown 1 lb. ground beef or sausage; drain fat. Stir in ¼ cup Spiced Tomato-Mushroom Blend, tomato sauce, and canned beans. Simmer to develop flavors.

GOULASH Cook and drain macaroni according to package directions. Combine with ¼ cup Spiced Tomato-Mushroom Blend, shredded cooked meat, and pasta sauce. Simmer to develop flavors.

SOUP Combine ¼ cup Spiced Tomato-Mushroom Blend, water, shredded cooked chicken, and vegetables; heat through.

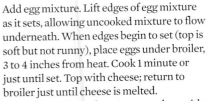
Everyday Easy
Flavorful Weeknight Meals

HERBED FRITTATA WITH EDAMAME
START TO FINISH: 20 MINUTES
BUDGET $1.66 PER SERVING

8	eggs
¼	cup finely chopped green onions (about 2)
¼	cup chopped fresh cilantro
1	Tbsp. olive oil
1	cup shredded Italian cheese blend (4 oz.)
1	medium carrot, shredded or cut in ribbons
1	cup frozen shelled sweet soybeans (edamame), thawed
	Fresh cilantro
	Shaved Parmesan cheese (optional)

1. Heat broiler. Break eggs into medium bowl. Whisk together eggs, ⅓ cup *water*, green onions, chopped cilantro, and ¼ teaspoon each *salt* and *ground black pepper*; set aside.
2. Heat olive oil in 12-inch broiler-proof skillet with flared sides over medium heat.

Add egg mixture. Lift edges of egg mixture as it sets, allowing uncooked mixture to flow underneath. When edges begin to set (top is soft but not runny), place eggs under broiler, 3 to 4 inches from heat. Cook 1 minute or just until set. Top with cheese; return to broiler just until cheese is melted.
3. Cut frittata in wedges. Serve wedges with carrot shreds, edamame, additional cilantro, and cheese. **MAKES 4 SERVINGS.**

EACH SERVING *306 cal, 22 g fat (8 g sat. fat), 443 mg chol, 6 g carbo, 2 g fiber, 23 g pro. Daily Values: 70% vit. A, 19% vit. C, 25% calcium, 16% iron.*

MEDITERRANEAN CHICKEN SALAD
START TO FINISH: 20 MINUTES
BUDGET $3.55 PER SERVING

⅔	cup bottled Greek salad dressing with feta cheese
12	oz. chicken tenders
8	cups mixed baby greens
1	16-oz. jar pickled mixed vegetables (giardiniera), drained and rinsed
½	cup pitted kalamata olives, halved
½	cup onion-and-garlic croutons (optional)

1. Brush 2 tablespoons of the dressing on chicken tenders. Lightly sprinkle *black pepper*.
2. Heat grill pan or large nonstick skillet over medium-high heat; add chicken. Reduce heat to medium. Cook 5 to 7 minutes, turning once, or until no pink remains. Slice chicken tenders in bite-size chunks.
3. In salad bowl toss together greens, chicken, drained vegetables, olives, and remaining dressing. Top with croutons.
MAKES 4 SERVINGS.

EACH SERVING *305 cal, 21 g fat (2 g sat. fat), 49 mg chol, 1,517 mg sodium, 9 g carbo, 2 g fiber, 21 g pro. Daily Values: 81% vit. A, 17% vit. C, 5% calcium, 7% iron.*

HERBED FRITTATA WITH EDAMAME

MEDITERRANEAN
CHICKEN SALAD

OPEN-FACE VEG
BURGERS WITH
SAUTÉED ONIONS

GINGERED BEEF AND BROCCOLI SALAD BOWL

FAST
OPEN-FACE VEG BURGERS WITH SAUTÉED ONIONS
START TO FINISH: 20 MINUTES
BUDGET $2.41 PER SERVING

2	Tbsp. olive oil
1	large sweet onion, halved and thinly sliced (about 3 cups)
4	refrigerated or frozen vegetable burgers (10-oz. pkg.)
2	Tbsp. mayonnaise or salad dressing
1	tsp. prepared yellow mustard
4	½-inch slices ciabatta bread, toasted
1	cup fresh baby spinach leaves
2	Tbsp. steak sauce

1. In large skillet heat olive oil over medium-high heat. Add onion slices and cook 8 to 10 minutes or until very tender, stirring frequently.
2. Meanwhile, prepare burgers according to package microwave directions.
3. In small bowl combine mayonnaise and mustard; spread mixture on one side of each bread slice. Top bread with spinach and burger. Stir steak sauce into cooked onions. Spoon onion mixture on burgers.
MAKES 4 SERVINGS.

EACH SERVING *329 cal, 20 g fat (3 g sat. fat), 3 mg chol, 688 mg sodium, 21 g carbo, 5 g fiber, 18 g pro. Daily Values: 16% vit. A, 10% vit. C, 6% calcium, 15% iron.*

SALMON SALAD SANDWICHES

FAST
SALMON SALAD SANDWICHES
START TO FINISH: 20 MINUTES
BUDGET $3.04 PER SERVING

4	sandwich rolls
½	cup ranch-style salad dressing
2	6-oz. cans skinless, boneless salmon
2	small tomatoes
½	a medium cucumber
1	cup coarsely shredded carrots (2) or shredded, peeled jicama (¼ jicama)

1. Split sandwich rolls. Lightly spread sliced rolls with some of the salad dressing. Drain salmon. Place salmon in bowl and flake with a fork. Add remaining salad dressing to salmon; mix to combine.
2. Thinly slice tomatoes and cucumber. Layer tomato slices on bottom halves of sandwich rolls. Top with salmon mixture, cucumber slices, shredded carrots or jicama, and roll tops. **MAKES 4 SERVINGS.**

EACH SERVING *575 cal, 25 g fat (4 g sat. fat), 64 mg chol, 1,094 mg sodium, 57 g carbo, 4 g fiber, 32 g pro. Daily Values: 107% vit. A 17% vit. C, 13% calcium, 21% iron.*

FAST   LOW FAT
GINGERED BEEF AND BROCCOLI SALAD BOWL
START TO FINISH: 20 MINUTES
BUDGET $3.57 PER SERVING

12	oz. beef sirloin steak
⅔	cup bottled ginger vinaigrette salad dressing
3	cups broccoli florets
1	medium red sweet pepper
8	cups mixed spring or baby salad greens

1. Trim fat from beef. Thinly slice beef across the grain into bite-size strips; set aside.
2. In a wok or large skillet heat 2 tablespoons of the salad dressing over medium-high heat. Add broccoli. Cook and stir for 3 minutes. Add beef to wok or skillet. Cook and stir 2 to 3 minutes or until beef is slightly pink in center. Remove beef and broccoli from wok or skillet. Remove stem end and seeds from sweet pepper. Cut sweet pepper in bite-size strips.
3. In large bowl combine greens, sweet pepper, beef, and broccoli. Drizzle remaining salad dressing; toss to coat.
MAKES 4 SERVINGS.

EACH SERVING *237 cal, 9 g fat (2 g sat. fat), 60 mg chol, 468 mg sodium, 17 g carbo, 4 g fiber, 22 g pro. Daily Values: 48% vit. A, 176% vit. C, 8% calcium, 21% iron.*

Good and Healthy

Nuts

Nuts are tiny storehouses of protein, fats, vitamins, and minerals that give trees a healthy start on life. Add nuts to your diet and those nutrients will work just as hard for you. See "Why Nuts are Good For You," page 108. Because they're high in calories, eat nuts in moderation—⅓ cup per day is about right. Even in small amounts, you'll get the benefits.

WALNUT-LEMON RICE PILAF

In addition to nutrients, walnuts contain a fat that helps the body absorb vitamin A from the sweet pepper.

START TO FINISH: 20 MIN.

- ½ cup coarsely chopped walnuts
- 1 small yellow sweet pepper, cut in bite-size strips
- ½ a small red onion, cut in slivers
- 2 cloves garlic, minced
- 2 tsp. olive oil
- 1 8.8-oz. pouch cooked brown rice
- ¼ cup coarsely chopped Italian (flat-leaf) parsley
- ½ tsp. finely shredded lemon peel
- 2 Tbsp. lemon juice

1. In large dry skillet heat walnuts over medium heat 3 to 5 minutes or until lightly toasted, stirring frequently. Remove from skillet; set aside. In same skillet cook sweet pepper, onion, and garlic in hot oil over medium heat 5 minutes or just until tender, stirring occasionally.

2. Add rice to skillet. Cook and stir to heat through. Stir in nuts, parsley, lemon peel and juice, and ¼ teaspoon *salt.*

MAKES 4 SIDE-DISH SERVINGS.

EACH SERVING *238 cal, 14 g fat (1 g sat. fat), 152 mg sodium, 26 g carbo, 2 g fiber, 5 g pro. Daily Values: 8% vit. A, 160% vit. C, 3% calcium, 7% iron.*

health nuts

1. BRAZIL NUTS
Rich in selenium and magnesium, minerals that contribute to heart health.

2. PEANUTS
High in protein. Source of B vitamins and beneficial phytosterols, which lower serum cholesterol.

3. HAZELNUTS
Also known as filberts and cobnuts. High in cholesterol-lowering oleic acid.

4. ALMONDS
Natural source of antioxidants for healthy cells. Rich source of calcium and potassium.

5. WALNUTS
Significantly high level of healthful omega-3 polyunsaturated fats.

6. PECANS
High in healthful oleic oils, fiber, and vitamin E.

WALNUT-LEMON
RICE PILAF

why nuts are good for you

"The evidence is consistent and robust that nuts reduce the risk of cardiovascular disease," says Janet Novotny, research physiologist at the USDA's Beltsville Human Nutrition Research Center. Three components of nuts work for the heart: Polyunsaturated fats help to lower cholesterol, phytosterols block natural cholesterol in food from absorbing, and fiber lowers "bad" LDL cholesterol.

Other health benefits:

MAINTAIN HEALTHY WEIGHT Though nuts are high in calories, studies have shown that people who regularly eat them tend to have healthy body weights. Subjects at Indiana's Purdue University who added 500 calories of peanuts to their diet found that they compensated for the added calories by eating less. "The high protein and fiber content in peanuts may play an important role in curbing hunger," says Purdue nutrition researcher Richard Mattes. In another study, 81 subjects added an average of 2½ ounces of almonds to their daily diets and lost weight, again despite the added calories of the nuts.

GOOD SOURCE OF MAGNESIUM According to the USDA, about 50 percent of Americans don't get enough magnesium in their diets, putting them at increased risk of osteoporosis. "Magnesium supports the underlying machinery of our body," says Novotny. "It helps absorb nutrients and helps cells grow and divide. Nuts are a great way to get magnesium."

ALMOND-CRUSTED
CHICKEN

LOW FAT

ALMOND-CRUSTED CHICKEN

PREP: 25 MIN.   COOK: 8 MIN.

- 4   small skinless, boneless chicken breast halves (1 to 1 ¼ lb.)
- 1   egg, lightly beaten
- 2   Tbsp. buttermilk
- ½   cup finely chopped almonds
- ½   cup panko (Japanese-style bread crumbs) or fine dry bread crumbs
- 2   tsp. snipped fresh rosemary
- ¼   tsp. salt
- 1   Tbsp. peanut oil or canola oil
- 1   shallot, chopped
- 8   cups fresh spinach leaves
- ¼   tsp. salt
       Freshly ground black pepper
       Fresh mint leaves (optional)

1. Place one chicken breast half between sheets of plastic wrap. With flat side of meat mallet, pound chicken to ¼- to ½-inch thickness. Repeat with the remaining breast halves.

2. In shallow dish whisk together egg and buttermilk. In another shallow dish combine almonds, panko, rosemary, and ¼ teaspoon salt. Dip chicken breasts, one at a time, in egg mixture, turning to coat. Allow excess to drip off, then dip chicken pieces in almond mixture, turning to coat.

3. In 12-inch nonstick skillet cook chicken, half at a time if necessary, in hot oil over medium heat for 4 to 6 minutes or until no longer pink, turning once halfway through cooking. Remove chicken from skillet; keep warm.

4. In same skillet cook shallot in drippings 3 to 5 minutes or just until tender, stirring frequently. Add spinach and ¼ teaspoon salt; cook and toss about 1 minute or just until spinach is wilted. Serve chicken with wilted spinach. Sprinkle pepper and mint.

MAKES 4 SERVINGS.

EACH SERVING *276 cal, 11 g fat (1 g sat. fat), 66 mg chol, 456 mg sodium, 11 g carbo, 3 g fiber, 33 g pro. Daily Values: 118% vit. A, 31% vit. C, 12% calcium, 18% iron.*

FAST

SPICY GREEN STIR-FRY WITH PEANUTS

PREP: 15 MIN.   COOK: 10 MIN.

- ¼   cup cold water
- 1   Tbsp. reduced-sodium teriyaki sauce
- ½   tsp. cornstarch
- 2   tsp. peanut oil or sesame oil
- 1   tsp. grated fresh ginger
- ⅓   cup lightly salted peanuts
- ⅛   tsp. cayenne pepper or crushed red pepper
- 4   ounces fresh green beans, trimmed (about ¾ cup)
- ½   large green or red sweet pepper, seeded and cut into thin bite-size strips
- ⅓   cup shelled frozen sweet soybeans (edamame), thawed
- 1   clove garlic, minced
- 2   baby bok choy, separated into leaves, or 3 cups coarsely shredded napa cabbage

1. In a small bowl stir together water, teriyaki sauce, and cornstarch; set aside.

2. In a wok or large nonstick skillet, heat 1 teaspoon oil over medium-high heat. Add ginger; cook and stir 15 seconds. Add peanuts; cook and stir 30 seconds. Transfer peanuts to a small bowl. Immediately sprinkle cayenne pepper over peanuts, tossing to coat. Set aside.

3. Heat remaining 1 teaspoon oil in the wok or large nonstick skillet. Add green beans; stir-fry for 3 minutes. Add green pepper, edamame, and garlic. Stir-fry for 3 to 5 minutes or until vegetables are crisp-tender. Stir water mixture; add to vegetables in wok. Cook and stir until thickened and bubbly. Cook and stir for 2 minutes more. Stir in bok choy or cabbage.

4. Top with peanuts before serving.

MAKES 4 SIDE DISH SERVINGS.

EACH SERVING *130 cal, 9 g fat (1 g sat. fat), 0 mg chol, 142 mg sodium, 8 g carbo, 3 g fiber, 6 g pro. Daily Values: 53% vit. A, 75% vit. C, 9% calcium, 7% iron.*

SPICY GREEN STIR-FRY WITH PEANUTS

American Classics
from Chef Scott Peacock
Pound Cake

CLASSIC POUND CAKE

PREP: 20 MIN. **BAKE:** 1¼ HR.

OVEN: 300°F

6	eggs
1	cup cold unsalted butter (8 oz.), cut in ½-inch pieces
1	8-oz. pkg. cold cream cheese, cut in 1-inch pieces
2¾	cups sugar
1	tsp. kosher salt
4	tsp. pure vanilla
3	cups sifted cake flour*

1. Let eggs stand at room temperature about 30 minutes or until they are room temperature (no more than 2 hours). Generously butter and lightly flour two 8×4×2-inch loaf pans or one 10-inch tube pan. Using large bowl of heavy-duty stand mixer with paddle attachment, beat cold butter about 2 minutes on low speed, occasionally raising to moderately high speed for 5 seconds to dislodge butter from paddle.

2. Add cream cheese. Beat on low speed 3 minutes with occasional short bursts on high speed to dislodge mixture from paddle. Beat butter and cream cheese mixture until waxy and well blended. Still mixing on low, add the sugar in a slow continuous stream. (This should take 1½ to 2 minutes.) Add salt. Continue creaming butter and cream cheese mixture for 5 minutes, scraping sides and bottom of bowl once halfway through. Increase speed to medium; continue mixing 2 minutes more, scraping once.

3. Add eggs, one at a time, beating 20 to 30 seconds after each addition or just until each egg is fully incorporated before adding the next egg. Scrape sides and bottom of bowl after first three eggs. Beat in vanilla with the last egg.

4. Gradually add about 2½ cups of the flour on low speed, mixing until just blended (This should take 1 to 1½ minutes). Turn off mixer. Fold in remaining flour by hand with a rubber spatula just until combined.

5. Turn batter into prepared pan(s). Shake pan(s) gently to distribute batter. Run a spatula in zigzag pattern through batter. Drop filled pan(s) from a height of about 6 inches onto kitchen counter to dislodge any large air pockets.

6. Place on center rack of cold oven. Turn oven setting to 300°F. Bake for 1 hour 15 minutes to 1 hour 30 minutes without opening oven door for the first 1 hour and 15 minutes. (Bake 1 hour 45 minutes for tube pan.) Test for doneness by carefully inserting a cake tester in center of cake or gently removing cake from oven and listening for light bubbling sounds that soften and slow as cake approaches doneness.

7. Transfer to cooling rack. Cool for 10 minutes before removing from pan(s). Cool completely before serving.

MAKES 2 LOAVES OR ONE 10-INCH TUBE CAKE (24 SERVINGS).

***NOTE** 2 ½ cups plus 2 tablespoons all-purpose flour can be used in place of the cake flour.

EACH SERVING *272 cal, 12 g fat (7 g sat. fat), 4 mg chol, 127 mg sodium, 37 g carbo, 1 g fiber, 4 g pro. Daily Values: 8% vit. A, 2% calcium, 9% iron.*

MEASURE WITH CARE
"Diligent, precise measuring is important for keeping the balance of ingredients. Evenly scoop, and level with a straight edge."

perfect batter: "Pale yellow and ribbony—this is what the batter should look like once all the eggs are blended," says Scott.

the ideal pound cake

... HAS A TENDER, FINE CRUMB and a velvety-rich texture.

... HAS A PERSONALITY ALL ITS OWN. No two pound cakes are alike. "Slight variations can be expected—splits and cracks are part of its charm."

... IS SIMPLE, uses the best ingredients, and gets its volume from diligent and patient mixing.

CAKE FLOUR AND SIFTING—A DUO FOR SUCCESS
"Cake flour is a soft-wheat flour that has a fine and silky texture. It makes the pound cake lighter and provides a more delicate crumb."

FINISH BY FOLDING
"Incorporating the last bit of the flour by hand, with quick and gentle turns with a rubber spatula, prevents overworking or deflating the carefully mixed batter."

GENEROSITY COUNTS
"Generously butter the pan with softened butter, then dust lightly with flour. Rap it on the edge of the sink to dislodge any excess flour."

EASY DOES IT
"Avoid losing volume by gently turning the batter into the pans. Once full, drop the pan on the counter to dislodge any stubborn air pockets that can cause tunneling."

"Place in the **middle** of a cold oven set to 300°F. Don't open the oven door while baking. It can cause the cakes to fall."

june

Fire up the grill for a feed-a-crowd barbecue and cool down with a trio of fabulously flavored lemonades.

116   118   134

BASIL-TOMATO SALAD
Recipe on page 123

Barbecue Bash

Meals for 12 people—under $100

1. Heat oven to 425°F. Place potatoes, onion, and garlic in 15×10×1-inch baking pan. Drizzle olive oil; toss to coat. Roast, uncovered, 20 minutes. Stir vegetables; add corn. Roast 15 to 20 minutes more or until vegetables are tender and browned.

2. For dressing, in large bowl whisk together mayonnaise, vinegar, salad dressing mix, and cayenne pepper. Add roasted vegetables; toss to coat. Stir in celery, eggs, and avocado. Season to taste with salt and black pepper. Transfer to serving dish. Sprinkle with parsley. Serve warm or chilled. **MAKES 12 SERVINGS.**

EACH SERVING *267 cal, 15 g fat (2 g sat. fat), 58 mg chol, 362 mg sodium, 19 g carbo, 2 g fiber, 4 g pro. Daily Values: 5% vit. A, 28% vit. C, 7% calcium, 5% iron.*

SWEET AND TANGY FOUR-BEAN SALAD

The longer the beans are in the dressing, the more flavorful they'll be. The green beans will lose some of their color as they chill; for bright green color, toss them in just before serving.

PREP: 30 MIN. CHILL: 4 TO 48 HR.

8	oz. fresh green beans, trimmed
¾	cup cider vinegar
⅔	cup tomato juice
¼	cup vegetable oil
3	Tbsp. dry red wine or apple juice
½	cup sugar
2	tsp. Worcestershire sauce
2	tsp. Dijon-style mustard
1	clove garlic, minced (½ tsp.)
1	12-oz. pkg. frozen shelled sweet soybeans (edamame), thawed
1	14.5-oz. can cut wax beans, rinsed and drained
1	15-oz. can red kidney beans, rinsed and drained
1	bunch green onions, finely chopped
4	large carrots, coarsely shredded

1. In large saucepan cook green beans in boiling lightly salted water for 10 minutes or just until tender; drain and rinse with cold water. Set aside.

2. In large bowl combine vinegar, tomato juice, oil, wine, sugar, Worcestershire, mustard, and garlic. Stir in beans, green onions, and carrots. Refrigerate, covered, 4 to 48 hours. Serve with a slotted spoon. **MAKES 12 (ABOUT 1-CUP) SERVINGS.**

EACH SERVING *174 cal, 6 g fat (1 g sat. fat), 0 mg chol, 231 mg sodium, 24 g carbo, 6 g fiber, 7 g pro. Daily Values: 75% vit. A, 24% vit. C, 8% calcium, 11% iron.*

POTATO SALAD WITH COUNTRY RANCH DRESSING

See tip on page 124 for a no-fail method for hard-cooking eggs. The avocado in this salad adds fresh, buttery flavor. Stir it in just before serving.

PREP: 25 MIN. ROAST: 35 MIN. OVEN: 425°F

3	lbs. round red potatoes, cut in 1-inch pieces
1	small red onion, cut in wedges (½ cup)
6	cloves garlic, minced
2	Tbsp. olive oil
1	cup frozen whole kernel corn
¾	cup mayonnaise
2	Tbsp. cider vinegar
1	1-oz. envelope dry ranch salad dressing mix
¼	tsp. cayenne pepper (optional)
1	stalk celery, bias-sliced
3	hard-cooked eggs, peeled and chopped
1	avocado, halved, seeded, peeled, and chopped (optional)
	Salt and ground black pepper
	Fresh Italian (flat-leaf) parsley, coarsely snipped (optional)

make it ahead

Divvy up the prep over a couple of days and relax before hosting a party.

COUNTRY RIBS The ribs can be baked up to 2 days ahead and stored, covered, in the refrigerator. Let the ribs stand at room temperature 30 minutes before grilling. On the day of the BBQ, grill ribs as directed and place in three 4- to 6-quart slow cookers (one for each sauce); borrow an extra slow cooker, if needed. Cover and keep warm on low-heat setting up to 2 hours. Except for Rosemary and Citrus sauce, which can be made up to 1 day ahead, the sauces can be made up to 2 days ahead.

FOUR-BEAN SALAD Assemble and refrigerate 4 to 48 hours. The fresh green beans will lose some color as they marinate in the dressing. For bright-color green beans, cook and chill as directed but do not add to salad. Cover and refrigerate separately. Toss beans with the salad just before serving.

POTATO SALAD Combine all ingredients except the avocado. Cover and refrigerate up to 24 hours. Just before serving, stir in avocado. Thin dressing with a little milk, if needed.

GARDEN SLIDERS Make the bean spread up to 2 days ahead; refrigerate, covered. Slice vegetables up to 24 hours ahead. Assemble sliders 2 hours ahead.

BASIL LEMONADE After removing fresh basil, cover and refrigerate up to 3 days.

COOL-AS-A-CUKE LEMONADE Make up to 24 hours ahead; cover and refrigerate. Stir before serving.

WATERMELON-BERRY LEMONADE Make up to 2 days ahead; cover and refrigerate. To serve, stir and add berries and watermelon wedges.

MINI CORN DOGS Make these fresh. Skewer hot dogs ahead of time; cover and refrigerate. Once fried, corn dogs can be kept warm in a 200°F oven up to 30 minutes.

PEACH PIE TWISTERS Store in an airtight container at room temperature for 24 hours. Reheat in a 350°F oven on a baking sheet for 8 minutes or until warm.

SAUCY COUNTRY RIBS

Start with these basic ribs. Add the trio of sauces (or triple one of the sauces) and grill.
PREP: 25 MIN. BAKE: 1¾ HR. OVEN: 350°F GRILL: 10 MIN.

12   to 15 lb. pork country-style ribs

1. Heat oven to 350°F. Trim fat from ribs. Place 1 cup of water in each of two large roasting pans.* Place ribs in a single layer, meaty sides up. Generously sprinkle with *salt* and *black pepper*. Cover with foil.
2. Bake ribs 1¾ to 2 hours or until tender. Carefully remove foil.
3. For charcoal grill, place ribs, in batches, on the grill rack directly over medium coals. Grill 10 to 15 minutes, brushing with sauces as directed in sauce recipes. (For gas grill, preheat grill. Reduce heat to medium. Place ribs on grill rack. Cover and grill as above.)
4. Serve or transfer to a slow cooker set on low to keep warm. **MAKES 4 SERVINGS.**

*NOTE If you don't have two large roasting pans, use two extra-large disposable roasting pans (placed on baking sheets for support), or one roasting pan and two 13×9×2-inch pans.

EACH SERVING *(ribs only) 351 cal, 13 g fat (5 g sat. fat), 187 mg chol, 330 mg sodium, 0 g carbo, 0 g fiber, 53 g pro. Daily Values: 5% calcium, 13% iron.*

FAST

A TRIO OF SAUCES
1. ROSEMARY AND CITRUS
PREP: 10 MIN.

¼   cup coarsely chopped fresh rosemary
¼   cup olive oil
2   Tbsp. finely shredded lemon peel
2   Tbsp. lemon juice
2   Tbsp. finely shredded orange peel
2   Tbsp. finely shredded grapefruit peel
½   tsp. sea salt or salt
⅓   recipe Saucy Country Ribs
     Lemon wedges (optional)

SAUCY COUNTRY RIBS
THREE WAYS

1. In bowl combine rosemary, oil, lemon peel and juice, orange peel, grapefruit peel, and salt. Brush half the mixture on ribs at the beginning of grilling. Brush remaining sauce on ribs the last 1 minute of grilling. Serve with lemon wedges. **MAKES 4 SERVINGS.**

EACH SERVING (ribs and sauce) 481 cal, 27 g fat (7 g sat. fat), 187 mg chol, 531 mg sodium, 3 g carbo, 1 g fiber, 53 g pro. Daily Values: 2% vit. A, 26% vit. C, 7% calcium, 14% iron.

FAST

2. RHUBARB-CHIPOTLE

PREP: 10 MIN. COOK: 20 MIN.

- 2 cups chopped fresh or frozen rhubarb (about 8 oz.)
- 1 small onion, chopped
- ¼ cup water
- ½ a 12-oz. jar strawberry jam (½ cup)
- ¼ cup ketchup
- 1 Tbsp. cider vinegar
- 1 Tbsp. yellow mustard
- 1 chopped canned chipotle peppers in adobo sauce
- 2 cloves garlic, minced
- 1 Tbsp. Worcestershire sauce
- ¼ tsp. ground black pepper
- ⅛ tsp. salt
- ⅓ recipe Saucy Country Ribs
  Fresh parsley or cilantro (optional)

1. In saucepan combine rhubarb, onion, and water; bring to boiling. Reduce heat; simmer, covered, 5 minutes. Add jam, ketchup, vinegar, mustard, chipotle peppers, garlic, Worcestershire, black pepper, and salt. Bring to boiling; simmer, uncovered, 15 minutes.

2. Generously brush on ribs at beginning of grilling. Occasionally brush with additional sauce during grilling. Sprinkle parsley. Pass remaining sauce. **MAKES 4 SERVINGS.**

EACH SERVING (ribs and sauce) 512 cal, 14 g fat (5 g sat. fat), 187 mg chol, 683 mg sodium, 39 g carbo, 2 g fiber, 54 g pro. Daily Values: 5% vit. A, 22% vit. C, 13% calcium, 17% iron.

FAST

3. SWEET MUSTARD

PREP: 10 MIN.

- ½ cup packed brown sugar
- ¼ cup yellow mustard
- ¼ cup ketchup
- ¼ cup dill relish
- 2 Tbsp. cider vinegar
- ½ tsp. ground black pepper
- ⅓ recipe Saucy Country Ribs

1. In bowl combine brown sugar, mustard, ketchup, dill relish, vinegar, and pepper. Generously brush ribs with sauce the last 5 minutes of grilling. Pass remaining sauce. **MAKES 4 SERVINGS.**

EACH SERVING (ribs and sauce) 488 cal, 14 g fat (5 g sat. fat), 187 mg chol, 916 mg sodium, 33 g carbo, 1 g fiber, 54 g pro. Daily Values: 3% vit. A, 4% vit. C, 9% calcium, 16% iron.

POTATO SALAD WITH COUNTRY RANCH DRESSING

SWEET AND TANGY FOUR-BEAN SALAD

L'EMONADE TRIO

BLUE CHEESE AND BACON MINI CORN DOGS

The crackly cornmeal crust of these pint-size appetizers is studded with bacon and blue cheese. For a retro-decadent splurge, serve with homemade blue cheese dip or prepared honey mustard.

PREP: 30 MIN. COOK: 2 TO 3 MIN. PER BATCH

1	cup all-purpose flour
⅔	cup yellow cornmeal
2	Tbsp. sugar
1½	tsp. baking powder
½	tsp. dry mustard
¼	tsp. salt
1	Tbsp. shortening
¾	cup milk
¼	cup blue cheese
1	egg
3	slices bacon, crisp-cooked and finely crumbled or chopped
	Oil for deep-frying
6	jumbo beef hot dogs, cut in half crosswise
12	6-inch wooden skewers
	Honey mustard or mustard
	Blue Cheese Dip (optional)
	Fresh Italian (flat-leaf) parsley (optional)

1. In large bowl combine flour, cornmeal, sugar, baking powder, dry mustard, and salt. Cut in the shortening until mixture resembles fine crumbs. In a blender combine milk, blue cheese, and egg; cover and blend until almost smooth. Add egg mixture to flour mixture along with bacon; mix well. (Batter will be thick.)

2. Meanwhile, heat 1 inch of oil in a heavy 10-inch skillet over medium heat to 365°F. (should take about 15 minutes).

3. Insert skewers into ends of hot dogs. Holding on to skewers, hold hot dogs over bowl of cornmeal mixture. Spoon cornmeal mixture on hot dogs and slightly spread to completely cover. Place coated hot dogs, 3 or 4 at a time, on their sides in hot oil. Turn hot dogs with tongs after about 10 seconds of cooking to prevent batter from sliding off. Cook for 2 to 3 minutes more or until golden brown, turning to brown evenly. Remove and drain on a baking sheet lined with paper towels. Keep warm in a 200°F oven while frying remaining hot dogs. Serve warm with honey mustard and/or Blue Cheese Dip. Sprinkle parsley.

MAKES 12 APPETIZER CORN DOGS.

BLUE CHEESE DIP In medium bowl combine ⅔ cup mayonnaise, ¼ cup sour cream, 2 ounces crumbled blue cheese, 1 teaspoon Worcestershire sauce, and ⅛ teaspoon ground black pepper. Cover and chill until ready to serve.

EACH CORN DOG *259 cal, 15 g fat (6 g sat. fat), 49 mg chol, 564 mg sodium, 23 g carbo, 1 g fiber, 9 g pro. Daily Values: 2% vit. A, 5% calcium, 9% iron.*

LOW FAT

BASIL LEMONADE

PREP: 15 MIN. CHILL: 8 HR.

12	cups cold water
2	12-oz. cans frozen lemonade concentrate, thawed
⅓	cup sugar
¼	cup fresh lime juice
½	cup firmly packed fresh basil leaves, torn (one 0.75-oz. pkg.)
	Lemon slices and fresh basil (optional)

1. In large bowl or pitcher combine water, lemonade concentrate, sugar, and lime juice. Stir well to combine. Stir in torn basil leaves. Cover; refrigerate 8 hours.

2. Strain through a fine-mesh strainer into serving container; discard basil leaves. Chill up to 3 days.

3. Serve over ice with lemon slices and fresh basil. **MAKES 12 SERVINGS.**

EACH SERVING *125 cal, 0 g fat, 0 mg chol, 9 mg sodium, 33 g carbo, 0 g fiber, 0 g pro. Daily Values: 19% vit. C, 1% calcium, 2% iron.*

FAST | LOW FAT

COOL-AS-A-CUKE LEMONADE

PREP: 10 MIN.

1	English cucumber, coarsely chopped
2	12-oz. cans frozen lemonade concentrate, thawed
10	cups water
	Cucumber slices (optional)

1. In blender combine cucumber and 1 can lemonade concentrate; blend until almost smooth. Transfer to serving container. Stir in remaining lemonade concentrate and water. Cover; chill up to 24 hours.

2. Stir before serving. Serve over ice with cucumber slices. **MAKES 12 SERVINGS.**

EACH SERVING *106 cal, 0 g fat, 0 mg chol, 8 mg sodium, 27 g carbo, 0 g fiber, 0 g pro. Daily Values: 1% vit. A, 18% vit. C, 1% calcium, 3% iron.*

LOW FAT

WATERMELON-BERRY LEMONADE

PREP: 25 MIN. CHILL: UP TO 24 HR.

8	cups cubed, seeded watermelon
3	cups hulled and quartered strawberries
2	12-oz. cans frozen lemonade concentrate, thawed
8	cups water
	Wedges of fresh watermelon (optional)
	Whole hulled strawberries (optional)

1. In blender combine half the watermelon, strawberries, and lemonade concentrate. Cover; blend until smooth. Transfer to serving container. Repeat with remaining. Add water; chill up to 2 days.

2. Serve over ice with watermelon wedges and strawberries. **MAKES 12 SERVINGS.**

EACH SERVING *145 cal, 0 g fat, 0 mg chol, 8 mg sodium, 37 g carbo, 1 g fiber, 1 g pro. Daily Values: 12% vit. A, 66% vit. C, 2% calcium, 4% iron.*

BLUE CHEESE AND
BACON MINI CORN DOGS

all this food for under $100?

Offer the crowd a generous spread while keeping your budget intact. The total is based on serving the entire menu. Spend less by serving plain lemonade or by making your favorite from-the-pantry barbecue sauce. Or spend more by serving grilled chicken or spareribs instead of country ribs. Here's what we spent:

Rosemary and Citrus Ribs	$12.99
Rhubarb-Chipotle Ribs	15.12
Sweet Mustard Ribs	12.14
Four-Bean Salad	8.26
Potato Salad	6.90
Garden Sliders	5.99
Basil Lemonade	7.41
Cool-as-a-Cuke Lemonade	4.53
Watermelon-Berry Lemonade	8.94
Mini Corn Dogs	9.59
Peach Pie Twisters	7.54
Total	**$99.41**

Costs are based on national brand prices in Des Moines, Iowa, supermarkets during February 2009 and do not include optional ingredients. Costs may vary by region or season.

FAST | LOW FAT

GARDEN SLIDERS

For a no-cook starter, serve the squash in these sandwiches fresh rather than grilled.

START TO FINISH: 30 MIN.

- 1   15- to 16-oz. can Great Northern or cannellini beans, rinsed and drained
- 2   Tbsp. olive oil
- 2   cloves garlic, minced (1 tsp.)
- ½   tsp. Italian seasoning, crushed
- 1   medium yellow summer squash, cut in ¼-inch-thick slices
- 24   ¼-inch-thick slices baguette
- 2   medium plum tomatoes, cut in ¼-inch-thick slices
- 1   small cucumber, cut in ¼-inch-thick slices
     Small celery top sprigs, small tomato wedges, and/or pickle slices (optional)

1. For bean spread, in blender or food processor combine beans, 1 tablespoon of the oil, the garlic, and Italian seasoning. Cover; blend or process until smooth. Season with *salt* and *ground black pepper*.
2. To grill squash, toss squash slices with remaining 1 tablespoon olive oil. Place in a grill basket. Place basket directly over medium coals for about 5 minutes or just until squash is tender, turning once.
3. Spread one side of each bread slice with bean spread. Top half the bread with tomato, squash, and cucumber slices. Top with remaining bread slices, spread sides down. Secure sandwiches with wooden picks. Top with celery sprigs, tomato wedges, and/or pickle slices.

MAKES 12 APPETIZER-SIZE SLIDERS.

EACH SLIDER *120 cal, 2 g fat, 0 mg chol, 289 mg sodium, 23 g carbo, 3 g fiber, 6 g pro. Daily Values: 3% vit. A, 5% vit. C, 3% calcium, 9% iron.*

KID-FRIENDLY

SUMMER PEACH PIE TWISTERS

Chopped fresh summer peaches and tiny marshmallows are all you need to make the filling for these stand-up hand pies. A dusting of chili powder gives the pies spicy kick; substitute cinnamon for milder flavor.

PREP: 40 MIN. BAKE: 15 MIN. OVEN: 400°F

- 1   15-oz. pkg. rolled refrigerated unbaked piecrust (2 crusts)
- 3   medium peaches, pitted and chopped, or one 16-oz. pkg. frozen unsweetened peach slices, thawed and chopped
- ⅔   cup tiny marshmallows
- ½   tsp. cinnamon sugar or chili powder
- 1   Tbsp. cinnamon sugar or 1 Tbsp. sugar mixed with ½ tsp. chili powder
     Vanilla ice cream (optional)

1. Let piecrusts stand at room temperature according to package directions. Preheat oven to 400°F. Line two large baking sheets with parchment paper or foil; lightly grease the foil if using. Set aside.
2. In medium bowl combine peaches, marshmallows, and the ½ teaspoon cinnamon-sugar or chili powder.
3. Unroll one piecrust. Cut crust in 6 wedges. Spoon a scant ¼ cup of the peach mixture along one long side of each wedge ½ inch from edge of crust. Brush edge of long sides of crust with a little water. Fold crust over filling. Using the tines of a fork, press long sides together to seal. Fold the top edge of the crust back to expose some of the filling.
4. Place pies on prepared baking sheets. Prick top crusts of pies two or three times with a fork. Sprinkle with the 1 tablespoon cinnamon sugar or chili powder-sugar mixture. Bake 15 to 18 minutes or until filling is bubbly and pastry is golden brown. Cool pies on pans slightly to serve warm, or cool completely.
5. Serve standing upright in paper cups or glasses with a scoop of ice cream.

MAKES 12 TWISTERS.

EACH SERVING *188 cal, 9 g fat (3 g sat. fat), 3 mg chol, 148 mg sodium, 24 g carbo, 1 g fiber, 1 g pro. Daily Values: 2% vit. A, 4% vit. C, 1% iron.*

GARDEN SLIDERS

What's Cooking

Stacked Summer Salads

PORK AND
NOODLE SALAD

PORK AND NOODLE SALAD

PREP: 25 MIN. BAKE: 25+5 MIN. OVEN: 425°F

1	recipe Ginger-Soy Dressing
1	¾- to 1-lb. pork tenderloin
1	3.75-oz. pkg. bean threads or cellophane noodles
2	cups shredded napa cabbage
2	medium carrots, shredded
1	cup thinly sliced radishes
2	cups torn bok choy or baby bok choy
½	cup cilantro leaves
1	recipe Wonton Crisps

1. Prepare Ginger-Soy Dressing; set aside.
2. Heat oven to 425°F. Line a 15×10×1-inch pan with foil; set aside. Trim fat from pork; place in prepared pan. Sprinkle *salt* and *black pepper*. Roast 25 minutes, or until internal temperature reaches 155°F, brushing with 1 tablespoon of the dressing the last 5 minutes of cooking. Cover with foil; let stand 15 minutes. Slice thinly.
3. Meanwhile, prepare noodles according to package directions. Rinse with cold water to cool; drain well. With scissors, snip noodles in short lengths. Add cabbage; toss.
4. In 3-quart dish layer noodle mixture, carrots, pork, and radishes. Drizzle half the Ginger-Soy Dressing. Top with bok choy and cilantro. Refrigerate, covered, until ready to serve or up to 24 hours. Serve with Wonton Crisps; pass remaining dressing.
MAKES 6 SERVINGS.

GINGER-SOY DRESSING In screw-top jar combine ⅓ cup vegetable oil, 3 tablespoons lime juice, 3 tablespoons rice vinegar, 1 tablespoon brown sugar, 1 tablespoon grated fresh ginger, 1 tablespoon soy sauce, 1 tablespoon honey, 1 teaspoon toasted sesame oil, ¼ teaspoon salt, and ¼ teaspoon crushed red pepper. Cover; shake well. Refrigerate up to 3 days.

WONTON CRISPS Line baking sheet with foil. Lightly coat with nonstick cooking spray. Place 12 wonton wrappers on baking sheet. Brush tops of wrappers with 1 tablespoon sesame or peanut oil. Bake in a 425°F oven for 5 to 6 minutes or until golden (wontons will continue to brown after baking). When cool, break into pieces.

EACH SERVING *351 cal, 17 g fat (2 g sat. fat), 8 mg chol, 529 mg sodium, 35 g carbo, 2 g fiber, 15 g pro. Daily Values 99% vit. A, 51% vit. C, 8% calcium, 10% iron.*

BASIL-TOMATO SALAD

FAST

BASIL-TOMATO SALAD

The flavors of pesto mix and mingle in this salad. For a meal, serve with chicken or fish drizzled with Lemon Vinaigrette.

START TO FINISH: 30 MIN. OVEN 425°F

1	recipe Lemon Vinaigrette
1	small baguette or French roll
2	Tbsp. olive oil
2	cloves garlic, minced
1	small head green leaf lettuce, torn (6 cups)
3	cups fresh basil, torn
2	cups grape tomatoes, halved, or chopped plum tomatoes
½	cup pine nuts, toasted
2	oz. Parmesan cheese, shaved

1. Prepare Lemon Vinaigrette; set aside.
2. Heat oven to 425°F. Split baguette in half horizontally. In small bowl combine olive oil and garlic. Brush on cut sides of baguette. Cut each bread piece lengthwise into 3 or 4 breadsticks. Place on baking sheet. Bake 3 to 5 minutes or until toasted. Transfer to wire rack; cool.
3. In large bowl combine lettuce and basil. In 3- to 4-quart glass canister layer greens, tomatoes, pine nuts, and cheese. Serve with breadsticks and Lemon Vinaigrette.
MAKES 6 SERVINGS.

LEMON VINAIGRETTE In small screw-top jar combine ½ cup olive oil, 1 teaspoon finely shredded lemon peel, ⅓ cup lemon juice (from 1 large lemon), 4 cloves minced garlic, 1 teaspoon sugar, ¼ teaspoon salt, and ¼ teaspoon ground black pepper. Cover; shake well.

EACH SERVING (WITH BREADSTICK) *449 cal, 33 g fat (6 g sat. fat), 8 mg chol, 502 mg sodium, 30 g carbo, 3 g fiber, 13 g pro. Daily Values: 87% vit. A, 43% vit. C, 19% calcium, 22% iron.*

SOUTHERN
COBB SALAD

SOUTHERN COBB SALAD

The creamy cheese dressing pulls together crisp fried chicken, black-eyed peas, sweet peppers, and pecans for a satisfying salad.

PREP: 30 MIN. COOK: 6 MIN.

1	recipe Pimiento-Cheese Dressing
3	hard-cooked eggs
2	skinless, boneless chicken breast halves
1	egg
1	Tbsp. milk
1	tsp. bottled hot pepper sauce
⅓	cup all-purpose flour
3	Tbsp. vegetable oil
1	Tbsp. cider vinegar
1	tsp. snipped fresh oregano (optional)
1	15.8-oz. can black-eyed peas, rinsed and drained
1	large head butterhead (Boston or Bibb) lettuce, torn (8 cups)
1	red sweet pepper, cut in strips
½	cup pecan halves, toasted

1. Prepare Pimiento-Cheese Dressing; set aside. Halve eggs lengthwise and scoop out yolks. In a bowl mash yolks with a fork. Stir in 1 to 2 tablespoons Pimiento-Cheese Dressing until smooth. Spoon yolk mixture into egg halves. Cover and refrigerate.

2. Place chicken in heavy-duty plastic bag (do not seal). Pound chicken lightly with meat mallet to even thickness of ½ inch. Sprinkle with *salt* and *black pepper*. In shallow dish, beat together egg, milk, and hot pepper sauce. In another shallow dish, place flour. Dip chicken in egg mixture; dredge in flour. In large skillet heat 2 tablespoons of the oil. Add chicken; cook 6 minutes, turning once, or until golden and chicken is no longer pink (170°F). Drain. Cool chicken slightly; cut in strips.

3. In bowl combine remaining oil, vinegar, and oregano. Add peas; toss to coat.

4. To serve, place lettuce on platter. Arrange chicken, peas, sweet pepper, pecans, and deviled eggs. Pass remaining Pimiento-Cheese Dressing. **MAKES 6 SERVINGS.**

PIMIENTO-CHEESE DRESSING Let 1 cup finely shredded sharp cheddar cheese stand at room temperature 30 minutes. In bowl beat cheese and ½ cup mayonnaise with electric mixer on medium to combine. Add ½ cup milk, one 2-ounce jar drained diced pimientos, ⅛ teaspoon *each* cayenne pepper, salt, and black pepper.

EACH SERVING *536 cal, 39 g fat (9 g sat. fat), 197 mg chol, 668 mg sodium, 22 g carbo, 5 g fiber, 26 g pro. Daily Values: 76% vit. A, 61% vit. C, 23% calcium, 20% iron.*

TEST KITCHEN TIP

Perfectly Hard-Cooked Eggs

Place eggs in single layer in a medium saucepan. Completely cover with cold water. Cook over medium-high heat until water comes to a rapid boil. Remove from heat, cover, and let stand 15 minutes. Drain. Run under cold water or place in a bowl of ice water until cool.

SMOKED SALMON AND MELON SALAD

Make this salad for brunch or a light no-cook dinner. Lively, spicy-sweet cardamom adds depth of flavor to the dish and complements the smoky salmon and cool melon.

START TO FINISH: 25 MIN.

1	recipe Yogurt-Cardamom Dressing
⅓	cup mint leaves, coarsely chopped
1	tsp. finely shredded lemon peel
¼	tsp. cracked black pepper
½	a cantaloupe, peeled and cut in thin wedges (about 2 cups)
2	cups thinly sliced fennel
2	cups blueberries or seedless red grapes
8	oz. smoked salmon, skin and bones removed, coarsely broken
½	a honeydew melon, cut in cubes and/or balls (about 2 cups)

1. Prepare Yogurt-Cardamom Dressing; set aside.
2. In small bowl combine mint, lemon peel, and pepper; set aside.
3. In a trifle dish or straight-sided glass serving bowl place cantaloupe, fennel, blueberries, salmon, and honeydew. Sprinkle with mint mixture. Serve with Yogurt-Cardamom Dressing.
MAKES 6 SERVINGS.

YOGURT-CARDAMOM DRESSING In small bowl combine one 6-ounce carton plain low-fat yogurt, ¼ cup olive oil, 2 tablespoons lemon juice, 1 tablespoon honey, 1 clove minced garlic, ½ teaspoon ground cardamom or ground nutmeg, ½ teaspoon cracked black pepper, and ¼ teaspoon salt.
EACH SERVING *239 cal, 12 g fat (2 g sat. fat), 10 mg chol, 452 mg sodium, 26 g carbo, 3 g fiber, 10 g pro. Daily Values: 33% vit. A, 77% vit. C, 9% calcium, 10% iron.*

a head start

TO MAKE THESE SALADS IN ADVANCE OR TO TOTE, prepare the dressings separately and store in a jar or other airtight container. Refrigerate dressings and undressed salads, covered, up to 24 hours. An exception: Half of the dressing should be added to the Pork and Noodle Salad before chilling. For picnics, any of these salads can be layered in glass jars for individual servings.

SMOKED SALMON AND MELON SALAD

Everyday Easy
Quick, budget-friendly meals

FAST

BLT SALAD WITH WARM VINAIGRETTE

START TO FINISH: 20 MINUTES
BUDGET $2.43 PER SERVING

8	slices bacon
4	slices country Italian bread
1½	cups cherry tomatoes
8	cups torn romaine
⅓	cup blue cheese crumbles
¼	cup cider vinegar
¼	cup olive oil
1	tsp. sugar
1	tsp. Dijon-style mustard
	Salt and ground black pepper

1. In large skillet cook bacon over medium heat until crisp, turning occasionally. Remove bacon from skillet; drain on paper towels.
2. Meanwhile, toast bread. Halve cherry tomatoes. Break bacon in 2-inch pieces. On plates layer toast, romaine, tomatoes, bacon, and blue cheese.

3. For vinaigrette, in screw-top jar combine vinegar, oil, sugar, and mustard. Shake well. Season to taste with salt and pepper. Drizzle vinaigrette on salads. **MAKES 4 SERVINGS.**
EACH SERVING *375 cal, 26 g fat (7 g sat. fat), 31 mg chol, 923 mg sodium, 24 g carbo, 4 g fiber, 14 g pro. Daily Values: 145% vit. A, 59% vit. C, 14% calcium, 14% iron.*

FAST

APRICOT PORK WITH GARLIC GREEN BEANS

START TO FINISH: 20 MINUTES
BUDGET $2.09 PER SERVING

1	Tbsp. olive oil
4	½-inch-thick pork rib chops
	Salt and ground black pepper
4	apricots, pitted and cut in wedges
2	Tbsp. honey
3	cloves garlic, sliced
1	lb. green beans, trimmed if desired

1. In large nonstick skillet heat the oil over medium-high heat; lower heat to medium. Lightly sprinkle chops with salt and pepper. Cook chops in hot oil for 5 minutes, turning once. Add apricots, honey, and garlic to chops in skillet; cover and cook 5 to 7 minutes or until apricots are tender and pork is slightly pink in center.
2. Meanwhile, in a 2-quart microwave-safe dish combine beans and ¼ cup water. Cook, covered, on 100% (high) power 6 minutes, stirring once; drain.
3. To serve, spoon cooking juices from skillet over pork, apricots, and beans.
MAKES 4 SERVINGS.
EACH SERVING *295 cal, 14 g fat (4 g sat. fat), 57 mg chol, 207 mg sodium, 20 g carbo, 4 g fiber, 22 g pro. Daily Values: 27% vit. A, 34% vit. C, 7% calcium, 11% iron.*

BLT SALAD WITH WARM VINAIGRETTE

APRICOT PORK WITH
GARLIC GREEN BEANS

TURKEY BURGERS WITH
MUSTARD SAUCE

FAST
TURKEY BURGERS WITH MUSTARD SAUCE

START TO FINISH: 25 MINUTES
BUDGET $1.93 PER SERVING

5	kaiser rolls or hamburger buns
1	lb. ground raw turkey
1	egg, lightly beaten
3	Tbsp. honey mustard
¼	tsp. *each* salt and black pepper
1	Tbsp. olive or cooking oil
⅓	cup light mayonnaise
1	medium tomato, sliced
1	medium avocado, pitted, peeled, and sliced

1. For bread crumbs, in blender or food processor coarsely process one roll. In large bowl combine turkey, egg, 1 cup of the crumbs, 1 tablespoon of the mustard, and the salt and pepper. Shape turkey mixture into four patties.
2. In large nonstick skillet cook turkey patties in hot oil over medium heat for 12 minutes, turning once, or until no longer pink (165°F).
3. For mustard sauce, in small bowl combine mayonnaise and remaining 2 tablespoons mustard. Spread some sauce on remaining four rolls. Layer turkey patty, tomato, avocado, a dollop of sauce, and roll top.
MAKES 4 SERVINGS.

EACH SERVING *610 cal, 31 g fat (6 g sat. fat), 149 mg chol, 778 mg sodium, 51 g carbo, 6 g fiber, 31 g pro. Daily Values: 9% vit. A, 29% vit. C, 11% calcium, 24% iron.*

FAST
STIR-FRY SHRIMP WITH CHEESY GRITS

START TO FINISH: 25 MINUTES
BUDGET $3.62 PER SERVING

2	red and/or yellow sweet peppers
½	cup quick-cooking hominy grits

CHICKEN-BROCCOLI
MAC AND CHEESE

½	cup shredded Mexican cheese blend (2 oz.)
1½	lb. medium shrimp, peeled and deveined, tails intact
½	tsp. chili powder
¼	cup olive oil
1	cup cilantro sprigs
1	Tbsp. cider vinegar
	Lemon wedges and cilantro sprigs (optional)

1. Halve, seed, and coarsely chop peppers. In medium saucepan heat 1¾ cups water to boiling. Stir in grits and peppers. Return to boiling. Reduce heat. Simmer, covered, 5 minutes, until most water is absorbed and grits are tender. Stir in cheese. Sprinkle *salt* and *black pepper*. Cover; keep warm.
2. In bowl toss shrimp with chili powder. Heat 1 tablespoon oil in large skillet over medium-high heat. Add shrimp. Cook and stir 3 to 4 minutes or until shrimp are opaque.
3. In food processor combine remaining oil, cilantro, vinegar, and 2 tablespoons *water*. Drizzle on shrimp and grits. Serve with lemon and cilantro. MAKES 4 SERVINGS.

EACH SERVING *385 cal, 21 g fat (5 g sat. fat), 185 mg chol, 423 mg sodium, 21 g carbo, 3 g fiber, 29 g pro. Daily Values: 68% vit. A, 164% vit. C, 17% calcium, 25% iron.*

STIR-FRY SHRIMP
WITH CHEESY GRITS

FAST   KID-FRIENDLY
CHICKEN-BROCCOLI MAC AND CHEESE

START TO FINISH: 21 MINUTES
BUDGET $3.60 PER SERVING

8	oz. dried rigatoni
2	cups fresh broccoli florets
1	2- to 2-¼ lb. whole roasted chicken
1	5.2-oz. pkg. semisoft cheese with garlic and fine herbs
¾	to 1 cup milk
¼	cup oil-packed dried tomatoes, drained and snipped
	Fresh Italian (flat-leaf) parsley (optional)

1. In large saucepan cook pasta according to package directions, adding broccoli florets during the last 3 minutes of cooking time. While pasta is cooking, remove meat from roasted chicken. Coarsely chop chicken. Drain pasta and broccoli; set aside.
2. In same saucepan combine cheese, the ¾ cup milk, tomatoes, and ¼ teaspoon freshly ground *black pepper*. Cook and stir until cheese is melted. Add pasta mixture and chicken. Heat through. If necessary, thin with additional milk. Sprinkle fresh parsley. MAKES 4 SERVINGS.

EACH SERVING *667 cal, 34 g fat (15 g sat. fat), 163 mg chol, 872 mg sodium, 52 g carbo, 3 g fiber, 40 g pro. Daily Values: 9% vit. A, 80% vit. C, 11% calcium, 24% iron.*

Good and Healthy

Fish

Fish is an almost-perfect source of protein. Fish and shellfish provide lean protein that's low in saturated fat and high in essential omega-3 fatty acids.

"We should all eat a variety of fish and seafood—at least a couple of servings per week," says Harvard researcher Dariush Mozaffarian, M.D. Analyzing more than 20 studies worldwide, he found that 1 to 2 servings of fish per week, especially those high in omega-3s such as salmon, reduced risk of fatal heart disease by 36 percent.

To maximize the benefits, it's important to choose fish low in harmful chemicals.

fresh fish to try

1 SNAPPER
BENEFITS Good source of protein and magnesium
FLAVOR Mild; firm large flakes

2 TILAPIA
BENEFITS Lean protein, heart-healthy omega-3s
FLAVOR Mild, slightly sweet; fine texture, meaty

3 CATFISH
BENEFITS Low in saturated fat, has heart-healthy omega-3s
FLAVOR Mild; tender, juicy, fine flakes

FAST | LOW FAT

GRILLED BASS WITH LEMON AND HERBS

Striped bass is high in heart-heathly omega 3 fatty acids.

PREP: 15 MIN. GRILL: 4 MIN.

1	lb. fresh or frozen striped bass fillets
2	tsp. olive oil
2	Tbsp. snipped fresh Italian (flat-leaf) parsley
1	Tbsp. snipped fresh basil and/or chives
2	tsp. finely shredded lemon peel
1	tsp. snipped fresh rosemary

1. Thaw fish, if frozen. Rinse; pat dry with paper towels. Cut in four serving-size pieces. Brush with oil; sprinkle ¼ teaspoon *salt* and ⅛ teaspoon *black pepper.* Measure thickness of fish.

2. For charcoal grill, place fish on greased rack of uncovered grill directly over medium coals. Grill 4 to 6 minutes per ½-inch thickness of fish or until fish flakes easily when tested with fork; carefully turn once halfway through grilling. (For gas grill, preheat. Reduce heat to medium. Place fish on greased grill rack over heat; cover. Grill as above.)

3. In bowl combine parsley, basil, lemon peel, and rosemary. Sprinkle on grilled fish.

MAKES 4 SERVINGS.

EACH SERVING *131 cal, 5 g fat (1 g sat. fat), 90 mg chol, 225 mg sodium, 0 g carbo, 0 g fiber, 20 g pro. Daily Values: 6% vit. A, 7% vit. C, 2% calcium, 6% iron.*

GRILLED BASS WITH
LEMON AND HERBS

making smart choices

Along with benefits of fish come warnings. Some species are laden with mercury and other toxins, and some teeter near the edge of extinction. Here's how to choose.

• Avoid species that are prone to methylmercury contamination. Women who are or may be pregnant, nursing women, and children under age 2 should limit white tuna to once per week, says Dariush Mozaffarian, M.D., a Harvard researcher who studies the relationship between diet and disease. Those at risk should also avoid large, long-lived fish, such as swordfish, king mackerel, shark, and tilefish. For all other healthy adults, there is limited evidence for harmful effects of low-level mercury exposure from eating fish, Mozaffarian says.

• PCBs, industrial compounds that made their way into waterways before being banned in 1977, can be found in the fatty tissue of some fish. To minimize consumption of this chemical, remove skin from fish before cooking.

CATFISH 'N' CHIPS

CATFISH 'N' CHIPS

This recipe has double benefits: Catfish is low in fat, and using sweet potatoes in place of white potatoes boosts vitamins.

PREP: 20 MIN. BAKE: 14 MIN. OVEN: 450°F

1	lb. fresh or frozen skinless catfish fillets
1	tsp. chili powder or paprika
½	tsp. salt
¼	tsp. dried dillweed
¼	tsp. ground black pepper
2	small sweet potatoes (10 oz.)
1	medium Yukon gold potato
1	Tbsp. canola oil
⅓	cup buttermilk
⅔	cup panko (Japanese-style bread crumbs)
2	cloves garlic, minced
	Fresh dill sprigs (optional)
	Malt vinegar (optional)

1. Thaw fish, if frozen. Rinse; pat dry with paper towels. Cut in 4 to 8 pieces. Set aside. Heat oven to 450°F. Line two baking sheets with foil; lightly coat with nonstick spray. In bowl combine chili powder, salt, dill, and pepper; set aside.

2. Scrub potatoes; cut in ½-inch-thick wedges. In bowl toss potatoes with oil to coat. Add ½ teaspoon of the chili powder mixture; toss to coat. Arrange potatoes in single layer on one prepared baking sheet. Bake 10 minutes.

3. Meanwhile, pour buttermilk in shallow dish. In another shallow dish combine panko, garlic, and remaining chili powder mixture. Dip fish in buttermilk, turning to coat and allowing excess to drip off. Dip in panko mixture, coating both sides. Place fish on second baking sheet. Lightly coat with nonstick spray. Measure thickness.

4. Bake 4 to 6 minutes per ½-inch thickness of fish or until fish flakes easily when tested with fork and potatoes are tender. Sprinkle fish with fresh dill. Serve with vinegar.

MAKES 4 SERVINGS.

EACH SERVING *317 cal, 13 g fat (2 g sat. fat), 54 mg chol, 449 mg sodium, 28 g carbo, 3 g fiber, 22 g pro. Daily Values: 206% vit. A, 16% vit. C, 7% calcium, 8% iron.*

TILAPIA PUTTANESCA

Low in saturated fats, tilapia takes well to a wide variety of flavors.

START TO FINISH: 25 MIN.

1	lb. fresh or frozen skinless tilapia fillets
⅛	tsp. salt
½	medium red onion, cut in wedges
1	Tbsp. olive oil
2	cloves garlic, minced
1	14.5-oz. can diced tomatoes
½	tsp. dried oregano, crushed
¼	tsp. crushed red pepper
¼	cup pitted kalamata olives
1	Tbsp. capers, drained (optional)
2	Tbsp. coarsely chopped fresh Italian (flat-leaf) parsley

1. Thaw fish, if frozen. Rinse; pat dry with paper towels. Sprinkle with salt. Set aside.

2. In large skillet cook onion in olive oil over medium heat 8 minutes or until tender, stirring occasionally. Stir in garlic, undrained tomatoes, oregano, and crushed red pepper. Bring to boiling; reduce heat. Simmer, uncovered, 5 minutes.

3. Add olives and capers to sauce. Top with tilapia fillets. Return sauce to boiling; reduce heat. Cook, covered, 6 to 10 minutes or until fish flakes when tested with fork. Remove fish. Simmer sauce, uncovered, 1 to 2 minutes more to thicken. To serve, spoon sauce over fish. Sprinkle with parsley.

MAKES 4 SERVINGS.

EACH SERVING *182 cal, 6 g fat (1 g sat. fat), 56 mg chol, 431 mg sodium, 8 g carbo, 2 g fiber, 24 g pro. Daily Values: 12% vit. A, 19% vit. C, 4% calcium, 6% iron.*

TILAPIA PUTTANESCA

American Classics
from Chef Scott Peacock

Succotash

LOW FAT

CLASSIC SUCCOTASH

In the South, butter beans are a popular variety of fresh shelled beans similar to baby limas.

PREP: 15 MIN. COOK: 30 MIN.

2	cups fresh shelled butter or lima beans
	Kosher salt
2	large ears fresh corn (about 2 cups)
2	Tbsp. unsalted butter
	Freshly ground black pepper
¼	cup heavy cream
¼	cup minced country ham

1. Place butter beans in large saucepan. Cover with water; add about 1 teaspoon kosher salt. Bring to boiling. Skim surface until clear. Cook, partially covered, 30 to 40 minutes, until tender. Strain beans into sieve. Set aside.

2. Shuck corn. Using clean terry cloth kitchen towel gently rub corn to remove silks. Using sharp knife, cut corn kernels from cobs.

3. In large skillet heat butter over medium-high heat until melted and foaming. Add corn. Lightly season with salt and pepper, stirring to coat corn in butter. Cook 1 to 2 minutes. Add beans. Lightly season with *salt* and *pepper*. Cook 1 minute more, taking care not to overcook corn and beans.

4. Add cream and ham. Cook just until heated through and slightly reduced. Season to taste. **MAKES 8 (½-CUP) SERVINGS.**
EACH SERVING *141 cal, 6 g fat (4 g sat. fat), 20 mg chol, 246 mg sodium, 18 g carbo, 3 g fiber, 5 g pro. Daily Values: 5% vit. A, 7% vit. C, 2% calcium, 4% iron.*

SIMMER AND STRAIN
"Simmering the butter beans in salted water until tender, but not mushy, is key. Once tender, strain to prevent overcooking. Cooking time will vary depending on maturity and freshness."

polishing act: "The simplest, most fuss-free way to remove stubborn silks from freshly shucked corn is by gently brushing the corn with a clean terry cloth kitchen towel," says Scott.

COOK IN BUTTER
"The butter should just be melted and foamy before adding corn. Watch that it doesn't become browned. Once the vegetables go in, stir well to evenly coat."

HAM FOR FLAVOR
"A generous sprinkling of country ham adds a rich and savory flavor finish to succotash. As a substitute, mince any ham you have on hand."

GLAZE WITH CREAM
"Think of the cream as a simple glaze that pulls together the sweetness of the corn and earthiness of the beans. Let the cream reduce slightly until the vegetables are lightly glazed."

the ideal succotash

... IS AS GOOD ON ITS OWN as it is as an accompaniment. Try this pure and simple version, then customize yours with tomatoes, squash, and herbs on hand.

... IS FLEXIBLE AND QUICK. To save time, cook the beans ahead and refrigerate in cooking liquid until ready to finish and serve. Frozen beans work well when fresh are not in season.

july

Beat the heat with fiery foods that cool you down—then chill out with creamy hand-churned vanilla ice cream.

139

147

151

GRILLED CORN AND
GREEN TOMATO SALSA
Recipe on page 143

GRILLED VEGETABLE
TOSTADAS WITH
QUICK MOLE SAUCE

Heat Wave

Summer fare with chiles and spices

3. For charcoal grill, on rack of uncovered grill cook vegetables directly over medium coals 5 to 8 minutes or until tender, turning once halfway through grilling. (For gas grill, preheat. Reduce heat to medium. Place vegetables on rack over heat. Cover and grill as above.) Cut vegetables in pieces.

4. Serve the grilled vegetables with Quick Mole Sauce, toasted tortillas, sour cream, cheese, avocado, and cilantro. **MAKES 8 SERVINGS.**

*TO TOAST CORN TORTILLAS (Find 4-inch tortillas in stores that stock Mexican foods.) Brush both sides of tortillas with 1 tablespoon olive oil. Place on baking sheet. Heat in 425°F oven 8 minutes or until golden. Or, after brushing with oil, grill directly over medium coals 30 seconds on each side or until warmed.

EACH SERVING *464 cal, 28 g fat (8 g sat. fat), 25 mg chol, 514 mg sodium, 48 g carbo, 9 g fiber, 11 g pro. Daily Values: 26% vit. A, 66% vit. C, 17% calcium, 12% iron.*

QUICK MOLE SAUCE

Refrigerate any remaining sauce, covered, for up to 5 days.

HOT 2 tsp. chili powder
HOTTER 3 tsp. hot chili powder
HOTTEST 4 tsp. hot chili powder + hot-style BBQ sauce

2	Tbsp. pumpkin seeds (*pepitas*)
1	tsp. sesame seeds
1	medium onion, chopped
2	cloves garlic, minced
1	Tbsp. olive oil
2	to 4 tsp. chili powder or hot chili powder
½	tsp. ground cumin
¼	tsp. ground cinnamon
1	cup barbecue sauce or hot-style barbecue sauce
½	oz. bittersweet chocolate, chopped
	Hot pepper sauce (optional)

1. In large dry skillet over medium heat toast pumpkin and sesame seeds 2 to 3 minutes or until toasted. Remove from skillet.

2. In same skillet cook onion and garlic in hot oil for 3 minutes or until tender. Stir in chili powder, cumin, and cinnamon. Cook 1 minute more or until fragrant. Stir in barbecue sauce, chocolate, and hot pepper sauce. Bring to boiling; reduce heat. Simmer until chocolate is melted. Cool slightly.

3. Transfer onion mixture and toasted seeds to blender or food processor. Cover and blend or process until smooth. Thin with water if needed; cool. **MAKES 1½ CUPS.**

GRILLED VEGETABLE TOSTADAS WITH QUICK MOLE SAUCE

Mole (MOH-lay) is a flavorful Mexican sauce traditionally made with dried chiles, seasonings, and, most notably, dark chocolate. The chocolate adds rich depth to the sauce without being overly sweet.

PREP: 1 HR. COOK: 10 MIN. GRILL: 5 MIN.

1	recipe Quick Mole Sauce
4	medium zucchini and/or yellow summer squash, quartered lengthwise
1	medium eggplant, cut in ½-inch slices
1	large red onion, cut in ½-inch slices
2	Tbsp. olive oil
16	4- to 6-inch toasted corn tortillas*
1	8-oz. carton sour cream
1	cup crumbled queso fresco or feta cheese
	Avocado slices and/or fresh cilantro
	Chili powder

1. Prepare Quick Mole Sauce.

2. Brush zucchini or squash, eggplant, and onion with olive oil; season with *salt* and *black pepper*.

SWEET-HOT PICKLED PEACHES

Serve alongside barbecue pork or chicken, or coarsely chop and pile on a burger. Save any remaining juices to drizzle on pound cake or grain salads.

PREP: 40 MIN. COOK: 10 MIN. CHILL: 24 HR.

HOT 2-inch piece fresh gingerroot

HOTTER 3-inch piece fresh gingerroot

HOTTEST 4-inch piece fresh gingerroot

6	lb. small fresh peaches or apricots (about 18 peaches)
2½	cups water
2½	cups cider vinegar
4	cups granulated sugar
3	cups packed brown sugar
4	sticks cinnamon
1	2- to 4-inch piece fresh gingerroot, peeled and cut in strips
1½	tsp. crushed red pepper
1	tsp. mustard seeds
8	whole cloves
1	small sweet onion, cut in wedges
1	medium red sweet pepper, seeded and cut in strips

1. To peel peaches (apricots may be used unpeeled), fill Dutch oven with water; bring to boiling. Carefully lower peaches, a few at a time, into boiling water; let stand 30 to 60 seconds. With slotted spoon transfer peaches to large bowl of ice water. When cool enough to handle, gently rub skin off peaches. Halve and pit any large peaches; set aside.

2. Drain water from Dutch oven. For pickling mixture, in same Dutch oven combine the 2½ cups water, vinegar, sugars, cinnamon, gingerroot, red pepper, 1 teaspoon *salt*, mustard seeds, and cloves. Bring to boiling, stirring to dissolve sugars. Reduce heat. Simmer, uncovered, 5 minutes.

3. Add peaches, onion, and sweet pepper to pickling mixture; return to boiling. Reduce heat; simmer, covered, 5 minutes or just until tender, gently stirring once or twice.

With slotted spoon divide peaches, onion, sweet pepper, and cinnamon evenly among four clean, hot 1-quart jars. (See "Safe Storage," *left*.) Pour pickling mixture into jars; cool. Cover and refrigerate at least 24 hours or up to 3 weeks. Serve peaches with a slotted spoon and drizzle with a little of the juices. **MAKES 18 SERVINGS.**

EACH SERVING (1 PEACH + 2 TBSP. JUICE) *167 cal, 0 g fat, 0 mg chol, 50 mg sodium, 42 g carbo, 2 g fiber, 1 g pro. Daily Values: 10% vit. A, 21% vit. C, 2% calcium, 3% iron.*

SPICY MELON SKEWERS

PREP: 40 MIN. MARINATE: 2 HR. OVEN: 400°F

HOT 1 tsp. ground ancho chile pepper

HOTTER 1 tsp. ground pasilla chile pepper

HOTTEST 1 tsp. ground cayenne chile pepper

1	recipe Chile Syrup
3	cups papaya or cantaloupe chunks or balls
3	cups honeydew melon chunks or balls
3	cups seeded watermelon chunks or balls
20	10-inch bamboo skewers
4	oz. thinly sliced prosciutto (6 slices)
1	Tbsp. packed brown sugar
1	tsp. ground ancho, pasilla, or cayenne chile pepper
½	tsp. paprika
½	tsp. ground cumin
	Snipped cilantro

1. Prepare Chile Syrup. Place papaya, honeydew, and watermelon in large self-sealing plastic bag. Pour in Chile Syrup. Seal; turn to coat. Marinate in refrigerator 2 to 4 hours, turning bag occasionally. Drain papaya and melon, reserving syrup. Thread papayas and melon pieces on skewers.

2. Heat oven to 400°F. Arrange prosciutto, cut in thin strips, in single layer on large baking sheet. Bake 6 to 8 minutes or until crisp. Transfer to paper towels; cool.

3. In bowl combine brown sugar, the ground chile pepper, the paprika, cumin, and ⅛ teaspoon *salt*. Sprinkle skewered papaya and melon with spice mixture, prosciutto, and cilantro. Drizzle Chile Syrup. Serve with any remaining spice mixture and syrup. **MAKES 10 SERVINGS.**

CHILE SYRUP In small saucepan bring 1 cup water; 1 cup sugar; and 1 teaspoon ground ancho, pasilla, or cayenne chile pepper to boiling. Stir to dissolve sugar. Remove from heat; cool.

EACH SERVING *171 cal, 3 g fat (0 g sat. fat), 0 mg chol, 249 mg sodium, 34 g carbo, 1 g fiber, 4 g pro. Daily Values: 43% vit. A, 53% vit. C, 2% calcium, 2% iron.*

Safe Storage

Before filling the jars, wash them in hot soapy water and rinse thoroughly. Pour boiling water in and over the jars and let them stand in the hot water until ready to fill. The pickled peaches are stored in canning jars but are not processed as canned. Therefore, keep refrigerated and eat within 3 weeks. If giving as a gift, include storage instructions.

SPICY MELON SKEWERS

CHILLY CHILE PEPPER GAZPACHO

PREP: 30 MIN. CHILL: 4 HR. OVEN: 425°F

HOT 4 medium jalapeño chile peppers
HOTTER 4 medium serrano chile peppers
HOTTEST 2 medium habañero chile peppers

- 6 large tomatoes, cored, halved, and seeded
- 1 medium onion, cut in wedges
- 4 cloves garlic, peeled
- 1 medium cucumber, peeled, seeded, and cut up
- 1 medium yellow sweet pepper, seeded and cut up
- 4 medium jalapeño or serrano chile peppers, or 2 medium habanero chile peppers, seeded and cut up, (see tip, right)
- 2 11.5-oz. cans hot-style vegetable juice
- 2 Tbsp. lemon juice
- 2 Tbsp. extra virgin olive oil
- 1 tsp. sugar
- 2 6-oz. cans crabmeat, drained, flaked, and cartilage removed
  Chopped fresh chives (optional)

1. Heat oven to 425°F. Place tomatoes (cut sides up), onion, and garlic on a rimmed baking sheet. Roast 30 minutes or until tomato skins are charred. Peel off tomato skins.

2. Place tomatoes in food processor. Cover; process until smooth. Transfer to large serving bowl. Place onion, garlic, cucumber, sweet pepper, and chile peppers in food processor. Cover; pulse with on/off turns until chopped to desired consistency.

3. Add processed vegetables, vegetable juice, lemon juice, olive oil, sugar, ½ teaspoon *salt*, and ¼ teaspoon *black pepper* to tomatoes. Stir to combine. Cover; chill at least 4 hours or up to 24 hours.

4. Spoon gazpacho in bowls. Top with crabmeat. Sprinkle chives.

MAKES 8 SERVINGS.

EACH 1-CUP SERVING *122 cal, 4 g fat (0 g sat. fat), 53 mg chol, 570 mg sodium, 12 g carbo, 2 g fiber, 10 g pro. Daily Values: 35% vit. A, 120% vit. C, 7% calcium, 5% iron.*

pick your heat

Whether serving family or feeding a table of daredevil eaters, these dishes make it easy to adjust the heat level to taste. Experiment with these ingredients to vary the level of fire and spice.

FRESH CHILES Icons of spiciness, chile peppers—from jalapeños to fiery habañeros—generate a hot burning sensation that can build on the palate, the heat varying from pepper to pepper. A general rule: The smaller the chile, the hotter.

PLAYING WITH FIRE Hot chile peppers and ground chiles (such as cayenne) contain oils that can cause minor skin irritations and burn the eyes if they come in contact. When working with fresh chile peppers, wear plastic gloves (or cover your hands with plastic bags), especially if you handle seeds and white veins. If using bare hands, wash well immediately after with soap and water.

CHILI POWDER Made from a mix of dried spices that can vary, chili powders are rich in smoky flavor and lightly spicy. Hot-style varieties usually have ground dried chiles in the blend, which give them an extra kick.

FRESH GINGERROOT A little has a subtle tinge, but when a lot of this aromatic seasoning is added to a dish, it provides surprisingly sharp heat. Its cool, citrusy flavor balances the heat, preventing it from overpowering.

GROUND CHILES Because drying and grinding chile peppers concentrate the heat, just a bit can add a big wallop. Available in large supermarkets and Mexican markets, these range from hot to very hot, depending on the chile. Look for them labeled by chile name.

BLACK PEPPER When added with a heavy hand, this familiar seasoning has a pungent bite. Pepper has more zing freshly cracked than ground.

WASABI Think sushi. This pungent condiment produces a head-clearing tingle rather than a burn. Add a little for a light bite—a lot for a blast of heat. It's available as paste, powder, and, less commonly, fresh.

CHILLY CHILE PEPPER
GAZPACHO

SHRIMP AND
NOODLES

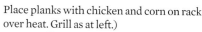

SHRIMP AND NOODLES

For even more kick, substitute wasabi peas for the cashews. And if there's a heat lover at the table, serve extra sliced jalapeños on the side.

START TO FINISH: 40 MIN.

HOT 1½ tsp. wasabi powder
HOTTER 2 tsp. wasabi powder
HOTTEST 3 tsp. wasabi powder

2	lb. medium fresh or frozen shrimp, peeled and deveined (tails may be left intact)
2	Tbsp. grated fresh gingerroot
3	cloves garlic, minced
1	Tbsp. vegetable oil
½	a 16-oz. pkg. wide rice noodles
1	Tbsp. toasted sesame oil
4	cups shredded napa cabbage or butterhead (Boston or Bibb) lettuce
3	medium carrots, coarsely shredded
1	cup thinly sliced radishes
½	cup fresh basil leaves, torn
1	to 2 medium jalapeño peppers, thinly sliced (see tip, page 141)
1	recipe Wasabi Dressing
½	cup honey-roasted cashews, coarsely chopped
	Thinly sliced jalapeño peppers (see tip, page 141) (optional)

1. Thaw shrimp, if frozen. In 10-inch skillet cook shrimp, gingerroot, and garlic in hot oil for 3 minutes or until shrimp are opaque; set aside.

2. Cook rice noodles according to package directions; drain. Rinse in cold water to cool; drain again. Toss noodles with toasted sesame oil. For easy-to-eat bites, use kitchen shears to snip noodles.

3. Arrange noodles, shrimp, cabbage, carrots, radishes, basil, and sliced jalapeño peppers in bowls. Serve with Wasabi Dressing. Sprinkle cashews and additional sliced jalapeños. **MAKES 8 SERVINGS.**

WASABI DRESSING In small bowl combine ⅓ cup soy sauce, ⅓ cup rice vinegar, 1 tablespoon lime juice, 3 tablespoons vegetable oil, 1 tablespoon sesame oil, 1 tablespoon sugar, and 1½ to 3 teaspoons wasabi powder. Sprinkle 1 teaspoon finely shredded basil.

EACH SERVING *351 cal, 14 g fat (2 g sat. fat), 129 mg chol, 903 mg sodium, 34 g carbo, 2 g fiber, 21 g pro. Daily Values: 85% vit. A, 32% vit. C, 10% calcium, 18% iron.*

PLANK-SMOKED CHICKEN WITH GRILLED CORN RELISH

To coarsely crack whole peppercorns, place them between two clean kitchen towels. Roll over them with a rolling pin or lightly hit them with the flat side of a meat mallet.

PREP: 45 MIN. GRILL: 50 MIN.

HOT 2 tsp. cracked black pepper
HOTTER 3 tsp. cracked black pepper
HOTTEST 4 tsp. cracked black pepper

2	14×6×¾-inch oak or hickory grilling planks
2	3- to 3½-lb. broiler-fryer chickens, quartered
2	to 4 Tbsp. bottled hot pepper sauce
2	to 4 tsp. cracked black pepper
6	ears fresh sweet corn, husked
1	4-oz. jar diced pimientos, drained
½	cup sliced green onions
2	Tbsp. olive oil
2	Tbsp. honey
1	Tbsp. lemon juice
1	recipe Fresh Ranch Dressing
¾	cup pecan halves, toasted (optional)
	Lemon wedges (optional)

1. At least 1 hour before grilling, soak grilling planks in water. (Top with heavy dish to keep submerged.)

2. Loosen skin on chicken. In small bowl combine hot pepper sauce, black pepper, and 1 teaspoon *salt*. Drizzle under skin of chicken. Rub to disperse pepper mixture.

3. For charcoal grill, place planks on rack of uncovered grill directly over medium coals until planks begin to crackle and smoke. Place chicken, bone sides down, on planks. Add corn to grill rack. Cover; grill 15 to 20 minutes or until corn is tender, turning two or three times. Remove corn from grill. Set aside; keep warm. Cover and grill chicken 35 to 40 minutes longer or until no pink remains (180°F in a thigh). (For gas grill, heat grill. Reduce heat to medium.

Place planks with chicken and corn on rack over heat. Grill as at left.)

4. For Grilled Corn Relish, cut corn from cobs. In medium bowl combine corn, pimientos, green onions, oil, honey, lemon juice, ½ teaspoon *salt* and ⅛ teaspoon *ground black pepper*; toss. Add ⅓ cup Fresh Ranch Dressing. Toss to coat.

5. On large platter spoon Grilled Corn Relish. Top with chicken and pecans. Drizzle remaining Fresh Ranch Dressing. Serve with lemon. **MAKES 8 SERVINGS.**

FRESH RANCH DRESSING In blender or food processor combine ⅓ cup buttermilk, ½ cup sour cream, 2 tablespoons mayonnaise, ½ teaspoon lemon juice, 1 tablespoon bottled hot pepper sauce (optional), 1 clove garlic, ¼ teaspoon salt, and ⅛ teaspoon ground black pepper. Cover and blend or process until smooth.

EACH SERVING *664 cal, 44 g fat (13 g sat. fat), 180 mg chol, 745 mg sodium, 20 g carbo, 2 g fiber, 46 g pro. Daily Values: 21% vit. A, 39% vit. C, 6% calcium, 17% iron.*

grilled corn and green tomato salsa

Peel back corn husks; remove corn silk. Strip about half the husks from each ear. In a large kettle or Dutch oven cook corn, covered, in boiling water for 5 minutes. Drain. Grill corn on rack of uncovered grill directly over medium coals for 10 minutes or until tender, turning several times. (For gas grill, preheat grill to medium. Cook as above.) To serve, brush ears with butter. Top with a handful of chopped green, yellow, or red tomatoes; a sprinkling of chopped fresh basil; and an ounce or two of crumbled feta cheese.

What's Cooking
from author Elizabeth Karmel

Grilling

SUMMERTIME HOT
DOGS WITH DR PEPPER
BARBECUE SAUCE

SUMMERTIME HOT DOGS WITH DR PEPPER BARBECUE SAUCE

This sauce ties together flavor ideas from all over, says Elizabeth. "I borrowed the sweetness from Kansas City, fun use of soda from the barbecue circuit, and balanced it with savory ingredients."

PREP: 15 MIN. COOK: 45 MIN. GRILL: 5 MIN.

1	large yellow onion, chopped
4	cloves garlic, chopped
4	Tbsp. (½ stick) unsalted butter
1	12-oz. can Dr Pepper
1	cup ketchup
½	cup packed brown sugar
½	cup cider vinegar
⅓	cup Worcestershire sauce
3	Tbsp. tomato paste
2	tsp. ancho chili powder
1	tsp. finely ground white pepper
1	tsp. kosher salt
8	hot dogs (1-lb. pkg.)
8	hot dog buns, split and toasted
	Toppers: pickles, sliced jalapeño peppers, chopped onion (optional)

1. For sauce, in medium saucepan cook and stir onion and garlic in hot butter over medium heat about 10 minutes until onions are tender. Add all ingredients except hot dogs, buns, and toppers. Reduce heat. Simmer, covered, 15 minutes. Cook, uncovered, until sauce begins to thicken, 20 to 30 minutes. Remove from heat. Cool sauce 10 minutes.

2. Puree sauce in pan with immersion blender; or transfer to a blender jar, cover, and blend until smooth.

3. Meanwhile, on charcoal grill cook hot dogs on rack directly over medium coals for 5 to 7 minutes or until heated through. (For gas grill, heat grill. Reduce heat to medium. Cook on grill rack over heat. Cover; grill as above.) Serve hot dogs on buns with toppers. **MAKES 8 HOT DOGS AND 4 CUPS SAUCE.**

EACH HOT DOG WITH BUN AND 2 TBSP. SAUCE *338 cal, 19 g fat (8 g sat. fat), 32 mg chol, 1,030 mg sodium, 30 g carbo, 1 g fiber, 11 g pro. Daily Values: 4% vit. A, 4% vit. C, 8% calcium, 13% iron.*

TEQUILA-HONEY-LIME MARINATED DRUMSTICKS

"I like to use untoasted walnut oil," Elizabeth says, "because it is light and enhances the flavor of the other ingredients."

PREP: 15 MIN. MARINATE: 4 HR. GRILL: 50 MIN.

½	cup blue agave tequila
½	cup untoasted walnut oil
½	cup honey
2	to 3 limes (1 tsp. finely shredded peel plus ¼ cup juice)
1	tsp. kosher salt

drums 101

ELIZABETH SAYS, "I love drumsticks because they taste great and take everyone back to a time when they were 5. You pick up a drumstick, and there's a smile on your face."

TECHNIQUE This recipe uses indirect grilling—food is not directly over the heat source. "Indirect is your secret weapon to perfectly prepared food. The inside will be done at the same time the outside is roasty, toasty, golden brown."

	Optional add-ins: 2 cloves garlic, minced; ½ tsp. ground cumin; 2 shallots, minced
12	chicken drumsticks
	Lime and/or orange slices
	Fresh cilantro

1. For marinade, in bowl whisk together tequila and oil. Whisk in honey, lime juice, peel, salt, and desired add-ins. Cover and refrigerate marinade up to 2 days.

2. Place drumsticks in self-sealing plastic bag in shallow dish. Add marinade; seal. Refrigerate 4 to 8 hours; turn occasionally. Drain; discard marinade.

3. For charcoal grill, arrange medium-hot coals around drip pan. Grill drumsticks 50 to 60 minutes over drip pan, covered, until chicken is no longer pink (180°F), turning once halfway. (For gas, heat grill. Reduce heat to medium. Adjust for indirect cooking. Grill as above.)

MAKES 6 (2-DRUMSTICKS) SERVINGS.

EACH DRUMSTICK *274 cal, 15 g fat (4 g sat. fat), 118 mg chol, 243 mg sodium, 4 g carbo, 0 g fiber, 28 g pro. Daily Values: 5% vit. A, 13% vit. C, 2% calcium, 9% iron.*

APPLE CIDER BRINE
PORK CHOPS

top chops

ELIZABETH SAYS, "Brining increases juiciness and flavor. Try this and you'll never cook a dry pork chop again. Before grilling, lightly brush meat with olive oil, but *don't* add more salt."

TECHNIQUE TIP
Direct grilling means cooking directly over coals or gas flame. It's best suited for thin cuts of meat, such as these chops, which require less than 20 minutes of cooking time.

LOW FAT

APPLE CIDER BRINE PORK CHOPS

Because the pork will be soaked in a salty solution, Elizabeth recommends buying chops that have not been preseasoned.

PREP: 30 MIN. MARINATE: 6 HR. GRILL: 11 MIN.

2	cups cold water
1	cup kosher salt
1	cup packed light brown sugar
2	tsp. dried thyme or 2 sprigs fresh thyme
1	tsp. whole black peppercorns
1	tsp. whole cloves
4	cups unfiltered apple cider
2	cups ice cubes
4	¾-inch-thick pork chops
	Olive oil
	Miniature sweet peppers (optional)
	Sliced French bread (optional)

1. For apple cider brine, in large saucepan over medium heat bring water, salt, brown sugar, thyme, peppercorns, and cloves to boiling. Cook, uncovered, 2 to 3 minutes, stirring occasionally until sugar and salt are dissolved. Remove from heat; stir in apple cider and ice cubes. Cool.

2. Place pork chops in extra-large resealable plastic bag. Pour cooled brine on chops; seal bag. Refrigerate 6 to 12 hours, turning bag occasionally to marinate evenly. Drain chops; discard brine. Pat chops dry with paper towels. Lightly brush chops with olive oil.

3. For charcoal grill, place oiled chops on rack directly over medium coals. Grill, covered, 11 to 13 minutes or until chops are slightly pink in center and juices run clear (160°F), turning once halfway through grilling. (For gas grill, heat grill. Reduce heat to medium. Grill as above.)

4. Brush peppers and bread slices with olive oil. Add peppers to grill with chops. Grill directly over heat about 8 minutes, turning occasionally, until tender. Add bread to grill during last 2 to 4 minutes of grilling, turning once. Serve chops with peppers and bread.

MAKES 4 SERVINGS.

EACH SERVING *214 cal, 6 g fat (2 g sat. fat), 105 mg chol, 1,481 mg sodium, 5 g carbo, 0 g fiber, 33 g pro. Daily Values: 2% calcium, 7% iron.*

BITTERSWEET CHOCOLATE BUTTER ON GRILLED STONE FRUIT

PREP: 25 MIN. CHILL: 3½ HR.
GRILL: 7 MIN.

- ½ cup (1 stick) unsalted butter
- 4 oz. bittersweet chocolate (70%), melted and cooled
- 2 tsp. superfine sugar
- ¼ tsp. vanilla extract
- ½ tsp. fleur de sel
- 4 nectarines or peaches, halved and pitted
- 2 Tbsp. untoasted nut oil or other neutral oil
- 1 Tbsp. superfine sugar

1. Make butter at least 3 hours before serving. In a medium bowl, mash or stir the butter with a fork until it is smooth and slightly fluffy. Add the chocolate, 2 teaspoons sugar, vanilla, and fleur de sel.

Mix together, mashing with the back of the fork to incorporate all the ingredients. Taste for seasoning and adjust if desired. Chill in refrigerator for 30 minutes or until firm enough to roll into a log.
2. On a piece of plastic wrap or parchment, drop the butter in spoonfuls to form a log. Roll the butter in plastic wrap and smooth out to form a round log about 1½ inches in diameter. Refrigerate until hard and easy to cut in pieces. The butter will keep, tightly wrapped, in the refrigerator up to 1 week and in the freezer up to 1 month.

3. Brush the nectarines with oil; sprinkle cut sides with 1 tablespoon sugar. For a charcoal grill, place nectarines, cut sides down, directly over medium coals for 4 minutes. Turn cut sides up; add a ¼-inch slice of chocolate butter to center. Grill 3 minutes more or until fruit is tender and chocolate begins to melt. (For a gas grill, preheat grill. Reduce heat to medium. Place nectarine halves on grill, cut sides down. Cover; grill as above.).
4. Serve at once or at room temperature.
MAKES 8 SERVINGS.

EACH SERVING *244 cal, 21 g fat (11 g sat. fat), 31 mg chol, 102 mg sodium, 17 g carbo, 2 g fiber, 2 g pro. Daily Values: 12% vit. A, 6% vit. C, 1% calcium, 7% iron.*

BITTERSWEET CHOCOLATE BUTTER ON GRILLED STONE FRUIT

Everyday Easy
Fresh time-saving dinners

FAST | **LOW FAT**

LINGUINE IN FRESH TOMATO SAUCE WITH GARLIC-BASIL TOAST

START TO FINISH: 20 MIN.
BUDGET $2.25 PER SERVING

10	oz. dried linguine
3	Tbsp. olive oil
6	cloves garlic, minced, or 1 Tbsp. bottled minced garlic
2	English muffins, split
⅔	cup fresh basil, chopped
1	pint small tomatoes, halved
½	cup chicken broth or pasta water
1	tsp. sugar
½	cup halved, pitted kalamata olives (optional)
	Grated Parmesan cheese (optional)
	Fresh basil (optional)

1. Heat broiler. Cook pasta according to package directions. Drain; set aside.
2. Meanwhile, in bowl combine 1 tablespoon of the oil and about one-third of the minced garlic; brush on cut sides of muffins. Place muffins on baking sheet. Broil 3 to 4 inches from heat, for 2 to 3 minutes, until golden. Sprinkle 1 tablespoon of the chopped basil; set aside.
3. In large saucepan heat remaining oil over medium-high. Add remaining garlic, basil, and the tomatoes. Cook 2 minutes; add broth and sugar. Cook 3 to 4 minutes, until tomatoes soften. Season with *salt* and *pepper*. Stir in pasta and olives; heat through. Sprinkle cheese and basil.
MAKES 4 SERVINGS.
EACH SERVING *450 cal, 12 g fat (2 g sat. fat), 1 mg chol, 403 mg sodium, 72 g carbo, 3 g fiber, 12 g pro. Daily Values: 22% vit. A, 24% vit. C, 5% calcium, 20% iron.*

FAST | **KID-FRIENDLY**

PAN-SEARED PORK BURGERS WITH PEPPERS AND MUSHROOMS

START TO FINISH: 25 MIN.
BUDGET $1.86 PER SERVING

2	small red and/or green sweet peppers
1	banana, jalapeño, or other chile pepper, seeded and chopped (optional)
1	lb. ground pork
1	Tbsp. Worcestershire or soy sauce
8	oz. sliced fresh mushrooms
4	pita bread rounds or other flatbread
½	cup mayonnaise

1. Slice half the peppers in rings; set aside. Chop remaining. In bowl combine chopped peppers, pork, 2 teaspoons of the Worcestershire, and 2 teaspoons *cracked black pepper*. Shape in four ¾-inch-thick patties. In large hot skillet cook patties over medium-high heat 10 to 12 minutes; turn once (160°F internal temp.). Transfer to plates; cover. In same skillet cook pepper rings and mushrooms 3 minutes; sprinkle *salt*.
2. Wrap bread in paper towels. Heat in microwave on 100% power (high) for 30 seconds. For sauce, combine mayonnaise, remaining Worcestershire, and *black pepper*. Serve burgers on bread with pepper and mushrooms. Pass sauce.
MAKES 4 SERVINGS.
EACH SERVING *693 cal, 47 g fat (12 g sat. fat), 92 mg chol, 734 mg sodium, 40 g carbo, 3 g fiber, 27 g pro. Daily Values: 27% vit. A, 89% vit. C, 9% calcium, 21% iron.*

LINGUINE IN FRESH TOMATO SAUCE WITH GARLIC-BASIL TOAST

PAN-SEARED PORK BURGERS
WITH PEPPERS AND
MUSHROOMS

POACHED SALMON
ON CITRUS SALAD

GINGERED CHICKEN
AND FRIED RICE

POACHED SALMON ON CITRUS SALAD

START TO FINISH: 25 MIN.
BUDGET $3.50 PER SERVING

1	lime
6	oranges (navel, blood, Cara Cara, or tangerines)
4	4-oz. skinless salmon fillets, about 1 inch thick
¼	cup olive oil
1	tsp. sugar
2	Tbsp. cooking oil
6	wonton wrappers, cut in ½-inch strips
1	7-oz. bunch watercress, trimmed, or 4 cups arugula or baby spinach

1. Finely shred 1 teaspoon peel from lime; set aside. Juice lime and 2 oranges; reserve ¼ cup juice for dressing. Pour remaining juice in large nonstick skillet with lime peel and ½ cup *water*. Bring to boiling; add salmon. Reduce heat. Simmer, covered, 8 to 12 minutes or until fish flakes easily with a fork.
2. Meanwhile, for dressing, in bowl whisk together reserved juice, olive oil, and sugar; season with *salt* and *pepper*.
3. In second large skillet heat cooking oil over medium-high. Cook wontons 1 to 2 minutes, stirring often, until crisp.
4. Peel and section remaining oranges. Drizzle dressing on greens, oranges, and salmon. Pass wontons. **MAKES 4 SERVINGS.**
EACH SERVING *557 cal, 36 g fat (6 g sat. fat), 63 mg chol, 302 mg sodium, 34 g carbo, 6 g fiber, 27 g pro. Daily Values: 42% vit. A, 225% vit. C, 16% calcium, 7% iron.*

GRILLED STEAK AND
ONION SALAD WITH BLUE
CHEESE TOAST

GRILLED STEAK AND ONION SALAD WITH BLUE CHEESE TOAST

START TO FINISH: 25 MIN.
BUDGET $3.27 PER SERVING

4	1-inch-thick slices crusty bread
2	to 3 oz. blue cheese, cut in 4 wedges
2	small red onions, cut in wedges
6	Tbsp. olive oil
1	lb. boneless beef breakfast steak, thinly cut
¼	cup cider vinegar
1	tsp. sugar
2	hearts romaine lettuce, halved
	Fresh basil leaves (optional)

1. On rack of uncovered grill directly over medium heat, toast bread 1 to 2 minutes, turning once. Top each bread slice with a cheese wedge; set aside.
2. Brush onion wedges with 2 tablespoons of the oil. Grill 1 to 2 minutes each side; move to side of grill. Sprinkle *salt* and *pepper* on steaks; grill about 4 minutes, turning once.
3. Meanwhile, for vinaigrette, in blender process one-third of the onions with the vinegar, sugar, and ½ teaspoon each *salt* and *pepper*. With blender operating, add remaining oil. Serve steak, grilled onions, and blue cheese toast on romaine leaves. Sprinkle basil. Pass vinaigrette.
MAKES 4 SERVINGS.
EACH SERVING *506 cal, 30 g fat (7 g sat. fat), 58 mg chol, 883 mg sodium, 25 g carbo, 4 g fiber, 32 g pro. Daily Values: 166% vit. A, 44% vit. C, 17% calcium, 22% iron.*

GINGERED CHICKEN AND FRIED RICE

START TO FINISH: 29 MIN.
BUDGET $2.48 PER SERVING

4	chicken drumsticks
1	1-inch piece fresh ginger, peeled and finely chopped (2 Tbsp.)
2	Tbsp. soy sauce
2	large carrots, chopped or sliced
1	14.8-oz. pkg. cooked long grain rice
8	oz. sugar snap peas
½	cup chopped red sweet pepper (optional)
4	eggs, beaten
	Sliced green onions (optional)
	Soy sauce

1. In large nonstick skillet heat 1 tablespoon *cooking oil* over medium-high. Add chicken, half the ginger, and soy sauce. Brown chicken on all sides. Add ½ cup *water*. Cook, covered, 15 minutes or until no pink remains in chicken.
2. In covered microwave-safe dish place carrots, remaining ginger, and 2 tablespoons *water*. Heat in microwave on 100% power (high) 4 minutes. Add rice, peas, and sweet pepper. Cover; cook 5 minutes more, stirring twice.
3. Remove chicken and juices. Wipe skillet with paper towels; return to heat. Add eggs; cook and stir 30 seconds to scramble. Stir in rice mixture; heat through. Serve chicken and juices with fried rice, onions, and soy sauce. **MAKES 4 SERVINGS.**
EACH SERVING *421 cal, 17 g fat (4 g sat. fat), 271 mg chol, 667 mg sodium, 42 g carbo, 4 g fiber, 25 g pro. Daily Values: 122% vit. A, 64% vit. C, 7% calcium, 19% iron.*

American Classics
from Chef Scott Peacock

Ice Cream

KID-FRIENDLY

CLASSIC VANILLA ICE CREAM

**PREP: 30 MIN. STAND: 20 MIN. CHILL: 8 HR.
FREEZE: ACCORDING TO MFG. DIRECTIONS
RIPEN: 4 HR.**

1	vanilla bean
2	cups whole milk
8	egg yolks
¾	cup sugar
2	cups whipping cream
2	to 3 Tbsp. pure vanilla extract
1	tsp. kosher salt
	Kosher or rock salt and crushed ice (for hand-crank ice cream freezers)

1. Twist vanilla bean to release flavor. In medium stainless-steel saucepan heat milk and vanilla bean until just below simmering point. Remove from heat. Cover; let stand 20 minutes to allow vanilla to infuse milk.
2. For custard, in medium mixing bowl whisk to blend egg yolks and sugar. Slowly whisk in the hot milk; return milk mixture to saucepan. Cook over medium heat, stirring constantly with rubber spatula until custard thickens enough to coat back of spatula.
3. Strain custard through fine-mesh sieve into large heatproof bowl placed in larger bowl of ice water. Stir custard until cooled. Return vanilla bean to custard. Stir in

whipping cream, vanilla extract, and the 1 teaspoon kosher salt. Taste for flavor balance, adding additional salt or vanilla as desired. Cover and refrigerate until thoroughly chilled or up to 48 hours before freezing.
4. Remove vanilla bean. Transfer custard to ice cream canister. Freeze according to manufacturer's instructions. Transfer ice cream to shallow glass dish. Cover with plastic wrap. Freeze to ripen before serving.
MAKES 12 (½-CUP) SERVINGS.

EACH SERVING *257 cal, 19 g fat (11 g sat. fat), 199 mg chol, 198 mg sodium, 16 g carbo, 0 g fiber, 4 g pro. Daily Values: 16% vit. A, 9% calcium, 2% iron.*

TEMPER THE EGG YOLKS
"Adding the hot milk slowly to the egg yolks keeps the yolks from curdling and helps ensure smooth and creamy texture."

STRAIN FOR SILKY TEXTURE
"Remove any small bits of cooked egg and the vanilla bean by straining the custard through a fine-mesh sieve."

SLOW-CHURN BY HAND
"Hand-churning is best and incorporates less air in the ice cream for dense texture and rich flavor. Aim for one even turn every two seconds."

Cook the Custard "Never allow custard to simmer or boil," says Scott. "Stir constantly until surface bubbles dissipate and the custard thickens enough to coat the spatula."

TASTE AND BALANCE
"After straining, it's important to taste the custard. The flavor should be rich with egg yolks and cream, yet full of vanilla goodness from both the vanilla bean and vanilla extract. The right amount of salt is key—its purpose is to heighten the flavor of the ingredients without adding salty flavor."

RIPEN AND SERVE
Fresh-churned ice cream is generally a soft-serve consistency. "For more scoopable ice cream, transfer it to a shallow glass dish, cover with plastic wrap, and freeze until ice cream is firmly set, about 4 hours."

the ideal ice cream

... IS A CELEBRATION of high-quality yet simple ingredients: eggs, milk, cream, and vanilla. I prefer using organic eggs and the best-quality cream I can find.

... IS SOCIAL. Gathering friends 'round the ice cream freezer is the essence of summer. It's the perfect cool-down on a hot day and easy to customize with the freshest fruits.

august

Plan a week of menus filled with peak-season produce—then get tickled by home-canned sweet pickles.

162

166

172

FRESH MELON
QUENCHERS
Recipe on page 163

monday

LAMB CHOPS WITH BARLEY
SALAD AND TOMATO VINAIGRETTE

Daily Specials

A week of healthful meals

Eat Healthfully
SEVEN DAYS A WEEK

Eating a healthful diet is easy (and better) when you take it one day at a time. "Our bodies work best when we eat a healthful mix of foods and nutrients throughout the week rather than eating well one day to make up for a day of eating poorly," says *Better Homes and Gardens*® Test Kitchen dietitian Laura Marzen. The latest thinking in health and weight management is that the focus should not be on which foods are good or bad but on striking a balance. "Keep the flavor and foods you love—grilled pork, beef skewers, fruit tarts—while including plenty of good-for-you whole grains, vegetables, and fruits," Laura says.

LAMB CHOPS WITH BARLEY SALAD AND TOMATO VINAIGRETTE

Because pearl barley has most of the bran removed, it cooks quickly. It's still high in fiber because not all the bran is removed. Whole grain (hull-less) barley, with bran intact, requires longer cooking and has a chewy texture. Find barley among other grains in supermarkets or health food stores.

START TO FINISH: 1 HR.

- ⅔ cup regular (pearl) barley
- 2 medium tomatoes, coarsely chopped
- 2 Tbsp. red wine vinegar
- 2 cloves garlic, minced
- 1 tsp. cinnamon
- 3 Tbsp. olive oil
- 4 small lamb loin chops, cut 1 inch thick
- 1 small cucumber, seeded and chopped
- ½ cup red sweet pepper strips
- ¼ cup sweet onion, chopped
- ½ cup Italian (flat-leaf) parsley or mint, snipped
- 4 oval-shape flatbreads, toasted*
- 4 cups mixed greens

1. Prepare barley following package directions. Drain. Rinse with cold water; drain. Set aside.

2. Meanwhile, for tomato vinaigrette, in blender or food processor combine tomatoes, vinegar, garlic, cinnamon, 1 teaspoon *black pepper*, and ½ teaspoon *salt*. Blend or process until almost smooth. Blend in olive oil. Set aside ¼ cup vinaigrette to brush on lamb.

3. Trim fat from lamb. Brush with reserved vinaigrette. Season with *salt* and *black pepper*. Place on unheated rack of broiler pan. Broil 4 to 5 inches from heat 10 to 15 minutes (160°F); turn chops once halfway through broiling time.

4. For salads, in large bowl combine cooked barley, cucumber, sweet pepper, onion, and parsley. Toss with about ¾ cup of the tomato vinaigrette. To serve, top flatbreads with greens, barley salad, and lamb chop. Pass remaining vinaigrette.

MAKES 4 SERVINGS.

* TO TOAST FLATBREADS Broil about 4 inches from heat for 1 to 2 minutes on each side or until lightly browned.

EACH SERVING *580 cal, 21 g fat (7 g sat. fat), 61 mg chol, 674 mg sodium, 71 g carbo, 9 g fiber, 28 g pro. Daily Values: 50% vit. A, 81% vit. C, 14% calcium, 29% iron.*

tuesday

CHIMICHURRI-STUFFED
PORK LOIN

how to butterfly a pork loin

Place loin on cutting board with one end toward you. Using a long sharp knife, make a lengthwise cut, starting 1 inch in from the right side of loin. Cut down to about 1 inch from the bottom of loin. Turn the knife and cut to the left, as if forming a right angle and stopping about 1 inch from the opposite side of the loin. Open roast nearly flat.

CHIMICHURRI-STUFFED PORK LOIN

Fresh herbs, garlic, and lime peel—in place of salt—flavor this pork loin.

PREP: 40 MIN. GRILL: 1 HR. STAND: 10 MIN.

1	cup loosely packed fresh Italian (flat-leaf) parsley leaves
1	cup loosely packed fresh cilantro leaves
1	Tbsp. finely shredded lime peel
3	Tbsp. olive oil
3	large cloves garlic, minced
1	2½- to 3-lb. boneless pork loin roast
1	recipe Grilled Sweet Corn
1	recipe Grilled Pineapple

1. Snip 2 tablespoons *each* of the parsley and cilantro. In small bowl combine snipped herbs with ½ teaspoon of the lime peel, 1 tablespoon of the oil, and one-third of the minced garlic; set aside.

2. Trim fat from pork. Butterfly pork loin (See "How to butterfly a pork loin," *page 158.*) Brush with 2 tablespoons of the olive oil. Spread remaining minced garlic on surface. Sprinkle ¼ teaspoon *black pepper* and remaining parsley, cilantro, and lime peel. Roll pork to original shape. Tie at 2-inch intervals with 100%-cotton kitchen string. Spread snipped herb mixture on roast. Sprinkle *black pepper.*

3. For charcoal grill, arrange medium-hot coals around a drip pan. Test for medium heat above pan. Place pork on grill rack over pan. Cover and grill 1 to 1½ hours or until an instant-read thermometer inserted in center of pork registers 150°F. Add more coals as needed to maintain medium heat above drip pan. (For a gas grill, preheat grill. Reduce heat to medium. Adjust for indirect cooking. Grill as above.)

4. Remove pork from grill. Cover with foil; let stand 10 minutes. (After standing, temperature should be 160°F.) Remove string. Slice and serve with Grilled Sweet Corn and Grilled Pineapple. **MAKES 4 TO 6 SERVINGS PLUS LEFTOVERS.**

GRILLED SWEET CORN Brush 4 to 6 husked ears of corn with 2 tablespoons melted butter. Sprinkle salt and pepper. Grill directly over coals, turning occasionally during last 20 minutes of grilling time.

GRILLED PINEAPPLE Grill 4 to 6 slices *pineapple* directly over coals, turning occasionally during the last 5 to 10 minutes of pork grilling time.

EACH SERVING (WITH CORN AND PINEAPPLE) *385 cal, 15 g fat (6 g sat. fat), 113 mg chol, 283 mg sodium, 30 g carbo, 4 g fiber, 35 g pro. Daily Values: 34% vit. A, 113% vit. C, 6% calcium, 14% iron.*

FAST

VEGETABLE BOWLS WITH YOGURT-LIME DRESSING

Butterhead (Bibb) lettuce is a good substitute when savoy cabbage isn't available.

PREP: 20 MIN. COOK: 10 MIN.

1	recipe Yogurt-Lime Dressing
1	Tbsp. soy sauce
1	Tbsp. lime juice
1	tsp. chili powder
1	tsp. fresh oregano, snipped, or ½ tsp. dried oregano, crushed
1	tsp. olive oil
1	lb. sweet potatoes (2 to 3 medium), peeled and cut in 1-inch cubes
1	15-oz. can black beans, rinsed and drained
1	cup cherry or grape tomatoes, halved
1	medium avocado, halved, seeded, peeled, and chopped
8	large savoy cabbage leaves
¼	cup thinly sliced green onions Lime wedges (optional) Toasted baguette slices (optional)

1. Prepare Yogurt-Lime Dressing; set aside.

2. In a small bowl stir together soy sauce, lime juice, chili powder, oregano, and olive oil; set aside. Place sweet potatoes in medium microwave-safe bowl. Place beans in small microwave-safe bowl. Evenly spoon half the soy sauce mixture on potatoes and half on beans; toss to coat. Cover bowls with vented plastic wrap. Microcook sweet potatoes on 100% power (HIGH) 9 minutes or until tender, stirring occasionally; set aside. Microcook beans on 100% power (HIGH) 1 to 2 minutes or until heated through, stirring once.

3. Divide potatoes, beans, tomatoes, and avocado among cabbage leaves. Sprinkle green onions. Pass Yogurt-Lime Dressing and lime wedges. Serve with toasted baguette slices. **MAKES 4 SERVINGS.**

YOGURT-LIME DRESSING In a small bowl combine ½ cup plain low-fat yogurt, 2 tablespoons lime juice, 1 tablespoon soy sauce, 1 tablespoon chili powder, and 1 clove minced garlic. Whisk in ¼ cup olive oil until well combined. Or stir 1 tablespoon chili powder into 1 cup bottled light ranch-style dressing.

EACH SERVING *409 cal, 21 g fat (3 g sat. fat), 2 mg chol, 896 mg sodium, 51 g carbo, 14 g fiber, 13 g pro. Daily Values: 355% vit. A, 53% vit. C, 17% calcium, 17% iron.*

wednesday
VEGETABLE BOWLS WITH YOGURT-LIME DRESSING

thursday

CREAMY LEMON-DILL
TUNA SALAD

CREAMY LEMON-DILL TUNA SALAD

This quick from-the-pantry salad has a good supply of protein, fiber, and vitamin C—and requires no cooking.

START TO FINISH: 20 MIN.

1	recipe Creamy Lemon-Dill Dressing
1	15- to 19-oz. can cannellini beans (white kidney beans), rinsed and drained
1	12-oz. can solid white tuna (water pack), drained and broken in chunks
½	cup halved red onion slices
½	cup bottled roasted yellow or red sweet peppers, drained and chopped
1	stalk celery, sliced
2	to 3 Tbsp. capers, drained, or ½ cup stuffed green olives, sliced (optional)
½	of a 5-oz. pkg. arugula or baby spinach
2	large tomatoes, sliced

1. Prepare dressing; set aside.
2. In a bowl combine beans, tuna, and half the dressing. Stir in onions, peppers, celery, and capers. Serve over greens and tomatoes. Pass remaining dressing.
MAKES 6 SERVINGS.
CREAMY LEMON-DILL DRESSING Combine ¾ cup mayonnaise or salad dressing, 1 tablespoon Dijon-style mustard, 1 tablespoon lemon juice, 1 tablespoon snipped fresh or ¼ teaspoon dried dill, 1 tablespoon honey, ¼ teaspoon salt, and ⅛ teaspoon ground pepper.
EACH SERVING *343 cal, 23 g fat (3 g sat. fat), 35 mg chol, 686 mg sodium, 18 g carbo, 5 g fiber, 20 g pro. Daily Values: 17% vit. A, 75% vit. C, 5% calcium, 7% iron.*

CHILLED CUCUMBER-CHICKPEA SOUP

With ingredients of hummus—chickpeas, tahini, lemon juice, garlic, plus cucumber—this soup is satisfying and refreshing. Look for tahini (sesame seed paste) in the ethnic foods section of the supermarket.

START TO FINISH: 25 MIN.

1	recipe Coriander-Paprika Spice Rub
½	lb. peeled and deveined cooked cocktail shrimp, chopped
2	medium cucumbers
1	15-oz. can chickpeas (garbanzo beans), rinsed and drained
¼	cup tahini (sesame seed paste)
¼	cup packed fresh mint leaves
2	Tbsp. lemon juice
1	Tbsp. olive oil
1	Tbsp. honey
2	cloves garlic, smashed
1½	tsp. ground coriander
¼	tsp. cayenne pepper
3	cups ice cubes
½	cup cherry tomatoes, halved
4	green onions, thinly sliced

1. Prepare Coriander-Paprika Spice Rub. In a medium bowl toss shrimp with spice rub; set aside.
2. Thinly slice enough cucumber to measure ⅓ cup; set aside. Peel, seed, and cut up remaining cucumbers.
3. In blender combine cut-up cucumbers, chickpeas, tahini, mint, lemon juice, olive oil, honey, garlic, coriander, cayenne pepper, and ¼ teaspoon *each* salt and *black pepper*. Cover; blend until smooth, scraping sides as needed.
4. With motor running, add ice cubes, a few at a time, through lid opening until smooth and thickened (blender will be full). Pour into bowls. Top soup with shrimp, sliced cucumber, tomatoes, and green onions. Serve immediately.
MAKES 4 TO 6 SERVINGS.
CORIANDER-PAPRIKA SPICE RUB In small bowl combine 1 teaspoon ground coriander, ½ teaspoon paprika, ¼ teaspoon salt, and ¼ teaspoon ground black pepper.
EACH SERVING *357 cal, 14 g fat (2 g sat. fat), 111 mg chol, 752 mg sodium, 41 g carbo, 7 g fiber, 22 g pro. Daily Values: 17% vit. A, 35% vit. C, 13% calcium, 30% iron.*

SPICED BEEF KABOBS WITH MASHED CARROTS

PREP: 30 MIN. MARINATE: 4 HR.
GRILL: 10 MIN.

¼	cup reduced-sodium soy sauce
3	Tbsp. vegetable oil
2	Tbsp. lemon juice
2	Tbsp. packed brown sugar
6	cloves garlic, smashed
1	tsp. crushed red pepper
1	lb. boneless beef chuck or sirloin, trimmed of fat and cut in 1-inch cubes
1	recipe Mashed Carrots
1	recipe Lemon Gremolata

1. In self-sealing plastic bag set in a shallow dish combine soy sauce, oil, lemon juice, brown sugar, garlic, and red pepper. Add beef to bag. Seal and turn to coat. Marinate, refrigerated, 4 to 24 hours, turning bag occasionally.
2. Drain and discard marinade. Thread beef ¼ inch apart on 8-inch wooden* or metal skewers.
3. For charcoal grill, cook kabobs on rack of uncovered grill directly over medium coals for 10 to 14 minutes or until desired doneness (160°F for medium), turning occasionally and moving to cooler areas of grill if they brown too quickly. (For gas grill, preheat. Reduce heat to medium. Place kabobs on grill. Cover; grill as above.)
4. Serve with Mashed Carrots. Sprinkle Lemon Gremolata. **MAKES 4 SERVINGS.**

MASHED CARROTS In medium saucepan cook 1 lb. peeled and sliced carrots, covered, in small amount of boiling salted water for 12 to 15 minutes or until tender. Drain; return to saucepan. Add 1 tablespoon lemon juice and 1 tablespoon olive oil. Mash until nearly smooth. Season to taste with black pepper.

LEMON GREMOLATA In a small bowl combine ¼ cup snipped fresh basil, 2 teaspoons shredded lemon peel, and 1 clove minced garlic.

* If using wooden skewers, soak in water for 30 minutes before using.

EACH SERVING 277 cal, 12 g fat (3 g sat. fat), 50 mg chol, 483 mg sodium, 16 g carbo, 3 g fiber, 27 g pro. Daily Values: 382% vit. A, 20% vit. C, 7% calcium, 15% iron.

PLUM-BERRY WHOLE WHEAT TARTS

This whole wheat pastry, made with canola oil and butter to cut down saturated fat, can be made and refrigerated a day ahead of baking.

PREP: 25 MIN. FREEZE: 1 HR. BAKE: 30 MIN.
COOL: 30 MIN. OVEN: 400°F

⅓	cup canola oil
¼	cup butter, melted
2	cups whole wheat flour
1	Tbsp. powdered sugar
½	tsp. salt
5	to 6 Tbsp. cold water
¼	cup apricot, cherry, or raspberry spreadable fruit
3	plums, halved, pitted, and cut in thin wedges
1	cup fresh blackberries and/or raspberries
1	Tbsp. fat-free milk
1	oz. semisoft goat cheese, crumbled (optional)
2	Tbsp. honey

1. In a small bowl stir together oil and melted butter until well combined. Cover and freeze for 1 hour or until nearly firm, stirring occasionally.
2. Preheat oven to 400°F. Line a large baking sheet with parchment paper or foil; set aside. In a medium bowl combine flour, powdered sugar, and salt. With pastry blender or fork cut or stir in butter mixture until pieces are about pea size. Sprinkle 1 tablespoon water over part of the flour mixture; gently toss with fork. Push moistened pastry to side of bowl. Repeat, using 1 tablespoon of water at a time, until all is moistened. Form pastry in a ball. (Dough may be wrapped and refrigerated up to 24 hours. Let stand at room temperature about 30 minutes or until easy to roll.)
3. Divide pastry in six equal portions. On lightly floured surface roll each portion to a 6-inch circle. Place on prepared baking sheet 1 inch between pastry rounds (some pastry may extend beyond edge of pan).
4. Spoon spreadable fruit on pastry; spread in 2-inch circle. Top with plums and berries, leaving 2 inches of pastry edge. Fold and pleat pastry over filling. Use spatula to evenly space tarts on pan. Brush crusts with milk.
5. Bake 30 to 35 minutes or until filling is bubbly and fruit is tender, covering tarts with foil the last 10 minutes of baking. Cool slightly on baking sheet on rack. Sprinkle cheese and drizzle honey. Serve warm. **MAKES 6 SERVINGS.**

EACH SERVING 389 cal, 21 g fat (6 g sat. fat), 20 mg chol, 252 mg sodium, 49 g carbo, 7 g fiber, 6 g pro. Daily Values: 8% vit. A, 18% vit. C, 3% calcium, 10% iron.

saturday
SPICED BEEF KABOBS WITH MASHED CARROTS

sunday
**PLUM-BERRY
WHOLE WHEAT TARTS**

FAST | LOW FAT

FRESH MELON QUENCHERS

Add a spoonful of yogurt to make this drink creamy without being heavy, or add a splash of vodka to turn it into a cocktail. Finish with a Frozen Melon Drink Skewer—the skewers can also dress up your favorite flavored water.

START TO FINISH: 10 MIN.

1	to 1½ cups cantaloupe, honeydew, or watermelon puree* (about one-fourth of a 4-lb. melon)
3	ice cubes
1	¼-inch slice fresh ginger, grated Plain low-fat yogurt
1	to 2 tsp. honey Shredded lime peel (optional) Plain or flavored sparkling water Frozen Melon Drink Skewers, *right*

1. In blender container combine melon puree, ice cubes, ginger, a teaspoon or two of yogurt, and honey. Blend just until mixture is frothy and smooth. Pour into serving glass. Add additional honey to adjust sweetness. Stir in lime peel to taste. Add sparkling water to fill glass. Serve with Frozen Melon Drink Skewers. Serve immediately.

MAKES 1 (16-OUNCE) SERVING.

*TO PUREE MELON coarsely chop melon and transfer to blender container. Cover and blend until smooth. If needed, stop motor and press fruit down into blades with rubber spatula or spoon and continue to blend until smooth.

EACH 16-OZ. SERVING (with cantaloupe; other melons are similar) *86 cal, 1 g fat, 0 mg chol, 57 mg sodium, 21 g carbo, 2 g fiber, 2 g pro. Daily Values: 122% vit. A, 142% vit. C, 4% calcium, 3% iron.*

FROZEN MELON DRINK SKEWERS

Using a small melon baller, scoop cantaloupe, honeydew, or watermelon into balls. Or use a knife to cut melons into cubes or ½-inch-thick wedges.

Thread melon balls and wedges onto wooden skewers. Arrange on parchment- or waxed paper- lined baking sheet. Freeze for 2 to 4 hours or until firm.

What's Cooking

Tacos reinvented

STEAK-AND-HERB
TACOS

STEAK-AND-HERB TACOS

A spicy rub for the beef gives this authentic taco Southwest flavor.

PREP: 25 MIN. CHILL: 2 HR. GRILL: 14 MIN.

1-	to 1½-lb. lean boneless beef top sirloin steak, 1 inch thick
2	Tbsp. snipped fresh marjoram or oregano, or 2 tsp. dried marjoram or oregano, crushed
1	Tbsp. chili powder
2	tsp. garlic powder
¼	tsp. salt
¼	tsp. cayenne pepper
1	Tbsp. olive oil or vegetable oil
12	6- to 8-inch corn or flour tortillas
2	tomatoes, chopped
1	small onion, chopped
4	to 6 radishes with tops, sliced
½	cup snipped fresh cilantro
8	to 10 oz. queso fresco, crumbled, or Monterey Jack cheese, shredded Lime wedges (optional)

1. Trim fat from beef; place in shallow dish. In bowl combine marjoram, chili powder, garlic powder, salt, cayenne pepper, and oil; spread on both sides of beef. Cover. Refrigerate 2 to 4 hours.

2. For charcoal grill, cook steak on rack of an uncovered grill directly over medium coals until desired doneness, turning once halfway through grilling. Allow 14 to 18 minutes for medium-rare (145°F) or 18 to 22 minutes for medium (160°F).

(For gas grill, preheat. Reduce heat to medium. Cook steak on grill rack over heat. Cover; grill as at left.)

3. While beef is grilling, wrap tortillas in foil. Place on grill during last 10 minutes of cooking time, turning occasionally.

4. Cut beef crosswise in slices or chunks. On each tortilla layer beef, tomatoes, chopped onion, radishes, and cilantro. Sprinkle crumbled cheese. Serve immediately with limes. **MAKES 12 TACOS.**

EACH TACO *189 cal, 8 g fat (2 g sat. fat), 18 mg chol, 115 mg sodium, 16 g carbo, 2 g fiber, 14 g pro. Daily Values: 13% vit. A, 13% vit. C, 20% calcium, 13% iron.*

CHICKEN-VEGETABLE TACOS

Gather the best from the garden or market in a tortilla.

START TO FINISH: 45 MIN.

1	lb. skinless, boneless chicken breasts, cut in bite-size strips
1	cup bottled green salsa
4	oz. fingerling potatoes
2	ears sweet corn
12	8-inch whole wheat tortillas, heated (see "Bring Out the Best in Tortillas," page 166)
2	tomatoes, seeded and chopped
½	cup coarsely chopped Italian (flat-leaf) parsley
2	red, yellow, and/or green sweet peppers, coarsely chopped
2	small zucchini, cut in thin wedges

1. In microwave-safe bowl combine chicken and ½ cup salsa. Heat in microwave on 100% power (high) 5 to 7 minutes, stirring once, until no pink remains. Remove with slotted spoon. Cover and keep warm.

2. In medium microwave-safe bowl combine potatoes and 1 tablespoon *water.* Cover with plastic wrap; heat in microwave on 100% power (high) 3 to 4 minutes or until tender, tossing once. Carefully open corner of plastic to let steam escape. Cool briefly. Cut in chunks; lightly sprinkle salt. Cut corn from cobs.

3. On each tortilla place chicken, corn, tomatoes, parsley, sweet peppers, potatoes, zucchini, and remaining salsa. Serve immediately. **MAKES 12 TACOS.**

EACH TACO *311 cal, 14 g fat (4 g sat. fat), 67 mg chol, 925 mg sodium, 24 g carbo, 12 g fiber, 24 g pro. Daily Values: 23% vit. A, 69% vit. C, 9% calcium, 19% iron.*

CHICKEN-VEGETABLE TACOS

LOW FAT

PORK-WASABI TACOS

At taco stands around the U.S., cooks are adding Asian flavors to these tasty creations.

PREP: 25 MIN. GRILL: 12 MIN.

1	1½-lb. pork tenderloin, cut in 1-inch pieces
⅓	cup hoisin sauce
6	flatbreads or flour tortillas
1	to 2 tsp. prepared wasabi paste
2	Tbsp. water
2	Tbsp. vegetable oil
½	tsp. white wine vinegar
½	tsp. sugar
¼	of a head napa cabbage, shredded
2	carrots, shredded
½	of an English cucumber, thinly sliced

1. Thread pork on wooden skewers.* Brush with hoisin sauce. For charcoal grill, cook pork on rack of uncovered grill directly over medium coals for 12 to 14 minutes or until no pink remains (160°F), turning once. Add flatbreads the last 1 minute of grilling time, turning once to heat through. (For gas grill, preheat. Reduce heat to medium. Place pork over heat. Cover and grill as above.)

2. Meanwhile, for wasabi oil, in a small bowl combine wasabi paste, water, oil, vinegar, and sugar. Whisk to combine.

3. Serve pork and vegetables on flatbreads. Drizzle wasabi oil. Serve immediately.

MAKES 6 TACOS.

* Soak skewers 30 minutes before using.

EACH TACO *447 cal, 13 g fat (5 g sat. fat), 89 mg chol, 470 mg sodium, 50 g carbo, 2 g fiber, 1 g pro. Daily Values: 74% vit. A, 16% vit. C, 9% calcium, 16% iron.*

TEST KITCHEN TIP

Bring Out the Best in Tortillas

At many taco stands, tortillas are heated on a grill to soften and bring out a slight toasty flavor. At home, heat a skillet over medium-low heat. Place a tortilla in the skillet. Toast for 10 to 20 seconds. With tongs or fork, flip and toast 10 to 20 seconds more or until hot and beginning to turn golden. Cover and keep warm while toasting remaining tortillas.

CATFISH-AND-SLAW TACOS

The flavors draw on two influences—a little bit Southern, a little bit city chic.

PREP: 15 MIN. COOK: 8 MIN.

- 1   lb. fresh or frozen catfish fillets
- 1   lime
- ¼   cup mayonnaise or salad dressing
- ½   tsp. bottled hot pepper sauce
- ½   a small head cabbage, shredded (about 2½ cups)
- 1   Tbsp. Cajun seasoning
- ¼   cup cornmeal
- ¼   cup all-purpose flour
- ¼   cup vegetable oil (more as needed)
- 16   4-inch corn tortillas or eight 8-inch flour tortillas
       Lime wedges
       Bottled hot pepper sauce (optional)

1. Thaw fish if frozen; set aside. For slaw, squeeze about 3 tablespoons juice from lime. In medium bowl combine juice, mayonnaise, and the ½ teaspoon hot pepper sauce. Add cabbage; toss to coat. Set aside.

2. Rinse fish; pat dry with paper towels. Cut fish in 1-inch strips. Toss strips with Cajun seasoning. In large bowl combine cornmeal and flour. Add catfish strips. Toss to coat with cornmeal mixture.

3. In large skillet cook catfish strips, half at a time, in hot oil over medium heat about 2 to 3 minutes on each side or until golden brown and fish flakes when tested with a fork. Remove from skillet.

4. Wrap tortillas in paper towels. Heat in microwave on 100% power (high) for 1 minute (or toast in a dry skillet; see "Bring Out the Best in Tortillas," *page 166*). If using corn tortillas, stack two for each taco; or use one flour tortilla for each taco. Top with 2 or 3 pieces of fish and some of the slaw. Reserve any remaining dressing to serve with tacos. Serve with limes, reserved dressing, and additional hot pepper sauce. Serve immediately.

MAKES 8 TACOS.

EACH TACO *310 cal, 18 g fat (3 g sat. fat), 29 mg chol, 150 mg sodium, 26 g carbo, 2 g fiber, 12 g pro. Daily Values: 4% vit. A, 23% vit. C, 3% calcium, 7% iron.*

pick a tortilla

1. **FLOUR** smooth texture, very mild
2. **CORN** robust texture, mild corn flavor
3. **WHOLE WHEAT** robust texture, wheaty flavor
4. **GLUTEN-FREE** made with rice flour; smooth texture, mild rice flavor

Everyday Easy

Economical, summer-fresh meals

FAST | **LOW FAT**

FRESH CORN AND CHICKEN CHOWDER

START TO FINISH: 30 MIN.

BUDGET $2.05 PER SERVING

12	oz. skinless, boneless chicken breast halves or chicken thighs
4	fresh ears of sweet corn, husked
1	32-oz. container reduced-sodium chicken broth
1	small green sweet pepper, chopped (½ cup)
1	cup milk
1¼	cups instant mashed potato flakes Salt and ground black pepper Crushed red pepper (optional)

1. In Dutch oven combine chicken, corn, and broth. Cover; bring to boiling over high heat. Reduce heat. Simmer for 12 minutes or until chicken is no longer pink. Remove chicken and corn to cutting board.

2. Add half the sweet pepper to broth in Dutch oven. Stir in milk and potato flakes.

3. Shred chicken using two forks. Return chicken to Dutch oven. Using a kitchen towel to hold hot corn, cut kernels from cobs. Place corn in Dutch oven; heat through. Season to taste with salt and pepper. Sprinkle each serving with remaining sweet pepper and crushed red pepper. **MAKES 4 SERVINGS.**

EACH SERVING *269 cal, 3 g fat (1 g sat. fat), 4 mg chol, 721 mg sodium, 33 g carbo, 3 g fiber, 29 g pro. Daily Values: 8% vit. A, 58% vit. C, 9% calcium, 8% iron.*

FAST | **LOW FAT**

GRILLED VEG SANDWICHES

START TO FINISH: 30 MIN.

BUDGET $1.54 PER SERVING

4	ciabatta rolls or other hearty rolls
1	lemon
2	Tbsp. olive oil
1	Tbsp. balsamic vinegar
3	small zucchini and/or yellow summer squash
1	small red onion
2	oz. feta cheese, crumbled Fresh mint leaves (optional)

1. Split rolls; halve and seed lemon. Lightly brush 1 tablespoon of the oil on cut sides of rolls and lemon halves; set aside. In small bowl combine remaining oil and the vinegar.

2. Cut zucchini lengthwise in ¼-inch-thick slices. Cut onion in ¼-inch slices. Brush both with some of the oil-vinegar mixture; sprinkle *salt* and *pepper.*

3. For charcoal grill, cook vegetables and lemon on uncovered rack directly over medium-hot coals for 2 to 3 minutes on each side or until tender. Add rolls, cut sides down, during last 3 minutes of grilling. (For gas grill, heat. Reduce heat to medium-hot. Grill as above.)

4. Serve vegetables on rolls. Top with feta and mint. Drizzle remaining oil-vinegar. Squeeze juice from lemon over vegetables. **MAKES 4 SERVINGS.**

EACH SERVING *294 cal, 11 g fat (3 g sat. fat), 13 mg chol, 684 mg sodium, 41 g carbo, 4 g fiber, 10 g pro. Daily Values: 5% vit. A, 65% vit. C, 13% calcium, 16% iron.*

FRESH CORN AND CHICKEN CHOWDER

GRILLED VEG
SANDWICHES

SHRIMP FRITTERS
WITH ROMAINE

FAST
SHRIMP FRITTERS WITH ROMAINE

START TO FINISH: 30 MIN.
BUDGET $2.53 PER SERVING

1	lb. peeled and deveined cooked shrimp, tails removed
1	egg
6	green onions, thinly sliced
¼	cup all-purpose flour
3	tsp. seafood seasoning blend
1	lime
⅓	cup mayonnaise or salad dressing
1	Tbsp. honey
1	head romaine, sliced crosswise

1. Coarsely chop shrimp. In a bowl beat the egg. Add shrimp, two-thirds of the onions, the flour, and 2 teaspoons seasoning.
2. In large skillet heat ¼ cup *oil* over medium-high heat. In ⅓-cup portions, carefully drop about half the shrimp mixture in hot oil; slightly flatten with spatula. Cook for 3 minutes on each side or until golden and heated through. Transfer to paper towels; cover and keep warm. Cook remaining shrimp mixture.
3. Shred 2 teaspoons peel from lime. Cut lime in half. Juice half into bowl. Stir in peel, mayonnaise, remaining seasoning, and honey. Cut remaining lime half in wedges. Serve fritters with romaine, mayonnaise mixture, and lime wedges.
MAKES 4 SERVINGS.

EACH SERVING *455 cal, 31 g fat (4 g sat. fat), 281 mg chol, 385 mg sodium, 17 g carbo, 2 g fiber, 28 g pro. Daily Values: 94% vit. A, 39% vit. C, 10% calcium, 30% iron.*

CHILI-PEANUT PORK CHOPS WITH CARROT-CUCUMBER SALAD

TURKEY-MANGO QUESADILLAS

FAST
CHILI-PEANUT PORK WITH CARROT-CUCUMBER SALAD

START TO FINISH: 20 MIN.
BUDGET $2.55 PER SERVING

1	cup dry-roasted peanuts
2	tsp. chili powder
4	½-inch-thick pork chops
2	Tbsp. olive oil
¼	cup vinegar
1	Tbsp. sugar
3	small carrots
1	small English (seedless) cucumber
½	cup fresh cilantro leaves

1. In food processor or by hand chop three-fourths of the peanuts. In a shallow dish combine chopped nuts and chili powder. Press pork chops into nut mixture to coat.
2. In 12-inch skillet cook pork in hot oil over medium heat for 5 minutes on each side or until internal temperature reaches 155°F.
3. Meanwhile, in a medium bowl combine vinegar and sugar; stir until sugar is dissolved. With vegetable peeler, cut carrots and cucumber lengthwise in ribbons. Add to bowl. Stir in remaining peanuts and the cilantro leaves.
4. Serve pork chops with carrots and cucumber mixture. Sprinkle additional chili powder. **MAKES 4 SERVINGS.**

EACH SERVING *444 cal, 32 g fat (6 g sat. fat), 52 mg chol, 97 mg sodium, 17 g carbo, 5 g fiber, 25 g pro. Daily Values: 124% vit. A, 25% vit. C, 7% calcium, 15% iron.*

FAST | KID-FRIENDLY
TURKEY-MANGO QUESADILLAS

START TO FINISH: 30 MIN.
BUDGET $2.70 PER SERVING

4	8-inch flour tortillas
1	Tbsp. vegetable oil
6	oz. Gouda or smoked Gouda cheese, thinly sliced or shredded
8	oz. cooked or smoked turkey or chicken, chopped
½	cup bottled roasted red peppers, drained and sliced
1	cup mango salsa or mango-peach salsa
¼	cup snipped fresh cilantro (optional)

1. Heat oven to 250°F. Brush one side of each tortilla with some of the oil. Place tortillas, oil sides down, on a large baking sheet. Top half of each tortilla with cheese, turkey, red peppers, one-fourth the salsa, and the cilantro. Fold tortillas in half; press gently.
2. In 12-inch skillet cook quesadillas, two at a time, over medium heat for 6 minutes, until lightly browned and crisp, turning once. Place cooked quesadillas on baking sheet; keep warm in oven while cooking the remaining quesadillas.
3. To serve, cut in wedges. Pass remaining salsa. **MAKES 4 SERVINGS.**

EACH SERVING *392 cal, 18 g fat (9 g sat. fat), 96 mg chol, 778 mg sodium, 27 g carbo, 5 g fiber, 32 g pro. Daily Values: 9% vit. A, 85% vit. C, 38% calcium, 16% iron.*

American Classics
from Chef Scott Peacock
Bread and Butter Pickles

CLASSIC BREAD AND BUTTER PICKLES

PREP: 60 MIN. CHILL: UP TO 24 HR.

12	cups ¼-inch slices small pickling cucumbers (about 4 lb.)
2	medium onions, thinly sliced
6	Tbsp. kosher or pickling salt
4	to 5 cups crushed ice
3	cups granulated sugar
3	cups cider vinegar
2	Tbsp. mustard seeds
2	tsp. celery seeds
4	¼-inch slices unpeeled fresh ginger

1. In a large bowl gently toss the sliced cucumbers, onions, and kosher salt. Transfer to a colander set in an extra-large bowl, layering with ice and finishing with a layer of ice. Weight with a heavy plate. Refrigerate overnight or up to 24 hours.

2. Meanwhile, for pickling syrup, in large nonreactive (stainless, enamel, or nonstick) saucepan combine sugar, vinegar, mustard seeds, celery seeds, and ginger. Bring to boiling; reduce heat and simmer, uncovered, 3 minutes. Remove from heat. Cool, cover, and refrigerate until ready to proceed with recipe.

3. After cucumbers have chilled, remove any unmelted ice and discard any liquid in bowl. Transfer cucumber mixture to nonreactive Dutch oven.

4. To remove seeds and ginger, strain syrup through a large sieve lined with cheesecloth over the Dutch oven with the sliced cucumbers. Bring mixture just to a low boil, stirring occasionally. Remove from heat.

5. With a large spoon transfer the cucumbers to hot sterilized pint canning jars, leaving ½-inch headspace. Bring syrup in Dutch oven to boiling. Ladle hot syrup over pickles to cover. Wipe jar rims with damp cloth. Put on lids and screw bands. To seal, invert jars until cool. Store in refrigerator.

MAKES 5 PINTS (40 ¼-CUP SERVINGS).

EACH SERVING *38 cal, 0 g fat, 0 mg chol, 291 mg sodium, 9 g carbo, 0 g fiber, 0 g pro. Daily Values: 1% vit. A, 2% vit. C, 1% calcium, 1% iron.*

> ## "For the best-tasting
> pickles, use fresh unwaxed pickling cucumbers. Choose only those that are vibrant green, firm, and blemish-free."

ADD THE RIGHT SALT
"Kosher or pickling salt is best. Table salt can discolor the pickles and make the brine cloudy."

PREPARE THE SYRUP
"Make the pickling syrup while the cucumbers are on ice, allowing time for the spices to impart their flavor."

CHILL AND WEIGHT
"The ice crisps the cucumber slices. The heavy plate presses out excess moisture, ensuring firm pickles."

STRAIN THE SYRUP
"I like a clear syrup without seeds clinging to pickles." To remove the spices, strain through a sieve lined with a double layer of cheesecloth.

the ideal pickle ...

... HAS JUST THE RIGHT SNAP, adding crunch to hamburgers and sandwiches yet satisfying on its own.

... IS IMMEDIATELY DELICIOUS and gets even better as flavors develop over days or weeks.

... IS CUSTOMIZED TO TASTE. Make the recipe as is or add garlic, chiles, or extra spices.

—CHEF SCOTT PEACOCK

HEAT CUCUMBERS AND PICKLING SYRUP
"Bring just to boiling, stirring occasionally and taking care to cook the cucumbers as little as possible."

SPOON PICKLES IN JARS
Fill sterilized jars with pickles, then ladle hot syrup to cover. Use a damp cloth to wipe jar rims before sealing.

september

Use your noodle in a new way, cook up a weeknight steak—and indulge in some good-for-you chocolate.

185

188

195

SPAGHETTI WITH
BEST-EVER BOLOGNESE SAUCE
Recipe on page 177

SPAGHETTI WITH
ROASTED BUTTERNUT
SQUASH

On Top of Spaghetti

Nine fresh ways with a favorite noodle

SPAGHETTI WITH ROASTED BUTTERNUT SQUASH

Garlic becomes soft and mild tasting when roasted. To peel the cloves before roasting, place them in a bowl, pour boiling water over, let stand 15 minutes, drain, and peel.

START TO FINISH: 40 MIN. OVEN: 425°F

1	2-lb. butternut squash, peeled and cut in 1-inch pieces
1	bulb garlic, separated in cloves and peeled (halve large cloves)
3	Tbsp. olive oil
1	14- to 16-oz. pkg. dried multigrain, whole wheat, or regular spaghetti
¼	cup butter
3	slices bacon, crisp-cooked and crumbled
½	cup walnuts, chopped and toasted
½	tsp. freshly grated nutmeg or ¼ tsp. ground nutmeg
⅓	cup shredded pecorino cheese Sliced green onions (optional)

1. Heat oven to 425°F. In 15×10×1-inch baking pan toss together squash, peeled garlic cloves, oil, and ¼ teaspoon *each salt* and *black pepper*. Evenly spread squash in pan. Bake 15 to 18 minutes or until squash is tender and lightly browned.

2. Meanwhile, cook spaghetti, with 1 tablespoon *salt* added to water, according to package directions. Drain; keep warm.

3. In small saucepan heat butter over medium heat until it turns the color of light brown sugar, stirring frequently.

4. In serving bowl toss spaghetti with about half the browned butter. Toss squash, garlic, bacon, nuts, and nutmeg with remaining browned butter. Serve squash mixture over spaghetti. Sprinkle cheese and green onions.

MAKES 8 SERVINGS.

EACH SERVING *398 cal, 19 g fat (6 g sat. fat), 22 mg chol, 250 mg sodium, 47 g carbo, 6 g fiber, 13 g pro. Daily Values: 206% vit. A, 36% vit. C, 12% calcium, 15% iron.*

SPAGHETTI WITH BEST-EVER BOLOGNESE SAUCE

This rich, hearty meat sauce is a natural with whole wheat spaghetti.

PREP: 25 MIN. COOK: 20 MIN.

1½	lb. 85% lean ground beef chuck
1	large onion, chopped (1 cup)
2	medium carrots, chopped (1 cup)
3	cloves garlic, minced
1	cup half-and-half or milk
1	cup chicken broth
1	Tbsp. white wine vinegar
1	28-oz. can crushed tomatoes
1	6-oz. can tomato paste
2	tsp. Italian seasoning, crushed
1	tsp. ground black pepper
½	tsp. salt
1	14- to 16-oz. pkg. dried whole wheat, multigrain, or regular spaghetti Grated Parmesan, Romano, or Asiago cheese (optional) Fresh oregano (optional)

1. For sauce, in 12-inch skillet brown beef, onion, carrots, and garlic until meat is no longer pink, stirring occasionally. Drain off fat.

2. Add half-and-half. Bring to boiling. Reduce heat; simmer, uncovered, for 5 minutes or until half-and-half is nearly evaporated. Stir in broth, then vinegar. Return to boiling. Reduce heat; simmer, uncovered, 15 minutes or until liquid is nearly evaporated. Stir in crushed tomatoes, tomato paste, seasoning, pepper, and salt. Bring to boiling. Reduce heat; simmer, uncovered, 5 minutes or until thickened.

3. Meanwhile, cook spaghetti, with 1 tablespoon salt added to water, according to package directions. Drain. Serve spaghetti with sauce. Sprinkle cheese and oregano. **MAKES 8 SERVINGS.**

EACH SERVING *474 cal, 18 g fat (7 g sat. fat), 69 mg chol, 645 mg sodium, 53 g carbo, 6 g fiber, 26 g pro. Daily Values: 73% vit. A, 28% vit. C, 10% calcium, 36% iron.*

LOW FAT

SPAGHETTI WITH TWO-TOMATO TOSS

Gluten-free corn or cornmeal pasta has texture and appetizing color. With all gluten-free pastas, it's important to follow package cooking directions exactly.

START TO FINISH: 35 MIN.

½ a 7- to 8-oz. jar oil-packed dried tomatoes

4 cloves garlic, minced

2 pints red and/or yellow cherry or grape tomatoes

1 tsp. cracked black pepper or ½ to 1 tsp. crushed red pepper

½ tsp. salt

1 14- to 16-oz. pkg. dried corn, multigrain, whole wheat, or regular spaghetti

4 oz. bite-size fresh mozzarella cheese balls (bocconcini), halved

½ cup chopped Italian (flat-leaf) parsley or fresh basil

1. For sauce, drain dried tomatoes, reserving 1 tablespoon oil. Halve large tomatoes. In 12-inch skillet cook garlic in oil from tomatoes over medium heat until tender, about 1 minute. Add cherry and oil-packed tomatoes. Cook, stirring, until fresh tomato skins blister, about 8 to 10 minutes. Season with pepper and salt.

2. Meanwhile, cook spaghetti, with 1 tablespoon *salt* added to water, according to package directions. Reserve 1 cup pasta cooking water. Drain pasta.

3. Toss spaghetti with tomato mixture in skillet, adding enough cooking water to thin sauce. Serve immediately with fresh mozzarella balls and parsley.

MAKES 8 SERVINGS.

EACH SERVING *264 cal, 6 g fat (2 g sat. fat), 10 mg chol, 229 mg sodium, 47 g carbo, 7 g fiber, 8 g pro. Daily Values: 28% vit. A, 49% vit. C, 12% calcium, 8% iron.*

SPAGHETTI WITH
TWO-TOMATO TOSS

SPAGHETTI WITH ITALIAN SAUSAGE AND SPINACH

Sweet peppers and onions balance the spiciness of this Italian-inspired dish.

START TO FINISH: 35 MIN.

- 1   19- to 20-oz. pkg. uncooked mild or hot Italian sausage links, cut in 1-inch pieces
- 2   medium yellow or green sweet peppers, cut in bite-size strips
- 1   small sweet onion, cut in wedges
- 1   14- to 16-oz. pkg. dried multigrain, whole wheat, or regular spaghetti
- 1   tsp. crushed red pepper
- ¼   tsp. salt
- ½   cup chicken broth
- 6   cups packaged fresh baby spinach
- 2   to 3 oz. Asiago cheese, shaved Crushed red pepper (optional)

1. In 12-inch skillet cook sausages, turning occasionally, for 15 minutes or until no longer pink.

2. Add sweet peppers and onion to sausage in skillet. Cook for 5 minutes, stirring occasionally, until vegetables are tender.

3. Meanwhile, cook spaghetti, with 1 tablespoon *salt* and 1 teaspoon crushed red pepper added to water, according to package directions. Reserve 1 cup pasta cooking water. Drain pasta; return to pan.

4. Toss sausage mixture and the ¼ teaspoon salt with spaghetti in pan. Stir in chicken broth and enough reserved pasta water to thin. Add spinach; toss just until combined and spinach is slightly wilted. To serve, sprinkle Asiago cheese and additional crushed red pepper.

MAKES 8 SERVINGS.

EACH SERVING *466 cal, 24 g fat (9 g sat. fat), 59 mg chol, 745 mg sodium, 41 g carbo, 5 g fiber, 21 g pro. Daily Values: 47% vit. A, 157% vit. C, 13% calcium, 18% iron.*

SPAGHETTI WITH
ITALIAN SAUSAGE
AND SPINACH

SHRIMP, CHICKPEA, AND
FETA CHEESE NESTS

SPAGHETTI-CORN
RELISH SALAD

SPAGHETTI-CORN RELISH SALAD

Make and refrigerate this pasta salad as long as 24 hours before serving.

START TO FINISH: 30 MIN.

1	14- to 16- oz. pkg. dried multigrain, whole wheat, or regular spaghetti
4	fresh ears of sweet corn, husks and silks removed, or 2 cups frozen whole kernel corn
1	small cucumber, seeded and chopped
1	small summer squash, chopped
1	small red onion, finely chopped
1	stalk celery, thinly sliced
1	large red sweet pepper, chopped
½	cup cider vinegar
⅓	cup olive oil
1	Tbsp. sugar
½	tsp. dry mustard
½	tsp. celery seeds

1. Cook spaghetti, with 1 tablespoon *salt* added to water, according to package directions; add sweet corn during the last 3 minutes of pasta cooking time. Use tongs to transfer ears of corn to cutting board. (If using frozen corn, drain with pasta.) Drain spaghetti; rinse in cold water and drain well.

2. Cool corn until easy to handle. Hold corn upright. With fingers away from knife blade and cutting down the length of the corn cob, cut off corn in planks.

3. In large serving bowl combine cooled drained spaghetti, cucumber, squash, onion, celery, and sweet pepper.

4. In jar combine vinegar, oil, sugar, dry mustard, celery seeds, and ½ teaspoon *salt.*

Cover; shake well to combine and dissolve sugar. Pour over spaghetti mixture; toss to coat. Gently fold in corn planks. Serve immediately or cover and refrigerate up to 24 hours. **MAKES 8 SERVINGS.**

EACH SERVING *320 cal, 11 g fat (1 g sat. fat), 0 mg chol, 181 mg sodium, 47 g carbo, 6 g fiber, 11 g pro. Daily Values: 15% vit. A, 51% vit. C, 3% calcium, 12% iron.*

SHRIMP, CHICKPEA, AND FETA CHEESE NESTS

START TO FINISH: 30 MIN.

1	14- to 16-oz. pkg. dried multigrain, whole wheat, or regular spaghetti
2	15- to 16-oz. cans chickpeas (garbanzo beans), rinsed and drained
1	16-oz. bag frozen peeled, cooked shrimp with tails, thawed
3	plum tomatoes, seeded and chopped
4	oz. feta cheese, crumbled (1 cup)
2	Tbsp. chopped fresh mint
1	tsp. finely shredded lemon peel
2	Tbsp. lemon juice
1	tsp. dried oregano, crushed
	Lemon wedges
	Green olives (optional)
	Olive oil

1. Cook spaghetti, with 1 tablespoon salt added to water, according to package directions; add drained chickpeas and shrimp during the last 1 minute of pasta cooking time. Drain.

2. Return pasta mixture to pan. Stir in tomatoes, cheese, mint, lemon peel, lemon juice, oregano, and ¼ teaspoon *each salt* and *black pepper.*

3. Serve with lemon wedges and green olives. Drizzle with olive oil.
MAKES 8 SERVINGS.

EACH SERVING *696 cal, 14 g fat (3 g sat. fat), 123 mg chol, 408 mg sodium, 102 g carbo, 23 g fiber, 44 g pro. Daily Values: 11% vit. A, 37% vit. C, 24% calcium, 58% iron.*

MAC AND CHEESE SPAGHETTI

START TO FINISH: 30 MIN. OVEN: 425°F

1½	cups coarse white bread crumbs
2	Tbsp. grated Parmesan cheese
1	Tbsp. butter, melted
1	14- to 16-oz. pkg. dried multigrain, whole wheat, or regular spaghetti
1	10-oz. pkg. frozen peas (2 cups) or 2 cups fresh broccoli florets
2	Tbsp. butter, melted
1	tsp. Dijon-style mustard
8	oz. sharp cheddar cheese, finely shredded (2 cups)
4	oz. American cheese, shredded (1 cup) Shredded thinly sliced prosciutto or cooked ham (optional)

1. Heat oven to 425°F. In 15×10×1-inch baking pan combine crumbs, Parmesan cheese, and the 1 tablespoon butter. Bake 5 minutes; remove from oven, stir, and set aside.

2. Meanwhile, in Dutch oven cook spaghetti, with 1 tablespoon *salt* added to water, according to package directions; add peas during last 3 minutes of pasta cooking time. Reserve 2 cups pasta cooking water; set aside. Drain pasta and vegetables; keep warm.

3. Return 1 cup reserved pasta water to Dutch oven. Bring to boiling. Add the 2 tablespoons butter and mustard. Add cheeses, a bit at a time, stirring after each addition until melted. Stir in more pasta water if needed. Add spaghetti mixture; toss. To serve, sprinkle crumb mixture and prosciutto.

MAKES 6 TO 8 SERVINGS.

EACH SERVING *456 cal, 20 g fat (12 g sat. fat), 56 mg chol, 561 mg sodium, 47 g carbo, 6 g fiber, 23 g pro. Daily Values: 14% vit. A, 6% vit. C, 33% calcium, 14% iron.*

MAC AND CHEESE SPAGHETTI

FAST

SPAGHETTI WITH FRESH PESTO

START TO FINISH: 30 MIN.

- 12 oz. green beans, trimmed
- 1 14- to 16-oz. pkg. dried multigrain, whole wheat, or regular spaghetti
- 1 medium onion, chopped
- 2 cloves garlic, minced
- 1 Tbsp. olive oil
- 1 cup packed fresh spinach
- ¾ cup packed fresh basil
- ½ cup toasted almonds
- ½ cup grated Parmesan cheese
- 1 tsp. lemon-pepper seasoning
- ½ cup olive oil
- 3 hard-cooked eggs, chopped
  Sliced green onions
  Fresh lemon juice
  Toasted baguette slices (optional)

1. Cut one-third of the green beans in 2-inch pieces; set aside. Cook spaghetti, with 1 tablespoon *salt* added to water, according to package directions; add cut beans the last 5 minutes of cooking time. Reserve 1½ cups pasta cooking water. Drain pasta; keep warm.

2. For pesto, in skillet cook onion and garlic in the 1 tablespoon oil until softened. Add whole beans. Cook, covered, 5 to 7 minutes, or until tender, stirring occasionally.

3. In food processor combine bean mixture, spinach, basil, almonds, cheese, and seasoning. Cover. Pulse to coarsely chop. With processor running, add ½ cup olive oil in thin stream; process until nearly smooth. Season with *salt* and *pepper*. Toss with spaghetti mixture, adding enough reserved pasta water to thin. To serve, sprinkle chopped eggs and green onions. Drizzle lemon juice. Serve with baguette slices. **MAKES 6 TO 8 SERVINGS.**

EACH SERVING *555 cal, 30 g fat (5 g sat. fat), 112 mg chol, 419 mg sodium, 54 g carbo, 8 g fiber, 21 g pro. Daily Values: 27% vit. A, 27% vit. C, 27% calcium, 21% iron.*

SPAGHETTI WITH FRESH PESTO

SPAGHETTI AND SPICY TURKEY MEATBALLS

PREP: 30 MIN. BAKE: 20 MIN. OVEN: 375°F

- 2 egg whites, lightly beaten
- 2 Tbsp. olive oil
- 1 Tbsp. milk
- 2 tsp. chili powder
- 2 lb. uncooked ground turkey breast or ground turkey
- ⅓ cup finely chopped onion
- ¼ cup fine dry bread crumbs
- 2 jalapeño peppers, seeded and minced*
- 1 Tbsp. chopped fresh cilantro
- 1 14- to 16-oz. pkg. dried multigrain, whole wheat, or regular spaghetti
- 2 3-oz. pkgs. cream cheese
- 2 cups milk
- 4 oz. Gouda cheese, shredded
  Fresh cilantro

1. Heat oven to 375°F. In bowl stir together egg whites, oil, milk, chili powder, 1 teaspoon *black pepper,* and ½ teaspoon *salt.*

2. In large bowl combine turkey, onion, bread crumbs, jalapeños, and chopped cilantro. Fold egg white mixture into turkey mixture; mix well. Shape in 1½-inch balls. Place on foil-lined 15×10×1-inch baking pan. Bake 20 minutes or until no longer pink (170°F).

3. Meanwhile, cook spaghetti, with 1 tablespoon *salt* added to water, according to package directions. Drain; keep warm.

4. In same pan used for pasta, melt cream cheese over low heat. Add milk. Cook, stirring, until bubbly. Return spaghetti to pan; toss to coat with cream cheese mixture. Serve spaghetti with meatballs, cheese, and cilantro. **MAKES 8 SERVINGS.**

*When working with hot peppers, wear plastic gloves. If peppers touch bare skin, wash immediately with soap and water.

EACH SERVING *507 cal, 18 g fat (8 g sat. fat), 115 mg chol, 247 mg sodium, 41 g carbo, 4 g fiber, 46 g pro. Daily Values: 15% vit. A, 7% vit. C, 24% calcium, 19% iron.*

SPAGHETTI AND SPICY
TURKEY MEATBALLS

What's Cooking
from food artisan Alisa Barry

Bella cucina

OLIVE AND ARUGULA
FLATBREAD PIZZA
SALAD

OLIVE AND ARUGULA FLATBREAD PIZZA SALAD

Alisa uses her Pane Rustico flatbread; any flatbread—pita or a thin Italian bread shell—works fine.

START TO FINISH: 30 MIN.

1	sheet purchased flatbread, about 12×14 inches
2	tsp. extra virgin olive oil
2	to 3 Tbsp. extra virgin olive oil
1	tsp. fresh lemon juice
1	tsp. red wine vinegar
2	cups baby arugula leaves
¼	cup olive pesto or tapenade
6	pimiento-stuffed green olives, sliced
1	oz. Parmesan cheese, shaved

1. Brush bread with the 2 teaspoons olive oil. In screw-top jar combine remaining olive oil, lemon juice, vinegar, ¼ teaspoon *salt*, and ⅛ teaspoon *cracked black pepper;* shake to combine. In a bowl toss the dressing with the arugula.

2. Place flatbread on grill rack directly over medium coals. Cook just until golden brown, about 1 to 2 minutes, turning once. Remove from grill. Evenly spread flatbread with olive pesto, leaving 2 inches of border uncoated. Top with dressed arugula, olives, and Parmesan shavings. **MAKES 4 SERVINGS.**

EACH SERVING *504 cal, 27 g fat (4 g sat. fat), 14 mg chol, 1,369 mg sodium, 51 g carbo, 1 g fiber, 16 g pro. Daily Values: 6% vit. A, 5% vit. C, 27% calcium, 5% iron.*

GRILLED FENNEL AND TOMATOES

A sprinkle of fresh bread crumbs adds crunch and flavor to tender grilled vegetables. Serve this vegetable dish warm from the grill or at room temperature.

PREP: 25 MIN. GRILL: 10 MIN.

2	bulbs fresh fennel
2	large tomatoes, quartered
3	Tbsp. extra virgin olive oil
1	slice bread
3	Tbsp. unsalted butter
⅓	cup finely shredded Parmesan cheese

1. Trim fronds from fennel bulbs. Cut fennel lengthwise in ¼- to ½-inch wedges. Brush vegetables with oil. Lightly sprinkle *salt* and *pepper.* Arrange coals around perimeter of grill. Place fennel in center of grill rack. Cover and grill 10 to 12 minutes or until fennel has grill marks and outer edges begin to caramelize, turning occasionally. During last 5 to 6 minutes of grilling, place tomatoes on rack directly over coals. Grill just until

GRILLED FENNEL AND TOMATOES

tomatoes soften, turning once. Transfer to platter.

2. Meanwhile, tear bread and place in blender. Cover and pulse with on-off turns for coarse crumbs. In skillet melt butter over medium heat. Add crumbs. Cook and stir 3 to 4 minutes, just until crumbs are browned. Remove from heat. Stir in cheese. Spoon vegetables. **MAKES 4 TO 6 SERVINGS.**

EACH SERVING *262 cal, 21 g fat (8 g sat. fat), 28 mg chol, 367 mg sodium, 15 g carbo, 5 g fiber, 5 g pro. Daily Values: 23% vit. A, 41% vit. C, 16% calcium, 8% iron.*

BAKED MOZZARELLA AND TOMATO-BASIL ANTIPASTI

PREP: 15 MIN. BAKE: 20 MIN. OVEN: 350°F

2	cups pasta sauce
1	clove garlic, minced
8	oz. fresh bocconcini mozzarella or mozzarella cheese, cut in cubes
1	Tbsp. extra virgin olive oil
¼	cup torn fresh basil leaves
1	recipe Parmesan-Toasted Baguette Slices

1. Heat oven to 350°F. In four 12- to 16-ounce or one 1½-quart shallow ovenproof dish layer pasta sauce, garlic, and mozzarella. Bake 20 minutes or until mozzarella is melted. Remove from oven; drizzle olive oil. Top with basil. Serve with bread or Parmesan Toasted Baguette Slices. **MAKES 4 SERVINGS.**

PARMESAN-TOASTED BAGUETTE SLICES
Diagonally cut baguette in ½-inch slices. Lightly brush with olive oil. Broil 3 to 4 inches from heat for 2 minutes. Turn slices; sprinkle shredded Parmesan and crushed dried basil. Broil 1 to 2 minutes or until lightly toasted. **MAKES 4 SERVINGS.**

EACH SERVING *405 cal, 17 g fat (9 g sat. fat), 40 mg chol, 929 mg sodium, 41 g carbo, 3 g fiber, 19 g pro. Daily Values: 19% vit. A, 11% vit. C, 49% calcium, 16% iron.*

MEDITERRANEAN EGGPLANT DIP

Make and refrigerate this dip up to 3 days before serving.

PREP: 20 MIN. GRILL: 8 MIN.

1	cup canned garbanzo beans (chickpeas), drained
1	Tbsp. fresh mint leaves
1	clove garlic
1	Tbsp. fresh lemon juice
½	tsp. kosher salt
1	cup grilled* or roasted eggplant
¼	cup extra virgin olive oil
	Olive oil and fresh mint
	Walnuts, toasted
	Grilled pita wedges or focaccia

1. In a food processor finely chop chickpeas, mint, and garlic. Add lemon juice, salt, and eggplant. With processor running, add olive oil in a steady stream; process until smooth. Transfer to serving dish; drizzle olive oil; sprinkle mint and walnuts. Serve with grilled pita. **MAKES 1¾ CUPS, 14 (2-TBSP.) SERVINGS.**

*GRILLED EGGPLANT Brush eight ½-inch eggplant slices with 2 tablespoons olive oil. Sprinkle ½ teaspoon kosher salt. Grill on rack of uncovered grill directly over medium coals for 8 to 10 minutes or until tender, turning once. Cool slightly; process in food processor until slightly chunky.

EACH 2-TBSP. SERVING *79 cal, 6 g fat (1 g sat. fat), 0 mg chol, 190 mg sodium, 6 g carbo, 2 g fiber, 1 g pro. Daily Values: 3% vit. C, 1% calcium, 2% iron.*

BAKED MOZZARELLA
AND TOMATO-BASIL
ANTIPASTI

MEDITERRANEAN
EGGPLANT DIP

Everyday Easy
Quick, budget-friendly meals

FAST

PAN-FRIED GARLIC STEAK AND POTATOES

START TO FINISH: 30 MIN.
BUDGET $2.87 PER SERVING

12	cloves garlic
1	lb. tiny new potatoes, scrubbed
2	Tbsp. olive oil
4	6-oz. boneless beef ribeye or beef strip steaks
1	cup grape or cherry tomatoes
	Fresh oregano (optional)

1. Using the side of large chef's knife smash garlic; discard skins. Halve any large potatoes. Place potatoes in microwave-safe bowl. Cover with vented plastic wrap; heat in microwave on 100% power (high) 5 minutes. Stir in garlic. Cover; cook 5 minutes more or until tender, stirring once. Drain.
2. Meanwhile, heat 1 tablespoon of the olive oil in a skillet over medium-high heat. Season steak with *salt* and *pepper*. Cook steaks, half at a time, 8 minutes for ribeye or 4 minutes for strip (145°F for medium-rare or 160°F for medium),

turning once. Keep steaks warm while cooking remaining steaks.
3. Add remaining 1 tablespoon oil to skillet. Add potatoes, garlic, and tomatoes. Season with *salt* and *pepper*. Cook 5 minutes or until potatoes are golden and tomatoes begin to wilt, stirring occasionally. Serve potato mixture with steak. Top with fresh oregano. **MAKES 4 SERVINGS.**
EACH SERVING *434 cal, 20 g fat (6 g sat. fat), 99 mg chol, 247 mg sodium, 25 g carbo, 3 g fiber, 38 g pro. Daily Values: 8% vit. A, 44% vit. C, 5% calcium, 26% iron.*

FAST

LEMON CHICKEN WITH OLIVES AND RICOTTA

START TO FINISH: 27 MIN.
BUDGET $2.78 PER SERVING

8	no-boil (oven-ready) lasagna noodles
1	Meyer lemon or lemon
4	small skinless, boneless chicken breast halves, halved crosswise
1	cup garlic-stuffed or pitted green olives
1	cup ricotta cheese
	Olive oil
	Fresh rosemary (optional)

1. In a Dutch oven bring 3 inches water to boiling. Add noodles and 1 teaspoon *olive oil*. Cover. Cook 6 minutes or until tender; drain. Lay noodles in single layer on waxed paper. Cover; set aside.
2. Meanwhile, shred lemon peel; halve lemon. Juice 1 half; cut remaining in wedges. Season chicken with *salt, pepper,* and half of the lemon peel. In skillet heat 1 tablespoon *oil* over medium-high heat. Add chicken; cook 10 minutes or until no pink remains, turning once. Add olives; heat through. Remove from heat.
3. In microwave-safe bowl combine ricotta, the lemon juice, and ½ teaspoon *each salt* and *pepper.* Heat in microwave on 100% power (high) 30 seconds, stirring once.
4. Spoon ricotta mixture into bowls. Top with noodles, chicken, olive mixture, remaining lemon peel, and fresh rosemary. Pass lemon wedges.
MAKES 4 SERVINGS.
EACH SERVING *443 cal, 19 g fat (7 g sat. fat), 130 mg chol, 1,053 mg sodium, 30 g carbo, 4 g fiber, 39 g pro. Daily Values: 11% vit. A, 44% vit. C, 17% calcium, 15% iron.*

PAN-FRIED GARLIC STEAK AND POTATOES

LEMON CHICKEN
WITH OLIVES AND
RICOTTA

BACON, EGG, SPINACH,
AND TUNA SALAD

FAST

BACON, EGG, SPINACH, AND TUNA SALAD

START TO FINISH: 25 MIN.
BUDGET $3.31 PER SERVING

4	eggs
6	slices bacon
12	oz. tuna steaks
½	cup white wine vinegar
2	to 3 Tbsp. honey
1	Tbsp. Dijon-style mustard
1	6-oz. pkg. fresh baby spinach

1. Place eggs in saucepan; cover with water. Bring to rapid boil. Remove from heat; cover. Let stand 10 to 15 minutes (yolks will be soft-set at 10). Drain. Rinse with cold water; cool. Peel and halve.
2. Meanwhile, in large skillet cook bacon over medium heat until crisp. Drain; reserve 2 tablespoons drippings for dressing. Crumble bacon and set aside. Add tuna to skillet; cook over medium-high heat 3 minutes per side or until slightly pink in center. Transfer to cutting board; cover and keep warm. Wipe skillet clean. For dressing, whisk in reserved drippings, vinegar, honey, and mustard to skillet. Bring to boiling.
3. Line plates with spinach. Top with sliced tuna, crumbled bacon, and eggs. Drizzle dressing. Sprinkle *pepper.*
MAKES 4 SERVINGS.
EACH SERVING *481 cal, 32 g fat (10 g sat. fat), 289 mg chol, 702 mg sodium, 11 g carbo, 1 g fiber, 34 g pro. Daily Values: 86% vit. A, 22% vit. C, 9% calcium, 18% iron.*

FAST

PORK CUTLETS WITH BRUSSELS SPROUTS

START TO FINISH: 28 MIN.
BUDGET $1.99 PER SERVING

4	½-inch-thick boneless pork chops
¼	cup all-purpose flour

PORK CUTLETS
WITH BRUSSELS
SPROUTS

CURRIED
VEGETABLE SOUP

2	tsp. paprika or smoked paprika
1	lb. Brussels sprouts, trimmed and halved
2	Tbsp. butter
1	8-oz. carton light sour cream
2	Tbsp. milk or half-and-half
1	tsp. packed brown sugar

1. Using meat mallet or heavy rolling pin, pound pork, layered between plastic wrap, to ¼-inch thickness. In shallow dish combine flour, half the paprika, and ½ teaspoon each *salt* and *pepper.* Coat pork in flour mixture; set aside.
2. In a large skillet cook sprouts in hot butter over medium-high for 5 to 8 minutes, until crisp-tender and edges are brown. Remove from skillet. Cover and keep warm.
3. In the same skillet add additional butter, if needed. Cook pork for 4 to 5 minutes, turning once, until golden outside and slightly pink in center. Remove from skillet. Cover; keep warm.
4. For sauce, combine sour cream, milk, and brown sugar. Whisk into skillet. Heat through (do not boil). To serve, sprinkle pork and sprouts with remaining paprika.
MAKES 4 SERVINGS.
EACH SERVING *395 cal, 22 g fat (11 g sat. fat), 108 mg chol, 480 mg sodium, 22 g carbo, 5 g fiber, 29 g pro. Daily Values: 36% vit. A, 164% vit. C, 17% calcium, 19% iron.*

FAST | LOW FAT

CURRIED VEGETABLE SOUP

START TO FINISH: 20 MIN.
BUDGET $1.87 PER SERVING

3	cups cauliflower florets
1	14-oz. can unsweetened coconut milk
1	14-oz. can vegetable or chicken broth
1	Tbsp. curry powder
¼	cup chopped fresh cilantro
2	cups frozen baby peas-vegetable blend
2	pita bread rounds, cut in wedges (optional)
1	Tbsp. olive oil (optional) Fresh cilantro sprigs and crushed red pepper (optional)

1. Heat broiler. In a Dutch oven combine cauliflower, coconut milk, broth, curry powder, and the ¼ cup cilantro. Bring to boiling over high heat. Reduce heat to medium-low. Simmer, covered, 10 minutes or until cauliflower is tender. Stir in vegetable blend. Cook, uncovered, until heated through. Season with ¼ teaspoon *salt.*
2. Meanwhile, place pita wedges on baking sheet. Brush both sides with oil. Sprinkle ¼ teaspoon *curry powder.* Broil 3 to 4 inches from heat for 4 minutes, turning once, until golden. Serve soup with pita wedges. Sprinkle cilantro and red pepper.
MAKES 4 SERVINGS.
EACH SERVING *138 cal, 6 g fat (4 g sat. fat), 0 mg chol, 620 mg sodium, 19 g carbo, 4 g fiber, 3 g pro. Daily Values: 34% vit. A, 71% vit. C, 3% calcium, 12% iron.*

Good and Healthy
Chocolate

Chocolate originates as beans grown on tropical trees. They're dried, ground, then blended with milk, sugar, and cocoa butter. Because chocolate comes from a plant, it's no surprise that some of its health benefits resemble those of other produce. However, chocolate is high in calories and fat, so eat it in moderation. One ounce of dark chocolate each day (155 calories) provides benefits.

CINNAMON-SPICE CHOCOLATE BROWNIES

PREP: 20 MIN. BAKE: 23 MIN. COOL: 10 MIN.
OVEN: 350°F

	Nonstick cooking spray
¼	cup butter
1	cup granulated sugar
⅓	cup cold water
3	eggs
3	Tbsp. canola oil
1	tsp. vanilla
1¼	cups all-purpose flour
½	cup unsweetened cocoa powder
1	tsp. baking powder
¼	tsp. ground cinnamon
⅛	tsp. salt
⅛	tsp. ground ancho chile pepper or cayenne pepper
⅓	cup miniature bittersweet or semisweet chocolate pieces
2	Tbsp. hot strong coffee (optional) Powdered sugar and/or cinnamon-sugar (optional)

1. Preheat oven to 350°F. Line a 9×9×2-inch baking pan with foil, extending foil over edges of pan. Lightly coat the foil with nonstick spray. Set aside.
2. In a medium saucepan melt butter; remove from heat. Whisk in sugar and water. Whisk in eggs, oil, and vanilla until combined. Stir in flour, cocoa powder, baking powder, cinnamon, salt, and ancho chile pepper. Stir in chocolate pieces. Pour batter in prepared pan.
3. Bake for 23 to 25 minutes or until a wooden toothpick inserted near the center comes out clean. Cool in pan on wire rack for 10 minutes. Remove from pan by lifting the foil. Brush hot brownies with coffee. Cool completely.
4. Cut into bars. Sprinkle with powdered sugar and/or cinnamon-sugar.
MAKES 16 BROWNIES.

EACH BROWNIE *184 cal, 8 g fat (3 g sat. fat), 47 mg chol, 67 mg sodium, 25 g carbo, 0 g fiber, 3 g pro. Daily Values: 3% vit. A, 4% calcium, 6% iron.*

why chocolate is good for you

Provides protection
Chocolate is high in flavonoids, compounds that plants manufacture as protection from disease and damage. Eating flavonoids provides those benefits. Consuming flavonoid-rich foods may also reduce inflammation in arteries that lead to the heart, keep blood vessels open, ward off cancer, and raise good cholesterol levels.

Improves brain power
A recent study published in the *Journal of Nutrition* shows that participants over age 70 who reported regularly consuming chocolate scored higher on cognitive performance tests. The more eaten, the higher the scores. Flavonoids in chocolate that improve blood flow to the heart could be at work, says Penny M. Kris-Etherton, Ph.D., R.D., professor of nutrition at Penn State University. "Again, it could be blood flow to the brain, and I have seen other impressive studies that show chocolate flavonoids improves blood flow to specific parts of the brain that have to do with cognitive function."

May reduce heart attacks
A recent article published by Harvard Medical School reports that researchers in the U.S. and Switzerland found a possible link between chocolate and blood clot reduction. The study suggests flavonoids in chocolate may reduce blood clot formation responsible for many heart attacks and strokes.

RICH AND CREAMY
CHOCOLATE PUDDING

RICH AND CREAMY CHOCOLATE PUDDING

The coffee in this pudding brings out chocolate flavor rather than adding the taste of coffee.

PREP: 30 MIN. CHILL: 2 HR.

¼	cup granulated sugar
¼	cup packed brown sugar
¼	cup unsweetened cocoa powder
2	Tbsp. cornstarch
1	tsp. instant espresso coffee powder or instant coffee crystals
2	cups fat-free milk
1	egg, lightly beaten
1	Tbsp. butter
1	tsp. vanilla
1	banana, sliced (optional)
1	Tbsp. chopped crystallized ginger (optional)

1. In a medium saucepan combine sugars, cocoa powder, cornstarch, and espresso powder. Gradually stir in milk. Cook and stir over medium heat until thickened and bubbly; reduce heat. Cook and stir for 2 minutes more. Remove from heat.

2. Gradually whisk about ½ cup of the hot milk mixture into egg in a medium bowl. Add egg mixture to milk mixture in saucepan, stirring constantly. Return saucepan to medium-low heat; cook and stir for 2 minutes more. Remove from heat. Stir in butter and vanilla.

3. Place saucepan in a large bowl half-filled with ice water. Constantly stir pudding for 2 minutes to cool quickly. Transfer to a medium bowl. Cover surface of pudding with plastic wrap. Refrigerate 2 to 24 hours. To serve, top with sliced banana and/or crystallized ginger.

MAKES 4 SERVINGS.

EACH SERVING *217 cal, 5 g fat (3 g sat. fat), 63 mg chol, 95 mg sodium, 39 g carbo, 2 g fiber, 7 g pro. Daily Values: 8% vit. A, 18% calcium, 6% iron.*

GERMAN CHOCOLATE COOKIES

To make these cookies more healthful, use dark baking chocolate. For classic German chocolate flavor, use sweet baking chocolate.

PREP: 25 MIN. BAKE: 8 MIN. COOL: 1 MIN.
OVEN: 350°F

¼	cup butter, softened
¾	cup packed brown sugar
½	tsp. baking soda
⅛	tsp. salt
1	egg
1	tsp. vanilla
⅔	cup all-purpose flour
⅔	cup rolled oats
¼	cup flaxseed meal
¼	cup unsweetened cocoa powder
3	oz. dark or sweet baking chocolate, chopped
⅓	cup flaked coconut
⅓	cup chopped pecans, toasted
	Chopped pecans, optional
	Flaked coconut, optional

1. Preheat oven to 350°F. In a large mixing bowl beat butter with an electric mixer on medium to high speed for 30 seconds. Add brown sugar, baking soda, and salt. Beat until well combined, scraping sides of bowl occasionally. Beat in egg and vanilla until combined. Beat in flour. Stir in rolled oats, flaxseed meal, and cocoa powder. Stir in chopped chocolate, coconut, and pecans (dough will be dense).

2. Drop dough by rounded teaspoons 2 inches apart onto ungreased cookie sheets. If desired, sprinkle tops with additional chopped pecans and flaked coconut. Bake for 8 to 10 minutes or just until edges are firm and tops are set. Cool on cookie sheet for 1 minute. Transfer cookies to wire racks to cool.

MAKES ABOUT 35 COOKIES.

STORAGE Store cookies for 2 days at room temperature or freeze up to 3 months.

EACH COOKIE *84 cal, 4 g fat (2 g sat. fat), 0 mg chol, 45 mg sodium, 11 g carbo, 1 g fiber, 2 g pro. Daily Values: 1% vit. A, 1% calcium, 3% iron.*

GERMAN CHOCOLATE COOKIES

SEPTEMBER

American Classics
from Chef Scott Peacock

Fried Pies

ADD WATER GRADUALLY
"Mound the flour mixture. With your fingers, draw a trench in the center to sprinkle ice water 1 tablespoon at a time."

Choose the best fats:
"Good-quality butter for its delicious flavor and a bit of lard for flakiness and wonderful melting quality," says Scott.

SMEAR FOR FLAKINESS
"With the heel of your hand, press egg-size portions of rough dough away from you, flattening and pressing the chunks of fat into the flour paste. This technique creates a layered, flaky crust."

FLUFF IN THE WATER
"Quickly and confidently fluff the flour to incorporate the water. Redraw the trench and repeat until the mixture begins to clump."

GATHER TWICE-SMEARED DOUGH "This dough, as unpromising as it may look, is exactly how it should be at this step. It is now ready to wrap and chill."

WRAP AND CHILL
"Wrap the dough in a double thickness of plastic wrap. Then press firmly with both hands to flatten into a disk, forming a cohesive dough. Refrigerate at least 2 hours or up to 24 hours."

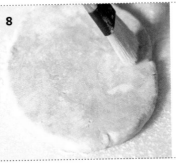

8

UNEVEN MARBLING
"The experience of making this pastry by hand is satisfying and rewarding, resulting in a dough that is beautifully marbled with obvious streaks of butter and lard. After the first rolling, be sure to brush off any excess flour before folding in thirds."

9

FOLD DOUGH IN THIRDS "Folding stacks the layers of fat and flour, which makes the pastry extra flaky. Chill again."

ROLL THINLY AND EVENLY
"Flour the rolling pin—not the dough. Using assertive pressure, quickly roll the cold dough from the center outward."

10

11

SPOON ON THE FILLING
"Resist the temptation to overfill. It's important to leave ⅓ inch around the edge."

12

MOISTEN THE EDGES
"Use a finger dipped in cold water to barely moisten around the edge of the dough, helping to ensure a good seal."

13

14

FRY UNTIL GOLDEN "Fry a few at a time, without crowding the pan, and remove the pies as they brown."

Make a tight seal.
"Carefully press the edges together, then gently pinch along the seam, flipping the pie over and pinching again to make sure both sides are well sealed."

15

COOL, ROLL IN SUGAR "A wire rack prevents the hot pies from steaming as they cool and keeps the pastry crisp."

CLASSIC FRIED PIES

PREP: 50 MIN. FREEZE: 10 MIN.
CHILL: 2½ HR. COOK: 3 MIN./BATCH

1	cup (2 sticks) unsalted butter
¼	cup lard
3	cups unbleached all-purpose flour
2	tsp. kosher salt
1	tsp. sugar
8	to 12 Tbsp. ice water
1	recipe Sweet Potato-Fig Filling
	Peanut oil for deep-fat frying
	Sugar

1. Place butter and lard in the freezer for 10 minutes.

2. Place flour, salt, and the 1 teaspoon sugar on a large cutting board. Mix them with your fingers to blend. Place cold butter and lard on flour mixture. Use a pastry scraper or large kitchen knife to roughly cut butter and lard into the flour mixture. (Some butter and lard will be finely cut in, and some will be in ½- to ¾-inch pieces.)

3. Working quickly, gather the flour mixture in a mound. Use your fingers to shape a lengthwise trench through center. Sprinkle 1 tablespoon of the ice water along the length of the trench. With upturned fingers toss and fluff flour mixture and water together. Repeat to reshape, sprinkle ice water, and toss and fluff. After incorporating 8 tablespoons of ice water, dough should begin to clump. If necessary, repeat to add more water.

4. Gather rough dough with a pastry scraper. Working quickly, use the heel of your hand to smear (push away) egg-size pieces of dough, one at a time. Regather dough and repeat the process.

5. Gather dough in mound. Wrap in a double thickness of plastic wrap. Press with palms of hands to flatten. Refrigerate at least 2 hours and up to 24 hours.

6. On a lightly floured surface roll chilled dough to about ½-inch thickness. Brush excess flour from surface of dough. Fold dough in thirds, brushing flour off the underside of dough as it is folded over. Lightly press layers together with a rolling pin. Wrap dough in plastic. Refrigerate at least 30 minutes or up to 24 hours.

7. On a lightly floured surface roll out cold dough to an even ⅛-inch thickness. With a 3-inch round cutter, cut 24 circles, rerolling dough as needed. (If dough becomes warm, transfer to a baking sheet and refrigerate about 5 minutes.)

8. Spoon a generous teaspoonful of filling on the center of each circle. Use fingers dipped in water to lightly moisten dough edges. Fold in half, pinching edges to seal. Refrigerate sealed pies until ready to fry.

9. Fill a very deep 10-inch cast-iron skillet half full with oil. Heat over medium heat to 365°F. Fry pies, a few at a time, about 3 minutes, until golden brown, turning as needed to cook evenly. Drain on cooling racks. Cool slightly; roll in sugar. Serve warm or at room temperature.

MAKES 24 PIES.

SWEET POTATO-FIG FILLING Heat oven to 350°F. On foil-lined baking sheet bake two medium-size sweet potatoes for 1½ hours or until very soft. Meanwhile, remove stems and halve dried figs (to equal ¼ cup, packed). Place in small saucepan; barely cover with water. Bring to boiling. Reduce heat; simmer, covered, about 15 minutes, until softened. Cool slightly, drain, and finely chop. Stir in 1 tablespoon honey; set aside. Remove potatoes from oven and cool slightly. Peel potatoes. In a large bowl mash potato flesh until smooth. Mix in 1 tablespoon unsalted butter, 1½ teaspoons granulated sugar, 1½ teaspoons packed brown sugar, ¼ teaspoon kosher salt, and ⅛ teaspoon freshly grated nutmeg. Stir figs into sweet potato mixture. Cool completely before filling pies.

EACH PIE 187 cal, 12 g fat (6 g sat. fat), 24 mg chol, 190 mg sodium, 19 g carbo, 1 g fiber, 2 g pro. Daily Values: 44% vit. A, 1% vit. C, 1% calcium, 5% iron.

the ideal fried pie

... IS WONDERFULLY FLAKY with a not-too-sweet filling.

... IS DELICIOUS as a snack, with a cup of hot tea, or as dessert.

... IS A SATISFYING handheld, go-anywhere treat. Just add milk.

—CHEF SCOTT PEACOCK

october

Warm up with a soup, salad, and bread supper—and discover new ways with pumpkin that go beyond pie.

207

208

217

ROASTED PUMPKINS WITH
BACON AND BROWN SUGAR
Recipe on page 211

SWEET POTATO AND HOMINY STEW

Comfort Zone

A soup dinner, a warm gathering

FIRESIDE CHILI

The bit of bittersweet chocolate in this chili is optional, but try it—it keeps the heat of the chili seasoning in check and adds richness.

PREP: 40 MIN. COOK: 1 HR 15 MIN. STAND: 30 MIN.

1	recipe Chili Seasoning Puree, *right*
1½	lb. ground beef chuck
1	large onion, chopped
2	stalks celery, sliced
2	Tbsp. smoked paprika
2	tsp. ground coriander
1	tsp. crushed red pepper
¼	to ½ tsp. ground cloves
1	28-oz. can whole tomatoes, cut up
1½	cups water
1	14-oz. can beef broth
1	6-oz. can tomato paste
1	to 2 oz. bittersweet chocolate, chopped (optional)
1½	cups dried plums (prunes) or raisins, chopped
1	recipe Cumin Polenta (optional), *right*

1. Prepare Chili Seasoning Puree. In 6-quart Dutch oven cook beef, onion, and celery until meat is browned, stirring as needed. Drain fat.
2. Stir in Chili Puree, paprika, coriander, crushed red pepper, and cloves. Cook and stir 2 minutes. Stir in *undrained* tomatoes, water, beef broth, and tomato paste. Bring to boiling; reduce heat. Add chocolate and plums. Simmer, covered, 1 hour, stirring occasionally. Serve with Cumin Polenta. **MAKES 8 SERVINGS.**

EACH SERVING *343 cal, 14 g fat (5 g sat. fat), 58 mg chol, 702 mg sodium, 38 g carbo, 7 g fiber, 20 g pro. Daily Values: 55% vit. A, 26% vit. C, 7% calcium, 22% iron.*

LOW FAT
SWEET POTATO AND HOMINY STEW

Posole, a hearty Mexican soup made with pork and hominy, is the inspiration here.

PREP: 30 MIN. COOK: 25 MIN.

6	cloves garlic, minced
1	medium onion, chopped
1	Tbsp. olive oil
2	14-oz. cans reduced-sodium chicken broth
2	cups water
3	sweet potatoes, peeled and chopped (5 cups)
1	Tbsp. chili powder
1	tsp. dried oregano, crushed
1	tsp. ground cinnamon
1	tsp. ground cumin
2	14.5- to 15.5-oz. cans golden hominy, rinsed and drained
1	large red sweet pepper, coarsely chopped
1	18-oz. tub refrigerated barbecue sauce with shredded pork Cilantro Lime wedges
1	recipe Cumin Polenta (optional), *below*

1. In saucepan or Dutch oven cook garlic and onion in hot oil until tender. Stir in broth and water; add sweet potatoes, chili powder, oregano, cinnamon, and cumin. Bring to boiling; reduce heat. Simmer, covered, 20 minutes. Stir in hominy, red pepper, and shredded pork. Cook and stir 5 minutes or until heated through.
2. Serve with cilantro, lime wedges, and Cumin Polenta. **MAKES 8 SERVINGS.**

EACH SERVING *250 cal, 5 g fat (1 g sat. fat), 17 mg chol, 994 mg sodium, 41 g carbo, 5 g fiber, 11 g pro. Daily Values: 163% vit. A, 52% vit. C, 7% calcium, 12% iron.*

CHILI SEASONING PUREE

2	dried chile peppers
1	fresh jalapeño pepper, seeded and chopped (see note, *page 213*)
¾	cup beef broth
5	pitted dried plums

1. Place chile peppers in a bowl. Add boiling water to cover. Let stand 30 minutes. Drain; remove stems and seeds.
2. In food processor or blender combine drained chile peppers, jalapeño pepper, broth, and dried plums. Cover and process or blend until smooth.

LOW FAT
CUMIN POLENTA

This recipe is from Better Homes and Gardens® *contributor Betty Rosbottom and her book* Sunday Soup *(Chronicle; $19.95).*

2	14-oz. cans reduced-sodium chicken broth
2	tsp. ground cumin
1	cup yellow cornmeal
½	cup whole milk
1	Tbsp. butter

1. In large heavy saucepan combine broth and cumin; bring to boiling. Reduce heat; gradually whisk in cornmeal. Cook and stir until thick, about 6 to 8 minutes. Whisk in milk and butter. Season with *salt* and *pepper*. **MAKES 8 SERVINGS.**

EACH SERVING *86 cal, 3 g fat (1 g sat. fat), 5 mg chol, 331 mg sodium, 13 g carbo, 1 g fiber, 3 g pro. Daily Values: 2% vit. A, 2% calcium, 3% iron.*

LOW FAT

AUTUMN SANGRIA

PREP: 15 MIN. CHILL: 2 TO 24 HRS.

2	to 3 fresh figs and/or 1 cup dried figs
2	to 3 fresh plums, pitted, and/or 1 cup dried plums (prunes)
2	to 3 fresh apricots, pitted, and/or 1 cup dried apricots
¼	cup molasses
1	750-ml. bottle light red wine, such as Pinot Noir or Gamay
1	750-ml. bottle sparkling apple cider or club soda, chilled
1	orange, peeled, if desired, and sliced

1. Halve, quarter, or slice fruit. In 3-quart glass container combine fruits and molasses; stir until well combined. Slowly pour in red wine. Cover and chill 2 to 24 hours.
2. To serve, add sparkling cider and orange. Stir gently with spoon. Fill glasses with ice and ladle in sangria.
MAKES 8 SERVINGS.

EACH SERVING *167 cal, 0 g fat (0 g sat. fat), 0 mg chol, 14 mg sodium, 25 g carbo, 1 g fiber, 1 g pro. Daily Values: 3% vit. A, 49% vit. C, 3% calcium, 4% iron.*

ROASTED BEETS AND GREENS WITH SPICY ORANGE VINAIGRETTE

PREP: 25 MIN. ROAST: 40 MIN. OVEN: 400°F

1	tsp. finely shredded orange peel
¼	cup orange juice
3	Tbsp. red wine vinegar
4	cloves garlic, minced
1	green onion, finely chopped
1	tsp. ground cinnamon
½	tsp. sea salt or salt
¼	tsp. cayenne pepper or paprika
½	cup extra virgin olive oil
1½	lb. baby beets, trimmed and roasted*
1	head red leaf lettuce or leaf lettuce, torn (8 cups)

AUTUMN SANGRIA

3	to 4 small blood oranges and/or oranges, peeled and sliced
½	cup dried cranberries

1. For the Spicy Orange Vinaigrette, in bowl combine orange peel, orange juice, vinegar, garlic, green onion, cinnamon, salt, and cayenne pepper. Gradually whisk in olive oil.
2. In salad bowl combine beets, lettuce, and orange slices. Toss with some of the Spicy Orange Vinaigrette; pass remaining. Serve with dried cranberries.
MAKES 8 SERVINGS.
*****ROASTED BEETS** Preheat oven to 400°F. Scrub beets; cut in halves or wedges. Place in 3-quart rectangular baking dish. Drizzle beets with 3 tablespoons olive oil. Sprinkle with ¼ teaspoon each *salt* and *black pepper*. Toss lightly to coat. Cover dish with foil. Bake 40 to 45 minutes or until tender. Cool before assembling salad.

EACH SERVING *180 cal, 14 g fat (2 g sat. fat), 0 mg chol, 153 mg sodium, 14 g carbo, 3 g fiber, 2 g pro. Daily Values: 46% vit. A, 58% vit. C, 5% calcium, 6% iron.*

LOW FAT

BUTTERNUT SQUASH BISQUE

PREP: 40 MIN. COOK: 35 MIN.

1	2½- to 3-lb. butternut squash or three, 12-oz. pkgs. frozen winter squash, thawed
¼	cup butter
1	medium onion, chopped
1	large carrot, coarsely chopped
1	stalk celery, coarsely chopped
2	cloves garlic, minced
2	large Braeburn or Gala apples, peeled, cored, and chopped
1	48-oz. box reduced-sodium chicken broth
1	cup apple cider or apple juice
2	canned chipotle peppers in adobo sauce, coarsely chopped
½	cup sour cream
3	oz. smoked Gouda or smoked cheddar cheese, finely shredded Crumbled cooked bacon, celery leaves, and/or shaved Gouda cheese (optional)

1. Peel, seed, and cube butternut squash. In 6-quart Dutch oven melt butter over medium-high heat. Add fresh squash (if using frozen squash, add with apples), onion, carrot, celery, and garlic. Cook 10 minutes, stirring frequently, or until vegetables are tender. Add apples, broth, cider, and chipotle peppers. Bring to a boil; reduce heat. Cover; simmer 25 minutes or until vegetables and apples are tender. Remove from heat; cool slightly.

2. When slightly cooled, puree in pot using an immersion blender. (Or puree in batches in a blender; return soup to Dutch oven.) Blend in sour cream. Heat through. Remove from heat; stir in shredded Gouda until melted. Top with bacon, celery leaves, and/or Gouda cheese.
MAKES 8 SERVINGS.

EACH SERVING *213 cal, 11 g fat (7 g sat. fat), 30 mg chol, 655 mg sodium, 26 g carbo, 3 g fiber, 6 g pro. Daily Values: 272% vit. A, 41% vit. C, 15% calcium, 6% iron.*

SOUP STICKS

PREP: 25 MIN. CHILL: OVERNIGHT RISE: 1 HR.
BAKE: 20 MIN. OVEN: 375°F

1¼	cups warm water (105°F to 115°F)
1	package active dry yeast
3½	cups all-purpose flour
½	cup whole wheat flour
⅓	cup olive oil
1	egg
¼	cup packed brown sugar
2	tsp. chili powder (optional)
1	tsp. salt
½	tsp. ground cinnamon
1	recipe Spicy Honey Butter

1. In mixing bowl combine warm water and yeast. Stir to dissolve. Add 1 cup of the all-purpose flour, the whole wheat flour, olive oil, egg, sugar, chili powder, salt, and cinnamon. Beat with electric mixer on low 1 minute.
2. Stir in remaining flour to make soft dough that pulls away from sides of bowl (dough will be sticky). Coat 2-quart container with *nonstick cooking spray*. Place dough in container. Cover; refrigerate overnight.
3. When ready to use, punch dough down. Turn out onto floured sheet of parchment paper. Pat or roll dough into 15×12-inch rectangle. Transfer parchment with dough to large baking sheet.
4. Using floured pizza cutter or knife, cut dough widthwise into 20 strips about ¾ inch wide. (Dip cutter in flour as necessary to prevent sticking.) Cover; let rise 1 hour or until doubled in size. Brush with *olive oil*.
5. Preheat oven to 375°F. Bake 20 minutes or until golden. Slide soup sticks onto cutting board; cool slightly. Cut apart. Serve with Spicy Honey Butter.
MAKES 20 STICKS.

SPICY HONEY BUTTER Whisk ¼ cup honey and ¼ teaspoon crushed red pepper into ½ cup (1 stick) softened butter.

EACH STICK *169 cal, 8 g fat (8 g sat. fat), 19 mg chol, 129 mg sodium, 21 g carbo, 1 g fiber, 3 g pro. Daily Values: 3% vit. A, 1% calcium, 6% iron.*

BUTTERNUT SQUASH
BISQUE

ROASTED BEETS AND
GREENS WITH SPICY ORANGE
VINAIGRETTE

SOUP STICKS

NO-KNEAD FOCACCIA TILES

Top each tile with different ingredients or use just one topper for all.

PREP: 20 MIN. STAND: 12 HRS. RISE: 1 HR.
BAKE: 30 MIN. OVEN: 400°F

4	cups all-purpose flour
¼	tsp. active dry yeast
1½	tsp. salt
	Olive oil
	Toppings such as toasted pumpkin seeds, oil-packed dried tomatoes, pitted olives, thinly sliced limes, and/or thinly sliced plum tomatoes
	Seasonings such as smoked paprika, ground cumin, oregano, and sea salt

1. In large bowl combine 3 cups of the flour, the yeast, and salt. Add 1⅔ cups *warm water* (120°F to 130°F). Stir until all is moistened. The mixture will be a soft, sticky dough. Cover and let stand at room temperature 12 to 24 hours.

2. Line a 15×10×1-inch baking pan with parchment paper. Brush parchment with olive oil. With a fork, stir remaining 1 cup flour into the dough. Turn dough out into prepared pan. Using well-oiled hands or a rubber spatula, gently push dough into pan (dough will be sticky). Cover; let rise for 1 to 1½ hours or until puffy.

3. Preheat oven to 400°F. Using a sharp floured knife, score dough into 6 portions. Gently press desired toppings into surface of dough. Brush lightly with olive oil. Sprinkle with desired seasonings. Bake for 30 to 35 minutes or until golden brown.

4. Transfer to wire rack. Cut into 6 tiles. Serve warm. **MAKES 6 TILES (12 SERVINGS).**
EACH SERVING *212 cal, 6 g fat (1 g sat. fat), 0 mg chol, 429 mg sodium, 35 g carbo, 2 g fiber, 6 g pro. Daily Values: 2% vit. A, 13% vit. C, 2% calcium, 15% iron.*

how to make focaccia tiles

The key to developing the texture and flavor of this bread is allowing the yeast to do its work without interference. Let the dough stand for 12 to 24 hours at room temperature. The dough will be wet and sticky, so use well-oiled hands or an oiled spatula to push and spread the dough into the pan. Loosely cover and let rise as directed. After the dough has risen, score it with a sharp floured knife or pizza cutter to make six tiles. Gently press in the toppings and bake as directed.

GRAPE AND
PEAR PIE

3. In small bowl combine egg white with 1 tablespoon *water*. Brush top of pie with egg white mixture. Cover edge of pie with foil. Bake 35 minutes; remove foil. Bake 35 to 40 minutes more or until top of pastry is golden and steam is escaping from slits in top crust. Remove from oven. Cool 6 hours. Store, loosely covered, in refrigerator up to 24 hours.
MAKES 8 SERVINGS.

PASTRY FOR DOUBLE-CRUST PIE In medium bowl stir together 2 ¼ cups all-purpose flour and ¾ teaspoon salt. Using pastry blender, cut in ⅔ cup shortening until pieces are pea size. Sprinkle 1 tablespoon cold water over part of flour mixture; gently toss with fork. Push moistened dough to side of bowl. Repeat, using 1 tablespoon water at a time, until all the flour mixture is moistened (8 to 10 tablespoons total). Divide dough in half. Form each half into ball.
EACH SERVING *411 cal, 20 g fat (6 g sat. fat), 8 mg chol, 250 mg sodium, 54 g carbo, 3 g fiber, 5 g pro. Daily Values: 3% vit. A, 7% vit. C, 3% calcium, 12% iron.*

RAISIN-PLUM PIE

Sweet, chewy raisins plump as they bake and balance the tangy-tart flavors of cranberries and plums.

PREP: 40 MIN. BAKE: 50 MIN. OVEN: 375°F

1	recipe Whole Wheat Pastry for Double-Crust Pie
¾	cup packed brown sugar
2	Tbsp. all-purpose flour
5	to 6 ripe plums (about 1 lb.), pitted and cut in bite-size pieces (2 cups)
½	cup raisins
½	cup currants
½	cup fresh cranberries
2	Tbsp. butter, cut up
	Milk
	Granulated sugar

1. Preheat oven to 375°F. Prepare pastry. On lightly floured surface, slightly flatten 1 ball of pastry. Roll from center to edges into circle about 12 inches in diameter. Wrap pastry around rolling pin; unroll in 9-inch pie plate. Ease into pie plate without stretching. Trim pastry to ½ inch beyond edge of pie plate.
2. For filling, in large bowl combine brown sugar and flour. Add plums, raisins, currants, and cranberries; toss to coat. Transfer to pastry-lined pie plate. Dot filling with butter.

GRAPE AND PEAR PIE

To crimp the bottom and top crust together as in the photo, pinch together with your thumb and forefinger and gently twist.

PREP: 30 MIN. BAKE: 1 HR. 10 MIN. COOL: 6 HRS. OVEN: 375°F

1	recipe Pastry for Double-Crust Pie or 2 rolled refrigerated unbaked piecrusts
¼	cup packed brown sugar
⅓	cup all-purpose flour
2	Tbsp. butter, melted
1	tsp. finely shredded orange peel
5	cups whole seedless red or black grapes
2	medium red pears, cored and sliced (2 cups)
1	egg white

1. Preheat oven to 375°F. Prepare Pastry for Double-Crust Pie. For filling, in large bowl stir together brown sugar, flour, melted butter, and orange peel. Add grapes and pears; toss.
2. On lightly floured surface, slightly flatten 1 ball of pastry. Roll dough from center to edges into 12-inch circle. Wrap pastry around rolling pin; unroll in 9-inch pie plate. Ease pastry into pie plate, being careful not to stretch. Trim even with rim of pie plate. Pour filling into pastry. Roll remaining dough into a circle about 12 inches in diameter. Cut slits in pastry to allow steam to escape. Place pastry on filling; trim to ½ inch beyond edge of pie plate. Fold top pastry edge under bottom pastry. Crimp edge as desired. Place on baking sheet.

3. Roll out remaining pastry into 10- to 12-inch circle. Cut into ½-inch-wide strips. Weave strips over filling in lattice pattern. Press strips into bottom pastry. Fold bottom pastry over strip ends; seal and crimp edge.

4. Brush top with milk and sprinkle with granulated sugar. To prevent overbrowning, cover edge of pie with foil. Bake 25 minutes. Remove foil. Bake pie 25 to 30 minutes more or until filling is bubbly and pastry is golden. Cool on wire rack.

MAKES 8 SERVINGS.

WHOLE WHEAT PASTRY FOR DOUBLE-CRUST PIE
In large bowl stir together 1½ cups all-purpose flour, 1 cup whole wheat flour, and ½ teaspoon salt. Using a pastry blender cut in ⅔ cup shortening until pieces are pea size. Sprinkle 1 tablespoon cold water over part of flour mixture; gently toss with fork. Push moistened pastry to side of bowl. Repeat moistening flour mixture, using 1 tablespoon of water at a time (7 to 9 tablespoons total), until all the flour mixture is moistened. Divide dough in half. Form each half into ball.

EACH SERVING *479 cal, 20 g fat (6 g sat. fat), 8 mg chol, 175 mg sodium, 72 g carbo, 5 g fiber, 6 g pro. Daily Values: 6% vit. A, 12% vit. C, 4% calcium, 14% iron.*

GRAPE AND PEAR PIE

RAISIN-PLUM PIE

What's Cooking

Pumpkin beyond pie

CREAMY PUMPKIN
RICE PUDDING

CREAMY PUMPKIN RICE PUDDING

Baking means less hands-on time for this creamy pudding. Make up to 24 hours ahead and prepare the topper just before serving.

PREP: 25 MIN. BAKE: 1 HR. 5 MIN. COOK: 15 MIN. STAND: 15 MIN. OVEN: 325°F

⅔	cup water
⅓	cup uncooked long grain rice
3	eggs, lightly beaten
1	cup milk
⅔	cup Pumpkin Puree, *page 212*, or canned pumpkin
⅓	cup packed brown sugar
1	tsp. pumpkin pie spice
1	tsp. vanilla
¼	tsp. salt
¾	cup dried cranberries or raisins
1	medium red apple and/or green pear, cored and thinly sliced (1 cup)
½	cup coarsely chopped walnuts, toasted
2	Tbsp. honey

1. Preheat oven to 325°F. In small saucepan combine water and rice. Bring to boiling; reduce heat. Simmer, covered, 15 minutes or until liquid is absorbed, stirring once.
2. In medium bowl combine eggs, milk, Pumpkin Puree, brown sugar, pumpkin pie spice, vanilla, and salt. Stir in rice and ½ cup of the cranberries. Pour mixture into 1½-quart straight-sided deep baking dish. Place dish in baking pan on oven rack. Pour boiling water into baking pan until water comes halfway up sides of baking dish.
3. Bake 30 minutes; stir. Bake 35 minutes more or until outside edge appears set. Remove dish from oven. Cool slightly on wire rack.
4. Meanwhile, in bowl combine remaining ¼ cup cranberries and boiling water to cover. Let stand 15 minutes; drain. Just before serving, toss together apple, walnuts, honey, and cranberries. Spoon over pudding. Serve warm.
5. To store, cover and refrigerate up to 24 hours. **MAKES 6 SERVINGS.**

EACH SERVING *295 cal, 10 g fat (2 g sat. fat), 109 mg chol, 156 mg sodium, 47 g carbo, 3 g fiber, 7 g pro. Daily Values: 89% vit. A, 4% vit. C, 10% calcium, 10% iron.*

ROASTED PUMPKINS WITH BACON AND BROWN SUGAR

ROASTED PUMPKINS WITH BACON AND BROWN SUGAR

Pie pumpkins are small sweet pumpkins grown for eating. Look for even coloring and no soft spots.

PREP: 15 MIN. ROAST: 20 MIN. OVEN: 400°F

2	2- to 4-lb. pie pumpkins slices bacon, crisp-cooked and drained, drippings reserved
1	tsp. salt
¼	tsp. coarsely ground black pepper
¼	cup packed brown sugar
2	tsp. fennel seeds, crushed
2	to 3 green onions, diagonally sliced

1. Preheat oven to 400°F. Cut off top one-fourth of pumpkins. Remove seeds and strings; reserve ⅔ cup pumpkin seeds.

2. Place pumpkins, cut sides up, in foil-lined baking pan. Brush insides with some of the bacon drippings and sprinkle with salt, pepper, and brown sugar. Replace lids. Roast pumpkins in oven 20 minutes.
3. Meanwhile, in ovenproof skillet stir together pumpkin seeds, fennel seeds, green onions, and remaining bacon drippings. Add skillet to oven during last 10 minutes of roasting.
4. Remove pumpkins and seed mixture from oven. Sprinkle insides of pumpkins with seed mixture and crumbled bacon. To serve, use a large spoon to scoop out insides or use knife to cut into wedges.
MAKES 8 TO 10 SERVINGS.

EACH SERVING *180 cal, 11 g fat (3 g sat. fat), 8 mg chol, 438 mg sodium, 19 g carbo, 1 g fiber, 7 g pro. Daily Values: 235% vit. A, 26% vit. C, 5% calcium, 15% iron.*

SPICED PUMPKIN
BUTTER

SPICED PUMPKIN BUTTER

PREP: 15 MIN. COOK: 25 MIN.

4	cups Pumpkin Puree, *below,* or two 15-oz. cans pumpkin
1¼	cups pure maple syrup
½	cup apple juice
2	Tbsp. lemon juice
2	tsp. ground ginger
½	tsp. ground cinnamon
½	tsp. ground nutmeg
¼	tsp. salt
	Chopped hazelnuts (optional)

1. In 5-quart Dutch oven combine all ingredients except nuts. Bring to boiling; reduce heat. Cook, uncovered, over medium heat, stirring frequently, 25 minutes or until thick. (If mixture spatters, reduce heat to medium-low.) Remove from heat; cool.

2. Ladle into jars or freezer containers, leaving a ½-inch headspace. Cover; store in refrigerator up to 1 week or freezer up to 6 months.

3. To serve, top with chopped nuts. **MAKES 4½ CUPS (36 TWO-TABLESPOON SERVINGS).**
EACH SERVING *35 cal, 0 g fat, 0 mg chol, 17 mg sodium, 9 g carbo, 0 g fiber, 0 g pro. Daily Values: 19% vit. A, 3% vit. C, 1% calcium, 1% iron.*

PUMPKIN PUREE

Use this puree when canned pumpkin is called for. It can be frozen and stored up to six months, allowing you to enjoy pumpkin no matter the time of year.

PREP: 15 MIN. BAKE: 1 HR. OVEN: 375°F

2	3½-lb. pie pumpkins

1. Preheat oven to 375°F. Cut pumpkins in 5×5-inch pieces. Remove seeds and strings. Arrange pieces in single layer, skin sides up, in foil-lined baking pan.

2. Bake, covered, 1 hour or until tender. When cool enough to handle, scoop pulp from rind. Place pulp in blender or food processor.

3. Cover and blend or process until smooth. Transfer to freezer bags. Store in refrigerator up to 3 days or freeze up to 6 months. Thaw in refrigerator to use.
MAKES 5 CUPS PUREE.
EACH ½-CUP SERVING *58 cal, 0 g fat (0 g sat. fat), 0 mg chol, 2 mg sodium, 14 g carbo, 1 g fiber, 2 g pro. Daily Values: 328% vit. A, 33% vit. C, 5% calcium, 10% iron.*

TEST KITCHEN TIP

Butter Up Pumpkin butter is one of fall's great all-purpose spreads. Spice up breakfast by using it on pancakes and muffins. For a quick appetizer, spread pumpkin butter on toasted bread with slices of your favorite cheese. Experiment with different flavors: Add a dash of cayenne pepper or a drizzle of honey.

PUMPKIN BLACK BEAN BAKE

This family-friendly dish puts a seasonal spin on an American classic, tamale pie.

PREP: 30 MIN. BAKE: 20 MIN. OVEN: 400°F

1	lb. ground beef
2	cups ½-inch pieces peeled pie pumpkin or winter squash
1	medium onion, coarsely chopped
1	15-oz. can black beans, rinsed and drained
1	cup frozen whole kernel corn
1	4-oz. can diced green chiles
½	tsp. salt
½	cup lower-sodium beef broth
1	3-oz. pkg. cream cheese, softened
1	8½-oz. pkg. corn muffin mix
1	egg, lightly beaten
⅓	cup milk
⅓	cup Pumpkin Puree, *page 212,* or canned pumpkin
	Jalapeño-Olive Relish (optional)

1. Preheat oven to 400°F. In large skillet cook ground beef, pumpkin, and onion over medium heat until meat is browned and onion tender, breaking up ground beef with spoon; drain fat. Stir in black beans, corn, chiles, and salt. Heat through. Stir in broth and cream cheese until blended. Transfer mixture to 2½-quart baking dish.

2. In medium bowl stir together corn muffin mix, egg, milk, and Pumpkin Puree until just combined. Spoon over beef mixture.

3. Bake 20 minutes or until toothpick inserted into topper comes out clean.

Serve with Jalapeño-Olive Relish.

MAKES 6 SERVINGS.

JALAPEÑO-OLIVE RELISH In small bowl combine ¼ cup halved pitted green olives; 1 to 2 jalapeño peppers,* sliced; 6 cherry tomatoes, quartered; and 1 to 2 tablespoons snipped fresh cilantro.

EACH SERVING *524 cal, 26 g fat (10 g sat. fat), 106 mg chol, 924 mg sodium, 51 g carbo, 7 g fiber, 25 g pro. Daily Values: 102% vit. A, 22% vit. C, 13% calcium, 23% iron.*

*NOTE Hot chile peppers contain oils that can burn skin and eyes. When working with them, wear plastic or rubber gloves.

what's in a can?

MOST SUPERMARKETS OFFER canned pumpkin and pumpkin pie filling. What's the difference? Pumpkin pie filling is canned pumpkin with added spices such as cinnamon, ginger, nutmeg, and allspice. Doublecheck pumpkin recipes to determine what type is called for.

Everyday Easy
Quick-to-the-table meals

FAST
GREEN CHILE AND CHICKEN ENCHILADAS

START TO FINISH: 28 MIN.
BUDGET $3.54 PER SERVING

1¼	lb. chicken breast tenders
1½	cups bottled green salsa
1	4-oz. can diced green chiles
1½	cups shredded Mexican-style four-cheese blend (6 oz.)
8	6- to 7-inch flour tortillas
	Refrigerated fresh salsa (optional)
	Lime wedges (optional)

1. Preheat broiler. Cut chicken into 1-inch pieces; place in a large microwave-safe bowl. Heat in microwave on 100% power (high) 7 minutes or until no pink remains, stirring twice. Drain liquid. Break up chicken slightly in bowl with back of wooden spoon. Add salsa and chiles. Cook 3 minutes more or until heated through, stirring once. Stir in 1 cup of the cheese.

2. Spoon chicken mixture evenly down centers of tortillas. Roll tortillas around filling and place in 13×9×2-inch baking pan. Sprinkle remaining cheese over enchiladas. Broil 3 to 4 inches from heat 1 to 2 minutes or until cheese is melted.
3. To serve, top with salsa and pass lime wedges. **MAKES 4 SERVINGS.**

EACH SERVING *569 cal, 24 g fat (8 g sat. fat), 120 mg chol, 1,081 mg sodium, 33 g carbo, 1 g fiber, 49 g pro. Daily Values: 11% vit. A, 33% vit. C, 45% calcium, 43% iron.*

FAST
CORNMEAL-CRUSTED CATFISH ROLLS

START TO FINISH: 28 MIN.
BUDGET $3.03 PER SERVING

1½	lb. catfish fillets
¼	cup cornmeal
2	tsp. Cajun or blackening seasoning
¼	cup vegetable oil
2	baby sweet peppers or ¼ a large sweet pepper
1	stalk celery
¼	a small red or sweet onion (optional)
⅓	cup mayonnaise
1	Tbsp. ketchup
¼	to ½ tsp. bottled hot pepper sauce (optional)
8	cocktail-size rolls, split and toasted

1. Rinse fish; pat dry. Cut in 8 pieces. In shallow dish combine cornmeal and 1½ teaspoons of Cajun seasoning; coat fish with cornmeal mixture.
2. In 12-inch skillet cook fish in hot oil over medium-high heat for 8 to 10 minutes or until browned and fish flakes when tested with fork.
3. Meanwhile, thinly slice peppers, celery, and onion and combine in medium bowl. In small bowl combine mayonnaise, ketchup, remaining ½ teaspoon Cajun seasoning, and hot pepper sauce. Add 1 tablespoon mayonnaise mixture to pepper-celery mixture. Spread some of remaining mayonnaise mixture on cut sides of rolls. Place catfish pieces on roll bottoms. Top with celery mixture and roll tops. Pass any remaining mayonnaise mixture. **MAKES 4 SERVINGS.**

EACH SERVING *636 cal, 38 g fat (7 g sat. fat), 88 mg chol, 638 mg sodium, 38 g carbo, 2 g fiber, 34 g pro. Daily Values: 8% vit. A, 20% vit. C, 13% calcium, 20% iron.*

GREEN CHILE AND CHICKEN ENCHILADAS

CORNMEAL-CRUSTED
CATFISH ROLLS

APPLE-GLAZED
PORK LOAF

"BEET" THE CLOCK STACK-UP

FAST
APPLE-GLAZED PORK LOAF
START TO FINISH: 28 MIN.
BUDGET $1.76 PER SERVING

½ cup apple jelly
1 Tbsp. Dijon-style mustard
2 small apples
2 eggs, lightly beaten
1 lb. ground pork
1 medium sweet potato, chopped
1 Tbsp. olive oil
⅛ tsp. cayenne pepper (optional)
2 ciabatta sandwich rolls, split and toasted

1. Heat oven to 425°F. For glaze, heat jelly in microwave on 100% power (high) 30 seconds. Stir in mustard. Set aside. Core and chop 1 apple.
2. Combine half of eggs, pork, half of chopped apple, and ½ teaspoon each *salt* and *pepper*. Form into 4 loaves (6×2) inches; place on greased 15×10×1-inch pan. Spoon some jelly glaze over loaves. Bake 10 minutes. Thinly slice remaining apple. Top loaves with apple slices; drizzle jelly glaze. Bake 5 minutes more or until internal temperature is 160°F.
3. Place chopped sweet potato in a microwave-safe bowl. Heat in microwave on 100% power (high) 4 minutes or until nearly tender. In skillet cook potato and remaining chopped apple in oil over medium-high. Sprinkle *salt, pepper,* and cayenne pepper. Cook 3 minutes or until tender. Serve pork loaves on ciabatta halves with sweet potatoes.
MAKES 4 SERVINGS.
EACH SERVING *697 cal, 32 g fat (11 g sat. fat), 187 mg chol, 842 mg sodium, 74 g carbo, 5 g fiber, 28 g pro. Daily Values: 96% vit. A, 9% vit. C, 9% calcium, 20% iron.*

BEER AND CHEESE SOUP

FAST
BEER AND CHEESE SOUP
START TO FINISH: 25 MIN.
BUDGET $3.62 PER SERVING

1 bunch green onions
3 Tbsp. olive oil
¾ cup bottled roasted red sweet peppers, drained
¾ cup pale lager or nonalcoholic beer
2 cups refrigerated shredded hash brown potatoes
2 cups milk
8 oz. American cheese, shredded
¼ tsp. paprika plus additional for sprinkling

1. Slice green onions, set aside green parts. In Dutch oven over medium heat cook white portion of green onions in 1 tablespoon hot oil until tender.
2. In blender combine red peppers, cooked onion, beer, and 1 cup potatoes; process until smooth. Transfer to Dutch oven. Bring to boiling. Reduce heat. Simmer, uncovered, 5 minutes.
3. Add milk and cheese to Dutch oven. Cook and stir over medium heat until cheese is melted and soup is hot (do not boil).
4. In skillet cook remaining potatoes in remaining hot oil over medium-high heat 8 minutes or until golden, stirring occasionally. Drain on paper towels; sprinkle with paprika. Top soup with potatoes, onion tops, and paprika.
MAKES 4 SERVINGS.

EACH SERVING *467 cal, 30 g fat (14 g sat. fat), 63 mg chol, 1,096 mg sodium, 28 g carbo, 2 g fiber, 19 g pro. Daily Values: 21% vit. A, 143% vit. C, 47% calcium, 5% iron.*

FAST
"BEET" THE CLOCK STACK-UP
START TO FINISH: 21 MIN.
BUDGET $3.60 PER SERVING

1 15-oz. can sliced beets, drained, or two 8-oz. pkgs. refrigerated cooked beets, sliced
1 14-oz. pkg. beef and pork sausage, low fat and low sodium
1 20-oz. pkg. refrigerated sliced potatoes
1 8-oz. pkg. shredded Colby and Monterey Jack cheese or cheddar cheese (2 cups)
⅓ cup sour cream
Freshly ground black pepper
Fresh Italian (flat-leaf) parsley (optional)

1. In greased microwave-safe 2-quart square baking dish layer half of beets, sausage, potato slices, and cheese; repeat layers. Cover with parchment paper. Heat in microwave on 100% power (high) 15 minutes or until potatoes are tender, turning the dish halfway every 5 minutes.
2. Cut stack-up into squares and top with sour cream, pepper, and parsley.
MAKES 4 SERVINGS.
EACH SERVING *594 cal, 30 g fat (15 g sat. fat), 82 mg chol, 1,268 mg sodium, 51 g carbo, 3 g fiber, 29 g pro. Daily Values: 13% vit. A, 22% vit. C, 42% calcium, 14% iron.*

Good and Healthy

Winter Greens

Winter greens are the hearty high-nutrition cousins of lettuce. They include familiar greens such as spinach as well as kale, chard, collard greens, and mustard greens.

Because greens are a little sturdier than lettuces, they keep their texture and shape when cooked, opening up many preparation options. These recipes include sautéing, boiling, wilting, and steaming.

FAST | LOW FAT

MINESTRONE

Swiss chard provides a bone-building mix of magnesium, manganese, and potassium.

START TO FINISH: 30 MIN.

1	medium onion, chopped
1	Tbsp. olive oil
2	14-oz. cans reduced-sodium chicken broth
1½	cups water
1	15-oz. can cannellini beans, rinsed and drained
1	medium zucchini, coarsely chopped
1	cup sliced carrots
3	cloves garlic, minced
¾	cup dried multigrain elbow macaroni
1	Tbsp. snipped fresh oregano or 1 tsp. dried oregano, crushed
6	cups coarsely torn, trimmed Swiss chard or 8 cups packaged fresh baby spinach leaves
1	14½-oz. can no-salt-added diced tomatoes

1. In 5- to 6-quart Dutch oven cook onion in hot oil over medium heat until tender, stirring occasionally. Add broth, water, beans, zucchini, carrots, and garlic. Bring to boiling. Add pasta and dried oregano, if using. Return to boiling; reduce heat.

Simmer, covered, 5 minutes. Stir in Swiss chard. (If using spinach, stir in with the tomatoes.) Simmer, uncovered, 5 to 7 minutes more or until pasta is tender, stirring occasionally.

2. Stir in tomatoes and fresh oregano, if using. Remove from heat. Season with *salt* and *black pepper*. Sprinkle with additional fresh oregano. **MAKES 6 (1½-CUP) SERVINGS.**

EACH SERVING *162 cal, 3 g fat (0 g sat. fat), 0 mg chol, 554 mg sodium, 30 g carbo, 7 g fiber, 10 g pro. Daily Values: 119% vit. A, 41% vit. C, 7% calcium, 13% iron.*

FAST | LOW FAT

KALE-GOAT CHEESE FRITTATA

Kale makes this dish a vitamin A powerhouse.

START TO FINISH: 25 MIN.

2	cups coarsely torn fresh kale
1	medium onion, halved and thinly sliced
2	tsp. olive oil
6	eggs
4	egg whites
¼	tsp. salt
⅛	tsp. ground black pepper
¼	cup drained oil-packed dried tomatoes, thinly sliced
1	oz. goat cheese, crumbled

1. Preheat broiler. In 10-inch ovenproof nonstick skillet cook and stir kale and onion in oil over medium heat for 10 minutes or until onion is tender.

2. Meanwhile, in medium bowl whisk together eggs, egg whites, salt, and pepper. Pour over kale mixture in skillet. Cook over medium-low heat. As egg mixture sets, run a spatula around the edge of the skillet, lifting egg mixture so the uncooked portion flows underneath. Continue cooking and lifting edge until egg mixture is almost set but still glossy and moist.

3. Sprinkle egg mixture with dried tomatoes and goat cheese. Broil 4 to 5 inches from the heat for 1 to 2 minutes or until eggs are set. Cut into wedges to serve. **MAKES 6 SERVINGS.**

EACH SERVING *145 cal, 9 g fat (3 g sat. fat), 216 mg chol, 242 mg sodium, 6 g carbo, 1 g fiber, 11 g pro. Daily Values: 76% vit. A, 55% vit. C, 11% calcium, 9% iron.*

MINESTRONE

KALE-GOAT CHEESE
FRITTATA

CREAMY
COLLARD DIP

CREAMY COLLARD DIP

Collards are a good source of vitamin A. One of its functions is helping the eyes adjust to light and dark.

PREP: 25 MIN. **COOK:** 15 MIN. **BAKE:** 10 MIN.
OVEN: 350°F

2	slices bacon
1	small sweet onion, chopped (about 1 cup)
1	medium red sweet pepper, seeded and chopped (¾ cup)
1	lb. fresh collard greens, trimmed and coarsely chopped (6 cups)
3	cloves garlic, minced
1	8-oz. pkg. reduced-fat cream cheese (Neufchâtel), cubed and softened
2	oz. reduced-fat Monterey Jack cheese, shredded (½ cup)
½	cup light sour cream
½	tsp. Cajun seasoning (optional)* Thin breadsticks or vegetable dippers, such as sweet pepper strips

1. Preheat oven to 350°F. In a 12-inch skillet cook bacon until crisp. Drain bacon on paper towel. Remove and discard all but 2 teaspoons of bacon drippings from skillet. Add onion and sweet pepper to skillet. Cook 5 minutes over medium heat or until vegetables are just tender, stirring occasionally. Add collard greens and garlic; cover and cook 10 minutes or until tender, stirring occasionally. Remove from heat.

2. Add cream cheese, Monterey Jack cheese, sour cream, and Cajun seasoning to the collard mixture, stirring until combined. If desired, trim fatty part from bacon and discard. Crumble remaining bacon and add to collard mixture. Spread mixture in a 1½-quart casserole dish or 9-inch pie plate.

3. Bake, uncovered, 10 minutes or until warmed through. Serve with vegetable dippers or breadsticks. **MAKES** 3⅓ **CUPS (12 TO 14 ¼-CUP) SERVINGS).**

*****NOTE:** If you do not use the Cajun seasoning, add ¼ teaspoon salt to dip.

EACH SERVING *104 cal, 8 g fat (4 g sat. fat), 23 mg chol, 208 mg sodium, 5 g carbo, 1 g fiber, 5 g pro. Daily Values: 41% vit. A, 36% vit. C, 10% calcium, 1% iron.*

FAST | **LOW FAT**

SHRIMP ON GREENS WITH GARLIC VINAIGRETTE

Chicory, a curly salad green, is high in lutein and zeaxanthin—which keep eyes healthy.

START TO FINISH: 20 MIN.

1½	lbs. fresh or frozen large shrimp Salt and freshly ground black pepper
2	Tbsp. olive oil
2	cloves garlic, minced
2	Tbsp. white wine or reduced-sodium chicken broth
2	Tbsp. white wine vinegar
2	tsp. snipped fresh thyme or ½ tsp. dried thyme, crushed
1½	cups fresh chicory leaves, trimmed and coarsely torn
1½	cups packed fresh baby spinach leaves
1	head Belgian endive, trimmed and thinly sliced crosswise
1	oz. Parmesan cheese, shaved

1. Thaw shrimp, if frozen. Peel and devein shrimp, leaving tails intact, if desired. Rinse shrimp; pat dry with paper towels. Sprinkle lightly with salt and pepper.

2. In small saucepan heat oil and garlic over low heat for 5 minutes to infuse oil with the garlic flavor. Whisk in wine, vinegar, and thyme. Keep warm over very low heat.

3. Meanwhile, heat a grill pan over medium-high heat. Add shrimp; cook for 3 to 5 minutes or until opaque, turning once halfway through cooking.

4. In a large bowl combine chicory, spinach, and endive. Add warm garlic mixture; toss gently to coat. Divide among 4 serving plates. Top with grilled shrimp and Parmesan cheese. **MAKES 4 SERVINGS.**

EACH SERVING *288 cal, 12 g fat (3 g sat. fat), 264 mg chol, 588 mg sodium, 4 g carbo, 1 g fiber, 38 g pro. Daily Values: 41% vit. A, 19% vit. C, 21% calcium, 27% iron.*

SHRIMP ON GREENS WITH GARLIC VINAIGRETTE

American Classics
from Chef Scott Peacock
Classic BBQ Chicken

CLASSIC BBQ CHICKEN
PREP: 1 HR. BAKE: 1 HR. 20 MIN.
OVEN: 325°F/450°F

2	3½-lb. whole chickens
	Kosher salt and freshly ground pepper
½	cup butter
1	cup finely chopped onion
1	Tbsp. chopped fresh garlic
2	Tbsp. kosher salt
1½	tsp. crushed red pepper
1	Tbsp. paprika
1	Tbsp. chili powder
½	tsp. freshly ground black pepper
2	cups cold water
1¼	cups cider vinegar
1	cup packed dark brown sugar
2	Tbsp. Worcestershire sauce
¼	cup molasses
1	cup tomato paste
	Peanut oil
	Water

1. Cut up chicken, leaving drumsticks and thighs attached. Season chicken with salt and black pepper. Refrigerate, covered, until ready to use (up to 24 hours).

2. For sauce, in large nonreactive saucepan melt butter. Add onion, garlic, and salt. Cook over low heat until onion is tender. Add crushed red pepper, paprika, chili powder, and black pepper; cook and stir for 1 minute.

3. Add water, vinegar, brown sugar, and Worcestershire sauce; bring to a simmer. Stir in molasses. Whisk in tomato paste until smooth. Bring to a simmer over low heat. Cook, uncovered, for 10 to 15 minutes or until sauce is thickened, stirring occasionally. Taste for seasoning, adding additional salt if needed. Remove 1½ cups of the sauce to prepare chicken. Store remaining sauce in the refrigerator; reheat to serve.

4. For chicken, heat ¼-inch peanut oil in a 12-inch skillet over medium heat. Working in batches, place chicken, skin sides down, in skillet. Cook until well browned, turning once, about 5 minutes.

5. Transfer browned chicken to two 2- to 3-quart rectangular glass or nonreactive baking dishes. Place skin sides up, adding breast portions to one dish and leg portions to the other. Add 2 tablespoons water to each baking dish.

6. Spoon reserved 1½ cups barbecue sauce over chicken.* Cover chicken with parchment paper and then cover tightly with foil. Preheat oven to 325°F. Bake leg portions for 70 to 75 minutes and breast portions for 30 to 40 minutes (170°F).

7. Increase oven temperature to 450°F. Uncover chicken and spoon on additional sauce. Bake, uncovered, for 10 to 15 minutes or until well glazed and meat is very tender. Serve with remaining barbecue sauce. Refrigerate any remaining barbecue sauce, covered, up to 1 week.

MAKES 12 SERVINGS.

*** FOOD SAFETY:** Be sure the sauce used on the uncooked chicken is kept separate from sauce for serving.

EACH SERVING (WITH ¼ CUP SAUCE) *626 cal, 40 g fat (14 g sat. fat), 158 mg chol, 1,381 mg sodium, 31 g carbo, 2 g fiber, 34 g pro. Daily Values: 25% vit. A, 12% vit. C, 7% calcium, 18% iron.*

COOK OVER LOW HEAT
"Gently sauté the onion and garlic, taking care not to let them brown."

ADD MOLASSES
"Much of the sauce's character comes from molasses, which gives a subtle yet distinctive flavor."

SIMMER SLOWLY
"Lightly simmer until the sauce bubbles thickly across the top and the texture becomes rich and coats the spoon."

"Begin building depth by stirring the spices into the onions and lightly cooking. This step is key to developing their aroma and flavor."

WHISK IN TOMATO PASTE
"Instead of chasing the tomato paste round and round in the pot with a spoon, scoop it up from the measuring cup with a whisk and blend it in."

SEAR FIRST
"Taking the time to brown the chicken well greatly contributes to the taste of the final dish. You're not cooking it through, just getting a nicely golden browned crust."

THE RIGHT-SIZE COOKWARE
"Create tight quarters by using baking dishes with just enough space for the chicken pieces so the chicken can cook in its own juices."

DOUBLE COVER
"The acidity in the sauce can react with foil, so place a layer of parchment paper over the chicken before covering with foil. A tight seal keeps the sauce from burning and creates an almost no-liquid braise."

"Brush generously with a final coat of sauce and finish in a hot oven for a blue ribbon-worthy glaze."

november

Fresh inspiration for Thanksgiving from a winery's executive chef, plus sweet ideas for holiday desserts.

232

237

240

MINI HOLIDAY PIES
Recipes on page 243

Thanks for Thanksgiving

Succulent turkey and all the trimmings from Justin Wangler, executive chef at Kendall-Jackson winery.

1. In Dutch oven melt 1 tablespoon of the butter over medium heat. Add shallots. Cook 1 minute. Add fresh cranberries; cook for 1 minute more. Add 2 cups chicken stock, the rice, and 1 teaspoon *kosher salt*. Bring to boiling; reduce heat. Simmer, covered, for 45 minutes. Drain.

2. Heat oven to 350°F. Return Dutch oven to medium heat. Add remaining butter, squash, and thyme. Cook and stir 2 minutes. Add onion and celery. Cook and stir 3 minutes more. Sprinkle *salt* and *pepper;* set aside.

3. In bowl whisk together cream, eggs, and 1½ cups stock. Stir in cooked rice, squash, dried cranberries, sage, and bread cubes. Transfer to shallow 3-quart casserole dish. Bake, covered, for 20 minutes. Uncover; bake for 30 minutes more or until golden.

MAKES 8 (½-CUP) SERVINGS + LEFTOVERS.

> **MAKE AHEAD** Prepare up to 2 days in advance; cover and refrigerate. Reheat, covered, in a 350°F oven, for 50 minutes.

EACH SERVING *149 cal, 5 g fat (2 g sat. fat), 79 mg chol, 426 mg sodium, 21 g carbo, 2 g fiber, 6 g pro. Daily Values: 55% vit. A, 11% vit. C, 5% calcium, 11% iron.*

LOW FAT

SPICED CRANBERRY SAUCE

"Pinot Noir verjus adds another layer of flavor to traditional cranberry sauce. And the next day, it's wonderful to serve any leftover sauce with sandwiches or pancakes," says Justin.

PREP: 25 MIN. COOK: 10 MIN. COOL: 2 HRS.

1	cup Pinot Noir verjus or ¾ cup grape juice + ¼ cup red wine vinegar
1	cup sugar
1	bay leaf
1	3- to 4-inch stick cinnamon
1	tsp. kosher salt
4	cups cranberries

1. In medium saucepan combine verjus, sugar, bay leaf, cinnamon, and kosher salt; bring to boiling. Add cranberries; return to boiling. Reduce heat; simmer, uncovered, 10 minutes, stirring frequently. Remove from heat; transfer to bowl. Cool to room temperature (about 2 hours). Remove and discard bay leaf and cinnamon stick.

MAKES 8 (¼-CUP) SERVINGS + LEFTOVERS.

EACH SERVING *99 cal, 0 g fat), 0 mg chol, 162 mg sodium, 22 g carbo, 2 g fiber, 0 g pro. Daily Values: 8% vit. C, 1% calcium, 1% iron.*

> **MAKE AHEAD** Prepare sauce. Refrigerate, covered, up to 5 days.

LOW FAT

SAVORY BUTTERNUT SQUASH STUFFING

"This bread pudding-like stuffing stays moist from the eggs and cream. It's great to make ahead and reheat."

PREP: 50 MIN. BAKE: 50 MIN. OVEN: 350°F

2	Tbsp. butter
2	shallots, finely chopped
1	cup fresh cranberries
2	cups chicken stock or reduced-sodium chicken broth
½	cup uncooked wild rice, rinsed
1	1½-lb. butternut squash, peeled, seeded, and cut in ½-inch cubes
1	Tbsp. finely chopped fresh thyme
1	medium onion, finely chopped
3	stalks celery, chopped
1½	cups half-and-half or light cream
8	eggs
1½	cups turkey or chicken stock or reduced-sodium broth
¾	cup dried cranberries
1	Tbsp. finely chopped fresh sage
8	cups dried sourdough bread cubes

SAVORY BUTTERNUT
SQUASH DRESSING

meet justin

WHEN HOSTING THANKSGIVING DINNER, KENDALL-JACKSON EXECUTIVE CHEF JUSTIN WANGLER FOCUSES ON THE HEART OF THE HOLIDAY.

"Christmas has the distractions of gifts and the hurry of it all. Thanksgiving day is all about the things that matter most—food, family, laughter."

Justin grew up in Asheville, N.C., where he worked in restaurants and attended culinary school. After moving to California, he began spending Thanksgiving with friends. "People are so far flung these days that many of us don't get home for holidays. Our friends become our family, and we celebrate with them," he says.

This new Thanksgiving routine allows him to play with flavors. "When you go to your family's house, you have the same things year after year. Now I mix things up a little. It's always fun to have a couple of new dishes, some conversation starters," he says.

To make sure he's not too busy to spend time with his guests, Justin prepares what he can in advance. "The turkey can be a bear—taking up the entire oven and a portion of the day," he says. "So I do things like roast sweet potatoes beforehand and reheat them with the pecans and marshmallows the day of. You can do everything for the Butternut Squash Stuffing ahead too. Mix it together in a Dutch oven and bake it the day of."

See additional make-ahead tips that follow recipes.

PUMPKIN CORN BREAD

"I add a little masa harina—a fine corn flour—to give the bread light texture with nice corn flavor," says Justin. Find masa harina in the ethnic section of supermarkets or in Mexican markets.

PREP: 30 MIN. BAKE: 22 MIN. OVEN: 350°F

6	Tbsp. butter, melted
2	cups cornmeal
⅓	cup sugar
2	Tbsp. masa harina or corn flour
2	tsp. baking powder
1	tsp. baking soda
1	tsp. salt
¼	tsp. pumpkin pie spice
1	cup buttermilk
1	8-oz. carton sour cream
1	egg, lightly beaten
¾	cup canned pumpkin
	Whipped butter (optional)

1. Heat oven to 350°F. Generously brush a 12-inch cast-iron skillet with 2 tablespoons of the butter; set aside remaining butter.
2. In large mixing bowl combine cornmeal, sugar, masa harina, baking powder, baking soda, salt, and pumpkin pie spice. In another bowl combine remaining butter, buttermilk, sour cream, egg, and pumpkin; whisk into cornmeal mixture. Pour into prepared pan.
3. Bake for 22 to 25 minutes or until a toothpick inserted off-center comes out clean. Cool on wire rack; serve warm with whipped butter. MAKES 8 TO 12 SERVINGS.

PUMPKIN CORN MUFFINS Prepare as directed except brush 22 1¾-inch muffin tins with the 2 tablespoons butter. Spoon in batter. Bake 8 to 10 minutes or until a toothpick inserted off-center comes out clean.
EACH SERVING *218 cal, 11 g fat (6 g sat. fat), 44 mg chol, 444 mg sodium, 27 g carbo, 2 g fiber, 4 g pro. Daily Values: 54% vit. A, 2% vit. C, 11% calcium, 4% iron.*

> MAKE AHEAD Prepare and bake as directed above. Wrap cooled corn bread in foil. Store in refrigerator up to 2 days. Reheat, wrapped in foil, in a 350°F oven for 15 minutes or until warm.

PRISCILLA'S PERSIMMON AND POMEGRANATE SALAD

"My wife's friend, Priscilla, made this salad—a cross between salad and relish—for a holiday party once, and everyone loved it."

PREP: 20 MIN. STAND: 30 MIN.

2	limes
1	jalapeño pepper, seeded and finely chopped*
4	ripe Fuyu persimmons
1	pomegranate, seeded (see "Getting at the Seeds," *page 250*)
¼	cup toasted pine nuts**
3	Tbsp. olive oil
½	cup cilantro leaves
	Cilantro sprigs

1. Squeeze juice from limes into large bowl. Add jalapeño. Let stand 2 minutes. Meanwhile, trim and discard tops and bottoms from persimmons. Thinly slice persimmons. Toss persimmons, pomegranate seeds, pine nuts, olive oil, and cilantro in lime juice. Season to taste with *salt*. Let stand 30 minutes or up to 2 hours. Top with cilantro sprigs.
MAKES 8 (¼-CUP) SERVINGS.

*NOTE Hot chile peppers contain oils that can burn skin and eyes. When working with them, wear plastic or rubber gloves.
**TO TOAST PINE NUTS Heat a skillet over medium heat; add pine nuts. Cook 3 minutes or until toasted, shaking pan frequently. Cool on paper towels.
EACH SERVING *90 cal, 7 g fat (1 g sat. fat), 0 mg chol, 1 mg sodium, 6 g carbo, 1 g fiber, 1 g pro. Daily Values: 7% vit. A, 21% vit. C, 1% calcium, 5% iron.*

PUMPKIN CORN BREAD

PRISCILLA'S PERSIMMON AND
POMEGRANATE SALAD

2 DAYS AHEAD: BRINE TURKEY

½ bunch fresh thyme (about 10 sprigs)
3 bay leaves
30 black peppercorns
1 cup kosher salt
1 cup sugar
1 19-lb. natural (not pre-brined or self-basting) fresh or frozen turkey, thawed

1. Prepare turkey brine: In large container combine thyme, bay leaves, peppercorns, salt, and sugar. Add 2 quarts hot *water* (about 130°F); stir. Add 2 quarts *ice;* let stand until ice is melted.

2. Meanwhile, prepare turkey for brining: Remove neck and giblets (reserve neck, heart, and gizzard for Pan Gravy, *right;* discard liver). Remove legs (see Step 1, *right*). Remove wings and backbone. Reserve for Braised Turkey Legs with Pan Gravy, *below.*

3. Place remaining whole turkey breast in brine, making sure to completely submerge. Cover; refrigerate for 2 days, turning occasionally.

1 DAY AHEAD: PREPARE BRAISED TURKEY LEGS WITH PAN GRAVY

Reserved turkey legs
½ bunch fresh thyme (about 10 sprigs)
Kosher salt and freshly ground pepper
2 tsp. cooking oil
2 large onions, quartered
5 stalks celery, cut in thirds
3 carrots, halved crosswise
½ cup Chardonnay or white wine
6 cups chicken stock or reduced-sodium chicken broth
2 bay leaves
20 black peppercorns
2 cups water

1. Heat oven to 400°F. Debone turkey legs (see Steps 2–4, *right*). Place leg bones, along with reserved neck, wings, and backbone in 15×10×1-inch baking pan. Roast, uncovered, about 45 minutes, until browned.

2. Meanwhile, remove and chop leaves from thyme. Season the insides of deboned legs with thyme, salt, and pepper. Roll and tie meat (see Step 5, *right*). Season rolled legs with salt and pepper.

3. Heat an oven-going extra-large deep skillet or braising pan over medium-high heat. Add oil. Carefully add turkey legs. Cook, turning as needed, until browned on all sides. Remove legs from pan. Drain fat, reserving 1 tablespoon in pan.

4. Add onions, celery, and carrots to pan. Cook, stirring occasionally, over medium heat for 5 minutes. Carefully add wine to pan; stir to scrape up browned bits. Add chicken stock, bay leaves, peppercorns, and water. Remove bones from oven and carefully add to pan. Reduce oven temperature to 350°F. Add browned legs to pan.

5. Cover and roast until tender, about 2½ hours. Cool. Remove legs; strain braising liquid; reserve for Pan Gravy. Remove strings from turkey legs. Slice legs; place slices in casserole dish with 1 cup reserved braising liquid. Cover and refrigerate overnight. See reheating instructions, *below.*

PAN GRAVY Chop reserved heart and gizzard. In a large saucepan melt ¼ cup butter; add giblets and cook 2 minutes. Stir in ½ cup flour and cook 2 minutes more. Whisk in ¼ cup of the braising liquid or turkey stock until smooth. Add 3¾ cups more of the braising liquid and 1 bay leaf. (Refrigerate or freeze additional reserved stock for another use.) Cook and stir until gravy comes to a simmer. Cook 5 minutes. Cool and refrigerate overnight. Just before serving, if desired sprinkle with fresh thyme and/or sage. See reheating instructions, *below.*
MAKES 8 (4-OZ.) SERVINGS + LEFTOVERS.
EACH SERVING *249 cal, 10 g fat (4 g sat. fat), 138 mg chol, 324 mg sodium, 6 g carbo, 1 g fiber, 31 g pro. Daily Values: 34% vit. A, 6% vit. C, 4% calcium, 16% iron.*

THANKSGIVING DAY: ROAST TURKEY BREAST AND REHEAT BRAISED LEGS

1. About 1 hour before roasting, remove turkey from brine. Pat with paper towels.
2. Heat oven to 350°F. Place breast, bone-side down, on rack in roasting pan. Insert oven-going meat thermometer into thickest portion. Roast 1 hour. Spoon juices over turkey. Roast about 1 hour 45 minutes more or until internal temperature reaches 170°F, spooning juices over turkey about every 30 minutes. Remove from oven. Cover with foil; let stand 20 minutes before carving.
3. To reheat legs, place casserole dish in oven with turkey breast during the last 20 to 30 minutes of roasting time. To reheat gravy, in large saucepan bring 2 tablespoons water to simmering. Whisk in gravy; heat through and discard bay leaf.
MAKES 8 (4 OZ.) SERVINGS + LEFTOVERS.
EACH SERVING *160 cal, 3 g fat (1 g sat. fat), 88 mg chol, 239 mg sodium, 0 g carbo, 0 g fiber, 30 g pro. Daily Values: 1% calcium, 8% iron.*

DEBONING STEP-BY-STEP

Ask a local butcher to debone the legs for you (be sure to call several days ahead) or follow these steps to debone them yourself.

1. To remove legs, pull leg away from body. With kitchen shears, cut through skin where leg attaches. Push leg back to dislocate from backbone. Cut through joint to remove.

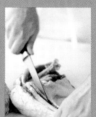

2. Place legs, skin sides down, on cutting board. With thin sharp knife, start at end of thigh and cut along length of bone to loosen bone from meat. Lift and use bone as guide to cut along underside.

3. Cut through the skin around the base of the drumstick. Cut the length of the drumstick all the way to the joint. Cut along bone, as with thigh, to remove bone (attached at joint). Cut around joint to completely remove bones.

4. Carefully remove tendons on the inside of each leg by holding each tendon (grip with a paper towel if needed) and cutting just below each tendon to separate it from the meat. Discard the tendons.

5. Season insides of deboned legs. Roll legs. Tie with kitchen string, beginning at each end. Continue to tie for a total of 6 to 8 ties per leg.

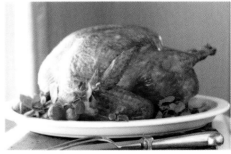

To serve a classic whole turkey or to serve a smaller crowd, see Justin's whole turkey recipe, *page 237.*

CHARDONNAY GLAZED CARROTS

2. Add arugula to pears; toss lightly to coat. Transfer to serving platter. Top with sunflower kernels, Parmesan, and lemon peel. Serve with remaining dressing. Cover and refrigerate remaining vinaigrette up to 1 week. **MAKES 8 SERVINGS.**

LEMON VINAIGRETTE In bowl combine 1 tablespoon lemon peel, ⅓ cup lemon juice, 1 teaspoon sugar, and ½ teaspoon kosher salt. Gradually whisk in ¾ cup extra virgin olive oil.

EACH SERVING *274 cal, 25 g fat (4 g sat. fat), 5 mg chol, 265 mg sodium, 11 g carbo, 2 g fiber, 5 g pro. Daily values: 15% vit. A, 20% vit. C, 14% calcium, 5% iron.*

> MAKE AHEAD Prepare Lemon Vinaigrette as directed. Refrigerate, covered, up to 1 week. To serve, bring to room temperature.

SWEET POTATOES WITH TOASTED PECANS

PREP: 45 MIN. ROAST: 32 MIN. OVEN: 350°F/450°F

4½	lb. sweet potatoes
2	Tbsp. olive oil
1	Tbsp. kosher salt
½	cup butter
⅔	cup whipping cream
2	Tbsp. pure maple syrup
¼	tsp. ground nutmeg
1	tsp. kosher salt
2	to 3 cups tiny marshmallows
¼	cup pecan halves, toasted

1. Heat oven to 350°F. Scrub potatoes and prick with a fork. Brush with olive oil. Sprinkle the 1 tablespoon salt. Place potatoes in 15×10×1-inch baking pan. Roast, uncovered, 30 to 40 minutes or until soft. Cool until easy to handle.

2. Increase oven temperature to 450°F. Halve potatoes; scoop out flesh and discard skin. Press through a fine-mesh sieve. Transfer to a large bowl.

3. In a small saucepan combine butter and whipping cream; cook over medium heat until mixture comes to a simmer. Fold into the sweet potatoes along with the maple syrup, nutmeg, and the 1 teaspoon salt. Transfer to a 2-quart baking dish.

4. Sprinkle marshmallows on potatoes. Bake, uncovered, 12 to 15 minutes or until marshmallows are golden brown. Sprinkle toasted pecans.

MAKES 8 (½-CUP) SERVINGS + LEFTOVERS.

EACH SERVING *255 cal, 14 g fat (7 g sat. fat), 33 mg chol, 670 mg sodium, 30 g carbo, 3 g fiber, 2 g pro. Daily Values: 305% vit. A, 4% vit. C, 4% calcium, 4% iron.*

> MAKE AHEAD Up to 1 day ahead, prepare through Step 3. Cover and refrigerate. To reheat, bake, covered, in a 350°F oven for 55 minutes, stirring once. Increase oven temperature to 450°F. Uncover and proceed with Step 4.

CHARDONNAY GLAZED CARROTS

"Verjus (vair-ZHOO), the pressed juice from unripe grapes, has sweet-tart flavor and is similar to, but less sharp than, vinegar. I use Kendall-Jackson Chardonnay verjus because it's not as acidic, but any white verjus will work."

PREP: 15 MIN. COOK: 25 MIN.

2	lb. assorted carrots
1	cup chardonnay verjus or ¾ cup white grape juice + ¼ cup white wine vinegar
½	cup honey
2	Tbsp. unsalted butter
1	tsp. kosher salt
1	cinnamon stick
2	bay leaves
2	Tbsp. sliced chives

1. Peel large carrots. Slice carrots lengthwise and/or crosswise. Heat a large skillet over medium-high heat. Add verjus, honey, butter, salt, cinnamon, and bay leaves. Bring to boiling, stirring to combine. Add carrots; return to boiling. Reduce heat to medium. Cook, uncovered, 25 minutes, stirring often, until carrots are tender and glaze thickens.

2. Remove from heat. Remove and discard cinnamon stick and bay leaves. Sprinkle chives. **MAKES 8 SERVINGS.**

EACH SERVING *156 cal, 3 g fat, (2 g sat. fat), 8 mg chol, 314 mg sodium, 28 g carbo, 3 g fiber, 1 g pro. Daily Values: 340% vit. A, 11% vit. C, 4% calcium, 3% iron.*

PEAR AND ARUGULA SALAD

"This is one of my favorite simple salads. It's refreshing and I love the way the sweetness of the pears complements the peppery arugula."

PREP: 20 MIN. STAND: 15 MIN.

1	recipe Lemon Vinaigrette
2	red Bartlett pears
12	cups arugula (about 8 oz.)
⅓	cup dry-roasted, salted sunflower kernels
2	oz. Parmesan cheese, shaved (¼ cup) Shredded lemon peel (optional)

1. Prepare Lemon Vinaigrette. Transfer ¼ cup of the vinaigrette dressing to large bowl. Quarter, core, and seed pears. Cut each quarter in thin slices; add to dressing in bowl. Let stand for 15 minutes.

PEAR AND
ARUGULA SALAD

SWEET POTATOES WITH
TOASTED PECANS

PAN-ROASTED
BRUSSELS SPROUTS

PAN-ROASTED BRUSSELS SPROUTS

"Roasting is a great way to get people to eat Brussels sprouts. And caramelizing gives them a mild nutty flavor. It's one of my favorite winter vegetable side dishes."

START TO FINISH: 30 MIN.

2	lb. Brussels sprouts, halved lengthwise
1	Tbsp. rice oil or olive oil
7	cloves garlic, minced
3	Tbsp. butter
12	sprigs fresh thyme
1	large sprig fresh rosemary, halved
2	tsp. fennel seeds
1¼	tsp. kosher salt or 1 tsp. salt
1	Tbsp. sherry or white wine vinegar

1. In a large saucepan cook Brussels sprouts, uncovered, in enough lightly salted boiling water to cover for 3 minutes; drain well. Pat dry with paper towels.
2. Place a very large heavy skillet or sauté pan over high heat for 1 to 2 minutes. Reduce heat to medium. Add oil and garlic; cook and stir 2 minutes. Add half the butter. Increase heat to medium-high; carefully arrange half the sprouts, cut sides down, in the hot skillet. Top with half the thyme, rosemary, fennel seeds, and salt. Cook, uncovered, 3 to 4 minutes or until the sprouts are well browned. Remove sprouts from pan. Repeat with remaining butter, sprouts, thyme, rosemary, fennel seeds, and salt.
3. Return all sprouts to skillet along with sherry. Quickly toss to distribute flavors.
MAKES 8 (½-CUP) SERVINGS + LEFTOVERS.
EACH SERVING *105 cal, 6 g fat (3 g sat. fat), 11 mg chol, 359 mg sodium, 11 g carbo, 4 g fiber, 4 g pro. Daily Values: 20% vit. A, 151% vit. C, 6% calcium, 11% iron.*

> **MAKE AHEAD** Step 1 may be done 1 day ahead. Cover and refrigerate the well-drained Brussels sprouts.

PECAN-CRANBERRY TART

"This tart has all the goodness of pecan pie with a sweet-tart hit from the cranberries."

PREP: 30 MIN. CHILL: 2 HRS. BAKE: 10 MIN./35 MIN. OVEN: 350°F

1	recipe Tart Shells
3	egg whites
2	whole eggs
⅓	cup butter
1½	cups packed brown sugar
1	cup light-color corn syrup
1	vanilla bean, halved lengthwise, or 2 tsp. vanilla extract
2	cups pecan halves, toasted
1	cup cranberries

1. Heat oven to 350°F. Prepare Tart Shells. In medium bowl beat egg whites and whole eggs until combined; set aside.
2. In small saucepan combine butter, brown sugar, and corn syrup. Scrape seeds from vanilla bean; add to pan with bean. Bring just to boiling over medium heat. Gradually whisk into egg mixture. With slotted spoon remove and discard vanilla bean.
3. Arrange pecans and cranberries in cooled tart shells. Pour syrup mixture over.
4. Place tarts on large baking sheet. Bake 35 to 40 minutes or until filling is set.
MAKES 2 TARTS (8 SERVINGS EACH).
TART SHELLS In mixing bowl beat ⅔ cup softened butter with electric mixer on medium-high until light. Add 1⅓ cups powdered sugar and 1 teaspoon kosher salt; beat for 1 minute. Beat in 2 eggs and 2 egg yolks; beat 1 minute more. Gradually beat in 3 cups all-purpose flour. Divide dough in half. Wrap in plastic; refrigerate 1 hour. On lightly floured surface, roll each half to a 16×6-inch rectangle about ¼ inch thick. Transfer to two 14×5-inch rectangular tart pans with removable bottoms. Trim edges. Chill 1 hour. Heat oven to 350°F. Bake 10 minutes or until edges begin to brown; cool.
EACH SERVING *369 cal, 19 g fat (7 g sat. fat), 88 mg chol, 196 mg sodium, 48 g carbo, 2 g fiber, 5 g pro. Daily Values: 7% vit. A, 1% vit. C, 4% calcium, 8% iron.*

> **MAKE AHEAD** Bake tart shells 1 day ahead. Wrap; store at room temperature.

SWEET BUTTERMILK ICE CREAM

PREP: 30 MIN. CHILL: 4 HRS. FREEZE: 20 MIN.

2	cups half-and-half or light cream
1	cup milk
1	vanilla bean, halved lengthwise, or 2 tsp. vanilla extract
1	cup sugar
8	egg yolks
¼	tsp. kosher salt or salt
2	cups buttermilk

1. In saucepan combine half-and-half and milk. Scrape seeds from vanilla bean into mixture. Add bean and half the sugar. Heat over medium until mixture comes to simmer.
2. Meanwhile, in bowl whisk yolks, salt, and remaining sugar until pale yellow and thick (2 minutes). Slowly drizzle 1 cup hot cream mixture into yolk mixture, whisking constantly. Stir yolk mixture into mixture in pan; cook over medium heat until thickened and mixture coats back of spoon. Remove from heat. Pour through fine-mesh sieve into large bowl; discard solids. Stir in buttermilk. Cover and refrigerate at least 4 hours or overnight.
3. Freeze in 4-quart ice cream freezer according to manufacturer's directions.
MAKES 2 QUARTS (16 ½-CUP SERVINGS).
EACH SERVING *135 cal, 6 g fat (3 g sat. fat), 118 mg chol, 85 mg sodium, 16 g carbo, 0 g fiber, 4 g pro. Daily Values: 5% vit. A, 1% vit. C, 10% calcium, 2% iron.*

> **MAKE AHEAD** Prepare and freeze up to 1 week in advance.

PECAN CRANBERRY TART WITH SWEET BUTTERMILK ICE CREAM

Turkey Roasting Guide
What you need to know

ROASTED BRINED
TURKEY

ROASTED BRINED TURKEY

Start with a turkey that has not been enhanced with tenderizing solution—otherwise the result will be too salty.

PREP: 20 MIN. ROAST: 2¾ HRS. STAND: 20 MIN.
MARINATE: 12 HRS. OVEN: 325°F.

- 1 8- to 12-lb. fresh or frozen turkey, thawed
- 1 recipe Brine

1. Rinse turkey, pat dry. Reserve neck and gizzards for Pan Gravy, *page 231,* or discard. Prepare brine. Add turkey. Weight down turkey with a clean dinner plate, or two if necessary. Refrigerate turkey 12 hours.

2. Preheat oven to 325°F. Remove turkey from brine; discard brine and drain turkey well. Pat turkey dry with paper towels.

3. Place turkey, breast side up, on a rack in a shallow roasting pan. Tuck drumsticks under band of skin across the tail, if available, or tie drumsticks to tail. Twist wing tips under back. Insert a meat thermometer into center of an inside thigh muscle.

4. Roast turkey, uncovered, for 2¾ to 3 hours, cutting the band of skin or string and rotating pan halfway through roasting. Thermometer should register 180°F. If necessary, cover turkey with foil during the last 30 minutes of roasting to prevent overbrowning.

5. Remove turkey from oven. Let stand, covered, for 20 minutes.

MAKES 8 TO 10 SERVINGS + LEFTOVERS.

BRINE In a 10-quart pot combine ½ bunch fresh thyme, 3 bay leaves, 30 black peppercorns (½ teaspoon), ½ cup kosher salt,* 1 cup sugar, and 2 quarts hot water; stir to combine. Add 2 quarts ice; let stand until ice is melted.

*Kosher salt has larger crystals than regular salt but is otherwise usually the same. If you use table salt, cut the amount by half.

EACH (4-OZ.) SERVING *184 cal, 5 g fat (2 g sat. fat), 109 mg chol, 651 mg sodium, 1 g carbo, 0 g fiber, 30 g pro. Daily Values: 2% calcium, 10% iron.*

TURKEY CHECKLIST

☑ **GET READY**

Buy To ensure plenty of leftovers, buy 1 to 1½ pounds of turkey per person.

Thaw Place in the refrigerator to thaw; allow one day for each 4 pounds of turkey plus one additional day. It's thawed when no ice crystals remain inside the body cavity.

☑ **PREP—1 HOUR**

Stuff Remove giblets; set aside for gravy or discard. Spoon desired stuffing loosely into turkey (stuffing won't reach a safe temperature if packed too tightly).

Arrange Skewer turkey neck skin to back. Tuck drumstick ends under band of skin across tail, if available. If there is no band of skin, tie drumsticks securely to tail. Twist wing tips under back. Place turkey, breast side up, on rack in shallow pan. Press foil over the drumsticks and neck to prevent skin from overbrowning.

☑ **ROAST—3 TO 5 HOURS**

Adjust With oven rack in lowest position, preheat oven to 325°F. Brush turkey with cooking oil. Push an oven-going meat thermometer into the center of an inside thigh muscle without touching bone.

Check When the bird has been in the oven for two-thirds of the time shown on the chart, *below,* cut the string between drumsticks. Remove foil for the last 30 to 45 minutes.

Test A meat thermometer inserted deep into the thigh must register 180°F, and the stuffing should be at least 165°F. Drumsticks should move easily in their sockets, and thickest part should feel soft when pressed. Juices from the thigh should run clear when pierced with a long-tined fork.

Stand Remove turkey from the oven and cover loosely with foil. Let stand 20 minutes. Remove stuffing; transfer to bowl.

roasting times at 325°F

READY-TO-COOK TURKEY WEIGHT	UNSTUFFED	STUFFED
8 to 12 lb.	2¾ to 3 hr.	3 to 3½ hr.
12 to 14 lb.	3 to 3¾ hr.	3½ to 4 hr.
14 to 18 lb.	3¾ to 4¼ hr.	4 to 4¼ hr.
18 to 20 lb.	4¼ to 4½ hr.	4¼ to 4¾ hr.
20 to 24 lb.	4½ to 5 hr.	4¾ to 5¼ hr.

SOURCE: NATIONAL TURKEY FEDERATION

by the numbers For the best turkey, here's what you need to know.

BUY	THAW	ROAST	TEST	STAND	CHILL
1½	**5**	**325°F**	**180°F**	**20**	**2**
LBS. PER PERSON	DAYS IN THE FRIDGE	IN OVEN	IN THIGH	MINUTES BEFORE SERVING	HOURS AFTER SERVING FOR LEFTOVERS

NOVEMBER

What's Cooking

Holiday dessert

HOLIDAY FRUIT PIE

HOLIDAY FRUIT PIE

Quickly stir together cranberries and golden raisins for a colorful pie.

PREP: 40 MIN. CHILL: 30 MIN. BAKE: 45 MIN.
COOL: 1 HR. OVEN 375°F

1	recipe Butter Pastry
1	12-oz. bag fresh cranberries or frozen cranberries, thawed
2	to 3 tsp. finely shredded orange peel
1	cup orange juice
½	cup golden raisins
½	cup dried cranberries
1	cup sugar
¼	cup all-purpose flour
1	egg, lightly beaten
1	Tbsp. sugar

1. Prepare Butter Pastry.

2. In saucepan combine cranberries, orange peel, orange juice, raisins, and dried cranberries; bring to boiling over medium heat. Cook, uncovered, 3 minutes. In bowl combine 1 cup sugar and flour; add to saucepan. Cook and stir until thickened and bubbly; cook 1 minute more. Remove from heat.

3. Preheat oven to 375°F. On floured surface, roll one dough portion to 12-inch circle. Wrap pastry around rolling pin. Unroll into 9-inch pie plate. Pour in filling. Trim bottom pastry to ½ inch beyond edge.

4. On floured surface, roll remaining dough to 13-inch circle; cut into ½-inch-wide strips. Weave strips over fruit filling in lattice pattern. Press strips into bottom pastry rim. Seal and crimp edge, if desired. Brush with egg and sprinkle with 1 tablespoon sugar.

5. Cover edge with foil. Bake 25 minutes. Remove foil. Bake 20 minutes more or until top is nicely browned and filling is bubbly. Let stand at least 1 hour.

MAKES 8 SERVINGS.

BUTTER PASTRY In bowl combine 2 ½ cups all-purpose flour, 2 tablespoons sugar, and 1 teaspoon salt. Using a pastry blender, cut in ⅓ cup chilled shortening and 6 tablespoons chilled unsalted butter until pieces are until crumbly. Using fork, stir in 8 to 9 tablespoons ice water, 1 tablespoon at a time, until dough just starts to form. Knead 2 or 3 times in bowl. Divide in half. Form halves into 2 discs. Wrap with plastic wrap; chill at least 30 minutes.

EACH SERVING 540 cal, 18 g fat (8 g sat. fat), 49 mg chol, 305 mg sodium, 84 g carbo, 4 g fiber, 6 g pro. Daily Values: 8% vit. A, 37% vit. C, 3% calcium, 13% iron.

CHOCOLATE LOAF WITH BUTTERSCOTCH GLAZE

CHOCOLATE LOAF WITH BUTTERSCOTCH GLAZE

PREP: 25 MIN. BAKE: 45 MIN. COOL: 45 MIN.
OVEN: 350°F

1	cup whipping cream
4	oz. semisweet chocolate, chopped
½	cup unsalted butter, softened
1	cup packed brown sugar
3	eggs
2	tsp. vanilla
1½	cups all-purpose flour
¼	cup unsweetened cocoa powder
1	Tbsp. baking powder
¼	tsp. baking soda
1	recipe Butterscotch Glaze

1. Preheat oven to 350°F. Butter and flour 9×5×3-inch loaf pan; set aside.

2. In small saucepan heat whipping cream over medium heat just until hot. Remove from heat; add chocolate. Stir until chocolate is melted. Let stand until cool.

3. Meanwhile, in bowl beat ½ cup butter with electric mixer on medium speed 30 seconds. Add 1 cup brown sugar; beat on high until fluffy, about 2 minutes, scraping bowl occasionally. Beat in eggs and vanilla. Beat in cooled chocolate mixture until smooth.

4. Combine flour, cocoa, baking powder, and baking soda; add to butter mixture. Beat on medium until well combined, 1 to 2 minutes. Pour in prepared pan; smooth with spatula.

5. Bake 45 minutes or until toothpick inserted in center comes out clean. While loaf bakes, prepare Butterscotch Glaze. Cool loaf in pan on rack 10 minutes. Remove from pan; cool completely. Pour half the Butterscotch Glaze on loaf. Pass remaining glaze. MAKES 8 SERVINGS.

BUTTERSCOTCH GLAZE In skillet combine ½ cup brown sugar, 1 tablespoon lemon juice, 3 tablespoons water, and 3 tablespoons unsalted butter; cook and stir over medium heat until sugar dissolves, about 1 minute. Stir in ½ cup sliced kumquats; 1 tangerine, sliced and seeded; and ¼ cup cranberries. Cook, stirring frequently, until kumquats start to soften, about 3 minutes. Remove from heat.

EACH SERVING 608 cal, 34 g fat (20 g sat. fat), 162 mg chol, 229 mg sodium, 73 g carbo, 3 g fiber, 7 g pro. Daily Values: 23% vit. A, 14% vit. C, 21% calcium, 17% iron.

CINNAMON APPLE SPICE CAKE

PREP: 25 MIN. BAKE: 40 MIN. COOL: 10 MIN.
OVEN: 350°F

- 1½ cups buttermilk
- ¾ cup canola oil
- ½ cup water
- 2 cups packed brown sugar
- 2 eggs
- 2 tsp. baking powder
- 1½ tsp. ground cinnamon
- ½ tsp. baking soda
- ½ tsp. salt
- 2 tsp. vanilla
- 2½ cups all-purpose flour
- 2 Gala apples, cored and cut in ½-inch chunks
- 1 recipe Fruit Topper

1. Preheat oven to 350°F. Line two 8×8×2-inch baking pans with parchment paper. Grease and flour the pans; set aside.
2. In mixing bowl whisk buttermilk, oil, water, brown sugar, eggs, baking powder, cinnamon, baking soda, salt, and vanilla until combined. Whisk in flour; stir in apples. Divide evenly between prepared pans.
3. Bake 40 minutes or until toothpick inserted near center comes out clean. Cool in pans on wire rack 10 minutes. Invert cake layers from pans onto racks; remove parchment paper. Cool completely on racks.

4. Prepare Fruit Topper. Place one cake layer, flat side up, on serving platter. Spoon on about two-thirds of topper. Top with second cake layer and remaining mixture. Serve immediately. **MAKES 10 SERVINGS.**

FRUIT TOPPER In skillet melt 2 tablespoons unsalted butter over medium heat. Add 4 small apples or firm pears, cored and cut in slices and/or wedges; add ¼ cup granulated sugar. Cook, stirring occasionally, just until fruit begins to soften, about 8 minutes. Remove from heat.

EACH SERVING *532 cal, 20 g fat (3 g sat. fat), 50 mg chol, 319 mg sodium, 84 g carbo, 3 g fiber, 6 g pro. Daily values: 3 % vit. A, 6 % vit. C, 17 % calcium, 12 % iron.*

KID-FRIENDLY

SHORTBREAD SANDWICHES WITH FUDGE SAUCE

PREP: 1 HR. BAKE: 30 MIN. COOL: 1 HR.
OVEN: 325°F

SHORTBREAD

½	cup dried tart cherries and/or dried cranberries
½	tsp. crushed red pepper (optional)
1½	cups all-purpose flour
½	cup granulated sugar
2	Tbsp. cornstarch
½	tsp. salt
¼	tsp. baking powder
¾	cup cold unsalted butter, cut in ½-inch pieces

WHIPPED FILLING

½	cup whipping cream
3	oz. cream cheese, softened
¼	cup powdered sugar
½	tsp. vanilla
1	recipe Fudge Sauce
	Snipped dried tart cherries and/or dried cranberries

1. Preheat oven to 325°F. In bowl combine cherries and/or cranberries and crushed red pepper; cover with boiling water. Let stand 10 minutes; drain.

2. In food processor bowl combine flour, granulated sugar, cornstarch, salt, and baking powder. Add butter and soaked cherries and/or cranberries. Pulse until dough begins to clump together. Remove from processor. Gather dough and press in free-form square. Roll between two sheets parchment paper to 12×9-inch rectangle. With knife, cut thirty-six 3×1-inch pieces (do not separate). Slide parchment onto baking sheet and remove top parchment.

3. Bake 30 to 35 minutes or until lightly golden. Remove from oven. Cool on wire rack.

4. For whipped filling, in bowl combine whipping cream, cream cheese, powdered sugar, and vanilla. Beat with electric mixer on high until stiff peaks form. Refrigerate until ready to use.

5. To assemble, spread flat sides of 18 rectangles with scant tablespoon of whipped filling each. Top with remaining shortbread, flat sides down.

6. Serve with Fudge Sauce. Sprinkle additional cherries and/or cranberries.

MAKES 18 SANDWICHES.

FUDGE SAUCE In saucepan combine ½ cup whipping cream and 3 tablespoons light corn syrup. Cook over medium-high heat until hot. Remove from heat; stir in 4 ounces chopped semisweet chocolate until melted. Let cool until thick, about 1 hour.

EACH SANDWICH *259 cal, 16 g fat (10 g sat. fat), 44 mg chol, 94 mg sodium, 27 g carbo, 1 g fiber, 2 g pro. Daily Values: 34% vit. A, 6% vit. C, 4% calcium, 16% iron.*

MINI PUMPKIN
PUDDING PIES

MINI HOLIDAY
FRUIT PIES

MINI PUMPKIN PUDDING PIES

**PREP: 30 MIN. CHILL: 2 HRS. BAKE: 10 MIN.
OVEN: 450°F**

- 1 Recipe Butter Pastry, *page 239*
- 1 cup milk
- 2 4-serving-size pkg. butterscotch instant pudding and pie filling mix
- 2 15-oz. cans pumpkin
- 1 tsp. pumpkin pie spice
- 1 recipe Spiced Whipped Cream (optional)

1. Preheat oven to 450°F. Divide chilled pastry into 8 portions. On a lightly floured surface roll each portion into a 7-inch circle. Line eight 4⅜- to 5-inch foil or metal tart pans with pastry. Fold edges under and crimp. Prick bottoms and sides with fork. Place on baking sheet. Bake 10 to 12 minutes or until golden. Cool on rack.
2. In a large mixing bowl combine milk, pudding mix, pumpkin, and pumpkin pie spice. Beat on medium speed for 2 minutes. Divide among tart shells. Cover and chill 2 hours. To serve, top with Spiced Whipped Cream; sprinkle pumpkin pie spice.
MAKES 8 PIES; EACH SERVES TWO.

SPICED WHIPPED CREAM In a chilled medium mixing bowl combine ½ cup whipping cream, 1 tablespoon sugar, and ¼ teaspoon pumpkin pie spice. Beat on medium speed until soft peaks form.

EACH SERVING (ONE-HALF OF A PIE) *222cal, 9 g fat, (4 g sat. fat), 13 mg chol, 350 mg sodium, 33 g carbo, 3 g fiber, 3 g pro. Daily Values: 156% vit. A, 2% calcium, 6% iron.*

MINI HOLIDAY FRUIT PIES

**PREP: 30 MIN. CHILL: 2 HRS. BAKE: 10 MIN.
COOL: 1 HR. OVEN: 450°F**

Prepare Holiday Fruit Pie, page 239, through step 2. Then begin step 1, below.
1. Divide pastry into 8 portions. On lightly floured surface roll four of the portions into 7-inch circles and four into 6-inch circles. Line four 4⅜- to 5-inch foil or metal tart pans with the 7-inch circles; trim pastry even with rim.
2. Reserve ½ cup cranberry filling. Divide remaining filling among pans. Cut top crust in ½-inch-wide strips and prepare lattice as in Step 4 on *page 239*. Place pies on foil-lined baking sheet. Bake for 30 to 35 minutes, until crust is golden and filling is bubbly. Cool on wire rack at least 1 hour. To serve, stir ¼ cup caramel-flavor ice cream topping into reserved filling; use to top pies. Add sliced kumquats and sage leaves.
MAKES 4 PIES; EACH SERVES TWO. (SEE EACH SERVING, *PAGE 239*.)

PUMPKIN PIE
CHEESECAKE

PUMPKIN PIE CHEESECAKE

Baking the cheesecake in a water bath results in a cake with a flat top and evenly creamy texture.

COOL: 2 HRS. CHILL: 4 HRS. OVEN: 350°F

- 1½ cups finely crushed gingersnaps (8 to 9 ounces)
- ¼ cup melted butter
- 2 tablespoons packed brown sugar
- 2 8-ounce packages cream cheese, softened
- 1¼ cups packed brown sugar
- 2 15-ounce cans pumpkin
- ¼ cup all-purpose flour
- 2 teaspoons pumpkin pie spice
- 5 eggs, slightly beaten

1. Preheat oven to 350°F. For crust, in a bowl combine crushed gingersnaps, butter, and 2 tablespoons brown sugar. Press the crumb mixture onto the bottom and about 1 inch up the sides of 9×3-inch springform pan; set aside. Bake 5 minutes or until firm. Cool completely.
2. For filling, in a large mixing bowl beat cream cheese and the 1¼ cups brown sugar until smooth. Beat in the pumpkin, flour, and pumpkin pie spice with an electric mixer until combined. Stir in eggs by hand.

3. Pour filling into crust-lined pan; spread filling to sides of pan. Place the pan in a shallow baking pan. Bake for 60 to 65 minutes or until filling appears set when gently shaken.
4. Cool in pan on a wire rack for 15 minutes. Using a small sharp knife, loosen the crust from sides of pan; cool for 30 minutes. Remove sides of the pan; cool cheesecake completely on rack. Cover and chill at least 4 hours before serving.
MAKES 12 SERVINGS.

WATER BATH METHOD: Prepare crust as directed. Place the crust-lined springform pan on a double layer of 18×12-inch heavy-duty aluminum foil. Bring edges of foil up and mold around sides of pan to form a watertight seal. Prepare filling as directed and pour into prepared pan. Place in a roasting pan and pour enough hot water around pan to reach halfway up the sides. Bake for 70 to 75 minutes or until filling appears set when gently shaken. Remove from water bath and cool and chill as directed in Step 4.

EACH SERVING *338 cal, 16 g fat (9 g sat. fat), 121 mg chol, 288 mg sodium, 41 g carbo, 3 g fiber, 7 g pro. Daily Values: 184% vit. A, 8% calcium, 10% iron.*

Everyday Easy
Quick, budget-friendly meals

FAST

RICE AND SWEET PEPPER BOWL

START TO FINISH: 30 MIN.
BUDGET $2.08 PER SERVING

4	medium green and/or red sweet peppers
1	8.8-oz. pkg. cooked Spanish-style rice
1	14.5-oz. can stewed tomatoes
4	1-oz. slices Monterey Jack cheese with jalapeño peppers
1	oz. Parmesan cheese, shaved
	Fresh oregano (optional)
1	Tbsp. olive oil

1. Quarter peppers; remove stems, seeds, and ribs. Place peppers in 2-quart square microwave-safe baking dish. Add 2 tablespoons water. Cover with parchment. Heat in microwave on 100% power (high) 4 minutes until crisp-tender; turn dish once if there is no turntable. Remove peppers from dish; drain and set aside.
2. Prepare rice according to microwave package directions. Drain tomatoes, reserving 2 tablespoons liquid. In baking dish layer half the peppers (cut sides up), the rice, drained tomatoes, Jack cheese, and remaining peppers (cut sides down). Drizzle reserved tomato liquid. Cover with parchment. Heat in microwave on 100% power (high) 5 to 6 minutes, turning once. Let stand 5 minutes. To serve, top with Parmesan and oregano; drizzle olive oil. **MAKES 4 SERVINGS.**

EACH SERVING *319 cal, 16 g fat (8 g sat. fat), 36 mg chol, 733 mg sodium, 31 g carbo, 3 g fiber, 14 g pro. Daily Values: 22% vit. A, 174% vit. C, 34% calcium, 13% iron.*

FAST

PORK AND PUMPKIN NOODLE BOWL

START TO FINISH: 30 MIN.
BUDGET $1.80 PER SERVING

8	oz. whole wheat linguine
1	small red onion, thinly sliced
1	lb. pork loin, cut in ½-inch-thick slices
3	Tbsp. reduced-sodium soy sauce
12	fresh sage leaves
1	tsp. minced garlic (2 cloves) or ½ tsp. garlic powder
1	cup canned or frozen pureed pumpkin or butternut squash
¼	cup blue cheese crumbles (optional)

1. Cook pasta according to package directions, adding onion during last 5 minutes of cooking time. Drain and keep warm.
2. Meanwhile, in 12-inch skillet heat 1 tablespoon *olive oil*. Brush pork with some soy sauce and generously sprinkle *black pepper*. Cook sage leaves in hot oil until crisp. Drain on paper towels. Add pork to skillet and cook for 2 minutes on each side or until golden outside and slightly pink inside. Remove pork from skillet; cover to keep warm. In the same skillet combine remaining soy sauce, garlic, ¼ cup pumpkin, and 1 cup *water*. Bring to boiling and reduce sauce slightly. Add pasta and onions to skillet; heat through. Divide pasta among four bowls. In the same skillet, heat remaining pumpkin. Serve pork with pasta, pumpkin, sage leaves, and blue cheese.
MAKES 8 SERVINGS.

EACH SERVING *414 cal, 9 g fat (2 g sat. fat), 71 mg chol, 645 mg sodium, 51 g carbo, 2 g fiber, 34 g pro. Daily Values: 197% vit. A, 16% vit. C, 8% calcium, 24% iron.*

RICE AND SWEET PEPPER BOWL

PORK AND PUMPKIN
NOODLE BOWL

PECAN-CRUSTED CHICKEN
THIGHS WITH BRAISED
GREENS AND GRAPES

PECAN-CRUSTED CHICKEN THIGHS WITH BRAISED GREENS AND GRAPES

START TO FINISH: 28 MIN.
BUDGET $2.82 PER SERVING

1	lb. boneless, skinless chicken thighs
1	egg
⅓	cup finely chopped pecans
⅓	cup crushed saltine or wheat crackers
¼	tsp. nutmeg
1	10-oz. bag mixed salad greens
4	small bunches grapes
⅓	cup frozen harvest blend or white grape juice concentrate, thawed

1. Pound chicken to slightly flatten; sprinkle *salt* and *pepper*. In shallow dish beat egg. In second dish combine pecans, crackers, and nutmeg. Dip chicken in egg, then nut mixture, pressing to coat.
2. Heat 1 tablespoon *olive oil* in 12-inch skillet over medium heat. Cook chicken 5 to 6 minutes on each side until crisp (180°F). Remove; cover. In hot skillet cook and stir greens until beginning to wilt. Remove greens from skillet; sprinkle with *salt* and *pepper*.
3. Heat 1 teaspoon *olive oil* in 10-inch skillet. Cook grapes 3 to 4 minutes, until skins begin to burst. Add grape juice concentrate; cook 1 minute more. To serve, drizzle juices over chicken and greens.
MAKES 4 SERVINGS.

EACH SERVING *367 cal, 18 g fat (3 g sat. fat), 147 mg chol, 485 mg sodium, 27 g carbo, 3 g fiber, 27 g pro. Daily Values: 21% vit. A, 46% vit. C, 7% calcium, 15% iron.*

CORNED BEEF, CABBAGE, CARROTS, AND NEW POTATOES

WHITE BEAN-TURKEY CHILI WITH CORN BREAD DUMPLINGS

CORNED BEEF, CABBAGE, CARROTS, AND NEW POTATOES

START TO FINISH: 25 MIN.
BUDGET $3.61 PER SERVING

1	lb. small new potatoes
1	lb. small carrots
1	small head savoy cabbage
2	Tbsp. olive oil
1	lb. cooked deli corned beef, unsliced
2	Tbsp. spicy brown mustard
2	Tbsp. honey

1. Scrub and halve potatoes. Trim, peel, and halve carrots lengthwise. In 2½- to 3-quart microwave-safe dish combine potatoes, carrots, and 2 tablespoons *water*. Heat in microwave on 100% power (high) covered, 8 minutes, stirring once. Cut cabbage in wedges; add to carrots and potatoes in dish. Cook, covered, on high 4 minutes or until cabbage is crisp-tender.
2. Heat broiler. Place potatoes, carrots, and cabbage in 15×10×1-inch baking pan. Drizzle oil; sprinkle *salt* and *pepper*. Broil 3 to 4 inches from heat 5 minutes. Slice beef; cook in hot 12-inch skillet over medium-high heat 1 minute on each side. Add 2 tablespoons *water*; reduce heat to low. Cover and heat through. To serve, drizzle with pan juices. Combine mustard and honey to pass. **MAKES 4 SERVINGS.**

EACH SERVING *537 cal, 29 g fat (8 g sat. fat), 111 mg chol, 1,657 mg sodium, 44 g carbo, 8 g fiber, 25 g pro. Daily Values: 393% vit. A, 85% vit. C, 9% calcium, 21% iron.*

WHITE BEAN-TURKEY CHILI WITH CORN BREAD DUMPLINGS

START TO FINISH: 22 MIN.
BUDGET $2.69 PER SERVING

1	lb. cooked turkey
1	16-oz. jar chunky salsa
1	15-oz. can cannellini beans, rinsed and drained
1	tsp. chili powder
1	8.5-oz. pkg. corn bread mix
1	egg
¼	cup shredded cheddar cheese (1 oz.) (optional)
	Slivered green onions (optional)
	Chili powder (optional)

1. Chop turkey. In Dutch oven combine turkey, salsa, beans, chili powder, and ⅔ cup *water*. Bring to boiling.
2. Meanwhile, for dumplings, in a medium bowl mix together corn bread mix, egg, and ¼ cup *water*. Drop batter by large spoonfuls on boiling turkey chili.
3. Cover; reduce heat and simmer for 10 to 15 minutes or until a wooden pick inserted into a dumpling comes out clean. To serve, top chili with cheese, green onions, and chili powder. **MAKES 4 SERVINGS.**

EACH SERVING *555 cal, 15 g fat (4 g sat. fat), 140 mg chol, 1,618 mg sodium, 64 g carbo, 11 g fiber, 47 g pro. Daily Values: 13% vit. A, 4% vit. C, 13% calcium, 24% iron.*

Good and Healthy

Pomegranates

why they're good for you

High in antioxidants
Pomegranates are usually enjoyed as seeds or juice—and the juice contains antioxidants at much higher levels than other fruit juices—more than red wine or tea, says Arpita Basu, assistant professor of nutritional sciences at Oklahoma State University. In both lab and human studies, antioxidants or polyphenols in pomegranates,, decreased the oxidative damage associated with cancer, diabetes, and heart disease. In several initial small studies, says Basu, "We've seen that one to two glasses a day can reduce blood pressure, the risk of recurrent heart attack, and clogged arteries." But, she adds, "While we do not yet have a lot of ata, the human studies for both heart disease and Type 2 diabetes are promising."

May slow prostate cancer
Researchers are optimistic about preliminary research on prostate cancer. "When we gave 40 men who had recurrent prostate cancer 8 ounces of juice a day, it slowed rising PSA by 50 percent," says Dr. David Heber, director of the UCLA Center for Human Nutrition. When PSA (the marker used to test for prostate cancer) rises, it indicates that cancer is spreading. In this test, says Heber, they were able to slow the time it took PSAs to double from 15 to 57 months.

Apple size with thin, dark red leathery skin, pomegranates grow on hardy, drought-tolerant shrubs. Native to Southwest Asia, the fruit is also grown in California and Arizona. Each pomegranate is packed with hundreds of bright red edible pulp-covered seeds, all of which are compartmentalized by thick cream-color membranes. The unique cherry-cranberry taste of the seeds of this fruit adds lively flavor to meats and side dishes as well as drinks and desserts. For commercial juicing, the entire fruit is used.

Domestic pomegranates—grown in California and Arizona—are available September through February in most grocery stores. The fruit is often used in holiday centerpieces, but don't overlook its high nutrition. Pomegranates are as healthful and delicious as they are beautiful.

LOW FAT

WILTED CHICKEN SALAD WITH POMEGRANATE DRESSING

START TO FINISH: 30 MIN.

¾	cup pomegranate juice
1	14- to 16-oz. pkg. chicken tenderloins
2	Tbsp. olive oil
½	medium red onion, cut lengthwise in thin wedges
1	Tbsp. snipped fresh oregano or ½ tsp. dried oregano, crushed
¾	tsp. coarsely ground black pepper
½	tsp. salt
2	Tbsp. red wine vinegar
2	6-oz. pkg. baby spinach leaves
½	cup pomegranate seeds
¼	cup slivered almonds, toasted*

1. In a small saucepan bring pomegranate juice to boiling; boil gently, uncovered, 5 to 8 minutes or until reduced to ¼ cup. Remove from heat; set aside. Meanwhile, in a 12-inch skillet cook chicken in 1 tablespoon hot olive oil over medium-high heat 6 to 8 minutes or until chicken is no longer pink, turning occasionally. Remove from skillet. Keep warm.

2. Add onion, remaining oil, dried oregano (if using), pepper, and salt to skillet; cook 3 to 5 minutes or just until onion is tender, stirring occasionally. Stir in reduced pomegranate juice and vinegar; bring to boiling. Boil 1 minute. Remove from heat and stir in fresh oregano (if using). Gradually add spinach, tossing just until spinach is wilted and combined.

3. Serve in large shallow dish. Top with chicken, pomegranate seeds, and nuts. Serve immediately. **MAKES 4 SERVINGS.**

*****NOTE** To toast nuts, spread slivered almonds in single layer in shallow baking pan. Bake in 350°F oven 5 to 10 minutes or until light golden brown, watching carefully and stirring once or twice to prevent burning. Toast nuts up to 1 day before using.

EACH SERVING *292 cal., 11 g total fat (2 g sat. fat), 58 mg chol., 425 mg sodium, 21 g carb., 4 g dietary fiber, 27 g protein. Daily Values: 111% vit. A, 51% vit. C, 12% calcium, 22% iron.*

WILTED CHICKEN SALAD
WITH POMEGRANATE
DRESSING

getting at the seeds

Peel and seed pomegranates in a bowl of water to make the job easy and less messy.

1. Score an "X" in the top of the pomegranate.

2. Cut the fruit in quarters.

3. Immerse each quartered section of the fruit in a bowl of cool water. Then use your fingers to loosen the seeds from the white membrane.

4. Discard peel and membrane. Drain off the water, retaining the seeds.

STORAGE Freeze pomegranate seeds in sealed freezer container up to 1 year.

POMEGRANATE RICE

POMEGRANATE RICE

PREP: 20 MIN. COOK: 14 MIN. STAND: 10 MIN.

1	shallot, chopped
1	Tbsp. canola oil
1	cup jasmine or long grain white rice
2	tsp. grated fresh ginger
⅛	tsp. ground cinnamon
1	14-oz. can reduced-sodium chicken broth
¼	cup water
½	cup roasted, salted pistachio nuts
1	cup pomegranate seeds
	Lemon peel strips

1. In a large saucepan cook shallots in hot oil over medium heat 3 to 5 minutes or just until tender, stirring occasionally. Add rice, ginger, and cinnamon. Cook and stir 5 minutes or until rice starts to brown.
2. Carefully add broth and water to rice. Bring to boiling; reduce heat. Simmer, covered, 14 minutes. Remove from heat; let stand, covered, 10 minutes or until the liquid is absorbed.
3. Stir in nuts and pomegranate seeds. Sprinkle lemon peel. **MAKES 6 TO 8 SERVINGS.**
EACH SERVING *235 cal, 8 g fat (1 g sat. fat), 0 mg chol., 203 mg sodium, 38 g carb, 3 g fiber, 5 g pro. Daily Values: 2% vit. A, 11% vit. C, 3% calcium, 4% iron.*

LOW FAT
POMEGRANATE GRAPE SAUCE

PREP: 15 MIN. COOK: 25 MIN.

1½	cups pomegranate juice or cranberry juice
1	teaspoon snipped fresh rosemary or ½ teaspoon dried rosemary, crushed
2	tablespoons honey
1	tablespoon balsamic vinegar (optional)
1	cup red seedless grapes, halved
1	medium pear, cored, peeled, and chopped
½	cup pomegranate seeds*
	Fresh rosemary (optional)

1. In a medium saucepan bring pomegranate juice and rosemary to boiling; reduce heat. Simmer, uncovered, about 25 minutes or until juice is reduced to ½ cup. Remove from heat.
2. Stir in honey and vinegar. Gently stir in grapes and pear.

3. Serve warm, at room temperature, or cover and chill up to 48 hours. Stir in pomegranate seeds just before serving. Top with fresh rosemary.
MAKES 8 (¼-CUP) SERVINGS.
EACH SERVING *91 cal, 1 g fat (0 g sat. fat), 0 mg chol, 21 g carbo, 2 g fiber, 0 g pro. Daily Values: 1% vit. A, 14% vit. C, 1% calcium, 1% iron.*

december

Bake something simple and sweet, then tuck into a traditional-yet-inspired holiday feast of stuffed pork loin.

256

264

266

SANTA'S CHOCOLATE AND VANILLA
SANDWICH COOKIES
Recipe on page 256

CHRISTMAS BLONDIES

'Tis the Gift to Be Simple

A confection box full of easy-to-bake sweets for the holidays

CHRISTMAS BROWNIES

PREP: 30 MIN. BAKE: 30 MIN. COOL: 2 HRS.
OVEN: 325°F

8	oz. semisweet chocolate, coarsely chopped
1	cup butter
2	Tbsp. cherry brandy or cherry juice (optional)
2	Tbsp. vanilla
1¼	cups granulated sugar
¾	cup packed brown sugar
6	eggs
2	cups all-purpose flour
¼	cup unsweetened cocoa powder
1	tsp. baking powder
½	tsp. salt
1	cup coarsely chopped candied cherries
4	oz. dark chocolate, coarsely chopped

1. Preheat oven to 325°F. Line a 15×10×1-inch baking pan with foil. Lightly grease foil. Set aside.
2. In small saucepan stir semisweet chocolate and butter over low heat until melted. Remove from heat. Stir in brandy and vanilla. Transfer to a large mixing bowl. Add granulated sugar, brown sugar, and eggs. Beat with an electric mixer on medium speed until well combined.
3. Combine flour, cocoa powder, baking powder, and salt. Add to chocolate mixture. Beat at medium speed until well combined. Stir in cherries and dark chocolate. Spread batter in prepared pan.
4. Bake for 30 minutes. Cool in pan on a wire rack. Cut in bars or sticks.*

MAKES 48 BARS OR ABOUT 54 STICKS.
*Freeze pan of brownies for 30 minutes before cutting.

EACH BAR *146 cal, 7 g fat (4 g sat. fat), 37 mg chol, 70 mg sodium, 20 g carbo, 1 g fiber, 8 g pro. Daily Values: 3% vit. A, 1% vit. C, 2% calcium, 4% iron.*

CHRISTMAS BLONDIES

The traditional ingredients for fruitcake— brandy, candied cherries, and walnuts—are stirred into a simple bar cookie.

PREP: 15 MIN. BAKE: 30 MIN. OVEN: 350°F

⅔	cup butter, softened
2	cups packed brown sugar
2	eggs
1	Tbsp. cherry brandy or cherry or cranberry juice
1½	tsp. baking powder
2	tsp. vanilla bean paste or vanilla extract
¼	tsp. salt
2¼	cups all-purpose flour
1	cup chopped walnuts, toasted*
¾	cup chopped white or dark sweet chocolate
½	cup coarsely chopped candied cherries

1. Preheat oven to 350°F. Lightly grease a 13×9-inch baking pan.
2. In a large mixing bowl beat butter on medium speed for 30 seconds. Add sugar, beating until well combined. Add eggs, brandy, baking powder, vanilla, and salt; beat well. Add flour; beat just until blended. Stir in nuts, chocolate, and cherries. Spread in prepared pan.
3. Bake for 30 minutes or until golden. Cool completely in pan on a wire rack. Cut in bars. **MAKES 24 BARS.**
*Toasting Nuts: Spread nuts in a single layer in a shallow baking pan. Bake in a 350°F oven 5 to 10 minutes, stirring every 2 minutes, or until golden brown.

EACH BAR *240 cal, 10 g fat (5 g sat. fat), 32 mg chol, 125 mg sodium, 34 g carbo, 1 g fiber, 3 g pro. Daily Values: 4% vit. A, 5% calcium, 5% iron.*

CHRISTMAS BROWNIES

KID-FRIENDLY
SANTA'S VANILLA SANDWICH COOKIES

Make these sandwich cookies in two flavors and two sizes to give Santa nibbling options.

PREP: 40 MIN. FREEZE: 2 HRS. BAKE: 9 MIN. PER BATCH COOL: 10 MIN. OVEN: 350°F

½	cup butter, softened
2	tsp. vanilla bean paste or vanilla extract
1	cup granulated sugar
1	egg
¼	tsp. baking soda
¼	tsp. salt
1¾	cups all-purpose flour
1	recipe Pink Filling

1. In large mixing bowl beat butter and vanilla bean paste with an electric mixer on medium speed for 30 seconds. Add sugar; beat until well combined. Add eggs, baking soda, and salt; beat well. Beat in as much of the flour as you can with mixer. Stir in remaining flour.

2. Divide dough in half. Shape each half in a 7-inch-long roll about 1½ inches in diameter. (For small cookies, shape dough in 10-inch-long rolls about 1 inch in diameter.) Wrap in plastic wrap or waxed paper. Freeze 2 to 3 hours or until firm enough to slice.

3. Preheat oven to 350°F. Cut rolls in ¼-inch slices. Place slices 1 inch apart on parchment-lined cookie sheets. Bake 9 to 10 minutes or just until cookies are firm. Transfer to wire rack to cool completely.

SANTA'S CHOCOLATE AND VANILLA SANDWICH COOKIES

4. For large cookies, spread the flat sides of half the cookies wish 1 tablespoon Filling (2 teaspoons for small cookies). Top with unfrosted cookies, flat sides down. **MAKES 22 LARGE OR 30 SMALL SANDWICH COOKIES.**

PINK FILLING In small saucepan melt 2 ounces chopped white chocolate over medium-low heat; cool. Meanwhile, in large mixing bowl beat ¼ cup softened butter with electric mixer until creamy. Beat in 2 tablespoons raspberry preserves and 1 teaspoons vanilla. Gradually beat in 3⅓ cups powdered sugar and cooled white chocolate, adding whipping cream (1 to 3 tablespoons) until spreading consistency.

EACH LARGE COOKIE *194 cal, 8 g fat (4 g sat. fat), 29 mg chol, 92 mg sodium, 31 g carbo, 0 g fiber, 1 g pro. Daily Values: 5% vit. A, 1% calcium.*

KID-FRIENDLY
SANTA'S CHOCOLATE SANDWICH COOKIES

PREP: 45 MIN. FREEZE: 2 HRS. BAKE: 10 MIN. PER BATCH COOL: 10 MIN. OVEN: 350°F

½	cup butter, softened
1	cup granulated sugar
¾	cup packed brown sugar
⅓	cup unsweetened Dutch-process cocoa powder
½	tsp. baking soda
¼	tsp. salt
2	tsp. vanilla
1	egg
1½	cups all-purpose flour
1	recipe Pink Filling, *above*

1. In large mixing bowl beat butter and vanilla with an electric mixer on medium speed 30 seconds. Add sugars; beat until well combined. Add cocoa powder, baking soda, and salt; beat well. Add vanilla and egg; beat well. Beat in as much flour as you can with mixer. Stir in remaining flour.

2. Divide dough in three portions. Shape each portion in a 8-inch-long roll about 1½ inches in diameter. (For small cookies, shape dough in four 9-inch-long rolls about 1 inch in diameter.) Wrap in plastic wrap or waxed paper. Freeze 2 to 3 hours or until firm enough to slice.

3. Preheat oven to 350°F. Cut rolls in ¼-inch slices. Place slices 1 inch apart on parchment-lined cookie sheets. Bake 10 to 12 minutes or just until cookies are firm. Transfer to wire rack to cool completely.

4. For large cookies, spread the flat sides of half the cookies with 1 tablespoon Filling (2 teaspoons for small cookies). Top with unfrosted cookies, flat sides down. **MAKES 30 LARGE OR 38 SMALL SANDWICH COOKIES.**

EACH LARGE COOKIE *187 cal, 6 g fat (4 g sat. fat), 20 mg chol, 80 mg sodium, 33 g carbo, 0 g fiber, 1 g pro. Daily Values: 3% vit. A, 1% calcium, 3% iron.*

CHOCOLATE-RASPBERRY TASSIES

The raspberry flavor in these tarts comes from a little liqueur in the gooey filling. Substitute your favorite liqueur or flavored syrup, or leave it out all together.

PREP: 40 MIN. BAKE: 12 MIN. COOL: 10 MIN. OVEN: 375°F

1	recipe Chocolate Pastry
6	oz. dark chocolate, chopped (1 cup)
2	Tbsp. butter
1	egg, lightly beaten
⅓	cup granulated sugar
1	Tbsp. raspberry liqueur or raspberry-flavored syrup
2	tsp. vanilla
1	recipe Chocolate Buttercream (optional)

1. Prepare Chocolate Pastry. Preheat oven to 375°F. Shape pastry in 24 balls. Press each ball on bottoms and sides of 24 ungreased 1¾-inch muffin cups, using floured fingers if necessary; set aside.

2. For filling, in small saucepan heat and stir chocolate and butter over medium-low heat until melted and smooth. Remove from heat. Stir in egg, sugar, liqueur, and vanilla. Spoon 1 scant tablespoon filling in each pastry shell.

3. Bake 12 to 15 minutes or until pastry is firm and filling is puffed. Cool in pans 10 minutes. Run a sharp thin-blade knife around tart edges; carefully remove from pans. Cool on wire rack. Pipe or spoon on a small amount of Chocolate Buttercream.

4. Refrigerate frosted tarts in single layer in airtight container up to 3 days. Freeze unfrosted tarts up to 3 months; thaw and top with buttercream. **MAKES 24 TASSIES.**

CHOCOLATE PASTRY In food processor combine 1¼ cups all-purpose flour, ⅓ cup sugar, ¼ cup unsweetened cocoa powder, and dash of salt; pulse to combine. Add ½ cup cold butter, cut up. Cover; process until crumbly. In small bowl whisk together 1 egg yolk and 2 tablespoons cold water. Add egg mixture; pulse until dough ball forms, adding water if needed. If dough is sticky, cover and refrigerate until easy to handle.

CHOCOLATE BUTTERCREAM In medium mixing bowl beat ¼ cup softened butter with an electric mixer on medium-high speed for 30 seconds. Gradually beat in 1 cup powdered sugar and 3 tablespoons unsweetened cocoa powder. Beat in 2 tablespoons milk. Gradually beat in 1 cup powdered sugar until piping consistency.

EACH TASSIE *138 cal, 7 g fat (5 g sat. fat), 30 mg chol, 52 mg sodium, 16 g carbo, 1 g fiber, 2 g pro. Daily Values: 3% vit. A, 1% calcium, 4% iron.*

CHOCOLATE-
RASPBERRY
TASSIES

SHORTBREAD ICICLES

Strawberry preserves and pink peppercorns add zing to shortbread. Find them at penzeys.com.

PREP: 45 MIN. BAKE: 18 MIN. COOL: 10 MIN.
OVEN: 300°F

- 1 cup butter, softened
- ½ cup granulated sugar
- 2 Tbsp. strawberry preserves
- 1 tsp. vanilla
- ½ tsp. ground pink peppercorns or crushed red pepper flakes (optional)
- 2⅔ cups all-purpose flour
  Coarse decorating sugar (optional)
- 1 recipe Icing (optional)
  Silver or white nonpareils (optional)

1. Preheat oven to 300°F. Line baking sheets with parchment; set aside.
2. In mixing bowl beat butter on medium speed for 30 seconds. Add granulated sugar, preserves, vanilla, peppercorns, and ¼ teaspoon *salt;* beat until well blended. Beat in as much flour as you can; stir in remaining flour by hand.
3. On lightly floured surface roll dough to ¼-inch thickness. Use 6- to 7-inch round scallop-edge or regular cutters or pans to cut dough, rerolling and cutting as needed. Transfer to prepared baking sheet, spacing 1 inch apart. Randomly cut rounds in wedges (do not separate). Lightly brush with *milk;* sprinkle with coarse sugar.
4. Bake 18 to 22 minutes or until centers are set and edges begin to brown. Remove baking sheets from oven; recut wedges. Transfer to wire racks to cool completely.
5. Ice cooled shortbread; sprinkle nonpareils. **MAKES 36 TO 48 WEDGES.**

ICING In bowl combine 2 cups powdered sugar, 1 tablespoon milk, and ½ teaspoon vanilla. Stir in additional milk for spreading consistency.

EACH WEDGE *93 cal, 5 g fat (3 g sat.fat), 14 mg chol, 53 mg sodium, 11 g carbo, 0 g fiber, 1 g pro. Daily Values: 3% vit. A, 2% iron.*

LEMON-GINGER
TEA COOKIES
Recipe on page 261

VANILLA
AND MOCHA
ANGEL WINGS

VANILLA AND MOCHA ANGEL WINGS

PREP: 30 MIN. **CHILL:** 30 MIN. **BAKE:** 12 MIN. PER BATCH **COOL:** 11 MIN. **OVEN:** 400°F

- 1 cup butter, softened
- ½ cup powdered sugar
- 2 tsp. vanilla bean paste or 4 tsp. vanilla
- ¼ tsp. salt
- 2⅓ cups all-purpose flour
- ½ cup toasted, finely chopped pine nuts (optional)
  Powdered sugar

1. Line baking sheets with parchment paper; set aside.
2. In a large mixing bowl beat butter with an electric mixer on medium to high speed for 30 seconds. Add ½ cup powdered sugar, the vanilla bean paste or vanilla, and salt; beat until well combined. Beat in as much flour as you can with mixer. Stir in any remaining flour and pine nuts. Refrigerate dough 30 minutes or until easy to handle.
3. Preheat oven to 400°F. Shape dough in 1-inch balls. Roll balls in 2½-inch ropes, then pinch into crescents. Place 2 inches apart on prepared baking sheets.
4. Bake for 12 to 13 minutes or until bottoms are golden brown. Cool 1 minute on baking sheet. Transfer to wire racks to cool completely. Roll cooled cookies in additional powdered sugar or dust lightly with powdered sugar.
MAKES 3½ TO 4 DOZEN COOKIES.

MOCHA CRESCENTS Prepare as above, except increase powdered sugar to ¾ cup. Reduce flour to 1⅔ cups and add ⅔ cup unsweetened cocoa powder and 1 tablespoon instant espresso powder or instant coffee crystals with the flour. Bake cookies for 8 to 9 minutes or until bottoms are browned. Dust cooled cookies lightly with additional unsweetened cocoa powder.
EACH COOKIE *71 cal., 4 g total fat (3 g sat. fat), 12 mg chol., 45 mg sodium, 7 g carb., 0 g fiber, 1 g pro. Daily Values: 3% vit. A, 2% iron.*

LEMON-GINGER TEA COOKIES

Loose tea provides just the right mix of bright flavor and spice in these cookies. Crush any large tea leaves.

PREP: 30 MIN. **CHILL:** 1 HR. **BAKE:** 10 MIN. **COOL:** 12 MIN. **OVEN:** 350°F

- ½ cup shortening
- 1 Tbsp. grated fresh ginger or finely chopped crystallized ginger
- 1 Tbsp. vanilla bean paste or vanilla extract
- 2 tsp. honey-lemon-ginseng flavor green tea*
- 1 tsp. finely shredded lemon peel
- 1 cup packed brown sugar
- 2 tsp. ground ginger
- 1 tsp. baking powder
- ½ tsp. baking soda
- ¼ tsp. salt
- 2 eggs
- 2½ cups all-purpose flour
  Granulated sugar
- 1 recipe Powdered Sugar Glaze
  Toppings: coconut, powdered sugar, white nonpareils

1. In large mixing bowl beat shortening, fresh ginger, vanilla, tea, and lemon peel on medium speed until fluffy. Add brown sugar; beat until combined. Beat in ground ginger, baking powder, baking soda, and salt. Beat in eggs. Beat in as much of the flour as you can; stir in remaining flour by hand. Refrigerate dough 1 hour or until easy to handle.
2. Preheat oven to 350°F. Shape dough in 1-inch balls. Roll in granulated sugar and place on ungreased baking sheets.
3. Bake for 10 minutes or until lightly browned. Cool 2 minutes on baking sheets. Transfer to wire racks to cool completely. Dip in Powdered Sugar Glaze and toppings; let stand on waxed paper to dry.
MAKES 4 DOZEN COOKIES.

POWDERED SUGAR GLAZE In medium bowl combine 1 cup powdered sugar and about 4 teaspoons water; stir to reach a thick drizzling consistency.
*NOTE Cut open tea bag to release the loose tea. Do not brew the tea.
EACH COOKIE *75 cal., 2 g fat (1 g sat. fat), 9 mg chol., 35 mg sodium, 11 g carbo, 0 g fiber, 1 g pro. Daily Values: 1% calcium, 2% iron.*

LEMON MERINGUE TASSIES

PREP: 40 MIN. **BAKE:** 10 MIN. **OVEN:** 375°F

- ½ cup butter, softened
- 1 3-oz. pkg. cream cheese, softened
- 1 cup all-purpose flour
- 1 recipe Lemon Filling
- 1 recipe Meringue or Lemon Buttercream Frosting

1. Preheat oven to 375°F. In a mixing bowl beat the butter and cream cheese until combined. Stir in the flour. Press a rounded teaspoon of pastry into the bottoms and sides of 24 ungreased 1¾-inch muffin cups.
2. Bake 10 to 15 minutes or until lightly browned. Cool in pans on a wire rack for 5 minutes. Transfer to racks to cool completely. Fill with Lemon Filling and pipe Meringue Frosting on filling. Serve immediately. **MAKES 24 TASSIES.**

LEMON FILLING In a medium saucepan combine ¾ cup sugar, 2 tablespoons all-purpose flour, 1 to 2 teaspoons finely shredded lemon peel, ¼ cup lemon juice, ¼ cup water, and ⅛ teaspoon salt. Whisk in 1 slightly beaten egg. Cook and stir over medium heat until thickened. Cool completely.
MERINGUE FROSTING In a small mixing bowl combine ¼ cup sugar, 2 tablespoons water, 1 tablespoon pasteurized liquid egg whites or 1 teaspoon meringue powder; ½ teaspoon vanilla, and ⅛ teaspoon cream of tartar. Beat at high speed until frosting holds soft peaks. Makes 1¼ cups frosting.
LEMON BUTTERCREAM FROSTING In a large mixing bowl beat ¼ cup butter with an electric mixer on medium speed for 30 seconds. Slowly add 1½ cups powdered sugar, beating well. Add 2 tablespoons milk and 1 teaspoon lemon juice. Gradually beat in an additional 1½ cups powdered sugar and enough milk (1 to 2 tablespoons) to reach spreading consistency.
STORAGE Unfilled tarts may be made ahead and stored up to 3 days at room temperature. Filling may be made 1 day ahead, covered, and refrigerated.
EACH TART *104 cal, 5 g fat (3 g sat. fat), 23 mg chol, 55 mg sodium, 13 g carbo, 0 g fiber, 1 g pro. Daily Values: 3% vit. A, 2% vit. C, 1% calcium, 2% iron.*

LEMON MERINGUE TASSIES

What's Cooking
from cookbook author Diane Morgan
Holiday Dinner

ROAST LOIN OF PORK
STUFFED WITH
DRIED APRICOTS AND PLUMS

SPINACH, PEAR, AND SHAVED PARMESAN SALAD

ROAST LOIN OF PORK STUFFED WITH DRIED APRICOTS AND PLUMS

"To stuff fruit to the center of the pork, use your fingers or the handle of a long wooden spoon to gently pack it in."

PREP: 25 MIN. ROAST: 80 MIN. STAND: 15 MIN. OVEN: 350°F

1	2½ lb. boneless pork top loin roast (single loin)
12	to 14 dried apricots
12	to 14 dried pitted plums (prunes)
¼	cup Dijon-style mustard
¼	tsp. garlic powder
¼	tsp. freshly ground pepper
2	carrots, cut in 1-inch chunks
2	stalks celery, cut in 1-inch chunks
1	yellow onion, cut in 1-inch chunks
1	cup dry white wine or reduced-sodium chicken broth
	Fresh herbs (optional)

1. Heat oven to 350°F. Stand roast on one end. Insert a 1-inch-wide long-blade knife through center of roast.* Stuff and pack the opening, alternating apricots and plums.

2. In a small bowl combine mustard, garlic powder, and pepper; rub all sides of meat with mustard mixture.

3. Place vegetables in 13×9×2-inch baking pan; place roast on vegetables. Pour wine over roast. Pour 2 tablespoon *water* in pan.

4. Roast, uncovered, 80 to 90 minutes or until instant-read thermometer inserted in meat (not touching fruit) registers 150°F. Transfer roast to warm platter. Reserve vegetables for another use. Cover roast with foil; let stand 15 minutes. Meat temperature after standing should reach 160°F. To serve, slice roast and sprinkle herbs. **MAKES 8 SERVINGS.**

*****TIP** If necessary, cut an opening in each side; stuff half the fruit from each side.

EACH SERVING *359 cal, 16 g fat (6 g sat. fat), 75 mg chol, 251 mg sodium, 17 g carbo, 2 g fiber, 26 g pro. Daily Values: 57% vit. A, 4% vit. C, 3% calcium, 8% iron.*

SPINACH, PEAR, AND SHAVED PARMESAN SALAD

"Have the cheese at room temperature and use a serrated vegetable peeler or the thin blade on a box grater to make the shavings."

START TO FINISH: 20 MIN.

8	cups fresh baby spinach
2	Bosc pears, quartered lengthwise, cored, and thinly sliced
2	oz. Parmesan or Parmigiano-Reggiano cheese, shaved
2	Tbsp. balsamic vinegar
1	Tbsp. whole grain mustard
½	cup extra virgin olive oil

1. In large bowl combine spinach and pears. Top with cheese. For dressing, in medium bowl whisk together vinegar, mustard, 1 teaspoon each *sugar* and *salt,* and ¼ teaspoon freshly ground *black pepper.* Slowly whisk in oil until well combined. Drizzle some on salad; pass remaining.

MAKES 8 SERVINGS.

MAKE AHEAD Up to 2 hours before assembling salad, shave the cheese, wrap it in plastic wrap, and store at room temperature.

EACH SERVING *200 cal, 16 g fat (3 g sat. fat), 6 mg chol, 474 mg sodium, 11 g carbo, 3 g fiber, 4 g pro. Daily Values: 74% vit. A, 30% vit. C, 14% calcium, 11% iron.*

holiday menu

Roast Loin of Pork Stuffed with Dried Apricots and Plums
Spinach, Pear, and Shaved Parmesan Salad
Parmesan Potatoes au Gratin
Sautéed Green Beans with Shallot Crisps
Eggnog Cheesecake with Candied Kumquats

PARMESAN POTATOES
AU GRATIN

SAUTÉED GREEN BEANS WITH SHALLOT CRISPS

PREP: 20 MIN. COOK: 14 MIN.

⅓	cup cooking oil
5	to 6 shallots, thinly sliced (½ cup)
2	lb. green beans, trimmed
1	Tbsp. butter
1	Tbsp. olive oil
	Salt and freshly ground black pepper

1. In 6-inch skillet heat oil over medium-high heat.* Using a slotted spoon, add half the shallots. Fry 3 to 4 minutes, until crisp and dark golden brown. Remove from oil; drain on double thickness of paper towels. Cook remaining shallots. Set aside.

2. Meanwhile, in large pot cook beans, covered, in enough boiling water to cover for 6 to 8 minutes or until crisp-tender. Drain and submerse in ice water to cool quickly; drain well.

3. Heat a 12-inch skillet over medium-high heat. Add butter and oil, swirling to coat skillet. Add beans. Cook about 5 minutes, stirring frequently, until beans are heated through. Season to taste with salt and pepper. Transfer to a serving bowl and top with shallot crisps. **MAKES 8 SERVINGS.**

***TIP** Test oil by adding 1 shallot slice to oil. When oil sizzles without spattering and shallot is golden, the oil is ready.

MAKE AHEAD Shallots may be prepared up to 2 hours ahead.

EACH SERVING *100 cal, 7 g fat (2 g sat. fat), 4 mg chol, 18 mg sodium, 10 g carbo, 4 g fiber, 2 g pro. Daily Values: 19% vit. A, 32% vit. C, 5% calcium, 7% iron.*

SAUTÉED GREEN BEANS
WITH SHALLOT CRISPS

PARMESAN POTATOES AU GRATIN

PREP: 40 MIN. BAKE: 1 HR. 35 MIN.
STAND: 10 MIN. OVEN: 350°F

3	cups whipping cream
1	large clove garlic, minced
2	Tbsp. butter, softened
4	lb. red potatoes, peeled, thinly sliced
4	oz. Parmigiano-Reggiano or Parmesan cheese, grated
2	Tbsp. minced fresh thyme
¼	tsp. freshly grated nutmeg
¼	tsp. freshly ground white pepper
	Toppings: Shaved Parmigiano-Reggiano or Parmesan cheese, fresh Italian (flat-leaf) parsley sprigs, and/or freeze-dried or dried tomato slices (optional)

1. Preheat oven to 350°F. In medium saucepan combine cream and garlic; bring just to a simmer over medium heat. Simmer, uncovered, 5 minutes (do not boil). Remove from heat; let stand.

2. Generously butter a 3- to 3½-quart au gratin or baking dish. Layer one-third of potato slices in dish. In small bowl combine grated cheese, thyme, 1 teaspoon *salt*, nutmeg, and pepper. Sprinkle one-third of cheese mixture. Repeat layers twice. Cover with foil.

3. Bake 1¼ to 1½ hours, until potatoes are almost tender and liquid mostly absorbed. Uncover; bake 20 to 30 minutes, until liquid is absorbed and potatoes are browned and moist. If dish is broiler-safe, broil 3 to 4 inches from heat for 2 to 3 minutes, until top is crisp and brown. Let stand 10 minutes. **MAKES 8 SERVINGS.**

EACH SERVING *382 cal, 27 g fat (17 g sat. fat), 96 mg chol, 384 mg sodium, 29 g carbo, 2 g fiber, 8 g pro. Daily Values: 20% vit. A, 40% vit. C, 16% calcium, 8% iron.*

EGGNOG CHEESECAKE WITH CANDIED KUMQUATS

This cheesecake can be made up to 3 days in advance. Cover and store in the refrigerator.

PREP: 30 MIN. BAKE: 50 MIN. STAND: 40 MIN.
COOL: 1 HR. 45 MIN. CHILL: 6 HRS.
OVEN: 375°F/350°F

5	Tbsp. butter, melted
1¼	cups whole-grain nugget cereal (such as Grape Nuts)
⅓	cup granulated sugar
¼	tsp. ground cinnamon
	Dash kosher or sea salt
3	8-oz. pkg. cream cheese, softened
1	cup granulated sugar
4	eggs, lightly beaten
1	Tbsp. pure vanilla
1	cup eggnog
1	Tbsp. bourbon
1	Tbsp. dark rum
1	Tbsp. brandy
1	recipe Candied Kumquats (optional)

1. Preheat oven to 375°F. Butter a 9- or 10-inch springform pan with 1 tablespoon of the butter; set aside.

2. In food processor bowl process cereal about 2 minutes, until a fine crumb forms. Add the ⅓ cup sugar, the cinnamon, and salt; process to combine. With processor running, add remaining butter through feed tube until combined. Press crumb mixture on bottom and 1 inch up sides of pan. Bake 10 to 12 minutes or until crisp and lightly browned. Cool on wire rack. Reduce oven temperature to 350°F.

3. In clean food processor bowl,* process cream cheese until smooth. Add 1 cup sugar until combined. Add eggs; process until creamy, scraping down sides once or twice. Add vanilla, eggnog, bourbon, rum, and brandy; process until combined.

4. Gently pour filling into baked crust. Bake 40 minutes or until sides are slightly puffed (center will be soft). Turn off oven and leave door ajar. Let cheesecake stand in oven for 40 minutes.

5. Transfer to wire rack; cool 15 minutes. Using a small thin knife, loosen crust from sides of springform pan. Cool 30 minutes. Remove sides from pan; cool 1 hour. Cover and refrigerate 6 hours or overnight. To serve, top with Candied Kumquats.
*Cheesecake filling may be prepared with electric mixer, beating on medium speed.
MAKES 12 SERVINGS.

EACH SERVING CHEESECAKE *435 cal, 28 g fat (16 g sat. fat), 156 mg chol, 321 mg sodium, 37 g carbo, 1 g fiber, 8 g pro. Daily Values: 20% vit. A, 1% vit. C, 4% calcium, 21% iron.*

CANDIED KUMQUATS Using a paring knife and piercing only the skin, cut four evenly spaced slits in each of 12 kumquats. Place kumquats in medium saucepan; add cold water to cover. Bring to a simmer over medium heat; cook 5 minutes. Drain. In medium saucepan stir to dissolve 1½ cups sugar in ¾ cup water; add kumquats. Bring to a simmer over medium heat. Reduce to low simmer. Cook, uncovered, 30 minutes, until glazed. Using a slotted spoon remove fruit from syrup. Place kumquats on wire rack over 15×10×1-inch pan. Cool 10 minutes. Place 1 cup sugar in small bowl. Roll kumquats in sugar and place 1 inch apart on rack. Let stand overnight. Store in airtight container in cool, dry place up to 3 months. Kumquats may be sliced before topping the cheesecake.

Everyday Easy

Fresh, time-saving meals

FAST | **LOW FAT**

GINGER SHRIMP AND RICE

START TO FINISH: 15 MIN.
BUDGET $3.81 PER SERVING

1	small bunch green onions
1	1-inch piece fresh ginger
1	Tbsp. olive oil
¼	cup water
1	Tbsp. soy sauce
2	8.8-oz. pkg. cooked long grain rice
1	lb. peeled and deveined cooked medium shrimp
¼	cup mango chutney

1. Slice green onions. Set aside ¼ cup of the onions to sprinkle on finished dish. Peel the ginger. Finely grate ginger using the smallest openings in a box or flat grater.
2. In a 12-inch skillet cook remaining green onions and grated ginger in hot oil for 1 to 2 minutes or until tender. Add water and soy sauce. Cover and bring to boiling. Add rice and shrimp. Cook until most of the liquid is absorbed and shrimp are heated through. Divide among four shallow bowls. Top with chutney and reserved green onions. **MAKES 4 SERVINGS.**
EACH SERVING *393 cal, 8 g fat (1 g sat. fat), 172 mg chol, 577 mg sodium, 53 g carbo, 3 g fiber, 27 g pro. Daily Values: 14% vit. A, 19% vit. C, 8% calcium, 20% iron.*

FAST

SAVORY FOCACCIA PIE

START TO FINISH: 22 MIN.
BUDGET $2.97 PER SERVING

¾	cup oil-packed dried tomato halves with Italian herbs (3 oz.)
1	12-inch round rosemary or garlic focaccia
8	oz. bulk Italian sausage
1	4-oz. pkg. baby spinach (4 cups)
2	oz. goat cheese (chèvre) or feta cheese

1. Preheat oven to 250°F. Drain tomatoes, reserving oil. Place focaccia on large baking sheet and brush with 2 teaspoons of the oil. Cut in 8 wedges. Arrange wedges in circle. Place in oven to warm.
2. Meanwhile, in a 12-inch skillet cook sausage over medium-high heat, breaking up with a wooden spoon. Drain sausage in a colander, reserving 2 teaspoons drippings in skillet. Cook spinach in drippings just until wilted.
3. Set oven to Broil. Top warmed focaccia with sausage, spinach, dried tomatoes, and cheese. Broil 4 to 5 inches from heat for 3 to 5 minutes or until cheese is softened and toppings are heated through. If desired, drizzle wedges with additional oil from tomatoes. **MAKES 4 SERVINGS.**
EACH SERVING *548 cal, 29 g fat (10 g sat. fat), 64 mg chol, 1,006 mg sodium, 55 g carbo, 2 g fiber, 22 g pro. Daily Values: 46% vit. A, 24% vit. C, 16% calcium, 16% iron.*

GINGER SHRIMP AND RICE

SAVORY
FOCACCIA PIE

PAPAYA AND COCONUT
CHICKEN SALAD

FAST
PAPAYA AND COCONUT CHICKEN SALAD

START TO FINISH: 30 MIN.
BUDGET $3.21 PER SERVING

1	lb. skinless, boneless chicken breast halves
1½	cups flaked coconut
1	medium papaya (12 oz.)
¼	cup cider vinegar
¼	cup vegetable oil
1	Tbsp. honey
	Dash cayenne pepper
1	5-oz. pkg. mixed salad greens
¾	cup blueberries

1. Preheat oven to 450°F. Line a baking sheet with foil; set aside. Cut chicken in strips; season with ½ teaspoon *salt*. Place coconut in shallow dish. Roll chicken in coconut to coat, pressing lightly to adhere. Transfer to prepared baking sheet. Bake 12 minutes or until coconut is golden and chicken is no longer pink.
2. Meanwhile, peel, seed, and cut papaya in cubes. For dressing, place ¼ cup papaya cubes in blender or food processor; add vinegar, oil, honey, ¼ teaspoon *salt*, and cayenne. Process until smooth. Toss ¼ cup dressing with greens; divide among four plates.
3. Top greens with chicken, remaining papaya, and blueberries. Pass remaining dressing. **MAKES 4 SERVINGS.**

EACH SERVING *526 cal, 30 g fat (15 g sat. fat), 66 mg chol, 639 mg sodium, 35 g carbo, 6 g fiber, 30 g pro. Daily Values: 27% vit. A, 90% vit. C, 5% calcium, 7% iron.*

CIRCLES AND SQUARES VEGETABLE PASTA SOUP

COWBOY STEAK TACOS

FAST LOW FAT
CIRCLES AND SQUARES VEGETABLE PASTA SOUP

START TO FINISH: 25 MIN.
BUDGET $2.09 PER SERVING

1	32-oz. box vegetable broth
1	cup medium-size pasta
2	cups frozen diced hash brown potatoes with onions and peppers
2	cups frozen peas and carrots
1	14.5-oz. can diced tomatoes with green chiles
	Snipped fresh parsley (optional)

1. In a large covered saucepan bring broth to boiling. Add pasta, potatoes, peas and carrots, and undrained diced tomatoes. Return to boiling. Reduce heat and simmer, covered, for 10 to 15 minutes or until pasta is tender.
2. Ladle soup into bowls. Sprinkle parsley. **MAKES 4 SERVINGS.**

EACH SERVING *171 cal, 0 g fat, 0 mg chol, 1,372 mg sodium, 36 g carbo, 6 g fiber, 7 g pro. Daily Values: 149% vit. A, 33% vit. C, 5% calcium, 11% iron.*

FAST
COWBOY STEAK TACOS

START TO FINISH: 30 MIN.
BUDGET $2.56 PER SERVING

1	lb. beef breakfast steaks (thinly sliced eye of round)
¼	tsp. salt
1	cup strong coffee
2	Tbsp. ketchup
2	tsp. chili powder
2	tsp. vegetable oil
1	small red onion, thinly sliced
1	red or green sweet pepper, thinly sliced
12	6-inch tortillas (flour, corn, or whole wheat)
¾	cup prepared corn relish
	Fresh cilantro leaves (optional)

1. Thinly slice steaks. Sprinkle steaks with salt; set aside. For sauce, in bowl whisk together coffee, ketchup, and chili powder.
2. In 12-inch skillet heat oil over medium-high heat; add steaks. Cook and stir 2 to 3 minutes or until brown on all sides. Add sauce, onion, and sweet pepper. Cook 6 to 8 minutes or until vegetables are tender.
3. Meanwhile, wrap tortillas in paper towels. Warm in microwave on high (100% power) for 30 seconds. Spoon steak and vegetable mixture on tortillas. Top with corn relish and sprinkle cilantro. **MAKES 4 SERVINGS.**

EACH SERVING *596 cal, 20 g fat (6 g sat. fat), 74 mg chol, 1,169 mg sodium, 71 g carbo, 4 g fiber, 32 g pro. Daily Values: 28% vit. A, 69% vit. C, 16% calcium, 29% iron.*

prize tested recipes®

Each year readers offer their creative best with award-winning recipes. This collection also features honor roll recipes that are too good not to share.

288

290

302

CARAMEL APPLE UPSIDE-DOWN
CORNMEAL CAKE
Recipe on page 310

Deborah Gelman, STATEN ISLAND, NY

FAST
SMOKED TURKEY SALAD WITH ORANGES
START TO FINISH: 30 MIN.

1	5-oz. pkg. arugula or baby spinach
12	oz. smoked turkey or duck breast, sliced
1	medium red sweet pepper, cut in strips (1 cup)
¼	cup fresh cilantro
½	cup peanut oil or canola oil
¼	cup orange juice
¼	cup honey
3	Tbsp. lemon juice
1	Tbsp. Dijon-style mustard
1	tsp. ground cumin
¼	tsp. salt
¼	tsp. ground black pepper
4	oranges, peeled and sectioned

1. In a large bowl toss together arugula, sliced turkey, sweet pepper strips, and cilantro.

2. For orange vinaigrette, in a screw-top jar combine oil, orange juice, honey, lemon juice, mustard, cumin, salt, and pepper. Cover and shake well. Drizzle desired amount of vinaigrette over salad; toss gently to coat. To serve, add orange sections to salad. Cover and refrigerate any remaining vinaigrette up to 2 weeks.
MAKES 4 SERVINGS.

EACH SERVING *242 cal, 8 g fat (1 g sat. fat), 37 mg chol, 1,092 mg sodium, 25 g carbo, 5 g fiber, 19 g pro. Daily Values: 46% vit. A, 210% vit. C, 13% calcium, 12% iron.*

LOW FAT
ORANGE, MINT, AND ASPARAGUS PASTA SALAD
PREP: 25 MIN. CHILL: 1 HR.

8	oz. dried campanelle or other medium-size pasta
1	lb. fresh asparagus spears, bias-sliced in 1-inch pieces
½	cup thinly sliced green onions (4)
⅓	cup chopped fresh mint
⅓	cup crumbled feta cheese
3	large navel, Cara Cara, or blood oranges
2	Tbsp. olive oil
1	Tbsp. white wine vinegar or cider vinegar
½	tsp. salt
¼	tsp. ground black pepper

1. Cook pasta according to package directions; add asparagus the last 2 minutes of cooking. Drain; rinse with cold water. Drain; transfer pasta and asparagus to large serving bowl. Add green onions, mint, and feta cheese to pasta mixture. Remove peel and white pith from two of the oranges. Halve oranges lengthwise, then slice crosswise. Add to pasta mixture.

2. For dressing, from remaining orange finely shred 2 teaspoons peel. In a screw-top jar squeeze 2 tablespoons orange juice. Add orange peel, olive oil, vinegar, salt, and pepper. Cover and shake. Pour over pasta mixture; toss to combine. Cover; refrigerate 1 hour.
MAKES 10 TO 12 SERVINGS.

EACH SERVING *145 cal, 4 g fat (1 g sat. fat), 4 mg chol, 175 mg sodium, 22 g carbo, 2 g fiber, 5 g pro. Daily Values: 8% vit. A, 34% vit. C, 6% calcium, 12% iron.*

Mary Ann Dell, PHOENIXVILLE, PA

ELEGANT BOW TIE SALAD

PREP: 25 MIN. CHILL: 2 HRS.

- 8 oz. bow tie pasta
- 2 grapefruit or 3 oranges
- 1 avocado, halved, seeded, peeled, and chopped
- 1 3.5-oz. (drained weight) pitted ripe olives, drained and halved
- ⅓ cup fresh lime juice
- 3 Tbsp. vinegar
- 2 Tbsp. olive oil
- 2 Tbsp. honey
- 2 Tbsp. finely chopped onion
- 1 tsp. salt
- ½ tsp. dried parsley
- ¼ tsp. dried basil, crushed
- ⅛ tsp. dried oregano, crushed
- ⅛ tsp. ground black pepper
- 2 oz. crumbled feta cheese

1. Cook pasta according to package directions; drain and rinse with cold water. **2.** Meanwhile, peel and section grapefruit. In a large bowl combine grapefruit, avocado, and olives. Add pasta; set aside. **3.** In a small bowl combine lime juice, vinegar, oil, honey, onion, salt, parsley, basil, oregano, and pepper; whisk to combine. Pour over pasta mixture; toss to coat. Cover and chill at least 2 hours or up to 24 hours. Sprinkle with feta cheese before serving. **MAKES 8 SERVINGS.**

EACH SERVING *237 cal, 9 g fat (2 g sat. fat), 6 mg chol, 482 mg sodium, 34 g carbo, 3 g fiber, 6 g pro. Daily Values: 14% vit. A, 45% vit. C, 7% calcium, 9% iron.*

SPICED PEARS WITH LEMON GINGER CREAM

PREP: 15 MIN. COOK: 18 MIN.

- 1 Tbsp. finely shredded lemon peel
- ¼ cup lemon juice
- 4 firm pears, peeled, cored, and halved
- 1½ cups apple cider
- ¼ tsp. ground nutmeg
- 4 whole cloves
- 1 cup whipping cream
- 2 Tbsp. maple syrup or maple-flavored syrup
- ¼ tsp. ground ginger
- ⅛ tsp. ground nutmeg

1. In a large skillet combine *half* of the peel and the lemon juice. Add pear halves, turning to coat. Add apple cider, ¼ teaspoon ground nutmeg, and whole cloves. Bring to boiling; reduce heat. Simmer, covered, about 10 minutes or until pears are tender. Use a slotted spoon to transfer pears to a serving dish. Simmer cooking liquid, uncovered, 8 minutes more or until reduced to ⅓ cup syrup. Discard whole cloves.

2. In a chilled mixing bowl beat whipping cream with electric mixer on medium speed until thickened. Add maple syrup, ginger, ⅛ teaspoon nutmeg, and remaining lemon peel; beat until soft peaks form.

3. To serve, spoon cooking liquid over pears in dessert bowls. Serve with whipped cream. **MAKES 4 SERVINGS.**

EACH SERVING *371 cal, 23 g fat (14 g sat. fat), 82 mg chol, 26 mg sodium, 37 g carbo, 5 g fiber, 2 g pro. Daily Values: 19% vit. A, 29% vit. C, 7% calcium, 4% iron.*

LOW FAT
DOUBLE GINGER LEMONADE

PREP: 15 MIN. STAND: 10 MIN. COOL: 2 HRS.

- 2 cups water
- 1 cup honey
- 2 tsp. freshly grated fresh ginger
- 2 12-oz. cans ginger ale, chilled
- 1 cup freshly squeezed lemon juice Ice cubes

1. In a medium saucepan bring water, honey, and ginger just to boiling, stirring occasionally; remove from heat. Cover and let steep for 10 minutes. Strain mixture through a fine-mesh sieve and discard ginger. Cool mixture to room temperature. Transfer mixture to a pitcher. Stir in the ginger ale and lemon juice. Serve in a glass over ice.

MAKES 6 SERVINGS.

EACH SERVING *219 cal, 0 g fat, 0 mg chol, 13 mg sodium, 60 g carbo, 0 g fiber, 0 g pro. Daily Values: 32% vit. C, 1% calcium, 2% iron.*

FAST LOW FAT
BLOOD ORANGE AND TOASTED ALMOND COUSCOUS

START TO FINISH: 12 MIN.

- 2 cups orange juice
- 1 Tbsp. butter
- ½ tsp. salt
- ½ tsp. ground cardamom
- 1 10-oz. pkg. couscous
- ½ cup dried cherries
- 2 large blood oranges, peeled, halved or quartered, and sliced
- ½ cup slivered almonds, toasted
- 1 tsp. finely shredded lime peel

1. In a large saucepan combine orange juice, butter, salt, and cardamom. Bring to boiling. Stir in couscous and cherries. Remove from heat; cover and let stand 5 minutes.

2. Stir in oranges, almonds, and lime peel. Serve warm. **MAKES 8 SERVINGS.**

EACH SERVING *402 cal, 5 g fat (1 g sat. fat), 4 mg chol, 167 mg sodium, 77 g carbo, 6 g fiber, 11 g pro. Daily Values: 8% vit. A, 91% vit. C, 7% calcium, 7% iron.*

COUSCOUS SALAD WITH ORANGE-LEMON DRESSING

PREP: 30 MIN. COOK: 12 MIN.
CHILL: UP TO 8 HRS.

- 1⅓ cups Israeli-style couscous (8 oz.)
- 1 Tbsp. canola oil
- 2¼ cups water
- ¾ cup dried cranberries
- 2 11-oz. cans mandarin orange sections, drained
- 1 recipe Orange-Lemon Dressing
- 1 cup pecans, toasted and chopped

1. In a medium saucepan cook couscous in hot oil over medium heat for 5 minutes or until couscous is lightly toasted, stirring occasionally. Carefully add water. Bring to boiling; reduce heat. Simmer, covered, about 12 minutes or until most of the liquid is absorbed and the couscous is tender. Drain if necessary. Cool to room temperature.

2. In a large bowl combine couscous and cranberries. Add mandarin oranges; toss to combine. Drizzle with Orange-Lemon Dressing; toss to coat. Serve immediately or cover and chill up to 8 hours. Stir in pecans just before serving.

MAKES 8 TO 10 SERVINGS.

ORANGE-LEMON DRESSING: In a small bowl whisk together ¼ cup white vinegar, 3 tablespoons snipped fresh mint, 2 tablespoons honey, 1 teaspoon finely shredded orange peel, 2 tablespoons orange juice, 1 teaspoon finely shredded lemon peel, 2 tablespoons lemon juice, 1 tablespoon snipped fresh chives, 1 tablespoon canola oil, ½ teaspoon salt, and ¼ teaspoon ground black pepper.

EACH SERVING *296 cal, 13 g fat (1 g sat. fat), 0 mg chol, 153 mg sodium, 42 g carbo, 4 g fiber, 4 g pro. Daily Values: 14% vit. A, 53% vit. C, 3% calcium, 8% iron.*

Party Appetizers and Nibbles

ANTIPASTO PINWHEELS

PREP: 15 MIN. STAND: 30 MIN. CHILL: 30 MIN.

- 12   thin slices provolone cheese (6 to 7 oz.)
- ½   cup Gorgonzola cheese, softened (2 oz.)
- 1   Tbsp. milk
- 12   thin slices sopressata or premium Genoa salami (4 oz.)
- 12   large fresh basil leaves
       Assorted crackers or flatbread (optional)

1. Let provolone cheese stand at room temperature for 30 minutes. Meanwhile, in a small bowl combine Gorgonzola and milk.

2. To make one of two rolls, on waxed paper slightly overlap 6 slices of provolone to form a rectangle. Top with 6 slices of salami and 6 basil leaves. Dollop half the Gorgonzola mixture on the basil leaves. Roll, beginning from the short side of the rectangle, using the waxed paper to lift and roll. Wrap roll in waxed paper or plastic wrap and place, seam side down, on a platter. Repeat to make second roll. Refrigerate wrapped rolls at least 30 minutes and up to overnight. Cut rolls in ½-inch slices. Serve with crackers or flatbread.

MAKES 10 (2-SLICE) SERVINGS.

EACH SERVING *122 cal, 10 g fat (5 g sat. fat), 28 mg chol, 426 mg sodium, 1 g carbo, 0 g fiber, 8 g pro. Daily Values: 6% vit. A, 16% calcium, 2% iron.*

FAST

CHÈVRE-FIG SPREAD

START TO FINISH: 25 MIN.

- ¾   cup snipped dried figs
- ¾   cup crumbled goat cheese (chèvre) (3 oz.)
- ½   cup light sour cream
- 3   Tbsp. snipped fresh basil
- 2   Tbsp. milk
- 1   Tbsp. snipped fresh thyme
       Salt
       Ground black pepper
- ½   cup chopped walnuts, toasted
       Fresh thyme sprigs (optional)
       Toasted baguette slices or crackers

1. In a small bowl pour boiling water over figs to cover; let stand 15 minutes. Drain.

2. Meanwhile, in a medium bowl stir together chèvre, sour cream, basil, milk, and thyme. Season to taste with salt and pepper. Stir in drained figs and half the walnuts. Cover and refrigerate up to 24 hours.

3. To serve, transfer spread to serving bowl. Sprinkle with remaining walnuts and fresh thyme sprigs. Serve with baguette slices or crackers. **MAKES ABOUT 1½ CUPS (TWELVE 2-TABLESPOON SERVINGS).**

EACH SERVING *100 cal, 7 g fat (3 g sat. fat), 10 mg chol, 45 mg sodium, 8 g carbo, 1 g fiber, 4 g pro. Daily Values: 4% vit. A, 1% vit. C, 10% calcium, 3% iron.*

FAST

ENDIVE SATAY BITES

START TO FINISH: 30 MIN.

1   2- to 2½-lb. purchased roasted chicken
⅔   cup bottled peanut sauce
2   Tbsp. lime juice
1   Tbsp. packed brown sugar
¼   cup snipped fresh cilantro
¼   cup honey-roasted peanuts, chopped
3   to 4 heads Belgian endive, separated into leaves (about 30)
     Fresh cilantro (optional)

1. Remove skin and bones from chicken; discard skin and bones. Chop chicken (you should have 3 cups). Place chopped chicken in a medium bowl; set aside.
2. In a large bowl combine peanut sauce, lime juice, brown sugar, snipped cilantro, and peanuts. Stir in chicken. Spoon mixture onto endive leaves. Garnish with additional sprigs of cilantro.
MAKES ABOUT 30 APPETIZERS.

EACH APPETIZER *77 cal, 5 g fat (1 g sat. fat), 27 mg chol, 310 mg sodium, 3 g carbo, 0 g fiber, 6 g pro. Daily Values: 1% vit. A, 3% vit. C, 1% calcium, 3% iron.*

SMOKED SALMON TOASTS

PREP: 20 MIN. BAKE: 14 MIN. OVEN: 325°F

8   slices pumpernickel bread
2   Tbsp. butter, melted
1   8-oz. pkg. cream cheese, softened
1   Tbsp. lemon juice
1   4-oz. piece smoked salmon, flaked, with skin and bones removed
1   3.5-oz. jar capers, drained
1   hard-cooked egg, chopped
¼   cup finely chopped red onion
     Dill sprigs

1. Preheat oven to 325°F. Remove crusts from bread slices. Flatten bread slices with a rolling pin. Cut each slice into four pieces. Brush each bread piece, on both sides, with melted butter. Press each bread piece into a 1¾-inch muffin cup. Bake for 14 minutes. Remove toast cups immediately from muffin cups and place on a wire rack to cool.
2. In a medium mixing bowl stir together cream cheese and lemon juice. Fold in salmon, capers, egg, and onion until combined. Spoon heaping tablespoons of mixture into toast cups. Serve at once or chill for 1 to 2 hours. Garnish with dill sprigs. **MAKES 32 APPETIZERS.**

EACH APPETIZER *59 cal, 4 g fat (2 g sat. fat), 17 mg chol, 201 mg sodium, 4 g carbo, 1 g fiber, 2 g pro. Daily Values: 3% vit. A, 1% vit. C, 1% calcium, 2% iron.*

MEDITERRANEAN CHICKEN PINWHEELS

PREP: 45 MIN. BAKE: 25 MIN. COOL: 15 MIN.
OVEN: 400°F

4   skinless, boneless chicken breast halves (about 1½ lb.)
     Ground black pepper
4   oz. sliced prosciutto
3   oz. goat cheese (chèvre), crumbled
¼   cup snipped fresh basil
¼   cup oil-packed dried tomatoes, drained and chopped
2   Tbsp. pine nuts, toasted and chopped
1   Tbsp. olive oil
⅔   cup Italian-style panko (Japanese-style bread crumbs)
     Pitted olives, drained
     marinated artichoke hearts,
     crackers, and/or toasted baguette
     slices (optional)
1   recipe Seasoned Mayonnaise

1. Preheat oven to 400°F. Place chicken breast halves between plastic wrap. Pound with the flat side of a meat mallet to about ¼ inch thickness. Remove top sheet of plastic wrap. Sprinkle chicken lightly with pepper. Place chicken narrow side toward you. Divide prosciutto among breast halves to within ½ inch of edges. Sprinkle with goat cheese, basil, tomatoes, and pine nuts. Roll up from a narrow side; secure with wooden toothpicks.
2. Brush chicken rolls with oil. Place bread crumbs in a shallow dish. Coat chicken rolls with bread crumbs; place in a 9×2-inch square pan. Bake, uncovered, 25 to 30 minutes or until cooked through (170° F). Cool 15 minutes. Cut in ½-inch-slices.
3. Serve pinwheels with olives, artichoke hearts, crackers, and/or baguette slices and Seasoned Mayonnaise.
MAKES ABOUT 20 APPETIZER SERVINGS.

SEASONED MAYONNAISE In a medium bowl stir together ½ cup mayonnaise, 1 teaspoon lemon or lime juice, and 2 cloves garlic, minced. Cover and chill.
EACH SERVING *137 cal, 8 g fat (2 g sat. fat), 29 mg chol, 392 mg sodium, 4 g carbo, 1 g fiber, 12 g pro. Daily Values: 3% vit. A, 4% vit. C, 2% calcium, 4% iron.*

TOMATILLO SALSA

PREP: 25 MIN. CHILL: 1 HR.

3   medium tomatillos, peeled and chopped
2   plum tomatoes, seeded, and chopped
2   medium oranges, peeled, seeded, and chopped
1   avocado, halved, seeded, peeled, and chopped
2   Tbsp. chopped fresh cilantro
2   Tbsp. lime juice
1   small jalapeño pepper,* halved, seeded, and finely chopped
1   Tbsp. extra virgin olive oil
1   clove garlic, minced
½   tsp. salt
¼   tsp. freshly ground black pepper
     Corn chips or tortilla chips

1. In a medium bowl stir together the tomatillos, tomatoes, oranges, avocado, cilantro, lime juice, jalapeño pepper, oil, garlic, salt, and black pepper. Cover and chill for 1 to 4 hours. Stir before serving. Serve with corn chips or tortilla chips.
MAKES 3 CUPS SALSA (SIXTEEN 2-TABLESPOON SERVINGS).
*NOTE Hot chile peppers contain volatile oils that can burn your skin and eyes. When working with them, wear plastic or rubber gloves.
EACH SERVING *193 cal, 11 g fat (1 g sat. fat), 0 mg chol, 274 mg sodium, 23 g carbo, 2 g pro. Daily Values: 5% vit. A, 29% vit. C, 6% calcium, 3% iron.*

CRANBERRY SPREAD

PREP: 10 MIN. STAND: 1 HR.

2   Tbsp. orange juice
2   Tbsp. amaretto or orange juice
½   cup dried cranberries
1   8-oz. pkg. cream cheese, softened
3   Tbsp. butter, softened
1   tsp. finely shredded orange peel
     Gingersnaps and/or crackers

1. In a small bowl combine orange juice and amaretto. Stir in dried cranberries. Cover and let stand for 1 hour. Drain and reserve liquid.
2. In medium bowl beat together cream cheese and butter until fluffy. Stir in cranberries, orange peel, and enough of the reserved liquid to make spreading consistency. Serve with gingersnaps and/or crackers. **MAKES ABOUT 1½ CUPS (TWELVE 2-TABLESPOON SERVINGS).**
EACH SERVING *114 cal, 10 g fat (6 g sat. fat), 28 mg chol, 77 mg sodium, 5 g carbo, 0 g fiber, 1 g pro. Daily Values: 7% vit. A, 3% vit. C, 2% calcium, 1% iron.*

Winter Vegetables

Debbie Reid, CLEARWATER, FL

CURRIED BUTTERNUT SQUASH SOUP

PREP: 25 MIN. COOK: 40 MIN.

1	medium onion, chopped (½ cup)
3	Tbsp. butter
2	tsp. red curry powder or curry powder
2	tsp. grated fresh ginger
½	tsp. salt
1	14-oz. can reduced-sodium chicken broth
1¼	cups water
1½	lb. butternut squash, peeled, seeded, and cut in 1-inch cubes (4 cups)
1	14-oz. can unsweetened coconut milk
½	cup half-and-half or light cream
⅓	cup chopped fresh cilantro
	Fresh cilantro (optional)

1. In a large saucepan cook onion in hot butter over medium heat 10 minutes or until tender and translucent. Stir in curry powder, ginger, and salt. Cook 30 seconds more.

2. Stir in chicken broth and water; bring to boiling. Add squash. Return to boiling; reduce heat. Simmer, covered, 40 minutes or until squash is tender.

3. Cool soup slightly. Transfer half the soup at a time to a blender or food processor. Blend or process until smooth. Return all soup to saucepan. Stir in coconut milk, half-and-half, and chopped cilantro. Heat through. Top with fresh cilantro. **MAKES 6 SIDE-DISH SERVINGS.**

EACH SERVING *237 cal, 9 g fat (2 g sat. fat), 6 mg chol, 482 mg sodium, 34 g carbo, 3 g fiber, 6 g pro. Daily Values: 213% vit. A, 46% vit. C, 9% calcium, 12% iron.*

Sheila Suhan, SCOTTDALE, PA

SWEET POTATOES WITH PECANS AND BLUE CHEESE

PREP: 30 MIN. ROAST: 30 MIN. OVEN: 375°F

2	large sweet potatoes, peeled and cut lengthwise in thin wedges (1½ lb.)
1	small sweet onion, cut in 1-inch pieces (⅓ cup)
4	Tbsp. olive oil
1	Tbsp. butter
⅓	cup pecan pieces
1	Tbsp. packed light brown sugar
4	tsp. cider vinegar
1½	tsp. honey
1	clove garlic, minced (½ tsp.)
2	Tbsp. crumbled blue cheese or finely shredded white cheddar cheese

1. Preheat oven to 375°F. In a 15×10×1-inch baking pan combine sweet potatoes and onion pieces. Drizzle with 2 tablespoons of the olive oil; sprinkle ½ teaspoon *salt* and ¼ teaspoon *pepper*. Toss gently to combine. Spread in a single layer. Bake for 30 to 35 minutes or until vegetables are tender, stirring once.

2. Meanwhile, in small skillet melt butter over medium heat. Stir in pecan pieces, brown sugar, and ¼ teaspoon *salt*. Cook and stir for 2 to 3 minutes or until pecans are coated in the brown sugar mixture. Remove from heat; spread on foil and let stand to cool completely.

3. For dressing, in a small bowl whisk together the vinegar, honey, garlic, ¼ teaspoon *salt*, and ¼ teaspoon *pepper*. Slowly whisk in remaining 2 tablespoons of the olive oil until combined. Whisk in 1 tablespoon of the blue cheese.

4. To serve, transfer potatoes and onions to serving plate. Drizzle with dressing. Sprinkle pecans and remaining blue cheese. **MAKES 6 SIDE-DISH SERVINGS.**

EACH SERVING *241 cal, 16 g fat (3 g sat. fat), 7 mg chol, 487 mg sodium, 23 g carbo, 3 g fiber, 63g pro. Daily Values: 210% vit. A, 5% vit. C, 5% calcium, 5% iron.*

FAST

CAULIFLOWER AND BROCCOLI PANCAKES

PREP: 25 MIN. COOK: 2 MIN. PER BATCH

1	cup chopped broccoli
1	cup chopped cauliflower
1¼	cups all-purpose flour
⅓	cup yellow cornmeal
¼	cup grated Parmesan cheese
2	tsp. baking powder
½	tsp. baking soda
¼	tsp. salt
1	egg, lightly beaten
1½	cups buttermilk or sour milk
3	Tbsp. cooking oil
1	recipe Lemon-Chive Sour Cream

1. In a medium saucepan cook broccoli and cauliflower in boiling salted water for 2 minutes; drain well.

2. In a large bowl stir together flour, cornmeal, Parmesan, baking powder, baking soda, and salt. In another bowl use a fork to combine egg, buttermilk, and oil. Add egg mixture all at once to flour mixture. Stir just until moistened (batter should be slightly lumpy). Stir in broccoli and cauliflower.

3. For each pancake, pour about ¼ cup batter onto a hot, lightly greased griddle or heavy skillet, spreading batter if necessary. Cook over medium heat for 1 to 2 minutes on each side or until pancakes are golden brown, turning to second side when pancakes have bubbly surfaces and edges are slightly dry. (For appetizer-size pancakes, use about 1 tablespoon batter. Cook as directed above.) Serve warm with Lemon-Chive Sour Cream.

MAKES 16 PANCAKES.

LEMON-CHIVE SOUR CREAM In a medium bowl combine one 8-ounce carton sour cream, 2 tablespoons snipped fresh chives, 1 teaspoon finely shredded lemon peel. Season to taste with salt and black pepper.

EACH PANCAKE *120 cal, 7 g fat (3 g sat. fat), 21 mg chol, 174 mg sodium, 12 g carbo, 1 g fiber, 4 g pro. Daily Values: 4% vit. A, 15% vit. C, 7% calcium, 3% iron.*

WINTER SQUASH AND SWEET POTATO PASTA

PREP: 30 MIN. BAKE: 30 MIN. OVEN: 375°F

1	medium winter squash, peeled, seeded, and diced (3 cups)
2	medium sweet potatoes, peeled and diced (3 cups)
2	Tbsp. olive oil
12	oz. dried penne pasta (4 cups)
1	15-oz. carton part-skim ricotta cheese
¾	cup grated Parmesan cheese
1¼	cups milk
1	Tbsp. dried Italian seasoning, crushed
¼	tsp. salt
¼	tsp. ground black pepper

1. Preheat oven to 375°F. Toss squash and sweet potatoes with oil. Spread in a 15×10×1-inch baking pan. Bake about 30 minutes or until tender.

2. Meanwhile, cook pasta according to package directions; drain. Return pasta to pan.

3. In a medium mixing bowl combine ricotta cheese, ½ cup of the Parmesan cheese, milk, Italian seasoning, salt, and pepper. Stir baked squash mixture and cheese mixture into the pasta. Cook and stir over low heat until heated through. Sprinkle with remaining Parmesan cheese. Serve immediately.

MAKES 6 MAIN DISH SERVINGS.

EACH SERVING *475 cal, 15 g fat (7 g sat. fat), 35 mg chol, 389 mg sodium, 63 g carbo, 4 g fiber, 22 g pro. Daily Values: 147% vit. A, 14% vit. C, 41% calcium, 18% iron.*

BUTTERNUT SQUASH GRATIN

PREP: 30 MIN. COOK: 20 MIN. BAKE: 20 MIN. OVEN: 375°F

3	oz. pancetta or bacon, chopped
3½	lb. butternut squash, peeled, seeded, and chopped (8 cups)
1	large onion, chopped
½	tsp. salt
¼	tsp. ground black pepper
1	5- to 6-oz. pkg. fresh baby spinach
2	Tbsp. butter
2	Tbsp. all-purpose flour
1⅓	cups half-and-half or whole milk
8	oz. Gruyère cheese, shredded (2 cups)
	Nonstick cooking spray

1. Preheat oven to 375°F. In a 12-inch large skillet cook pancetta over medium heat until crisp. Remove pancetta from skillet with a slotted spoon and drain on paper towels. If using bacon, drain all but 2 tablespoons drippings from the skillet.

2. Add squash, onion, salt, and pepper to the skillet. Cook, covered, stirring occasionally, for 12 to 15 minutes or until tender. Remove from skillet.

3. Add spinach to the skillet; cook and stir until spinach is wilted. Drain spinach in a colander, squeezing out as much excess liquid as possible.

4. For cheese sauce, in a small saucepan melt butter. Stir in flour until combined. Add half-and-half all at once. Cook and stir over medium heat until thickened and bubbly. Stir in 1½ cups of the cheese until melted.

5. Lightly coat a 3-quart rectangular baking dish with nonstick cooking spray. In a large bowl combine squash, spinach, and pancetta. Add cheese sauce; toss to coat. Transfer to prepared dish. Sprinkle with remaining ½ cup cheese. Bake, uncovered, for 20 minutes or until heated through. MAKES 12 SIDE-DISH SERVINGS.

EACH SERVING *217 cal, 14 g fat (7 g sat. fat), 41 mg chol, 329 mg sodium, 17 g carbo, 3 g fiber, 9 g pro. Daily Values: 265% vit. A, 46% vit. C, 29% calcium, 7% iron.*

LOW FAT

CHEESY BBQ POTATOES

PREP: 20 MIN. COOK: 6 HRS. (LOW) OR 3 HRS. (HIGH)

1½	lb. sweet potatoes, peeled
1½	lb. russet potatoes, peeled
2	medium onions
1	Tbsp. barbecue seasoning or spice
1	10.75-oz. can condensed cheddar cheese soup
¼	cup bottled barbecue sauce

1. Using the slicing blade of a food processor, thinly slice potatoes and onions. (Or use a knife or mandoline to thinly slice potatoes and onions.) In a large bowl toss potato mixture with barbecue seasoning. In a medium bowl combine soup and barbecue sauce; stir into potato mixture.

2. Line a 4- to 6-quart slow cooker with a slow cooker liner. Spoon in potato mixture. Cover and cook on low-heat setting for 6 to 8 hours or on high-heat setting for 3 to 3½ hours.

MAKES 8 TO 10 SERVINGS.

EACH SERVING *200 cal, 2 g fat (1 g sat. fat), 3 mg chol, 701 mg sodium, 43 g carbo, 5 g fiber, 4 g pro. Daily Values: 251% vit. A, 17% vit. C, 6% calcium, 5% iron.*

Angela Huse, EATONTOWN, NJ

LOW FAT

SLOW-COOKED MOROCCAN CHICKEN

PREP: 20 MIN. **COOK:** 8 HRS. (LOW) OR 4 HRS. (HIGH)

1	medium onion, coarsely chopped (½ cup)
8	oz. baby carrots with tops, trimmed, or baby carrots, halved lengthwise if large
½	cup pitted dried plums (prunes)
1	14-oz. can reduced-sodium chicken broth
8	bone-in chicken thighs, skinned
1¼	tsp. curry powder
½	tsp. salt
½	tsp. ground cinnamon

1. In a 4- to 5-quart slow cooker combine onion and carrots. Add plums and broth. Top with chicken. In a small bowl combine curry powder, salt, and cinnamon. Sprinkle over chicken.

2. Cover and cook on low-heat setting for 8 to 10 hours or on high-heat setting for 4 to 5 hours. Remove chicken, fruit, and vegetables from cooker with a slotted spoon. Spoon some of the cooking juices on each serving. **MAKES 4 SERVINGS.**

EACH SERVING *255 cal, 6 g fat (1 g sat. fat), 115 mg chol, 691 mg sodium, 22 g carbo, 4 g fiber, 30 g pro. Daily Values: 162% vit. A, 6% vit. C, 5% calcium, 13% iron.*

LOW FAT

GREEK LAMB WITH SPINACH AND ARTICHOKES

PREP: 25 MIN. **COOK:** 8 HRS. (LOW) OR 4 HRS. (HIGH)

2	to 2½ lb. boneless lamb shoulder roast
1	19-oz. can cannellini beans (white kidney beans), rinsed and drained
1	14.5-oz. can diced tomatoes
1	Tbsp. minced garlic (6 cloves)
½	tsp. salt
½	tsp. dried oregano, crushed
1	14-oz. can artichoke hearts, drained and quartered
3	cups fresh baby spinach
3	cups hot cooked orzo (6 oz. uncooked)
	Crumbled feta cheese (optional)

1. Trim fat from meat. Cut meat in 1-inch pieces. In a 3½- or 4-quart slow cooker stir together meat, beans, undrained tomatoes, garlic, salt, and oregano.

2. Cover and cook on low-heat setting for 8 to 10 hours or on high-heat setting for 4 to 5 hours. Stir in drained artichoke hearts and spinach.

3. To serve, spoon lamb mixture over hot cooked orzo. Sprinkle with crumbled feta cheese. **MAKES 6 SERVINGS.**

EACH SERVING *432 cal, 11 g fat (4 g sat. fat), 100 mg chol, 905 mg sodium, 43 g carbo, 9 g fiber, 41 g pro. Daily Values: 36% vit. A, 19% vit. C, 12% calcium, 38% iron.*

Marie Rizzio, INTERLOCHEN, MI

LOW FAT

PORK CHOPS WITH SWEET ONION SAUCE

PREP: 20 MIN. COOK: 6 HRS. (LOW) OR
3 HRS. (HIGH)

2	medium onions, thinly sliced and separated into rings
6	boneless pork loin chops, cut 1 inch thick (about 2¾ lb.)
¾	cup ketchup
¼	cup grape jelly
2	Tbsp. quick-cooking tapioca, crushed
2	Tbsp. red wine vinegar
1	tsp. dried Italian seasoning, crushed
¼	tsp. salt
¼	tsp. ground black pepper
1	24-oz. pkg. frozen potatoes for steaming and mashing

1. Place onion in a 3½- or 4-quart slow cooker. Arrange pork chops in cooker, overlapping as necessary. In a medium bowl combine ketchup, jelly, tapioca, vinegar, Italian seasoning, salt, and pepper; pour over chops. Cover and cook on low-heat setting for 6 to 7 hours or on high-heat setting for 3 to 3½ hours.
2. Meanwhile, prepare potatoes according to package directions. Serve chops and sauce with potatoes. **MAKES 6 SERVINGS.**
EACH SERVING *458 cal, 9 g fat (3 g sat. fat), 131 mg chol, 854 mg sodium, 44 g carbo, 3 g fiber, 47 g pro. Daily Values: 6% vit. A, 28% vit. C, 5% calcium, 15% iron.*

ASIAN-STYLE BARBECUE RIBS

PREP: 15 MIN. COOK: 6 HRS. (LOW) OR
3 HRS. (HIGH)

3	lb. pork loin back ribs, cut into 2- to 3-rib portions
½	cup plum jelly or jam
⅓	cup soy sauce
¼	cup packed brown sugar
¼	cup chopped green onions
2	Tbsp. molasses
2	cloves garlic, minced
2	tsp. ground ginger
2	Tbsp. cornstarch
2	Tbsp. cold water
	Hot cooked rice

1. Place ribs in a 3½- or 4-quart slow cooker.
2. In a small bowl whisk together plum jelly, soy sauce, brown sugar, green onions, molasses, garlic, and ginger. Pour jelly mixture over ribs in cooker.
3. Cover and cook on low-heat setting for 6 to 7 hours or on high-heat setting for 3 to 3½ hours. Remove ribs from cooker with a slotted spoon.
4. Pour cooking juices into a measuring cup; skim off fat. Strain into a small saucepan. In a small bowl whisk together cornstarch and cold water. Stir cornstarch mixture into cooking juices. Bring to boiling. Cook and stir until thickened and bubbly. Cook and stir 2 minutes more. Serve ribs with sauce over hot cooked rice.
MAKES 4 SERVINGS.
EACH SERVING *819 cal, 50 g fat (18 g sat. fat), 171 mg chol, 1,533 mg sodium, 57 g carbo, 1 g fiber, 36 g pro. Daily Values: 2% vit. A, 3% vit. C, 11% calcium, 18% iron.*

NUEVO LATINO SHORT RIBS

PREP: 25 MIN. COOK: 8 HRS. (LOW) OR
4 HRS. (HIGH) PLUS 30 MIN.

4	lb. boneless beef short ribs
¾	cup orange juice
¼	cup maple syrup
1	1.25-oz. pkg. savory chipotle gravy mix for steak
½	cup bottled mango salsa
1	Tbsp. smoked paprika
2	medium mangoes, seeded, peeled, and cut into ¾-inch pieces
	Hot cooked rice (optional)
	Snipped fresh cilantro

1. Trim fat from ribs. Place ribs on the rack of an unheated broiler pan. Broil 4 to 5 inches from heat for 10 to 12 minutes or until browned on all sides, turning occasionally. Drain fat from ribs and place ribs in a 4- to 5-quart slow cooker. In a medium bowl combine orange juice, maple syrup, and gravy mix. Pour over ribs in cooker.
2. Cover and cook on low-heat setting for 8 to 9 hours or on high-heat setting for 4 to 4½ hours. In a small bowl combine salsa and paprika. Add to cooker and top with mangoes. Cover and cook 30 minutes more. Serve ribs and sauce with hot cooked rice and sprinkle with cilantro.
MAKES 6 SERVINGS.
EACH SERVING *607 cal, 26 g fat (11 g sat. fat), 172 mg chol, 543 mg sodium, 31 g carbo, 2 g fiber, 58 g pro. Daily Values: 25% vit. A, 62% vit. C, 5% calcium, 40% iron.*

ITALIAN BEEF SANDWICHES

PREP: 20 MIN. COOK: 10 HRS. (LOW) OR
5 HRS. (HIGH) STAND: 15 MIN.

1	3-lb. boneless beef chuck pot roast, trimmed of fat
1	15-oz. can tomato sauce with Italian seasonings
2	medium green sweet peppers, sliced
2	medium onions, sliced
1	12- to 16-oz. jar pepperoncini salad peppers, drained and stems removed
1	0.65-oz. envelope cheese-garlic dry salad dressing mix
12	crusty sandwich rolls, split and toasted
1	8-oz. pkg. shredded Italian-blend cheeses

1. Place beef in a 5- to 6-quart slow cooker. Pour tomato sauce over roast. Top with green peppers, onions, and pepperoncini peppers. Sprinkle with dressing mix. Cover and cook on low-heat setting for 10 to 12 hours or on high-heat setting for 5 to 6 hours.
2. Remove beef to a cutting board. Using two forks, shred beef. Return shredded beef to slow cooker. Let stand in juices for 15 minutes. Remove beef and vegetables from cooker with a slotted spoon; reserve juices. Spoon about ½ cup beef mixture on each roll; top with cheese and roll top. Serve reserved juices with sandwiches for dipping.
MAKES 12 SANDWICHES.
EACH SERVING *486 cal, 27 g fat (11 g sat. fat), 88 mg chol, 1,292 mg sodium, 29 g carbo, 2 g fiber, 31 g pro. Daily Values: 8% vit. A, 35% vit. C, 22% calcium, 20% iron.*

LOW FAT

BRACIOLE

PREP: 20 MIN. COOK: 5 HOURS (LOW)

½	cup chopped onion
1	Tbsp. butter
⅔	cup Burgundy or reduced-sodium beef broth
⅓	cup water
1¼	cups herb-seasoned stuffing mix
1½	lb. beef cubed steaks (2 or 3 steaks)
2	cups chopped carrots and/or celery
1	10.75-oz. can condensed golden mushroom soup
¾	cup mushroom pasta sauce
	Hot cooked pasta

1. In a large skillet cook onion in hot butter over medium heat for 5 minutes or until tender. Add 2 tablespoons of the wine and 2 tablespoons of the water. Bring to boiling. Remove from heat and stir in stuffing mix.
2. Spread stuffing mixture on top of steaks. Roll up steaks, starting from a narrow side. Secure with wooden toothpicks. Place in a 3½- or 4-quart slow cooker.
3. In a medium bowl combine carrots, soup, pasta sauce, and remaining wine and water. Pour over meat in slow cooker. Cover and cook on low-heat setting for 5 to 6 hours. Remove toothpicks; cut meat in six serving portions. Serve meat and sauce over hot cooked pasta. **MAKES 6 SERVINGS.**
EACH SERVING *430 cal, 11 g fat (4 g sat. fat), 76 mg chol, 750 mg sodium, 44 g carbo, 4 g fiber, 32 g pro. Daily Values: 147% vit. A, 8% vit. C, 5% calcium, 26% iron.*

Down-to-Earth Classics

Maggie Brudnok, NEWBERG, OR

LOW FAT

PORK ROAST AND VEGETABLE STEW

PREP: 45 MIN. COOK: 1½ HRS.

2	lb. boneless pork shoulder roast
1	Tbsp. olive oil
1	Tbsp. butter
2	stalks celery, chopped
1	large onion, chopped
1	Tbsp. dried chives
1	tsp. dried parsley, crushed
1	tsp. dried basil, crushed
½	tsp. dried dill weed
½	tsp. ground black pepper
1	26-oz. jar traditional pasta sauce
1	14.5-oz. can diced tomatoes, undrained
2	cups frozen whole kernel corn
1	cup packaged peeled fresh baby carrots, halved lengthwise
3	medium Yukon gold potatoes, peeled, if desired, and cut in 1-inch pieces

1. Trim fat from pork; discard fat. Cut pork in 1- to 2-inch pieces.

2. In a 4- to 5-quart Dutch oven cook pork, half at a time, in hot oil over medium-high heat until browned, stirring occasionally. Remove from pan. Add butter to pan. Add celery, onion, chives, parsley, basil, dill weed, and pepper; cook for 8 to 10 minutes or until vegetables are tender, stirring occasionally.

3. Add pasta sauce, undrained tomatoes, corn, carrots, potatoes, and browned pork to onion mixture. Bring to boiling; reduce heat. Simmer, covered, about 1½ hours or until meat and vegetables are tender, stirring occasionally. Season to taste with *salt.* **MAKES 8 (1⅓-CUP) SERVINGS.**

EACH SERVING *363 cal, 12 g fat (4 g sat. fat), 72 mg chol, 532 mg sodium, 40 g carbo, 6 g fiber, 26 g pro. Daily Values: 70% vit. A, 26% vit. C, 8% calcium, 17% iron.*

TURKEY SALISBURY STEAKS WITH WHITE BEAN MASH

START TO FINISH: 35 MIN.

1	lb. uncooked ground turkey
1	envelope beef-flavored onion soup mix (half of a 2.2-oz. pkg.)
2	Tbsp. Worcestershire sauce
2	tsp. olive oil
1	clove garlic, minced
1	Tbsp. butter
2	cups sliced fresh mushrooms
½	cup reduced-sodium chicken broth
¼	cup dry red wine or reduced-sodium chicken broth
¼	cup tomato paste
1	recipe White Bean Mash (optional) Fresh thyme leaves (optional)

1. In a bowl Combine turkey, 2 tablespoons soup mix, and 1 tablespoon Worcestershire sauce; mix well. Shape in 4 oval patties about ½ inch thick.

2. In skillet cook patties in hot oil over medium-high heat for 3 minutes or until browned; turning once. Remove; set aside. In hot skillet cook garlic in butter 30 seconds. Add mushrooms. Cook and stir 5 minutes or until tender. Add broth, wine, tomato paste, remaining soup mix, and Worcestershire sauce. Stir, scraping up browned bits. Return patties to skillet; spoon sauce over. Cover; cook over medium-low heat for 8 minutes or until patties are 160°F. Serve with White Bean Mash; sprinkle with thyme. **MAKES 4 SERVINGS.**

WHITE BEAN MASH In saucepan cook 2 cloves minced garlic in 2 tablespoons hot olive oil 1 minute. Stir in two 15-ounce cans white beans, rinsed and drained; coarsely mash. Add chicken broth to moisten beans. Add ½ teaspoon crushed dried thyme and 1 teaspoon lemon juice. Season to taste; heat through. Drizzle with olive oil.

EACH SERVING *285 cal, 15 g fat (5 g sat. fat), 97 mg chol, 1,008 mg sodium, 12 g carbo, 1 g fiber, 23 g pro. Daily Values: 7% vit. A, 10% vit. C, 3% calcium, 15% iron.*

Deepa Tuli, WESTBURY, NY

CHICKEN PASTA CASSEROLE

PREP: 30 MIN. BAKE: 35 MIN. OVEN: 350°F

8	oz. dried bow tie pasta
2	Tbsp. olive oil
1	Tbsp. minced garlic (6 cloves)
1	lb. skinless, boneless chicken breast halves, cut into 1-inch pieces
1	tsp. dried basil, crushed
½	tsp. salt
¼	tsp. ground black pepper
1	medium onion, chopped
1	small red sweet pepper, chopped
1	cup frozen cut asparagus
1	8-oz. tub cream cheese spread with chive and onion
¾	cup half-and-half, light cream, or milk
½	cup panko (Japanese-style bread crumbs)
¼	cup sliced almonds
1	Tbsp. butter, melted

1. Preheat oven to 350°F. Cook pasta according to package directions; drain. Return pasta to pan.
2. Meanwhile, in a large skillet heat oil; add garlic and cook for 30 seconds. Season chicken with basil, salt, and pepper. Add chicken to the skillet; cook 3 minutes or until no pink remains. Remove from skillet. Add onion and sweet pepper to skillet; cook until tender. Stir in asparagus and cooked chicken. Remove from heat and set aside.
3. Stir cheese into pasta until melted. Stir in chicken mixture and cream. Transfer to a 2-quart rectangular baking dish. In a small bowl combine bread crumbs, almonds, and butter; sprinkle over casserole.
4. Bake, uncovered, for 35 minutes or until heated through. **MAKES 5 OR 6 SERVINGS.**

EACH SERVING *615 cal, 31 g fat (16 g sat. fat), 116 mg chol, 531 mg sodium, 48 g carbo, 4 g fiber, 33 g pro. Daily Values: 36% vit. A, 71% vit. C, 15% calcium, 13% iron.*

KID-FRIENDLY
SKILLET TUNA AND NOODLES

PREP: 20 MIN. COOK: 10 MIN.

2	cups dried rotini pasta (5½ oz.)
2	Tbsp. butter
½	cup soft bread crumbs
1	Tbsp. olive oil
½	cup chopped onion
½	cup chopped green sweet pepper
⅓	cup chopped celery
1	tsp. dried herbes de Provence
½	tsp. salt
1¼	cups half-and-half or light cream
1	12-oz. can chunk white tuna (water pack), drained
2	Tbsp. dry white wine (optional)

1. Cook pasta according to package directions; drain.
2. Meanwhile, in a large skillet melt 1 tablespoon of the butter over medium heat; stir in bread crumbs to coat. Cook over medium heat 3 minutes or until lightly browned, stirring occasionally. Remove from skillet and set aside.
3. In the same skillet heat olive oil and remaining butter. Add onion, sweet pepper, celery, dried herbs, and salt. Cook over medium heat for 4 to 5 minutes or until vegetables are tender, stirring occasionally. Add half-and-half; heat just until bubbly. Reduce heat and simmer, uncovered, about 5 minutes or until slightly thickened, stirring occasionally. Add cooked pasta, tuna, and wine. Heat through. Just before serving, sprinkle toasted bread crumbs over the top. **MAKES 4 SERVINGS.**

EACH SERVING *451 cal, 21 g fat (10 g sat. fat), 79 mg chol, 725 mg sodium, 36 g carbo, 2 g fiber, 28 g pro. Daily Values: 11% vit. A, 29% vit. C, 12% calcium, 13% iron.*

ZESTY APRICOT BEEF STEW

PREP: 30 MIN. COOK: 1½ HRS.

1	Tbsp. olive oil
1	lb. 1-inch cubes beef stew meat
1	medium onion, cut in thin wedges (½ cup)
1	large clove garlic, minced
1	14-oz. can beef broth
1	cup dry red wine or cranberry juice
1½	cups water
½	cup dried apricot halves
2	Tbsp. Dijon-style mustard
1½	tsp. dried thyme, crushed
¼	tsp. ground black pepper
3	large carrots, sliced (2 cups)
⅓	cup water
3	Tbsp. all-purpose flour
1	Tbsp. snipped fresh Italian (flat-leaf) parsley
3	cups dried medium noodles, cooked and drained

1. In a 4-quart Dutch oven heat oil over medium heat. Brown meat in hot oil. Add onion; cook 4 minutes more or until just tender. Add garlic; cook and stir 1 minute more. Add broth, wine, 1½ cups water, apricot halves, mustard, thyme, and pepper. Bring to boiling; reduce heat. Simmer, covered, for 1 hour, stirring occasionally.
2. Stir in carrots. Return to boiling; reduce heat. Simmer, covered, for 30 to 40 minutes more or until meat and carrots are tender, stirring occasionally.
3. In a small bowl whisk together ⅓ cup water and flour until smooth; stir into stew. Cook and stir until thickened and bubbly. Cook and stir 1 minute more.
4. Sprinkle with parsley and serve with noodles. **MAKES 4 TO 6 SERVINGS.**

EACH SERVING *448 cal, 10 g fat (3 g sat. fat), 74 mg chol, 693 mg sodium, 45 g carbo, 4 g fiber, 32 g pro. Daily Values: 218% vit. A, 11% vit. C, 7% calcium, 28% iron.*

SKILLET MEAT LOAF

PREP: 20 MIN. COOK: 41 MIN.

1	egg, lightly beaten
1½	cups soft bread crumbs (2 slices)
⅔	cup chopped green onions
¼	cup milk
2	tsp. Worcestershire sauce
½	tsp. salt
½	tsp. ground black pepper
⅛	tsp. garlic powder
1½	lb. (85%) lean ground beef
1	14-oz. can beef broth
½	tsp. ground sage
1	pound potatoes, cut into 2-inch pieces
1	1½-lb. butternut squash, peeled, seeded, and cut in 1-inch pieces

1. In a large bowl combine egg, bread crumbs, green onions, milk, Worcestershire sauce, salt, pepper, and garlic powder. Add ground meat and mix well. Divide in half. Shape each half in a 6×3-inch loaf.
2. Heat a large nonstick skillet over medium-high heat for 2 minutes; place meat loaves in skillet. Cook 4 minutes or until browned. Carefully turn with a large spatula; cook 2 minutes more. Add broth and sage to the skillet. Add potatoes and squash; bring to boiling. Reduce heat to medium-low. Cover and simmer about 35 minutes or until potatoes and squash are tender and the internal temperature of the meat loaves registers 160°F.
MAKES 8 SERVINGS.

EACH SERVING *310 cal, 14 g fat (5 g sat. fat), 85 mg chol, 476 mg sodium, 24 g carbo, 3 g fiber, 20 g pro. Daily Values: 155% vit. A, 47% vit. C, 9% calcium, 19% iron.*

Lillian Murphy, FLORAL PARK, NJ

LOADED OATMEAL COOKIES

PREP: 30 MIN. **BAKE:** 9 MIN. PER BATCH
OVEN: 350°F

¼	cup butter, softened
½	cup packed brown sugar
⅓	cup granulated sugar
1	tsp. ground cinnamon
½	tsp. baking soda
⅛	tsp. salt
1	egg
1	tsp. vanilla
¾	cup all-purpose flour
¾	cup rolled oats
¼	cup flax seed meal
¼	cup wheat germ
2	oz. dark chocolate, finely chopped
¼	cup dried cranberries
¼	cup chopped walnuts, toasted

1. Preheat oven to 350°F. In a large mixing bowl beat butter with an electric mixer on medium to high speed for 30 seconds. Add brown sugar, granulated sugar, cinnamon, baking soda, and salt. Beat until combined, scraping sides of bowl occasionally. Beat in egg and vanilla until combined. Beat in flour. Stir in rolled oats, flax seed meal, wheat germ, chocolate, cranberries, and walnuts (dough will be a little crumbly).
2. Drop dough by rounded teaspoons 2 inches apart onto ungreased cookie sheets. Bake for 9 to 11 minutes or until tops are lightly browned. Let cookies cool on cookie sheet for 1 minute. Transfer cookies to wire rack to cool.
MAKES ABOUT 30 COOKIES.
EACH COOKIE 79 cal, 4 g fat (2 g sat. fat), 11 mg chol, 45 mg sodium, 12 g carbo, 1 g fiber, 2 g pro. Daily Values: 1% vit. A, 1% calcium, 3% iron.

DOUBLE DARK CHOCOLATE COOKIES

PREP: 30 MIN. **BAKE:** 12 MIN. PER BATCH
OVEN: 350°F

¼	cup butter, softened
¼	cup canola oil
½	cup packed brown sugar
¼	cup granulated sugar
1	egg
1	tsp. vanilla
½	cup whole wheat pastry flour
½	cup all-purpose flour
¼	cup unsweetened cocoa powder
½	tsp. baking powder
⅛	tsp. salt
4	oz. bittersweet chocolate, chopped

1. Preheat oven to 350°F. Line cookie sheets with parchment paper. In a large mixing bowl beat butter with an electric mixer on medium speed for 30 seconds. Beat in oil, brown sugar, and granulated sugar until well combined. Beat in egg and vanilla until combined. In a medium bowl whisk together flours, cocoa powder, baking powder, and salt; beat into sugar mixture. Stir in chocolate.
2. Drop dough by slightly rounded teaspoons 2 inches apart onto prepared cookie sheets. Bake about 12 minutes or just until edges are set. Let cool 1 minute on cookie sheets. Transfer cookies to wire rack to cool. **MAKES ABOUT 36 COOKIES.**
EACH COOKIE 237 cal, 9 g fat (2 g sat. fat), 6 mg chol, 482 mg sodium, 34 g carbo, 3 g fiber, 6 g pro. Daily Values: 14% vit. A, 45% vit. C, 7% calcium, 9% iron.

Susan Jasin, SAN DIEGO, CA

PUMPKIN BLONDIES

PREP: 15 MIN. BAKE: 20 MIN. OVEN: 350°F

	Nonstick cooking spray
⅓	cup canola oil
3	Tbsp. butter, melted
1	Tbsp. molasses
1⅓	cups packed dark brown sugar
½	cup canned pumpkin
1	egg
1	egg white
1	tsp. vanilla
1	cup white whole wheat flour
½	cup unbleached all-purpose flour
1	Tbsp. flax seed meal
1½	tsp. baking powder
½	tsp. salt
½	tsp. ground cinnamon
¼	tsp. baking soda
¼	tsp. ground nutmeg
⅛	tsp. ground allspice
½	cup coarsely chopped walnuts

1. Preheat oven to 350°F. Coat a 13×9×2-inch baking pan with nonstick cooking spray; set aside.
2. In a large mixing bowl beat oil, butter, and molasses with an electric mixer on medium speed until combined. Add sugar and beat until smooth. Add pumpkin, beating until combined. Beat in egg, egg white, and vanilla until combined.
3. In a medium bowl combine flours, flaxseed meal, baking powder, salt, cinnamon, baking soda, nutmeg, and allspice. Add to sugar mixture, beating just until dry ingredients are moistened.
4. Spread batter in prepared pan. Sprinkle with walnuts. Bake for 20 to 22 minutes or until a wooden toothpick inserted near the center comes out clean. Cool completely in pan on a wire rack. Cut into squares. **MAKES 24 SQUARES.**

EACH SQUARE *137 cal, 6 g fat (1 g sat. fat), 13 mg chol, 104 mg sodium, 19 g carbo, 1 g fiber, 2 g pro. Daily Values: 5% vit. A, 4% calcium, 3% iron.*

SMART CHOCOLATE CHIP COOKIES

PREP: 30 MIN. BAKE: 9 MIN. PER BATCH OVEN: 375°F

1½	cups turbinado sugar
1	cup tub-style 60% to 70% vegetable oil spread
1	tsp. baking soda
¼	tsp. salt
1	egg
1	tsp. vanilla
½	cup finely shredded zucchini
¼	cup ground flaxseed meal
2	cups whole wheat flour
¾	cup all-purpose flour
1	cup semisweet chocolate pieces

1. Preheat oven to 375°F. In a large mixing bowl beat sugar, vegetable oil spread, baking soda, and salt with an electric mixer on medium speed until well combined, scraping sides of bowl as needed. Beat in egg and vanilla. Beat in zucchini and flaxseed meal. Beat in as much of the flours as you can with the mixer. Stir in any remaining flours and chocolate pieces.
2. Drop dough by rounded teaspoons 2 inches apart on ungreased cookie sheets. Bake for 9 to 11 minutes or until cookies are set and tops are lightly browned. Let cookies cool on cookie sheets for 1 minute. Transfer cookies to wire racks to cool. **MAKES ABOUT 48 COOKIES.**

TO STORE Layer cookies between sheets of waxed paper in an airtight container; cover. Freeze up to 3 months.

EACH COOKIE *95 cal, 4 g fat (2 g sat. fat), 4 mg chol, 71 mg sodium, 14 g carbo, 1 g fiber, 1 g pro. Daily Values: 3% vit. A, 2% iron.*

WHOLE WHEAT CARROT-RAISIN COOKIES

PREP: 30 MIN. BAKE: 8 MIN. PER BATCH OVEN: 375°F

½	cup butter, softened
1	cup packed brown sugar
2	tsp. baking soda
1	tsp. ground cinnamon
1	tsp. ground ginger
¼	tsp. salt
1	egg
¼	cup applesauce
1	tsp. vanilla
2	cups whole wheat flour
1	cup finely shredded carrots
¾	cup raisins
¾	cup finely chopped walnuts

1. Preheat oven to 375°F.
2. In a large mixing bowl beat butter with an electric mixer on medium speed for 30 seconds. Add brown sugar, baking soda, spices, and salt; beat until combined. Beat in egg, applesauce, and vanilla. Beat in as much of the flour as you can with the mixer. Stir in any remaining flour, carrots, raisins, and walnuts just until combined.
3. Drop by slightly rounded teaspoons 2 inches apart onto ungreased cookie sheets. Bake for 8 to 9 minutes or until edges are firm. Transfer cookies to a wire rack to cool. **MAKES ABOUT 36 COOKIES.**

EACH COOKIE *98 cal, 4 g fat (2 g sat. fat), 13 mg chol, 111 mg sodium, 14 g carbo, 1 g fiber, 2 g pro. Daily Values: 12% vit. A, 1% vit. C, 1% calcium, 3% iron.*

LEMON CHERRY OAT COOKIES

PREP: 25 MIN. BAKE: 8 MIN. PER BATCH OVEN: 375°F

½	cup 60% vegetable oil spread
¾	cup packed brown sugar
2	tsp. baking powder
¼	tsp. salt
2	egg whites, lightly beaten
1	tsp. vanilla
1	cup all-purpose flour
1¼	cups quick-cooking oats
¾	cup dried tart cherries, coarsely chopped
1	tsp. finely shredded lemon peel

1. Preheat oven to 375°F. In a large mixing bowl beat vegetable oil spread with an electric mixer on medium to high speed for 30 seconds. Add sugar, baking powder, and salt. Beat until fluffy. Add egg whites and vanilla. Beat until combined. Beat in as much of the flour as you can with the mixer. Stir in any remaining flour. Stir in oats, cherries, and lemon peel.
2. Drop dough by rounded teaspoons onto ungreased cookie sheets. Bake for 8 to 9 minutes or until edges are lightly browned. Cool on cookie sheets 1 minute. Transfer cookies to a wire rack to cool. **MAKES ABOUT 30 COOKIES.**

TO STORE Place cookies between sheets of waxed paper in an airtight container; cover. Store at room temperature for 3 days or freeze up to 3 months.

EACH COOKIE *84 cal, 3 g fat (0 g sat. fat), 0 mg chol, 80 mg sodium, 15 g carbo, 1 g fiber, 1 g pro. Daily Values: 1% vit. A, 3% calcium, 3% iron.*

Cupcakes

Suzanne Conrad, FINDLAY, OH

CREAM SODA-TOFFEE CUPCAKES

PREP: 25 MIN. BAKE: 18 MIN. COOL: 5 MIN.
OVEN: 350°F

2	cups all-purpose flour
1½	tsp. baking powder
½	tsp. baking soda
½	cup butter, softened
¾	cup granulated sugar
¼	cup packed brown sugar
3	eggs
1	Tbsp. molasses
1½	tsp. vanilla
½	cup buttermilk
½	cup cream soda (not diet)
¾	cup toffee pieces
1	recipe Brown Butter Frosting

1. Preheat oven to 350°F. Line eighteen 2½-inch muffin cups with paper bake cups; set aside. Combine flour, baking powder, baking soda, and ¼ teaspoon *salt*; set aside.
2. In large bowl beat butter with electric mixer on medium to high 30 seconds. Add sugars; beat until well combined. Beat in eggs, one at a time, on low until combined. Beat in molasses and vanilla.

3. Alternately add flour mixture, buttermilk, and cream soda to butter mixture, beating on low speed after each addition until combined. Stir in ½ cup of the toffee. Fill cups three-fourths full. Bake about 18 minutes or until tops spring back when lightly touched. Cool in pans on racks 5 minutes. Remove from pans; cool. Frost; top with remaining toffee.
MAKES 18 CUPCAKES.

BROWN BUTTER FROSTING For brown butter, in saucepan heat ¼ cup butter over medium-low heat until lightly browned, about 8 minutes; cool. In bowl beat ¼ cup softened butter with mixer on medium 30 seconds. Add cooled brown butter; beat until combined. Add 2 cups powdered sugar, ½ teaspoon vanilla, ⅛ teaspoon ground nutmeg, and dash salt. Beat in 1 to 2 tablespoons buttermilk until spreadable. Use immediately. If frosting begins to set up, stir in a small amount of boiling water.
EACH CUPCAKE *307 cal, 14 g fat (8 g sat. fat), 69 mg chol, 241 mg sodium, 42 g carbo, 0 g fiber, 3 g pro. Daily Values: 7% vit. A, 5% calcium, 5% iron.*

CHOCOLATE CUPCAKES WITH A KICK

PREP: 35 MIN. BAKE: 18 MIN. OVEN: 350°F

1	pkg. two-layer chocolate or devil's food cake mix
1¼	cups sour cream
3	eggs
⅓	cup cooking oil
2	Tbsp. instant coffee crystals
½	to 1 tsp. ground chipotle chile pepper
1	11.5-oz. pkg. semisweet chocolate chunks
2	tsp. all-purpose flour
1	recipe White Frosting
2	oz. semisweet chocolate, chopped
¼	cup whipping cream

1. Preheat oven to 350°F. Line twenty-four 2½-inch muffin cups with paper bake cups; set aside. In bowl combine cake mix, sour cream, eggs, oil, coffee crystals, and chipotle pepper. Beat with electric mixer on low to combine. Beat on medium 2 minutes.
2. In bowl toss chocolate chunks with flour. Fold into batter. Spoon into prepared cups. Bake 18 to 22 minutes or until tops spring back when lightly touched. Cool in pans on wire rack 5 minutes. Remove from pans; cool completely. Frost with White Frosting.
3. For chocolate drizzle, place chopped chocolate in bowl. In saucepan bring cream to boiling. Pour over chocolate; do not stir. Let stand 5 minutes; whisk until smooth. Place in resealable plastic bag; seal bag and snip off a small corner. Drizzle over frosted cupcakes.
MAKES 24 CUPCAKES.

WHITE FROSTING In bowl beat one 8-ounce package softened cream cheese and ½ cup softened butter on medium to high for 30 seconds. Beat in ½ teaspoon vanilla. Gradually beat in 2 to 2½ cups powdered sugar until spreadable.
EACH CUPCAKE *335 cal, 21 g fat (10 g sat. fat), 55 mg chol, 251 mg sodium, 37 g carbo, 2 g fiber, 4 g pro. Daily Values: 8% vit. A, 6% calcium, 9% iron.*

Christina Jordan, WOODSTOCK, GA

KID-FRIENDLY

PB AND J CUPCAKES

PREP: 30 MIN. BAKE: 20 MIN. COOL: 5 MIN.
OVEN: 350°F

- 1 cup creamy peanut butter
- 1 8-oz. carton sour cream
- ¼ cup butter, softened
- ¾ cup water
- 3 eggs
- 1 pkg. two-layer butter golden cake mix
- 1 8-oz. pkg. cream cheese, softened
- ½ cup butter, softened
- 6 cups powdered sugar
- ¼ cup strawberry preserves

1. Preheat oven to 350°F. Line twenty-four 2½-inch muffin cups with paper bake cups. In a large mixing bowl beat peanut butter, sour cream, and ¼ cup butter with an electric mixer on medium to high speed until smooth. Add water and eggs; beat until combined. Add cake mix; beat well.
2. Spoon ¼ cup batter into each muffin cup. Bake for 20 to 25 minutes or until the tops springs back when lightly touched. Cool in pans on a wire rack for 5 minutes. Remove from pans and cool completely.
3. For frosting, in a large mixing bowl beat cream cheese and the ½ cup butter with an electric mixer on medium to high speed until light and fluffy. Gradually beat in powdered sugar until frosting is smooth. Beat in strawberry preserves. Frost cooled cupcakes. Store in an airtight container in the refrigerator. **MAKES 24 CUPCAKES.**
EACH CUPCAKE 387 cal, 18 g fat (9 g sat. fat), 6 mg chol, 273 mg sodium, 53 g carbo, 1 g fiber, 6 g pro. Daily Values: 8% vit. A, 1% vit. C, 7% calcium, 5% iron.

KID-FRIENDLY

PEACHES 'N' CREAM CUPCAKES

PREP: 25 MIN. BAKE: 18 MIN. COOL: 5 MIN.
OVEN: 350°F

- 1 pkg. 2-layer white cake mix
- 2 eggs
- 1 6-oz. carton peach yogurt
- ⅔ cup peach nectar
- ½ cup vegetable oil
- 1 medium peach, pitted and finely chopped, or 1 cup frozen unsweetened peaches, thawed, well drained, and finely chopped
- 1 recipe Peach Buttercream Frosting

1. Preheat oven to 350°F. Line twenty-four 2½-inch muffin cups with paper bake cups; set aside.
2. In a large bowl combine cake mix, eggs, yogurt, peach nectar, and oil. Beat with electric mixer on low speed until combined. Beat 2 minutes on medium speed. Fold in peaches. Divide batter evenly among prepared cups, filling each

about three-fourths full.
3. Bake for 18 to 22 minutes or until tops spring back when lightly touched. Cool n pans on wire racks for 5 minutes. Remove from pans and cool completely on wire racks.
4. Spread Peach Buttercream Frosting on cooled cupcakes. **MAKES 24 CUPCAKES.**
PEACH BUTTERCREAM FROSTING In a large mixing bowl beat ⅓ cup softened butter with an electric mixer on medium speed until smooth. Gradually add 1 cup powdered sugar, beating well. Beat in 3 tablespoons peach nectar. Gradually beat in 3 cups powdered sugar. Beat in additional peach nectar to reach spreading consistency. **MAKES ABOUT 2 CUPS.**
EACH CUPCAKE 254 cal, 10 g fat (3 g sat. fat), 25 mg chol, 174 mg sodium, 40 g carbo, 0 g fiber, 2 g pro. Daily Values: 3% vit. A, 2% vit. C, 7% calcium, 2% iron.

LAVENDER-HONEY CUPCAKES

PREP: 30 MIN. BAKE: 18 MIN. COOL: 10 MIN.
OVEN: 350°F

- 1 cup all-purpose flour
- ¾ cup whole wheat flour
- 1½ tsp. baking powder
- 1½ tsp. dried lavender
- ½ tsp. salt
- ½ cup butter, softened
- 1 cup granulated sugar
- 2 Tbsp. honey
- 1 tsp. vanilla
- 2 eggs
- ⅔ cup milk
- 1 recipe Lavender Frosting

1. Preheat oven to 350°F. Line eighteen 2½-inch muffin cups with paper bake cups; set aside. In a medium bowl combine flours, baking powder, lavender, and salt; set aside.
2. In a large mixing bowl beat butter with an electric mixer on medium to high speed for 30 seconds. Add sugar, honey, and vanilla; beat until well combined. Add eggs, one at a time, beating well after each addition. Alternately Add flour mixture and milk to butter mixture, beating on low speed after each addition just until combined. Spoon batter in muffin cups.
3. Bake for 18 to 20 minutes or until a wooden toothpick comes out clean. Cool in pans on wire racks for 10 minutes. Remove from pans. Cool thoroughly on racks. Frost with Lavender Frosting. Chill to store. **MAKES 18 CUPCAKES.**
LAVENDER FROSTING Beat together half of an 8-ounce package cream cheese (Neufchâtel), softened; 2 tablespoons butter, softened; ½ teaspoon vanilla; and ¼ teaspoon dried lavender until light and fluffy. Gradually add 1 cup powdered

sugar, beating well. Gradually beat in 1 to 1¼ cups additional powdered sugar to reach spreading consistency. If desired, tint lavender with 2 drops each of blue and red food coloring.
EACH CUPCAKE 237 cal, 9 g fat (6 g sat. fat), 48 mg chol, 161 mg sodium, 36 g carbo, 1 g fiber, 3 g pro. Daily Value: 7% vit. A, 3% calcium, 4% iron.

CHOCOLATE-ORANGE CUPCAKES

PREP: 25 MIN. BAKE: 18 MIN. COOL: 10 MIN.
OVEN: 350°F

- 2 oranges
- 1 8-oz. pkg. reduced-fat cream cheese (Neufchâtel), softened
- ¼ cup granulated sugar
- 4 eggs
- 1 pkg. 2-layer devil's food cake mix
- ½ cup cooking oil
- ¾ cup butter, softened
- 2½ cups powdered sugar
- 1 Tbsp. milk
  Orange peel strips (optional)

1. Preheat oven to 350°F. Line twenty-four 2½-inch muffin cups with paper bake cups; set aside. Finely shred peel from the oranges; set aside. Squeeze juice from oranges; add enough water to equal 1 cup; set aside.
2. In a medium bowl combine the cream cheese and granulated sugar; beat with an electric mixer on medium-high speed until combined. Beat in 1 egg; stir in 1 tablespoon of the orange peel. Set aside.
3. In a large mixing bowl combine cake mix, orange juice/water mixture, oil, and remaining 3 eggs. Beat on low speed until moistened, about 30 seconds. Beat on medium speed for 2 minutes. Divide batter evenly among prepared muffin cups. Drop a slightly rounded teaspoon of cream cheese mixture into each batter-filled muffin cup.
4. Bake for 18 to 22 minutes or until tops spring back when lightly touched. Cool in pans on wire rack for 10 minutes. Remove from pans; cool completely.
5. For frosting, in a medium bowl combine softened butter, powdered sugar, milk, and remaining orange peel. Beat with an electric mixer on medium speed until smooth. If necessary, add additional milk to reach spreadable consistency. Frost cupcakes. Garnish with orange peel strips.
MAKES 24 CUPCAKES.
EACH CUPCAKE 275 cal, 15 g fat (6 g sat. fat), 58 mg chol, 256 mg sodium, 34 g carbo, 1 g fiber, 3 g pro. Daily Values: 7% vit. A, 1% vit. C, 4% calcium, 6% iron.

Sensational Salmon

Margee Berry, TROUT LAKE, WA

HERBED CHEESE-STUFFED SALMON

PREP: 20 MIN. BAKE: 14 MIN. OVEN: 425°F

6	6-oz. fresh or frozen skinless salmon fillets
1	lemon
1	5.2-oz. container semisoft cheese with garlic and herbs
	Sea salt or salt
1	cup soft bread crumbs (about 1½ slices)
⅓	cup freshly shredded Parmesan cheese (1½ oz.)
¼	cup butter, melted
2	Tbsp. pine nuts, toasted

1. Thaw fish, if frozen. Rinse fish; pat dry. Preheat oven to 425°F. Finely shred enough peel from lemon to equal 2 teaspoons; cut lemon in wedges and set aside. In small bowl combine semisoft cheese and lemon peel. In top of each fillet, from about ½ inch from one edge, cut a pocket, taking care not to cut all the way through the fish. (If fillet is thin, cut into the fish at an angle.) Spoon cheese mixture into pockets. Season fish with salt. Place in shallow baking pan. Set aside.

2. In small bowl combine bread crumbs, Parmesan cheese, butter, and pine nuts; sprinkle over fillets, pressing lightly. Bake, uncovered, about 14 minutes or until salmon flakes when tested with a fork. Serve with lemon wedges.
MAKES 6 SERVINGS.

EACH SERVING *537 cal, 40 g fat (17 g sat. fat), 125 mg chol, 561 mg sodium, 7 g carbo, 1 g fiber, 38 g pro. Daily Values: 7% vit. A, 34% vit. C, 10% calcium, 7% iron.*

PEPPER JELLY AND SOY-GLAZED SALMON

PREP: 25 MIN. MARINATE: 1 HR. GRILL: 15 MIN. COOK: 10 MIN.

1	2-lb. fresh or frozen skinless salmon fillet, about 1 inch thick
⅔	cup green jalapeño pepper jelly
⅓	cup rice vinegar
⅓	cup soy sauce
3	green onions, sliced
1	Tbsp. grated fresh ginger
2	tsp. toasted sesame oil
3	cloves garlic, minced
¼	tsp. crushed red pepper
¼	cup snipped fresh cilantro
¼	cup sliced fresh jalapeño chile peppers (see Note, *page 275*) and/or sliced green onions

1. Thaw fish, if frozen. Rinse fish; pat dry. For marinade, in saucepan melt jelly over low heat; remove. Stir in next 7 ingredients. Place fish in shallow dish; pour jelly mixture on fish. Cover; refrigerate 1 to 2 hours, turning fish occasionally.

2. Remove fish from marinade; reserve marinade. For charcoal grill, arrange medium-hot coals around edge of grill. Test for medium heat in center of grill. Place fish on greased heavy-duty foil in center of grill. Cover; grill 15 to 18 minutes or until fish flakes when tested with a fork. (For gas grill, adjust for indirect cooking. Grill over medium heat as above.)

3. Bring reserved marinade to boiling; reduce heat. Simmer, uncovered, 10 to 15 minutes or until reduced to ½ cup. Drizzle over fish; sprinkle cilantro, peppers, and onions. **MAKES 8 SERVINGS.**
EACH SERVING *237 cal, 9 g fat (2 g sat. fat), 6 mg chol, 482 mg sodium, 34 g carbo, 3 g fiber, 6 g pro. Daily Values: 6% vit. A, 15% vit. C, 3% calcium, 6% iron.*

Dawn Forsberg, ST. JOSEPH, MO

FAST

CHIPOTLE-GLAZED SALMON
PREP: 15 MIN. GRILL: 4 MIN.

4	6-oz. fresh or frozen skinless salmon fillets
2	tsp. finely shredded lemon peel
¼	tsp. salt
¼	tsp. ground black pepper
¼	cup honey
2	Tbsp. lemon juice
1	small canned chipotle pepper in adobo sauce, chopped
1	Tbsp. adobo sauce

1. Thaw salmon, if frozen. Rinse salmon; pat dry. Sprinkle salmon with lemon peel, salt, and pepper; set aside.
2. For chipotle glaze, in a small bowl combine honey, lemon juice, chipotle pepper, and adobo sauce. Set aside half the glaze.
3. For a charcoal grill, place salmon on the greased rack of an uncovered grill directly over medium coals. Grill for 4 to 6 minutes per ½-inch thickness or until fish flakes easily when tested with a fork, turning once halfway through grilling and brushing with half the glaze during the last 2 minutes of grilling. (For a gas grill, preheat grill. Reduce heat to medium. Place salmon on a greased grill rack over heat. Cover; grill as above.) To serve, drizzle salmon with reserved glaze.
MAKES 4 SERVINGS.

EACH SERVING *382 cal, 19 g fat (4 g sat. fat), 100 mg chol, 282 mg sodium, 19 g carbo, 0 g fiber, 34 g pro. Daily Values: 3% vit. A, 19% vit. C, 2% calcium, 5% iron.*

STUFFED SALMON
PREP: 25 MIN. BAKE: 10 MIN. OVEN: 425 F

	Nonstick cooking spray
6	6-oz. fresh or frozen skinless salmon fillets
1	cup packaged fresh baby spinach
⅓	cup fresh basil leaves
⅓	cup crumbled feta cheese
3	Tbsp. chopped red onion
2	Tbsp. pine nuts, toasted
1	clove garlic, sliced
¼	tsp. salt
⅛	tsp. ground black pepper
1	Tbsp. olive oil
	Salt and ground black pepper

1. Preheat oven to 425°F. Line a large baking sheet with foil; lightly coat foil with nonstick spray. Set aside. Thaw salmon, if frozen. Rinse fish and pat dry with paper towels. Set aside. In a food processor combine spinach, basil, feta cheese, red onion, pine nuts, garlic, ¼ teaspoon salt, and ⅛ teaspoon pepper. Cover and process with several on/off turns until mixture is finely chopped and combined.

2. Using a small sharp knife cut 3- to 4-inch horizontal slits into the side of each fillet, cutting to, but not through, the opposite side. Fill pockets with spinach mixture. Brush salmon with oil. Lightly sprinkle salmon with salt and pepper.
3. Place fillets on prepared baking sheet. Bake for 10 to 12 minutes or until salmon flakes when tested with a fork.
MAKES 6 SERVINGS.

EACH SERVING *377 cal, 24 g fat (5 g sat. fat), 108 mg chol, 392 mg sodium, 2 g carbo, 0 g fiber, 36 g pro. Daily Values: 14% vit. A, 15% vit. C, 7% calcium, 6% iron.*

FAST

SALMON QUESADILLAS
PREP: 25 MIN. COOK: 2 MIN. PER BATCH OVEN: 300°F

2	tsp. chili powder
1	tsp. ground cumin
¼	tsp. salt
12	oz. skinless salmon fillets, cut into ½-inch pieces
1	Tbsp. cooking oil
1	cup chopped green onions
¾	cup frozen whole kernel corn
6	8-inch flour tortillas
6	Tbsp. tub-style cream cheese spread with chive and onion
1½	cups shredded Monterey Jack cheese (6 oz.)
1	avocado, halved, seeded, peeled, and chopped
	Nonstick cooking spray

1. Preheat oven to 300°F. In a small bowl combine chili powder, cumin, and salt. Toss salmon with spice mixture to coat.
2. In a large skillet cook salmon in hot oil for 2 minutes. Add green onions and corn. Cook 1 minute more. Remove from skillet; carefully wipe skillet clean with paper towels.
3. Spread one side of each tortilla with the cream cheese spread. Divide salmon mixture, shredded cheese, and avocado among the tortillas. Fold tortillas in half. Lightly spray tortillas with nonstick cooking spray.
4. Heat a 10-inch nonstick skillet over medium heat for 1 minute. Cook quesadillas, two at a time, for 1 to 2 minutes per side or until golden brown and cheese melts. Remove quesadillas; keep warm in 300°F oven. Repeat with remaining quesadillas. Serve immediately.
MAKES 6 MAIN-DISH OR 18 APPETIZER SERVINGS.

EACH MAIN-DISH SERVING *457 cal, 30 g fat (12 g sat. fat), 73 mg chol, 484 mg sodium, 25 g carbo, 23 g pro. Daily Values: 19% vit. A, 25% vit. C, 29% calcium, 10% iron.*

CREAMY CHEESY SALMON ENCHILADAS
PREP: 25 MIN. BAKE: 35 MIN. OVEN: 375°F

1	3-oz. pkg. cream cheese, softened
1	8-oz. pkg. shredded Mexican-style four-cheese blend (2 cups)
1	16-oz. jar salsa
1	4-oz. can diced green chile peppers, drained
2	14.75-oz. cans salmon, drained, flaked, and skin and bones removed
6	10- to 12-inch flour tortillas

1. Preheat oven to 375°F. In a large bowl stir together cream cheese, 1 cup of the cheese, 2 tablespoons of the salsa, and the chile peppers. Fold in salmon. Spoon about ¾ cup filling across each tortilla, slightly below center. Fold in ends and roll up. Place in a 3-quart rectangular baking dish. Top with remaining salsa and cheese.
2. Bake, covered, 25 minutes. Uncover and bake about 10 minutes more or until heated through. **MAKES 6 SERVINGS.**

EACH SERVING *547 cal, 29 g fat (13 g sat. fat), 125 mg chol, 1,820 mg sodium, 29 g carbo, 2 g fiber, 41 g pro. Daily Values: 11% vit. A, 9% vit. C, 6% calcium, 18% iron.*

NUT-CRUSTED BAKED SALMON
PREP: 25 MIN. BAKE: 20 MIN. OVEN: 400°F

4	5- to 6-oz. fresh or frozen skinless salmon fillets
	Kosher salt or salt
	Freshly ground black pepper
2	Tbsp. Dijon-style mustard
2	Tbsp. butter, melted
2	tsp. honey
¼	cup fine dried bread crumbs
¼	cup finely chopped pecans or walnuts
2	Tbsp. snipped fresh parsley
	Lemon wedges

1. Preheat oven to 400°F. Thaw fish, if frozen. Rinse fish and pat dry with paper towels; place in a 9×2-inch square baking pan. Season fish with salt and pepper.
2. In a small bowl combine the mustard, butter, and honey; set aside. In a small bowl combine the bread crumbs, pecans, and parsley. Brush the salmon with the mustard mixture. Top fish with bread crumb mixture.
3. Bake, uncovered, about 20 minutes or until fish flakes when tested with a fork. Serve with lemon wedges.
MAKES 4 SERVINGS.

EACH SERVING *403 cal, 26 g fat (7 g sat. fat), 98 mg chol, 481 mg sodium, 9 g carbo, 1 g fiber, 30 g pro. Daily Values: 8% vit. A, 15% vit. C, 4% calcium, 7% iron.*

Not-Your-Mother's Meatballs

Cheryl Woodson, LIBERTY, MO

LAMB MEATBALLS WITH POMEGRANATE SAUCE

PREP: 30 MIN. BAKE: 15 MIN. OVEN: 300°F

1	egg or 2 egg whites, lightly beaten
1	cup fine dry bread crumbs
¼	cup chopped fresh mint
2	or 3 cloves garlic, minced
½	tsp. salt
¼	tsp. ground black pepper
2	lb. ground lamb
1	16-oz. bottle pomegranate juice
1	tsp. sugar
3	Tbsp. olive oil
1½	cups plain Greek yogurt
2	Tbsp. snipped fresh chives
1	clove garlic, minced
	Fresh mint leaves (optional)
	Toasted pita bread wedges (optional)

1. Preheat oven to 300°F. In large bowl combine egg, bread crumbs, mint, garlic cloves garlic, salt, and pepper. Add ground lamb; mix well. Shape into 32 meatballs; set aside.
2. For sauce, in medium saucepan bring pomegranate juice to boiling; reduce heat. Simmer, uncovered, 25 minutes or until reduced to about ½ cup. Add sugar; stir to dissolve.
3. Meanwhile, in large skillet brown half the meatballs at a time in hot olive oil, turning to brown evenly. Transfer to 15×10×1-inch baking pan. Bake 15 to 20 minutes or until an instant-read thermometer registers 160° F. In medium bowl combine yogurt, 1 tablespoon of the chives, and 1 garlic clove. To serve, drizzle meatballs with pomegranate sauce; sprinkle with remaining chives and mint. Serve with seasoned yogurt and pita wedges. **MAKES 6 TO 8 SERVINGS.**
EACH SERVING *695 cal, 50 g fat (21 g sat. fat), 156 mg chol, 449 mg sodium, 27 g carbo, 1 g fiber, 32 g pro. Daily Values: 7% vit. A, 3% vit. C, 12% calcium, 22% iron.*

FONTINA-STUFFED MEATBALL KABOBS

PREP: 30 MIN. GRILL: 10 MIN.

1	egg, lightly beaten
⅓	cup grated Parmesan cheese
2	cloves garlic, minced
1	tsp. dried Italian seasoning
1½	lb. lean ground beef
2	oz. thinly sliced prosciutto, chopped
16	½-inch fontina cheese cubes (1½ oz.)
8	canned artichoke hearts, drained and halved
1	6- to 8-oz. pkg. fresh cremini mushrooms
1	pint grape tomatoes
1	recipe Balsamic Glaze
	Fresh basil (optional)

1. Combine egg, Parmesan, garlic, Italian seasoning, ½ teaspoon *salt*, and ⅛ teaspoon ground *black pepper*. Add beef and prosciutto; mix well. Divide in 16 portions; shape around cheese cubes. On sixteen 8- to 10-inch skewers thread meatballs, artichokes, mushrooms, and tomatoes, leaving a ¼-inch between. Prepare Balsamic Glaze; set aside.
2. On charcoal grill, place kabobs on greased rack of grill directly over medium coals. Grill 10 to 12 minutes or until meat is no longer pink (160°F), turning and brushing with half the glaze halfway through. To serve, drizzle with remaining glaze; sprinkle with fresh basil. **MAKES 8 MAIN-DISH OR 16 APPETIZER SERVINGS.**
BALSAMIC GLAZE In small saucepan combine ⅓ cup balsamic vinegar; 2 teaspoons olive oil; 1 clove garlic, minced; ¼ teaspoon salt; ¼ teaspoon dried Italian seasoning; and ⅛ teaspoon black pepper. Bring to boiling; reduce heat. Simmer, uncovered, 4 minutes or until reduced to about ¼ cup.
EACH SERVING *269 cal, 15 g fat (5 g sat. fat), 91 mg chol, 673 mg sodium, 8 g carbo, 2 g fiber, 24 g pro. Daily Values: 12% vit. A, 12% vit. C, 11% calcium, 20% iron.*

Patricia A. Harmon, BADEN, PA

BEER-BRAISED MEATBALLS
PREP: 35 MIN. BAKE: 25 MIN. OVEN: 400°F

2 eggs, slightly beaten
1 cup soft bread crumbs
4 slices bacon, crisp cooked and crumbled
½ cup chopped fresh parsley
2 Tbsp. chopped onion
1 clove garlic, minced
1 tsp. dried thyme, crushed
1 tsp. ground black pepper
1 lb. lean ground beef
2 Tbsp. chopped onion
2 Tbsp. butter
⅓ cup beer
1 Tbsp. stone-ground mustard
1½ cups beef broth
2 Tbsp. cornstarch
1 Tbsp. honey
   Mashed potatoes (optional)

1. Preheat oven to 400°F. In a large bowl combine eggs, bread crumbs, bacon, parsley, 2 tablespoons onion, garlic, thyme, and pepper. Add ground beef and mix until well combined. Shape meat mixture into twenty-four 1½-inch meatballs.
2. Place meatballs in a shallow baking pan. Bake about 25 minutes or until meatballs are no longer pink (160°F).
3. In a large skillet cook 2 tablespoons onion in hot butter for 5 minutes or until onion is tender. Add the beer and mustard to skillet. Combine beef broth and cornstarch and add to skillet. Cook and stir until thickened and bubbly. Cook and stir 2 minutes more. Stir in honey.
4. Serve meatballs on mashed potatoes. Pour gravy over meatballs.
MAKES 4 SERVINGS.

EACH SERVING *408 cal, 23 g fat (10 g sat. fat), 204 mg chol, 819 mg sodium, 15 g carbo, 1 g fiber, 31 g pro. Daily Values: 19% vit. A, 19% vit. C, 6% calcium, 23% iron.*

BREAKFAST MEATBALLS WITH COUNTRY GRAVY
START TO FINISH: 30 MIN.

1 lb. bulk pork sausage
½ cup sage-and-onion flavored or herb-seasoned stuffing cubes, crushed
3 Tbsp. pure maple syrup or maple-flavored syrup
½ tsp. ground black pepper
1 to 2 Tbsp. cooking oil
2 Tbsp. all-purpose flour
2 cups half-and-half or light cream
   Salt and ground black pepper
8 biscuits, warmed (optional)

1. In a large bowl combine sausage, crushed stuffing, 2 tablespoons of the maple syrup, and the ½ teaspoon pepper. Shape into 16 meatballs.
2. In a 12-inch skillet heat 1 tablespoon oil over medium-high heat. Add meatballs; cook 8 to 10 minutes or until done (160°F), turning occasionally to brown evenly (reduce heat to medium if meatballs brown too quickly). Remove from skillet, reserving 2 tablespoons drippings in pan. (Add 1 tablespoon oil if needed to equal 2 tablespoons drippings.)
3. Stir flour into drippings; add half-and-half and remaining maple syrup all at once, stirring until smooth. Cook and stir until thickened and bubbly. Return meatballs to skillet. Reduce heat to medium-low. Cook, uncovered, for 2 minutes. Season to taste with salt and pepper. Serve with warm biscuits. **MAKES 4 (4-MEATBALL) SERVINGS.**

EACH SERVING *613 cal, 48 g fat (19 g sat. fat), 126 mg chol, 1,017 mg sodium, 24 g carbo, 1 g fiber, 22 g pro. Daily Values: 1% vit. A, 3% vit. C, 16% calcium, 12% iron.*

SALMON KOFTA CURRY
PREP: 25 MIN. COOK: 20 MIN.

1½ lb. fresh or frozen skinless, boneless salmon fillet
1 egg yolk
2 Tbsp. finely chopped green onion
¼ cup snippped fresh cilantro
4 cloves garlic, minced
½ tsp. salt
1¼ cups soft bread crumbs
3 Tbsp. cooking oil
1 large onion, thinly sliced
1 large tomato, chopped
1 Tbsp. curry powder
½ tsp. salt
½ cup water
   Snipped fresh cilantro
   Hot cooked basmati rice

1. Thaw salmon, if frozen. Cut salmon in 1-inch pieces. Place salmon in a food processor. Cover and pulse with several on/off turns until salmon is finely chopped (do not process into a paste). Transfer salmon to a large bowl. Stir in egg yolk, green onion, ¼ cup cilantro, 1 clove garlic, and ½ teaspoon salt. Add bread crumbs and mix until combined. Form salmon into 1½-inch balls.
2. Heat 2 tablespoons of the oil in a 12-inch skillet over medium heat. Add salmon balls. Cook, turning occasionally, about 6 minutes, until balls are lightly browned on all sides. Remove from skillet.

3. In the same skillet heat remaining oil over medium heat. Add onion and remaining garlic to skillet. Cook about 5 minutes or just until onion is golden and tender. Stir in the tomato, curry powder, and the ½ teaspoon salt. Cook and stir for 3 minutes. Carefully add the water to the skillet. Cover and simmer for 5 minutes. Return salmon balls to the skillet. Cover and cook about 5 minutes more or until cooked through.
4. To serve, sprinkle with cilantro. Serve with rice. **MAKES 6 SERVINGS.**

EACH SERVING *417 cal, 20 g fat (4 g sat. fat), 101 mg chol, 806 mg sodium, 30 g carbo, 2 g fiber, 26 g pro. Daily Values: 12% vit. A, 24% vit. C, 6% calcium, 13% iron.*

TURKEY MEATBALLS IN PEACH SAUCE
PREP: 35 MIN. COOK: 22 MIN.

1 egg, beaten
¼ cup fine dry bread crumbs
¼ cup finely chopped shallot
1 tsp. grated fresh ginger
⅛ tsp. salt
1 lb. ground raw turkey
1 Tbsp. cooking oil
1 15- to 16-oz. can peach slices (juice pack)
¼ cup ketchup
2 Tbsp. soy sauce
2 Tbsp. butter, melted
¼ cup dried tart cherries

1. In a large mixing bowl combine egg, bread crumbs, shallot, ½ teaspoon of the ginger, and the salt; add turkey and mix well. Shape in 24 meatballs.
2. In a 12-inch skillet cook meatballs in hot oil over medium heat for 18 to 20 minutes or until browned and no longer pink (165°F), turning occasionally to brown evenly. Drain off fat.
3. Meanwhile, drain peaches, reserving ¼ cup of the juice. In a blender or food processor combine drained peaches, reserved juice, ketchup, soy sauce, melted butter, and remaining ginger. Cover and blend or process until smooth. Add peach mixture and cherries to skillet. Bring to boiling. Reduce heat and simmer, uncovered, for 1 to 2 minutes or until heated through, stirring gently to coat the meatballs. Serve warm.
MAKES 6 APPETIZER SERVINGS.

EACH SERVING *264 cal, 14 g fat (5 g sat. fat), 105 mg chol, 632 mg sodium, 20 g carbo, 1 g fiber, 16 g pro. Daily Values: 15% vit. A, 8% vit. C, 4% calcium, 10% iron.*

Creative Corn Breads

Angela Sams, TEMPE, AZ

PINEAPPLE-CHEDDAR CORN BREAD

PREP: 20 MIN. BAKE: 35 MIN. OVEN: 375°F

1	cup all-purpose flour
1	cup cornmeal
½	cup sugar
2	tsp. baking powder
1	tsp. salt
½	cup butter, softened
4	eggs, lightly beaten
1	14.75-oz. can cream-style corn
1	8-oz. can crushed pineapple (juice pack), drained
4	oz. cheddar cheese or Monterey Jack cheese, shredded (1 cup)

1. Preheat oven to 375° F. Grease and flour a 2-quart rectangular baking dish; set aside.
2. In medium bowl combine flour, cornmeal, sugar, baking powder, and salt; set aside.
3. In large mixing bowl beat butter with electric mixer on medium speed 30 seconds. Add eggs, one at a time; beat well after each addition. Beat in flour mixture on low speed just until combined. Stir in corn, drained pineapple, and cheese. Spoon batter into prepared dish.
4. Bake about 35 minutes or until toothpick inserted near center comes out clean. Cut in squares. Serve warm.
MAKES 12 SERVINGS.
EACH SERVING *273 cal, 13 g fat (7 g sat. fat), 101 mg chol, 474 mg sodium, 34 g carbo, 2 g fiber, 7 g pro. Daily Values: 9% vit. A, 6% vit. C.*

Char Antuzzi, COLFAX, CA

TUSCAN POLENTA BREAD

PREP: 25 MIN. BAKE: 30 MIN. OVEN: 375°F

1½	cups cornmeal
½	cup all-purpose flour
2	Tbsp. sugar
1	tsp. baking soda
¼	tsp. salt
2	Tbsp. olive oil
1¾	cups half-and-half or light cream
2	eggs, lightly beaten
9	slices bacon or ¾ cup chopped pancetta, crisp-cooked and drained
1	8-oz. jar oil-packed dried tomatoes, drained and snipped
1	Tbsp. chopped shallot
1	Tbsp. snipped fresh rosemary
	Butter, softened (optional)

1. Preheat oven to 375°F. In medium bowl stir together cornmeal, flour, sugar, baking soda, and salt; set aside. Add 1 tablespoon of the oil to a 10-inch cast-iron skillet or 9×1½-inch round baking pan. Place in oven for 5 minutes. Remove skillet or pan from oven; carefully swirl oil to coat bottom and sides.
2. Meanwhile, for batter, in large bowl combine half-and-half, eggs, and remaining oil. Crumble bacon. Stir tomatoes, bacon, shallot, and rosemary into egg mixture until combined. Add cornmeal mixture all at once to egg mixture. Stir just until moistened. Pour batter into hot skillet or pan. Bake 30 to 35 minutes or until wooden toothpick inserted near center comes out clean. Cut in wedges. Serve warm with softened butter. **MAKES 8 TO 10 SERVINGS.**
EACH SERVING *367 cal, 18 g fat (6 g sat. fat), 82 mg chol, 553 mg sodium, 46 g carbo, 2 g fiber, 11 g pro. Daily Values: 13% vit. A, 49% vit. C.*

DOUBLE BLUE CORNBREAD

PREP: 20 MIN. STAND: 5 MIN. BAKE: 25 MIN.
COOL: 15 MIN. OVEN: 400°F

- 1¼ cups milk
- 1 cup blue cornmeal
- 1 egg
- ⅓ cup cooking oil
- 1 cup all-purpose flour
- ¼ cup granulated sugar
- 1½ tsp. baking powder
- ½ tsp. salt
- ¾ cup fresh blueberries
- 1 Tbsp. coarse sugar

1. Preheat oven to 400°F. Lightly grease a 10-inch cast-iron or oven-going skillet. In a medium bowl combine milk and cornmeal. Let stand for 5 minutes. Whisk egg and oil into milk mixture.
2. In a large bowl combine flour, granulated sugar, baking powder, and salt; make a well in the center of the flour mixture. Add milk mixture all at once to flour mixture; stir just until combined.
3. Pour cornmeal mixture into prepared skillet. Top with blueberries; sprinkle with coarse sugar. Bake for 25 to 30 minutes or until toothpick inserted near center comes out clean. Cool 15 minutes on a wire rack. Serve warm. **MAKES 8 SERVINGS.**

EACH SERVING *253 cal, 11 g fat (2 g sat. fat), 29 mg chol, 238 mg sodium, 33 g carbo, 3 g fiber, 9 g pro. Daily Values: 2% vit. A, 2% vit. C, 11% calcium, 7% iron.*

OVERNIGHT CORNBREAD MUFFINS

PREP: 25 MIN. RISE: 1½ HRS CHILL: 8 HRS.
BAKE: 12 MIN. OVEN: 375°F

- 2 cups all-purpose flour
- 1 pkg. active dry yeast
- 1 cup milk
- ⅓ cup butter
- 3 tbs. sugar
- 1 tsp. salt
- ¼ tsp. coarsely ground black pepper
- 2 eggs
- 1 cup yellow cornmeal
  Nonstick cooking spray
- 1 recipe Peppered Honey Butter

1. In a large mixing bowl combine 1¼ cups flour and the yeast; set aside. In a saucepan combine milk, ⅓ cup butter, sugar, salt, and pepper; cook and stir over low heat just until warm (120°F to 130°F) and butter is almost melted. Add to flour mixture along with eggs; beat with an electric mixer on low speed 30 seconds. Beat on high speed for 3 minutes. Stir in cornmeal and remaining flour. Cover and let rise in a warm place for 1 hour. Stir batter. Cover; refrigerate 8 hours or overnight.

2. Lightly coat eighteen 2½-inch muffin cups with nonstick cooking spray. Stir muffin batter and spoon into muffin cups, filling cups half full. Let stand in a warm place for 30 minutes. Preheat oven to 375°F.
3. Bake for 12 to 15 minutes or until golden and sound hollow when lightly tapped. Serve warm with Peppered Honey Butter. **MAKES 18 MUFFINS.**

PEPPERED HONEY BUTTER In a medium mixing bowl beat together ½ cup softened butter, 1 tablespoon honey, and ¼ teaspoon coarsely ground pepper.

EACH MUFFIN *267 cal, 15 g fat (9 g sat. fat), 71 mg chol, 309 mg sodium, 30 g carbo, 1 g fiber, 5 g pro. Daily Values: 1% vit. A, 4% calcium, 9% iron.*

CORN BREAD WITH TOMATO-BACON RIBBON

PREP: 25 MIN. BAKE: 35 MIN. COOL: 15 MIN.
OVEN: 350°F

- Nonstick spray coating
- 1 8-oz. pkg. cream cheese, softened
- 2 Tbsp. butter, softened
- 2 Tbsp. cornstarch
- ½ tsp. ground black pepper
- 2 eggs
- ¼ cup milk
- 4 slices bacon, crisp-cooked, drained, and crumbled
- ¼ cup oil-packed dried tomatoes, drained and chopped
- 2 8.5-oz. pkgs. corn muffin mix

1. Preheat oven to 375°F. Lightly coat a 13×9×2-inch baking pan with nonstick cooking spray; set aside.
2. In medium bowl beat cream cheese, butter, cornstarch, and pepper with an electric mixer on medium speed until smooth. Beat in egg and milk until combined. Stir in bacon and tomatoes; set aside.
3. In another bowl prepare corn muffin mix according to package directions. Spread about two-thirds of the muffin mix (2 cups) in prepared pan. Pour cream cheese mixture evenly over batter. Drop remaining batter in small mounds over filling. Bake about 35 minutes or until top springs back when lightly touched. Cool 15 to 20 minutes before serving. **MAKES 12 TO 15 SERVINGS.**

EACH SERVING *290 cal, 16 g fat (7 g sat. fat), 65 mg chol, 597 mg sodium, 31 g carbo, 3 g fiber, 7 g pro. Daily Values: 9% vit. A, 4% vit. C, 5% calcium, 8% iron.*

KID-FRIENDLY

MAPLE-SAUSAGE CORN MUFFINS

PREP: 20 MIN. BAKE: 13 MIN. COOL: 5 MIN.
OVEN: 425°F

- 1 cup all-purpose flour
- 1 cup yellow cornmeal
- 2 Tbsp. packed brown sugar
- 1 Tbsp. baking powder
- 1 tsp. dry mustard
- ½ tsp. salt
- 2 large eggs, beaten
- ½ cup milk
- ½ cup pure maple syrup or maple-flavored syrup
- ¼ cup butter, melted
- 8 oz. cooked smoked sausage, chopped (about 1½ cups)

1. Preheat oven to 425°F. Lightly grease eighteen 2½-inch muffin cups or line with paper bake cups; set aside.
2. In a large bowl combine flour, cornmeal, brown sugar, baking powder, dry mustard, and salt. In a medium bowl whisk together eggs, milk, syrup, and butter. Add egg mixture all at once to flour mixture. Stir just until moistened. Stir in sausage. Spoon batter into muffin cups, filling cups two-thirds full.
3. Bake for 13 to 15 minutes or until a wooden toothpick inserted near centers comes out clean. Cool in muffin cups on a wire rack for 5 minutes. Remove muffins from pans. Serve warm. **MAKES 18 MUFFINS.**

EACH MUFFIN *156 cal, 7 g fat (4 g sat. fat), 36 mg chol, 239 mg sodium, 19 g carbo, 1 g fiber, 4 g pro. Daily Values: 3% vit. A, 3% calcium, 5% iron.*

Picnic Sandwiches

PRIZE TESTED RECIPES® $400 WINNER
Wendy Sternberg, SIMI VALLEY, CA

SKILLET CHICKEN SALAD PITAS

PREP: 30 MIN. MARINATE: 1 HR. COOK: 11 MIN.
CHILL: 1 HR.

⅓	cup snipped fresh cilantro
¼	cup Asian sweet chili sauce
2	Tbsp. lime juice
1	Tbsp. minced garlic
1	tsp. olive oil
⅛	tsp. kosher salt or salt
2	lb. skinless, boneless chicken breast halves, cut in 1-inch pieces
1	large red sweet pepper, cut in bite-size strips
⅔	cup mayonnaise
½	cup snipped fresh cilantro
2	Tbsp. lime juice
8	pita bread rounds
8	leaves red or green leaf lettuce

1. In resealable plastic bag set in shallow dish combine ⅓ cup cilantro, chili sauce, 2 tablespoons lime juice, garlic, oil, and salt. Add chicken. Seal bag; turn to coat. Marinate, refrigerated, 1 hour.
2. Heat 12-inch skillet over medium-high heat. Add chicken mixture, half at a time, and cook 3 minutes per batch, stirring occasionally. Return all chicken to skillet. Add sweet pepper; continue cooking 5 minutes more or until chicken is no longer pink, stirring occasionally. Using a slotted spoon transfer chicken mixture to large bowl. Cover; refrigerate 1 to 8 hours.
3. For dressing, in bowl combine mayonnaise, ½ cup cilantro, and 2 tablespoons lime juice. To serve, top each pita with a lettuce leaf. Spoon chicken mixture on half of each pita. Drizzle with dressing.
MAKES 8 PITA SANDWICHES.
EACH SANDWICH *456 cal., 18 g fat (3 g sat. fat), 73 mg chol, 644 mg sodium, 38 g carbo, 2 g fiber, 33 g pro. Daily Values: 51% vit. A, 64% vit. C, 9% calcium, 17% iron.*

**PRIZE TESTED RECIPES®
$200 WINNER**
Karen Johnson, McMINNVILLE, OR

FAST

TOTE-AND-SLICE LOAF SANDWICH

START TO FINISH: 25 MIN.

¾	cup dried tomatoes (not oil-packed)
1	1-lb. loaf Italian or French bread
½	an 8-oz. pkg. cream cheese, softened
⅓	cup basil pesto
4	oz. thinly sliced provolone cheese
8	oz. thinly sliced peppered or regular salami
1	medium fresh banana pepper or 8 bottled banana peppers, stemmed, seeded, and sliced
½	medium red onion, thinly sliced Small salad peppers and/or pimiento-stuffed green olives (optional)

1. Place tomatoes in a small bowl. Add enough boiling water to cover and let stand for 10 minutes. Drain tomatoes and place in a food processor; cover and process until finely chopped. Or finely chop tomatoes by hand.

2. Split loaf in half horizontally. Remove some soft bread from the bottom half of the loaf, leaving a ½-inch shell.
3. Spread cream cheese on cut sides of both bread halves. Spread top half with dried tomatoes and bottom half with pesto. On bottom half layer provolone cheese, salami, banana peppers, onion, and loaf top, spread side down.
4. If toting, tightly wrap loaf in plastic. To serve, slice loaf crosswise into six sandwiches. Spear a salad pepper and olive on long toothpicks; insert through sandwiches. **MAKES 6 SANDWICHES.**
EACH SANDWICH *588 cal, 34 g fat (14 g sat. fat), 69 mg chol, 1,645 mg sodium, 46 g carbo, 4 g fiber, 24 g pro. Daily Values: 12% vit. A, 16% vit. C, 28% calcium, 21% iron.*

CASHEW-CURRY CHICKEN SALAD

PREP: 20 MIN. CHILL: 2 HRS.

3	cups shredded cooked chicken
¾	cup red grapes, quartered
½	cup finely chopped red onion
¼	cup finely chopped radish or daikon
¼	cup shredded coconut
1	5-oz. carton piña colada or pineapple low-fat yogurt
⅓	cup mango chutney, chopped
1	tbsp. curry powder
½	cup dry-roasted cashews, coarsely chopped
1	cup fresh basil leaves
12	slices whole grain bread, toasted (optional)

1. In a large bowl combine chicken, grapes, onion, radish, and coconut; toss to combine. Set aside.
2. In a small bowl stir together yogurt, chutney, and curry powder. Stir into chicken mixture to coat. Cover and chill for 2 to 24 hours.
3. To serve, stir cashews into chicken mixture. Divide basil leaves among half the bread slices. Spread chicken salad over basil; top with remaining bread slices. **MAKES 6 SANDWICHES.**

EACH SANDWICH *410 cal, 14 g fat (4 g sat. fat), 63 mg chol, 501 mg sodium, 41 g carbo, 5 g fiber, 30 g pro. Daily Values: 11% vit. A, 9% vit. C, 13% calcium, 19% iron.*

FAST

MEDITERRANEAN SMOKED CHICKEN SALAD SANDWICHES

START TO FINISH: 25 MIN.

¾	cup light mayonnaise or salad dressing
1	tsp. smoked paprika
1	tsp. bottled hot pepper sauce
1	clove garlic, minced
4	6-inch hoagie rolls
2½	cups chopped cooked chicken
¼	cup pitted kalamata olives, chopped
1	cup shredded romaine lettuce
1	medium red sweet pepper, stem, seeds, and membranes removed, and thinly sliced into rings
¼	cup crumbled feta cheese Freshly ground black pepper

1. In a medium bowl combine mayonnaise, paprika, hot pepper sauce, and garlic.
2. Split rolls in half horizontally; scoop out some of the soft insides, leaving a ¼-inch shell. Spread the inside of each roll half with 1 tablespoon of the mayonnaise mixture; set aside.

3. Add chicken and olives to the remaining mayonnaise mixture and mix well. Spread chicken mixture on bottom halves of rolls. Top with lettuce, sweet pepper, feta cheese, and black pepper. Add top halves of rolls. Serve immediately or wrap and chill up to 6 hours. **MAKES 4 SANDWICHES.**

EACH SANDWICH *624 cal, 28 g fat (7 g sat. fat), 102 mg chol, 1,089 mg sodium, 58 g carbo, 4 g fiber, 35 g pro. Daily Values: 48% vit. A, 7% vit. C, 27% calcium, 24% iron.*

FAST

FRENCH CHICKEN SALAD SANDWICHES

PREP: 20 MIN.

½	cup mayonnaise
½	cup sour cream
1	shallot, minced
1	Tbsp. snipped fresh tarragon
1	Tbsp. Dijon-style mustard
¼	tsp. salt
⅛	tsp. ground black pepper
2	cups chopped cooked chicken (8 oz.)
1	cup seedless green grapes, halved
½	cup chopped walnuts or pecans, toasted
4	oz. Brie cheese, chilled and sliced
4	large (sandwich size) croissants, split
2	cups baby arugula

1. In a large bowl stir together mayonnaise, sour cream, shallot, tarragon, mustard, salt, and pepper. Add chicken, grapes, and walnuts; stir to coat. Set aside.
2. Place Brie slices on bottom halves of croissants; top with chicken mixture and arugula. Add top halves of croissants. **MAKES 4 SANDWICHES.**

EACH SANDWICH *830 cal, 61 g fat (21 g sat. fat), 151 mg chol, 1,072 mg sodium, 35 g carbo, 3 g fiber, 34 g pro. Daily Values: 25% vit. A, 8% vit. C, 15% calcium, 17% iron.*

FAST

GREEK HAM-AND-EGG SANDWICHES

START TO FINISH: 25 MIN.

⅓	cup cucumber ranch salad dressing
⅓	cup crumbled feta cheese
8	Greek olives, pitted and chopped
1	tsp. dried basil, crushed
¼	tsp. dried oregano, crushed
⅛	tsp. ground black pepper
4	hard-cooked eggs, chopped
8	slices sourdough bread, toasted
12	oz. thinly sliced smoked ham
16	to 20 spinach leaves, stems removed

1. In a medium bowl stir together salad dressing, cheese, olives, basil, oregano, and pepper; fold in chopped eggs.
2. Layer four slices of toasted bread with ham, the egg mixture, and spinach. Top with remaining bread. Serve immediately or wrap and chill up to 4 hours.
MAKES 4 SANDWICHES.

EACH SANDWICH *456 cal, 22 g fat (6 g sat. fat), 260 mg chol, 1,704 mg sodium, 34 g carbo, 2 g fiber, 30 g pro. Daily Values: 83% vit. A, 8% vit. C, 16% calcium, 28% iron.*

ITALIAN TUNA SANDWICHES

PREP: 20 MIN. CHILL: 4 HRS.

4	individual uncut French or ciabatta rolls
½	of an 8-oz. carton roasted garlic hummus
1½	cups shredded romaine or leaf lettuce
⅓	cup bottled creamy Italian salad dressing
1	small fennel bulb, quartered, cored, and thinly sliced
½	cup bottled roasted red sweet peppers, chopped
⅓	cup finely chopped red onion
1	12-oz. can light tuna, drained and flaked

1. Cut a ½-inch slice from the top of each roll. Hollow bottoms of rolls, leaving a ¼-inch shell. Spread hummus in bottoms of rolls. Sprinkle with lettuce.
2. In a medium bowl combine salad dressing, fennel, red sweet peppers, and red onion; fold in tuna. Spoon onto lettuce. Add roll tops. Serve immediately or wrap and chill up to 4 hours.

MAKES 4 SANDWICHES.

EACH SANDWICH *624 cal, 19 g fat (3 g sat. fat), 15 mg chol, 1,502 mg sodium, 75 g carbo, 6 g fiber, 40 g pro. Daily Values: 33% vit. A, 101% vit. C, 9% calcium, 35% iron.*

Beat-the-Heat Drinks

Paula Marchesi, LENHARTSVILLE, PA

LOW FAT

WATERMELON COOLER

START TO FINISH: 15 MIN.

3	cups coarsely chopped, seeded watermelon
¾	cup sugar
½	cup lightly packed fresh mint leaves
2	cups white grape juice
1	tsp. finely shredded lime peel
¾	cup fresh lime juice, chilled
32	oz. (4 cups) club soda, chilled
	Fresh mint sprigs (optional)
	Watermelon wedges or balls (optional)

1. Place watermelon in a blender or food processor. Cover and blend until smooth. Strain watermelon puree through a fine-mesh sieve; discard pulp.

2. In a large bowl combine sugar and mint. Using the back of a wooden spoon, lightly crush, mint by pressing it against the side of the bowl. Add grape juice, lime peel, lime juice, and watermelon puree, stirring until sugar is dissolved. Stir in club soda. Serve in glasses over ice. Garnish with fresh mint sprigs and watermelon wedges or balls. Serve immediately.

MAKES 9 SERVINGS.

EACH SERVING *121 cal, 0 g fat, 0 mg chol, 31 mg sodium, 31 g carbo, 1 g fiber, 1 g pro. Daily Values: 6% vit. A, 45% vit. C, 2% calcium, 5% iron.*

LOW FAT | KID-FRIENDLY

SPARKLING PEACH PUNCH

PREP: 20 MIN. FREEZE: 8 HRS. STAND: 1 HR.

3	cups water
1½	cups sugar
1	3-oz. pkg. peach-flavored gelatin
1	29-oz. can peach slices in light syrup
4	11.3-oz. cans peach nectar
½	cup lemon juice
8	10-oz. bottles ginger ale or club soda

1. In a large saucepan combine water, sugar, and gelatin. Bring to boiling, stirring to dissolve.

2. Place undrained peach slices in blender. Cover; blend until smooth. In a large bowl (3-to 4-gallon capacity) combine gelatin mixture, pureed peaches, peach nectar, and lemon juice. Divide peach mixture among four 1-quart containers. Cover and freeze overnight or until firm.

NOTE Mixture can be frozen up to 3 months. Use as many containers as needed to continue with Step 3. (Each quart makes 6 servings.)

3. To serve, place one or more containers at room temperature for 1 hour. Break in chunks with large fork. Place in punch bowl or jug. Stir in 2 bottles of ginger ale per container of peach mixture until slushy. **MAKES 24 SERVINGS (FOUR 6-SERVING BATCHES).**

EACH SERVING *143 cal, 0 g fat, 0 mg chol, 26 mg sodium, 37 g carbo, 1 g fiber, 1 g pro. Daily Values: 5% vit. A, 10% vit. C, 1% calcium, 2% iron.*

Tonya Wilson, BLACKSHEAR, GA

FAST | KID-FRIENDLY
PEACHES AND CREAM COOLER
PREP: 5 MIN.

- 2 medium peaches, peeled, pitted, and cut up, or 2 cups frozen unsweetened peach slices
- 1 cup peach ice cream
- 1 cup ice cubes
- 1 6-oz. container low-fat peach yogurt
- 1 Tbsp. honey
- ¼ tsp. almond extract
  Ground nutmeg (optional)

1. In a blender combine peaches, ice cream, ice, yogurt, honey, and almond extract. Blend until smooth. Sprinkle with nutmeg. **MAKES 3 SERVINGS.**

EACH SERVING *271 cal, 8 g fat (5 g sat. fat), 52 mg chol, 69 mg sodium, 44 g carbo, 2 g fiber, 5 g pro. Daily Values: 13% vit. A, 14% vit. C, 13% calcium, 3% iron.*

FAST | LOW FAT
SOUTH-OF-THE-BORDER SANGRIA
START TO FINISH: 10 MIN.

- 1 cup dry red wine
- ¾ cup margarita mix
- ½ cup orange juice
- ¼ cup tequila
- 2 Tbsp. orange liqueur
- 1 Tbsp. lemon juice
- 1 Tbsp. lime juice
- 1 12-oz. can lemon-lime carbonated beverage, chilled
  Ice cubes
  Orange, lemon, and/or lime slices

1. In a 1½-quart pitcher stir together wine, margarita mix, orange juice, tequila, orange liqueur, lemon juice, and lime juice; slowly add carbonated beverage. Serve in glasses over ice. Garnish each serving with citrus slices.

MAKES 4 (ABOUT 9-OUNCE) SERVINGS.

EACH SERVING *201 cal, 0 g fat, 0 mg chol, 50 mg sodium, 29 g carbo, 0 g fiber, 1 g pro. Daily Values: 2% vit. A, 45% vit. C, 2% calcium, 4% iron.*

FAST
SPARKLING CITRUS REFRESHER
PREP: 15 MIN. STAND: 30 MIN. CHILL: 8 HR.

- 3 lemons
- ⅓ cup sugar
- ¼ cup loosely packed fresh mint leaves
- 2 cups freshly squeezed tangerine or orange juice
- ¼ cup limoncello (Italian lemon liqueur)
- 2 cups crushed ice
- 2 cups Prosecco or other sparkling wine, chilled
  Fresh mint leaves

1. Finely shred 2 teaspoons lemon peel. Squeeze juice from lemons (you should have about ½ cup). In a small saucepan combine lemon juice, lemon peel, sugar, and ¼ cup mint leaves. Cook and stir until mixture comes to boiling; simmer, uncovered, 2 minutes. Let stand at room temperature 30 minutes. Strain out mint leaves and discard. Cover and chill overnight, if desired.

2. In a pitcher combine tangerine juice, the lemon syrup, and limoncello. Stir in crushed ice and Prosecco. Garnish with mint leaves. **MAKES 6 SERVINGS.**

EACH SERVING *174 cal, 0 g fat, 0 mg chol, 3 mg sodium, 31 g carbo, 3 g fiber, 1 g pro. Daily Values: 4% vit. A, 142% vit. C, 5% calcium, 6% iron.*

LOW FAT
SWEET SUMMERTIME TEA
PREP: 15 MIN. STAND: 5 MIN. CHILL: 4 HRS.

- 3 cups water
- 6 bags black tea
- 4 bags black cherry-berry or wild berry herb tea
- ½ cup sugar
- 1 cup cranberry juice
- 5 cups cold water
  Ice cubes

1. In a large saucepan bring 3 cups water to boiling. Remove from heat. Add tea bags; cover and let stand for 5 minutes. Remove and discard tea bags. Stir in sugar until dissolved. Stir in cranberry juice. Stir in 5 cups cold water. Cover and refrigerate at least 4 hours or until completely chilled. Serve in glasses over ice.

MAKES 8 (8-OUNCE) SERVINGS.

EACH SERVING *69 cal, 0 g fat, 0 mg chol, 8 mg sodium, 17 g carbo, 0 g fiber, 0 g pro. Daily Values: 22% vit. C, 1% calcium.*

Roxanne Chan, ALBANY, CA

LOW FAT

GOLDEN GRILLED CHICKEN THIGHS WITH APRICOTS

PREP: 30 MIN. MARINATE: 2 HRS. GRILL: 35 MIN.
OVEN: 350°F

- 1 lb. skinless, boneless chicken thighs
- ½ cup apricot nectar
- 6 Tbsp. apricot preserves
- ¼ cup snipped fresh mint
- 1 Tbsp. plus 1 tsp. olive oil
- 1 Tbsp. sherry vinegar
- ½ tsp. curry powder
- 1 clove garlic, minced
- 4 medium apricots, halved and pitted
- 2 green onions, chopped
- ¼ cup chopped pistachios
- 1 Tbsp. Dijon-style mustard
- ½ tsp. mustard seeds

1. Sprinkle chicken with *salt* and *black pepper.* Place in large resealable plastic bag set in shallow dish. For marinade, in bowl combine half the nectar, 2 tablespoons of the preserves, half the mint, 1 tablespoon of the olive oil, the sherry vinegar, curry, and garlic. Pour over chicken. Seal bag; turn to coat. Refrigerate 2 to 4 hours.
2. Remove chicken from marinade; discard marinade. For charcoal grill, place chicken on rack directly over medium coals. Grill, uncovered, 12 to 15 minutes or until chicken is no longer pink (180°F), turning once halfway through. Place apricots on grill, cut sides down, during last 5 minutes of grilling; grill until lightly browned and softened. (For gas grill, preheat grill. Reduce heat to medium. Place chicken on grill rack over heat. Cover; grill as above.)
3. For sauce, in bowl combine the *remaining* apricot nectar, preserves, mint, olive oil, the chopped green onions, pistachios, mustard, mustard seeds, and ¼ teaspoon *salt.* To serve, drizzle chicken and apricots with sauce. **MAKES 4 SERVINGS.**
EACH SERVING *237 cal, 9 g fat (2 g sat. fat), 6 mg chol, 482 mg sodium, 34 g carbo, 3 g fiber, 6 g pro. Daily Values: 25% vit. A, 19% vit. C, 5% calcium, 17% iron.*

KID-FRIENDLY

OPEN-FACE PESTO-CHICKEN BURGERS

PREP: 25 MIN. GRILL: 11 MIN.

- 1 lb. uncooked ground chicken or ground turkey
- 4 Tbsp. basil pesto
- ¼ cup finely shredded Parmesan cheese
- 3 cloves garlic, minced
- ¼ tsp. kosher salt or salt
- 2 3-inch slices ciabatta or four ¾-inch slices rustic Italian bread
- 2 Tbsp. olive oil
- 4 slices fresh mozzarella cheese
- 2 cups fresh basil leaves, arugula, or spring garden mix
- 8 small tomato slices
  Ground black pepper

1. In bowl combine chicken, half the pesto, the Parmesan cheese, garlic, and salt. Shape in four ½-inch-thick oval patties.
2. Horizontally halve ciabatta. Brush cut sides of ciabatta or both sides of Italian bread with olive oil; set aside.
3. For charcoal grill, place patties on greased rack directly over medium coals. Grill, uncovered, 10 to 13 minutes or until chicken is no longer pink (165°F), turning once halfway through grilling. Top each patty with mozzarella cheese. Cover grill; grill 1 to 2 minutes more or until cheese is melted. Add bread to grill rack; grill 1 to 2 minutes each side or until toasted. (For gas grill, preheat grill. Reduce heat to medium. Place patties on grill rack over heat. Cover; grill as above.)
4. Arrange basil or greens on toasted bread. Top with chicken patties, tomato slices, and remaining pesto. Sprinkle coarsely ground *black pepper.*
MAKES 4 SERVINGS.
EACH SERVING *348 cal, 13 g fat (2 g sat. fat), 194 mg chol, 504 mg sodium, 33 g carbo, 2 g fiber, 25 g pro. Daily Values: 25% vit. A, 19% vit. C, 5% calcium, 17% iron.*

Deborah Biggs, OMAHA, NE

GRILLED SPICED CHICKEN KABOBS

PREP: 25 MIN. CHILL: 1 HR. GRILL: 8 MIN.

- 1 Tbsp. olive oil
- 1 Tbsp. paprika
- 2 tsp. garlic powder
- 2 tsp. dried thyme, crushed
- 2 tsp. dried oregano, crushed
- 1 tsp. salt
- 1 tsp. Asian chili sauce
- 1 to 1¼ lb. skinless, boneless chicken breast halves, cut in 1-inch pieces
- 12 to 16 baby pattypan squash or 2 small yellow summer squash, cut in chunks

1. In a large bowl combine the olive oil, paprika, garlic powder, thyme, oregano, salt, and chili sauce. Add chicken pieces and squash; toss to coat. Cover and chill for 1 hour or up to 24 hours. Thread chicken pieces and squash onto eight 8-inch skewers, leaving ¼-inch space between each piece. (If using wooden skewers, soak them in water for at least 30 minutes before threading with food to prevent burning when grilling.)
2. For a charcoal grill, cookl chicken kabobs on the rack of an uncovered grill directly over medium coals for 8 to 10 minutes or until chicken is no longer pink, turning occasionally to brown chicken evenly. (For a gas grill, preheat grill. Reduce heat to medium. Place kabobs on grill rack over heat. Cover and grill as above.) Drizzle kabobs with additional *olive oil* before serving. **MAKES 4 SERVINGS.**

EACH SERVING *174 cal, 5 g fat (1 g sat. fat), 66 mg chol, 672 mg sodium, 4 g carbo, 1 g fiber, 27 g pro. Daily Values: 19% vit. A, 21% vit. C, 3% calcium, 8% iron.*

GRILLED LIME CHICKEN WITH WATERMELON SALSA

PREP: 35 MIN. GRILL: 12 MIN. CHILL: 1 HR.

- 2 cups chopped seeded watermelon
- ½ cup chopped cucumber
- ½ cup chopped orange or yellow sweet pepper
- ½ an ear fresh sweet corn, cut from the cob
- 2 Tbsp. chopped fresh cilantro
- 1 to 2 jalapeño peppers, seeded and chopped*
- 1 Tbsp. finely chopped red onion
- 1 tsp. finely shredded lime peel
- ¼ cup lime juice
- 1 tsp. packed brown sugar
- ¼ tsp. salt
- ¼ tsp. crushed red pepper
- 6 skinless, boneless chicken breast halves
- 1 tsp. lemon-pepper seasoning
- 1 Tbsp. cooking oil

1. For salsa, in a medium bowl combine watermelon, cucumber, sweet pepper, corn, cilantro, jalapeño pepper, and onion. In a small bowl combine ½ teaspoon of the lime peel, 2 tablespoons of the lime juice, the brown sugar, salt, and crushed red pepper. Add to watermelon mixture and toss to coat. Cover and chill for 1 hour.
2. Sprinkle chicken with lemon-pepper seasoning. In a small bowl combine remaining lime peel, lime juice, and the oil.
3. For a charcoal grill, cook chicken on the rack of an uncovered grill directly over medium coals for 12 to 15 minutes or until chicken is no longer pink (170°F), turning once halfway through grilling and brushing with oil mixture during the last 2 minutes of grilling. (For a gas grill, preheat grill; reduce heat to medium. Place chicken on grill rack over heat. Cover; grill as above.) Serve chicken with salsa.
MAKES 6 SERVINGS.
*****NOTE** Hot chile peppers contain oils that can burn skin and eyes. When working with them, wear plastic or rubber gloves.

EACH SERVING *221 cal, 4 g fat (1 g sat. fat), 88 mg chol, 360 mg sodium, 9 g carbo, 1 g fiber, 36 g pro. Daily Values: 17% vit. A, 47% vit. C, 3% calcium, 8% iron.*

GRILLED THAI-GINGER CHICKEN

PREP: 25 MIN. GRILL: 50 MIN.

- 2½ to 3 lb. meaty chicken pieces, (breast halves, thighs, and drumsticks)
- ¼ cup honey
- 1 Tbsp. cooking oil
- 1 small jalapeño pepper, seeded and finely chopped (see Note, *above*)
- 1 Tbsp. lemon juice
- 1 tsp. grated fresh ginger
- ½ tsp. salt
- ½ tsp. red or green curry paste
- ⅓ cup sliced green onions
- ¼ cup chopped fresh cilantro
- ¼ cup honey-roasted peanuts, chopped
- 2 Tbsp. shredded coconut, toasted

1. Skin chicken, if desired; set aside. In a small saucepan stir together honey, cooking oil, jalapeño pepper, lemon juice, ginger, salt, and curry paste. Bring to boiling; reduce heat. Boil gently, uncovered, for 2 minutes.
2. For a charcoal grill, arrange medium-hot coals around a drip pan. Test for medium heat above the pan. Place chicken pieces, bone sides up, on the grill rack over the drip pan. Cover and grill for 50 to 60 minutes or until chicken is no longer

pink (170°F for breasts; 180°F for thighs and drumsticks); turn once halfway through grilling and brush occasionally with glaze during the last 10 minutes of grilling. (For a gas grill, preheat grill. Reduce heat to medium. Adjust for indirect cooking. Cover and grill as directed.)
3. Meanwhile, in a medium bowl combine green onions, cilantro, peanuts, and coconut. Serve chicken sprinkled with green onion mixture.
MAKES 4 TO 6 SERVINGS.

EACH SERVING *555 cal, 32 g fat (9 g sat. fat), 161 mg chol, 452 mg sodium, 21 g carbo, 1 g fiber, 46 g pro. Daily Values: 12% vit. A, 2% vit. C, 4% calcium, 13% iron.*

BARBECUE CHICKEN WITH RASPBERRY GLAZE

PREP: 20 MIN. GRILL: 50 MIN.

- 1 3½- to 4-lb. whole roasting chicken
- ½ cup balsamic vinegar
- 2 Tbsp. snipped fresh rosemary
- 1 tsp. salt
- ¼ tsp. cayenne pepper
- ½ cup seedless raspberry jam
- ¼ cup dry red wine or cranberry juice

1. To butterfly chicken, using kitchen shears, cut along both sides of backbone to remove. Turn chicken skin side up and press down between the breasts to break the keel bone.
2. In a small bowl combine vinegar, rosemary, salt, and pepper; divide mixture in half. Use half of the mixture to brush on both sides of chicken.
3. In a small saucepan combine remaining half of the vinegar mixture, the jam, and wine or cranberry juice. Cook and stir over medium heat until mixture comes to boiling; reduce heat and cook, uncovered, for 3 to 4 minutes or until slightly thickened. Set aside.
4. For a charcoal grill, arrange medium-hot coals around a drip pan. Test for medium heat above the pan. Place chicken, skin side up, flat on the grill rack over the drip pan. Cover; grill for 50 to 60 minutes or until chicken is no longer pink (180°F in the thigh), brushing with raspberry glaze during the last 5 minutes of grilling. (For a gas grill, preheat grill. Reduce heat to medium. Adjust for indirect cooking. Cover and grill as above.)
MAKES 4 SERVINGS.

EACH SERVING *730 cal, 39 g fat (11 g sat. fat), 201 mg chol, 753 mg sodium, 35 g carbo, 1 g fiber, 50 g pro. Daily Values: 7% vit. A, 12% vit. C, 4% calcium, 15% iron.*

Melon Magic

Grace A. Eckstorm, HOLDEN BEACH, NC

FAST

MELON SALAD WITH SWEET SESAME DRESSING

START TO FINISH: 30 MIN.

⅓	cup sugar
3	Tbsp. champagne vinegar or white wine vinegar
½	tsp. kosher salt or salt
½	tsp. ground ginger
3	Tbsp. vegetable oil
3	Tbsp. extra virgin olive oil
1½	tsp. sesame seeds, toasted
½	tsp. toasted sesame oil
	Dash cayenne pepper
	Lettuce leaves
2	cups cut up seedless watermelon
2	cups cut up cantaloupe
2	cups cut up honeydew
1	cup sliced seedless (English) cucumber
	Snipped fresh cilantro
	Crisp-cooked bacon, drained and crumbled (optional)

1. For sweet sesame dressing, in small saucepan combine sugar, vinegar, salt, and ginger. Stir over medium heat until sugar is dissolved. Remove from heat. Transfer to medium bowl. In a thin steady stream, slowly add vegetable and olive oils to sugar mixture, whisking constantly until thickened. Stir in sesame seeds, sesame oil, and cayenne pepper; set aside.

2. Line salad bowls or platter with lettuce; top with watermelon, cantaloupe, honeydew, and cucumber. Drizzle with some of the dressing (about ½ cup). Sprinkle cilantro and bacon. Pass remaining dressing. **MAKES 6 SERVINGS.**

EACH SERVING *233 cal, 15g fat (2 g sat. fat), 0 mg chol, 186 mg sodium, 26 g carbo, 2 g fiber, 2 g pro. Daily Values: 68 % vit. A, 59% vit. C, 3% calcium, 4% iron.*

LOW FAT

HONEY-LIME LAMB AND MELON KABOBS

PREP: 25 MIN. MARINATE: 30 MIN. GRILL: 12 MIN.

1¼	to 1½ lb. boneless lamb sirloin steak, cut in 1-inch cubes
3	tsp. shredded lime peel
⅓	cup lime juice
⅓	cup honey
1	Tbsp. snipped fresh tarragon or ½ tsp. dried tarragon, crushed
1	clove garlic, minced
½	tsp. salt
½	tsp. ground black pepper
12	1-inch cubes cantaloupe
12	1-inch cubes honeydew
1	6-oz. carton plain yogurt
6	soft flatbreads, warmed
	Fresh arugula (optional)

1. Place lamb in resealable plastic bag set in dish. For marinade, in bowl whisk together 2 teaspoons of the peel, lime juice, honey, 2 teaspoons of the fresh tarragon (1 teaspoon dried), garlic, salt, and pepper. Reserve ¼ cup marinade. Pour remaining over lamb. Seal bag; turn to coat. Refrigerate ½ to 2 hours, turning once. Remove lamb; discard marinade.

2. On twelve 6-inch skewers thread lamb and melon pieces, leaving ¼-inch between. For charcoal grill, place on rack directly over medium coals. Grill, uncovered, 12 to 14 minutes or until meat is slightly pink in center, turning and brushing often with reserved marinade.

3. Stir remaining peel and tarragon into yogurt. Serve kabobs with yogurt, flatbreads, and arugula. **MAKES 6 SERVINGS.**

EACH SERVING *409 cal., 6 g fat (2 g sat. fat), 62 mg chol, 616 mg sodium, 62 g carbo, 3 g fiber, 27 g pro. Daily Values: 38% vit. A, 62% vit. C, 13% calcium, 21% iron.*

Angela Buchanan, LONGMONT, CO

FAST

GRILLED WATERMELON SALAD

PREP: 20 MIN. GRILL: 8 MIN.

¼	cup lemon juice
¼	cup olive oil
2	Tbsp. honey
1	tsp. crushed red pepper
¼	tsp. kosher salt
4	1½-inch slices seedless watermelon (2¼ to 2½ lb. total)
1	5- to 6-oz. pkg. torn mixed salad greens
2	oz. Gorgonzola cheese, crumbled

1. In a small bowl whisk together lemon juice, olive oil, honey, crushed red pepper, and salt. Brush 2 to 3 tablespoons lemon juice mixture on the watermelon wedges. Set aside.

2. For a charcoal grill, cook watermelon wedges on the rack of an uncovered grill directly over medium coals for 8 to 10 minutes or until watermelon has grill marks and is warm, turning once halfway through grilling.

3. Divide salad greens among four plates. Top with grilled watermelon wedges. Whisk remaining lemon juice mixture to combine; drizzle over salads. Sprinkle with Gorgonzola cheese.
MAKES 4 SERVINGS.

EACH SERVING 294 cal, 18 g fat (5 g sat. fat), 11 mg chol, 328 mg sodium, 32 g carbo, 2 g fiber, 5 g pro. Daily Values: 4% vit. A, 51% vit. C, 11% calcium, 6% iron.

WATERMELON-HONEY SHORTCAKES

PREP: 30 MIN. BAKE: 10 MIN. OVEN: 450°F

2	cups all-purpose flour
⅓	cup sugar
1	Tbsp. baking powder
½	tsp. baking soda
½	tsp. salt
½	cup butter
½	cup buttermilk
1	egg
¼	cup honey
3	cups seedless watermelon chunks
1	Tbsp. snipped fresh mint
1	7-oz. container Greek-style plain yogurt or one 6-oz. container vanilla yogurt
	Honey

1. Preheat oven to 450°F. Grease a baking sheet or line with parchment paper; set aside.

2. For shortcake, In a large bowl stir together the flour, sugar, baking powder, soda, and salt. Cut in butter until mixture resembles coarse crumbs. In a small bowl whisk together buttermilk, egg, and 1 tablespoon of the honey. Add buttermilk mixture to flour mixture. Stir with a fork just until combined.

3. Transfer dough to a lightly floured surface. Gently knead 5 to 6 times just until dough comes together. Gently pat or roll to ¾-inch thickness. Use a 3-inch round cutter to make 6 rounds, rerolling dough as necessary. Place rounds on prepared baking sheet. Bake for 10 minutes or until golden brown. Place baking sheet on a wire rack and let shortcake cool slightly.

4. Meanwhile, in a medium bowl stir together watermelon, remaining 3 tablespoons honey, and mint. Set aside.

5. To serve, split warm shortcake. Place bottoms on dessert plates. Top each with some of the yogurt, the watermelon, and shortcake tops; drizzle with additional honey. MAKES 6 SERVINGS.

EACH SERVING 470 cal, 18 g fat (11 g sat. fat), 78 mg chol, 574 mg sodium, 71 g carbo, 1 g fiber, 10 g pro. Daily Values: 19% vit. A, 12% vit. C, 12% calcium, 14% iron.

FAST

MELON-MANGO SMOOTHIE

START TO FINISH: 15 MIN.

½	a medium cantaloupe, seeded, peeled, and cubed (about 3 cups)
½	mango, halved, seeded, peeled, and cubed
1	8¼-oz. can unpeeled apricot halves in light syrup, chilled
1	small seedless orange, peeled and sectioned
1	cup frozen vanilla yogurt or low-fat or light vanilla ice cream

1. In a blender combine cantaloupe, mango, undrained apricot halves, orange sections, and frozen yogurt. Cover and blend until smooth.
MAKES 4 (1 CUP) SERVINGS.

EACH SERVING 169 cal, 2 g fat (1 g sat. fat), 1 mg chol, 53 mg sodium, 36 g carbo, 3 g fiber, 3 g pro. Daily Values: 104% vit. A, 117% vit. C, 8% calcium, 4% iron.

FAST

MIDSUMMER'S MELON SALAD

START TO FINISH: 25 MIN.

1	8-oz. tub light cream cheese
¼	cup honey
½	tsp. finely shredded lemon peel
2	Tbsp. lemon juice
1	cantaloupe, halved and seeded
1	honeydew melon, halved and seeded
1	cup seedless red grapes, halved Freshly ground black pepper (optional)

1. For dressing, stir together cream cheese, 2 tablespoons of the honey, lemon peel, and lemon juice. Set aside.

2. Using a melon baller, scoop balls from melon halves. Place in a large serving bowl. Add grapes, remaining honey, and pepper. Toss to combine. Serve immediately with dressing or cover and chill for 1 hour before serving.
MAKES 10 TO 12 SERVINGS (6 CUPS).

EACH SERVING 130 cal, 3 g fat (2 g sat. fat), 11 mg chol, 134 mg sodium, 24 g carbo, 1 g fiber, 3 g pro. Daily Values: 44% vit. A, 67% vit. C, 4% calcium, 2% iron.

FAST

SPINACH, WATERMELON, AND BLUEBERRY SALAD

START TO FINISH: 15 MIN.

1	6-oz. pkg. fresh baby spinach
1½	cups coarsely chopped seedless watermelon and/or cantaloupe
1	cup blueberries
¼	cup thin red onion slivers
1	recipe Orange Vinaigrette
4	oz. goat cheese (chèvre), crumbled

1. In a large salad bowl combine spinach, watermelon, blueberries, and onion. Add Orange Vinaigrette and toss to coat. Top with goat cheese. MAKES 8 TO 10 SERVINGS.

ORANGE VINAIGRETTE In a screw-top jar combine ¼ cup olive oil, 2 tablespoons vinegar, ½ teaspoon finely shredded orange peel, 1 tablespoon orange juice, ¼ teaspoon salt, and ⅛ teaspoon ground black pepper. Cover and shake well.

EACH SERVING 125 cal, 10 g fat (3 g sat. fat), 7 mg chol, 142 mg sodium, 6 g carbo, 1 g fiber, 4 g pro. Daily Values: 43% vit. A, 19% vit. C, 5% calcium, 6% iron.

Crave-Worthy Vegetable Suppers

Ilene S. Whitehead, PUEBLO, CO

VEGGIE-STUFFED PORTOBELLO MUSHROOMS

PREP: 25 MIN. BAKE: 17 MIN. OVEN: 425°F

1	small yellow sweet pepper, cut in bite-size strips
1	small red onion, chopped
1	medium zucchini, coarsely shredded
1	carrot, coarsely shredded
1	stalk celery, thinly sliced
2	cloves garlic, minced
2	to 3 Tbsp. olive oil
1	Tbsp. snipped fresh basil
1	Tbsp. lemon juice
1	5-oz. pkg. fresh baby spinach
½	cup fine dry bread crumbs
½	cup finely shredded Parmesan cheese
4	4- to 5-inch portobello mushroom caps, stems removed
4	slices provolone cheese

1. Preheat oven to 425°F. Line 15×10×1-inch baking pan with foil. In 12-inch skillet cook and stir sweet pepper, onion, zucchini, carrot, celery, and garlic in hot oil over medium-high heat 4 minutes. Stir in basil, lemon juice, and ¼ teaspoon each *salt* and ground *black pepper*. Top with spinach; cover. Cook for 2 minutes or until spinach is wilted. Remove from heat. Stir crumbs and half of the Parmesan cheese into spinach mixture; set aside.

2. Remove gills from mushrooms, if desired. Arrange mushrooms, stem sides up, on prepared pan. Top each with a slice of provolone. Divide spinach mixture among mushroom caps. Bake 15 minutes (mushrooms will water out slightly). Top with remaining Parmesan. Bake 2 minutes more or until cheese is slightly melted.

MAKES 4 SERVINGS.

EACH SERVING *296 cal, 17 g fat (7 g sat. fat), 625 mg chol, 617 mg sodium, 24 g carbo, 4 g fiber, 6 g pro. Daily Values: 129% vit. A, 135% vit. C, 33% calcium, 16% iron.*

VEGETABLE FLATBREADS WITH GOAT CHEESE

PREP: 25 MIN. BROIL: 6 MIN.

⅓	cup olive oil
1	medium yellow summer squash, quartered lengthwise and sliced
½	small red onion, sliced
1	small green sweet pepper, chopped
1	small red sweet pepper, chopped
1	medium carrot, chopped
½	cup fresh broccoli florets
4	cloves garlic, minced
2	plum tomatoes, chopped
12	pimiento-stuffed green olives, halved, plus 1 Tbsp. liquid from jar
4	6- to 7½-inch flatbreads
8	oz. goat cheese (chèvre), crumbled

1. Preheat broiler. In 12-inch skillet heat 2 tablespoons of the olive oil over medium-high heat. Add squash, onion, sweet peppers, carrot, broccoli, and garlic. Cook and stir 3 minutes. Add tomatoes, olives, and olive liquid. Cook, uncovered, 2 minutes more or until tender.

2. Place flatbreads on baking sheets. Brush both sides with some of the remaining olive oil. Broil half at a time 4 inches from the heat 1 to 2 minutes on each side or until lightly browned.

3. Using slotted spoon, remove vegetable mixture from skillet; spoon on toasted flatbreads. Top with cheese. Season with *black pepper*. Broil 4 inches from heat 2 minutes or until cheese softens. Drizzle with remaining olive oil. Sprinkle with *sea salt* and freshly ground *black pepper*.

MAKES 4 SERVINGS.

EACH SERVING *611 cal, 40 g fat (15 g sat. fat), 45 mg chol, 894 mg sodium, 45 g carbo, 5 g fiber, 20 g pro. Daily Values: 92% vit. A, 103% vit. C, 26% calcium, 19% iron.*

Inga Fouquette, GIG HARBOR, WA

LOW FAT

SUMMER RATATOUILLE TART

PREP: 25 MIN. BAKE: 40 MIN. COOK: 30 MIN. STAND: 20 MIN. OVEN: 400°F/350°F

- ½ a 15-oz. pkg. rolled refrigerated unbaked piecrust (1 crust)
- ¼ cup chopped yellow onion
- 2 cloves garlic, minced
- 1 Tbsp. extra virgin olive oil
- 1 medium zucchini, sliced (about 1¼ cups)
- 1 small eggplant, peeled and cubed (about 4 cups)
- 1 medium red sweet pepper, cut in bite-size pieces (about ¾ cup)
- 3 medium tomatoes, peeled, seeded, and chopped
- ½ tsp. sea salt or salt
- ½ tsp. herbes de Provence or dried Italian seasoning, crushed
- ½ tsp. freshly ground black pepper
- 8 oz. asparagus, trimmed and cut into 2-inch pieces
- ¼ cup finely shredded Parmesan cheese

1. Preheat oven to 400°F. Let piecrust stand according to package directions. Line bottom and sides of a 9- to 10-inch tart pan with removable bottom with pie crust. Line pastry with foil. Bake 10 minutes. Remove foil and bake 5 minutes more. Cool on a wire rack. Reduce oven temperature to 350°F.
2. Meanwhile, in a large saucepan cook onion and garlic in hot oil for 3 minutes or until onion is tender. Stir in zucchini, eggplant, and half of the sweet pepper. Cook and stir 10 minutes or until vegetables are tender. Stir in the tomatoes, salt, herbes de Provence, and black pepper. Cover and simmer 10 minutes. Uncover and simmer 10 minutes more or until mixture has thickened and most of the liquid is gone.
3. Spoon mixture into the partially baked pastry shell. Bake 10 minutes. Top with remaining sweet pepper and asparagus. Bake 15 minutes more. Sprinkle with Parmesan. Let stand 20 minutes before serving. **MAKES 6 MAIN-DISH SERVINGS.**
EACH SERVING *237 cal, 13 g fat (4 g sat. fat), 6 mg chol, 344 mg sodium, 27 g carbo, 4 g fiber, 4 g pro. Daily Values: 29% vit. A, 71% vit. C, 7% calcium, 7% iron.*

PORTOBELLO MUSHROOMS WITH GRILLED HERBED VEGETABLES

PREP: 30 MIN. GRILL: 30 MIN.

- 4 medium red-skinned potatoes, cut in ½-inch cubes (4 cups)
- 1 medium onion, cut into very thin wedges
- 1 medium sweet pepper, cut in strips
- 1 medium zucchini, cut in ¼-inch slices
- 1 medium yellow summer squash, cut in ¼-inch slices
- 4 Tbsp. olive oil
- 2 Tbsp. chopped fresh rosemary
- 2 Tbsp. chopped fresh basil
- 3 cloves garlic, minced
- ½ tsp. salt
- 4 6- to 8-oz. portobello mushrooms Salt and ground black pepper
- ½ cup finely shredded Parmesan cheese
- 12 grape or cherry tomatoes, quartered
- ¼ cup pine nuts, toasted and coarsely chopped Olive oil

1. In a large saucepan bring lightly salted water to boiling. Add potatoes and return to boiling. Reduce heat and simmer, covered, for 5 minutes; drain.
2. In a disposable foil roasting pan combine the potatoes, onion, sweet pepper, zucchini, and yellow summer squash. Drizzle with 2 tablespoons of the olive oil. Sprinkle with rosemary, 1 tablespoon of the basil, the garlic, and ½ teaspoon salt. Cover with heavy foil.
3. For a charcoal grill, place pan directly over medium coals. Grill 30 minutes, stirring twice. Meanwhile, brush mushrooms with remaining 2 tablespoons olive oil. Sprinkle with salt and black pepper. Grill mushroom caps, rounded side down, on the rack of an uncovered grill directly over medium coals for 5 minutes. Turn and grill for 5 to 7 minutes more or until slightly softened and tender. (For a gas grill, preheat grill. Reduce heat to medium. Place pan and mushrooms over heat. Cover and grill as above.)
4. Place 1 mushroom on each of 4 serving plates. Spoon vegetable mixture on top of mushrooms. In a small bowl combine Parmesan, tomatoes, pine nuts, and remaining basil; sprinkle over vegetable mixture. Drizzle with additional olive oil. **MAKES 4 SERVINGS.**
EACH SERVING *427 cal, 26 g fat (5 g sat. fat), 7 mg chol, 635 mg sodium, 42 g carbo, 8 g fiber, 15 g pro. Daily Values: 31% vit. A, 142% vit. C, 19% calcium, 21% iron.*

DEEP-DISH GARDEN VEGETABLE PIZZA

PREP: 30 MIN. BAKE: 20 MIN. OVEN: 400°F

- 1 egg, lightly beaten
- 1 8.5-oz. pkg. corn muffin mix
- ⅓ cup all-purpose flour
- 3 Tbsp. milk
- 1 Tbsp. dried Italian seasoning, crushed
- 2 medium carrots, shredded
- 1 cup fresh or frozen whole kernel corn, thawed
- 2 small red or green sweet peppers, chopped
- 2 plum tomatoes, seeded and chopped
- 1 fresh jalapeño pepper, seeded and finely chopped*
- 1 Tbsp. snipped fresh oregano
- ¼ cup bottled Italian salad dressing
- 1½ cups finely shredded Italian-style cheese blend
- 1 Tbsp. snipped fresh Italian (flat-leaf) parsley

1. Preheat oven to 400°F. Generously grease a 13×9×2-inch baking pan; set aside. In a medium bowl combine egg, corn muffin mix, flour, milk, and dried Italian seasoning. Mix until combined. On a well-floured surface, knead 10 to 12 times or until easy to handle (dough will be soft). Using floured hands, pat dough into the bottom of prepared pan. Sprinkle carrots, corn, sweet peppers, tomatoes, jalapeño pepper, and oregano over dough; drizzle with Italian dressing. Sprinkle cheese.
2. Bake for 20 minutes or until a toothpick inserted near the center comes out clean. Sprinkle with parsley. **MAKES 6 SERVINGS.**
*****NOTE** Hot chile peppers contain oils that can burn skin and eyes. When working with them, wear plastic or rubber gloves.
EACH SERVING *368 cal, 15 g fat (5 g sat. fat), 56 mg chol, 675 mg sodium, 47 g carbo, 2 g fiber, 13 g pro. Daily Values: 97% vit. A, 71% vit. C, 24% calcium, 12% iron.*

Frozen Desserts

Erika Rohr Luke, DAVIS, CA

BANANAS FOSTER GELATO

PREP: 30 MIN. CHILL: 8 HRS.
FREEZE: PER MANUFACTURER'S DIRECTIONS

- ⅔ cup packed brown sugar
- 5 egg yolks
- ¼ tsp. ground cinnamon
- 1¾ cups whole milk
- ¼ cup whipping cream
- 2 ripe bananas
- 1 tsp. lemon juice
- 2 Tbsp. dark rum or ½ tsp. rum extract
- 1 tsp. vanilla
  Sliced bananas (optional)
  Caramel-flavored ice cream topping (optional)

1. In medium mixing bowl beat brown sugar, egg yolks, and cinnamon with an electric mixer about 4 minutes or until light; set aside.

2. In medium saucepan heat and stir the milk, cream, and ½ teaspoon *salt* just until simmering. Slowly stir about 1 cup of the hot milk mixture into the egg yolk mixture. Return all egg yolk mixture to saucepan. Heat and stir constantly (do not boil) until mixture thickens. Remove pan from heat and place in bowl of ice water; stir 2 to 3 minutes to cool.

3. Mash the two bananas with the lemon juice. Stir into thickened milk mixture along with rum and vanilla (mixture may appear slightly curdled). Transfer to large bowl. Cover; refrigerate overnight.

4. Freeze in 1½- or 2-quart ice cream freezer according to manufacturer's directions. Serve with sliced bananas and caramel topping. **MAKES ABOUT 8 (½-CUP) SERVINGS.**
EACH SERVING *198 cal, 7 g fat (4 g sat. fat), 147 mg chol, 180 mg sodium, 28 g carbo, 1 g fiber, 4 g pro. Daily Values: 7% vit. A, 5% vit. C, 10% calcium, 3% iron.*

RASPBERRY-PEAR SORBET

PREP: 20 MIN. FREEZE: 10 HRS. COOK: 3 MIN. STAND: 5 MIN.

- ½ cup sugar
- 1 pint fresh raspberries
- 1 medium pear, peeled, cored, and cut up
- ⅓ cup lime juice
- 1 Tbsp. pear liqueur or vodka (optional)
- ⅛ tsp. salt
  Fresh raspberries (optional)

1. For simple syrup, in small saucepan bring 1 cup *water* and the sugar to boiling, stirring to dissolve sugar. Reduce heat. Simmer, uncovered, 3 minutes. Remove from heat. Place in refrigerator to cool.

2. Meanwhile, for puree, in food processor combine the 1 pint raspberries, pear, lime juice, pear liqueur, and salt. Cover; process 30 seconds or until smooth. Strain mixture through fine-mesh sieve to remove seeds; discard seeds. Stir in chilled simple syrup.

3. Spread mixture in an 8×2-inch square baking pan. Cover; freeze 4 hours or until solid. Break up mixture with a fork; place in food processor. Cover; process 30 seconds or until smooth. Transfer to 1-quart freezer container; cover and freeze sorbet 6 to 8 hours or until solid. To serve, let stand at room temperature 5 minutes before scooping. Serve with additional raspberries. **MAKES 6 (½-CUP) SERVINGS.**
EACH SERVING *106 cal, 0 g fat, 0 mg chol, 51 mg sodium, 27 g carbo, 4 g fiber, 1 g pro. Daily Values: 1% vit. A, 27% vit. C, 2% calcium, 2% iron.*

Jill Zahniser, ST. PAUL, MN

GERMAN CHOCOLATE PIE WITH COCONUT PECAN CRUST

PREP: 25 MIN. BAKE: 20 MIN. FREEZE: 4 HRS.
STAND: 15 MIN. OVEN: 325°F

3	Tbsp. butter, melted
1	Tbsp. packed brown sugar
1½	cups flaked coconut
½	cup pecans, chopped
1½	pkg. (6 oz.) sweet baking chocolate, chopped
⅓	cup milk
1	3-oz. pkg. cream cheese, softened
2	Tbsp. sugar
1	8-oz. container frozen whipped dessert topping, thawed
	Toasted flaked coconut and/or chocolate shavings (optional)

1. Preheat oven to 325°F. In a medium bowl combine melted butter and brown sugar; stir in coconut and pecans. Press into the bottom and up the sides of a 9-inch pie plate. Bake for 20 minutes; remove from oven and cool on wire rack.

2. In a large microwave-safe bowl combine chocolate and 2 tablespoons of the milk. Microwave on 100% power (high) for 1½ minutes or until chocolate is almost melted. Stir until chocolate is melted.

3. Add cream cheese and 2 tablespoons sugar to melted chocolate. Beat with an electric mixer on medium speed until combined. Gradually beat in remaining milk on low speed. Fold in dessert topping. Spoon into prepared crust.

4. Cover and freeze 4 hours or until firm. Let stand for 15 minutes before serving. Sprinkle with toasted coconut and/or chocolate shavings.

MAKES 8 SERVINGS.

EACH SERVING 427 cal, 31 g fat (20 g sat. fat), 24 mg chol, 129 mg sodium, 35 g carbo, 4 g fiber, 5 g pro. Daily Values: 6% vit. A, 3% calcium, 5% iron.

COCONUT-LIMEADE FREEZE

PREP: 30 MIN. CHILL: 1 HR. FREEZE: 4 HRS.
STAND: 15 MIN.

1	recipe Macadamia-Graham Cracker Crust
1	envelope unflavored gelatin
½	cup sugar
1	14-oz. can coconut milk
½	of a 12-oz. can frozen limeade concentrate, thawed (¾ cup)
1½	tsp. finely shredded lime peel
1	cup whipping cream
	Macadamia nuts, toasted and chopped (optional)
	Flaked coconut, toasted (optional)

1. Prepare graham cracker crust. In a small saucepan combine gelatin and sugar; add coconut milk. Cook and stir over medium heat until gelatin is dissolved. Transfer to a large bowl. Stir in limeade concentrate and lime peel. Chill 1 to 2 hours or until partially set; stirring occasionally.

2. In a large mixing bowl beat whipping cream with an electric mixer on medium speed until soft peaks form. Fold into gelatin mixture. Pour into crust. Cover and freeze 4 hours or overnight until firm.

3. Let stand at room temperature for 15 to 30 minutes before serving. Top with toasted macadamia nuts and/or coconut.

MAKES 8 SERVINGS.

MACADAMIA-GRAHAM CRACKER CRUST In a medium bowl combine ⅓ cup butter, melted; ¼ cup sugar; 1 cup finely crushed graham crackers; and ⅓ cup very finely chopped macadamia nuts. Press in the bottom of a 2-quart rectangular baking dish. Place in freezer.

EACH SERVING 478 cal, 33 g fat (21 g sat. fat), 61 mg chol, 137 mg sodium, 44 g carbo, 1 g fiber, 4 g pro. Daily Values: 14% vit. A, 6% vit. C, 3% calcium, 6% iron.

KID-FRIENDLY

PORTABLE PEANUT BUTTER PARFAITS

PREP: 20 MIN. CHILL: 20 MIN. FREEZE: 2 HRS.

¾	cup crushed pretzels
½	cup honey-roasted peanuts, chopped
¼	cup miniature semisweet chocolate pieces or miniature candy-coated semisweet chocolate pieces
2½	cups tiny marshmallows
½	cup creamy peanut butter
¼	cup milk
1	Tbsp. sugar
1½	cups whipping cream

1. In a small bowl combine pretzels, peanuts, and chocolate pieces. Place 1 tablespoon in eight 5- to 6-oz. disposable plastic cups.

2. In a medium saucepan combine marshmallows, peanut butter, milk, and sugar; heat and stir over medium-low heat just until melted. Transfer to a medium bowl. Chill 20 minutes, stirring once. In a large mixing bowl beat whipping cream on medium speed with an electric mixer until soft peaks form; gradually beat in peanut butter mixture (do not overbeat). Spoon half of the mixture into crumb-lined cups. Top with some of the pretzel mixture, then remaining whipped mixture. Top with remaining pretzel mixture.

3. Freeze at least 2 hours.

MAKES 8 SERVINGS.

EACH SERVING 429 cal, 30 g fat (14 g sat. fat), 62 mg chol, 34 g carbo, 2 g fiber, 7 g pro. Daily Values: 14% vit. A, 5% calcium, 5% iron.

FROZEN TIRAMISU

PREP: 45 MIN. FREEZE: 8 HRS. STAND: 15 MIN.

1	cup crushed chocolate wafer cookies (20)
½	cup finely chopped pecans, toasted
¼	cup butter, melted
1	3-oz. pkg. ladyfingers, split
¼	cup brewed espresso or strong coffee, cooled
⅔	cup whipping cream
2	Tbsp. sugar
1	8-oz. pkg. mascarpone cheese, at room temperature
2	Tbsp. white cream de cacao
1	quart chocolate ice cream
1	quart coffee ice cream
	Chocolate-covered espresso beans, chopped (optional)
	Chocolate shavings or curls (optional)

1. In a medium bowl combine crushed wafers, pecans, and melted butter. Press firmly into bottom of a 10-inch springform pan.

2. Lightly brush flat sides of the ladyfingers with half of the brewed espresso. Line, round sides to the outside, vertically around the outside of the pan on the chocolate crust. Set aside.

3. In a large bowl beat whipping cream and sugar with an electric mixer on medium to high speed to soft peaks. In a medium bowl beat mascarpone, cream de cacao, and remaining espresso with electric mixer until well combined. Fold in whipped cream until combined.

4. Stir chocolate ice cream to soften; spoon into lined pan. Spoon mascarpone mixture on top. Freeze about 3 hours or until firm.

5. Stir coffee ice cream to soften; spread on whipped cream layer. Cover and freeze overnight.

6. Let stand at room temperature 15 minutes before serving. Remove sides of pan. Sprinkle with chopped espresso beans and chocolate shavings.

MAKES 12 SERVINGS.

EACH SERVING 469 cal, 33 g fat (18 g sat. fat), 100 mg chol, 172 mg sodium, 39 g carbo, 1 g fiber, 9 g pro. Daily Values: 15% vit. A, 1% vit. C, 11% calcium, 7% iron.

Weeknight Steak Dishes

PRIZE TESTED RECIPES® $400 WINNER

PRIZE TESTED RECIPES® $400 WINNER
Leslie Clark, GRANDVIEW, MO

ESPRESSO-RUBBED STEAK WITH GREEN CHILE PESTO

START TO FINISH: 30 MIN.

- 1½ lb. beef flank steak
- 2 tsp. chili powder
- 1 tsp. kosher salt or salt
- 1 tsp. instant espresso coffee powder
- ½ tsp. garlic powder
- ½ tsp. dried oregano, crushed
- ½ tsp. ground black pepper
- 1 recipe Green Chile Pesto
  Cilantro leaves (optional)

1. Score both sides of steak by making diagonal cuts in a diamond pattern. In small bowl combine chili powder, salt, espresso powder, garlic powder, oregano, and pepper. Sprinkle over steak; rub in.
2. Coat a 12-inch nonstick skillet with *nonstick cooking spray.* Heat over medium-high heat until very hot; add steak. Reduce heat to medium. Cook 12 to 14 minutes for medium-rare (145°F) or 14 to 16 minutes for medium (160°F), turning once halfway through. Transfer to cutting board. Keep warm while preparing Green Chile Pesto.
3. To serve, thinly slice steak against grain. Pass Green Chile Pesto. Sprinkle with cilantro leaves. **MAKES 8 SERVINGS.**
GREEN CHILE PESTO Halve 2 medium fresh Anaheim or poblano chile peppers lengthwise; remove stems, seeds, and veins. Coarsely chop peppers. In food processor combine peppers, ½ cup fresh cilantro, ¼ cup crumbled Cotija cheese, 2 tablespoons pine nuts, 2 cloves garlic, ¼ teaspoon crushed red pepper, and salt and black pepper to taste. Process to finely chop mixture. With processor running, add ⅓ cup olive oil in steady stream through feed tube to combine into a coarse paste. **MAKES 1⅓ CUPS PESTO.**
EACH SERVING *244 cal, 17 g fat (3 g sat. fat), 31 mg chol, 335 mg sodium, 4 g carbo, 1 g fiber, 20 g pro. Daily Values: 15% vit. A, 131% vit. C, 7% calcium, 15% iron.*

PEACH-HORSERADISH SAUCED RIBEYES

PREP: 10 MIN. GRILL: 11 MIN.

- 2 beef ribeye steaks, cut 1 inch thick (about 1½ lb. total)
- 1 Tbsp. olive oil
- 1 Tbsp. steak seasoning
- ⅓ cup peach preserves
- 2 Tbsp. prepared horseradish
- 2 Tbsp. bottled plum sauce
  Grilled peaches (optional)*

1. Trim fat from steaks. Brush steaks with oil; sprinkle with steak seasoning. For charcoal grill, grill steaks on rack of uncovered grill directly over medium coals for 10 to 12 minutes for medium-rare (145°F) or 12 to 15 minutes for medium (160°F), turning once halfway through. Remove from grill. (For gas grill, preheat grill. Reduce heat to medium. Place steaks on rack over heat. Cover; grill as above.)
2. Meanwhile, for Peach-Horseradish Sauce, in small bowl stir together preserves, horseradish, and plum sauce. Slice steaks. Serve with sauce and grilled peaches. **MAKES 4 SERVINGS.**
EACH SERVING *399 cal, 18 g fat (6 g sat. fat), 100 mg chol, 700 mg sodium, 23 g carbo, 1 g fiber, 35 g pro. Daily Values: 7% vit. C, 3% calcium, 22% iron.*
***TO GRILL PEACHES,** halve and pit peaches. Grill on rack of uncovered grill directly over medium coals for 8 to 10 minutes or until tender and lightly browned, turning once.

PRIZE TESTED RECIPES®
$200 WINNER
Joyce Stanek, REYNOLDSBURG, OH

STEAK WITH BLUE CHEESE AND APPLES

PREP: 25 MIN. COOK: 10 MIN.

- 1 small sweet onion, cut into thin wedges (½ cup)
- 1 Tbsp. butter
- 2 Tbsp. vegetable oil
- 4 small or 3 medium cooking apples, cored and cut into thin wedges (about 4 cups)
- 4 beef tenderloin steaks, cut 1 inch thick (1 to 1½ lb. total) Salt and ground black pepper
- 1 oz. Roquefort or blue cheese, crumbled

1. In a large skillet cook onion in hot butter and 1 tablespoon of the oil over medium heat for 5 minutes. Reduce heat. Add apples and cook, covered, for 3 minutes. Remove from skillet to a serving dish; cover to keep warm (apples will continue to soften as they stand).

2. Season steaks with salt and pepper. Add remaining oil to same skillet and heat over medium heat. Add steaks and cook for 10 to 13 minutes over medium heat for medium-rare (145°F) to medium doneness (160°F), turning once. Top steaks with cheese during the last 1 minute of cooking time. Serve steaks with apple mixture.

MAKES 4 SERVINGS.

EACH SERVING *462 cal, 33 g fat (12 g sat. fat), 88 mg chol, 327 mg sodium, 19 g carbo, 3 g fiber, 25 g pro. Daily Values: 4% vit. A, 12% vit. C, 82% calcium, 2% iron.*

GRILLED STEAK, CUCUMBER, AND RADISH SALAD

PREP: 20 MIN. CHILL: 30 MIN. GRILL: 10 MIN.

- 1 lb. beef top loin steak or ribeye steak, cut 1 inch thick
- 1 Tbsp. packed brown sugar
- 1 tsp. five-spice powder
- ½ tsp. salt
- ½ tsp. ground black pepper
- 2 Tbsp. seasoned rice vinegar
- 2 Tbsp. orange juice
- 1 Tbsp. toasted sesame oil
- 1 Tbsp. honey Dash salt Dash ground black pepper
- 3 cups thinly sliced cucumber (2 large Japanese or 1 large English cucumber)
- 2 large radishes, sliced
- ½ a small sweet onion, halved and thinly sliced
- ¼ cup snipped fresh cilantro
- 1 Tbsp. black sesame seeds or toasted sesame seeds

1. Trim fat from steak. In a small bowl combine brown sugar, five-spice powder, salt, and pepper. Sprinkle rub evenly over both sides of the steaks; rub in with your fingers. Cover and chill for 30 minutes.

2. For a charcoal grill, grill steak on the rack of an uncovered grill directly over medium coals until desired doneness, turning once halfway through grilling. Allow 10 to 12 minutes for medium-rare (145°F) or 12 to 15 minutes for medium (160°F). Remove steak from grill.

3. Meanwhile, for vinaigrette, in a large bowl whisk together vinegar, orange juice, oil, honey, dash salt, and dash pepper. Remove about half of the vinaigrette and set aside. Add cucumber, radishes, onion, and cilantro to remaining vinaigrette. Toss to coat.

4. Arrange cucumber mixture on a serving platter. Thinly slice steak across the grain; place on cucumber mixture. Drizzle with reserved vinaigrette and sprinkle with sesame seeds. **MAKES 4 SERVINGS.**

EACH SERVING *360 cal, 22 g fat (8 g sat. fat), 65 mg chol, 470 mg sodium, 15 g carbo, 1 g fiber, 25 g pro. Daily Values: 8% vit. A, 22% vit. C, 8% calcium, 15% iron.*

STRIP STEAK WITH CHEESY ARTICHOKE TOPPER

PREP: 20 MIN. BROIL: 12 MIN.

- ¼ tsp. salt
- ¼ tsp. crushed red pepper
- 2 10- to 12-oz. beef top loin steaks (strip steaks), cut 1 inch thick
- 1 6-oz. jar marinated artichoke hearts, drained
- ½ an 8-oz. container whipped cream cheese with garlic and herbs
- ½ cup walnuts, toasted and coarsely chopped
- 2 Tbsp. grated Parmesan cheese

1. Preheat broiler. Combine the salt and crushed red pepper. Sprinkle evenly on steaks. Place meat on the unheated rack of a broiler pan. Broil meat 3 to 4 inches from heat for 12 to 14 minutes for medium-rare doneness (145°F) or 15 to 18 minutes for medium doneness (160°F), turning meat over after half of the broiling time.

2. Meanwhile, coarsely chop artichokes. In a medium bowl combine the artichokes, cream cheese, walnuts, and Parmesan. Cut steaks in half. Top with some of the cream cheese mixture. Cover and chill any remaining artichoke mixture. Serve spread on bagels and/or use as a sandwich spread. **MAKES 4 SERVINGS.**

EACH SERVING *584 cal, 46 g fat (17 g sat. fat), 124 mg chol, 569 mg sodium, 6 g carbo, 2 g fiber, 32 g pro. Daily Values: 6% vit. A, 6% vit. C, 8% calcium, 18% iron.*

FLANK STEAK WITH MUSHROOMS

PREP: 25 MIN. MARINATE : 1 HR. BROIL: 15 MIN. COOK: 8 MIN.

- 1½ lb. beef flank steak
- ¾ cup dry red wine
- 1 Tbsp. sherry or red wine vinegar
- 1 Tbsp. finely shredded orange peel
- ¼ tsp. fennel seeds, crushed
- 2 medium shallots, chopped (¼ cup)
- 2 cloves garlic, minced
- 1 Tbsp. butter
- 3 cups fresh mushrooms, sliced (cremini, oyster, or button)
- 1 Tbsp. cornstarch
- ¾ cup beef broth Salt and ground black pepper

1. Trim fat from steak. Score steak on both sides by making shallow cuts at 1-inch intervals in a diamond pattern. Place steak in a large resealable plastic bag set in a shallow dish. For marinade, combine red wine, vinegar, orange peel, and fennel seeds. Pour over steak; seal bag. Marinate in the refrigerator for 1 hour, turning bag occasionally. Drain steak; reserve ⅓ cup marinade.

2. Preheat broiler. Place steak on the unheated rack of a broiler pan. Broil 3 to 4 inches from the heat for 15 to 18 minutes (160°F), turning meat over after half of the broiling time.

3. Meanwhile, for mushroom sauce, in a medium saucepan cook shallots and garlic in hot butter over medium heat for 2 minutes, stirring occasionally. Add mushrooms; cook and stir until tender. Combine reserved marinade and cornstarch; add to saucepan along with beef broth. Cook and stir until thickened and bubbly. Cook and stir 2 minutes more. Season to taste with salt and pepper.

4. To serve, slice steak across the grain and serve with mushroom sauce.

MAKES 6 SERVINGS.

EACH SERVING *240 cal, 9 g fat (4 g sat. fat), 53 mg chol, 291 mg sodium, 6 g carbo, 1 g fiber, 27 g pro. Daily Values: 3% vit. A, 5% vit. C, 4% calcium, 13% iron.*

Breakfast Sweets

Marie McConnell, SHELBYVILLE, IL

KID-FRIENDLY

DOUBLE OAT BREAKFAST COOKIES

PREP: 30 MIN. BAKE: 10 MIN. OVEN: 375°F

½	cup butter, softened
½	cup smooth peanut butter
1¼	cups sugar
½	tsp. baking soda
¼	tsp. salt
¼	cup water
1	egg
1	Tbsp. vanilla
1½	cups all-purpose flour
1	cup rolled oats
1	cup golden raisins and/or milk chocolate pieces
3	cups round toasted oat cereal (such as Cheerios)

1. Preheat oven to 375°F. In large mixing bowl beat butter and peanut butter with electric mixer on medium to high speed for 30 seconds. Add sugar, baking soda, and salt. Beat until combined, scraping sides of bowl. Beat in water, egg, and vanilla until combined. Beat in flour until combined. Beat in as much of the rolled oats as you can with mixer. Stir in any remaining rolled oats. Stir in raisins and oat cereal.

2. Drop dough by scant ¼ cupfuls about 3 inches apart onto an ungreased cookie sheet. Flatten slightly. Bake for 10 to 12 minutes or until edges are lightly browned. Cool on cookie sheet for 5 minutes. Transfer to a wire rack and let cool completely. Store cookies in a tightly covered container up to 5 days or freeze up to 3 months.

MAKES 24 (2-COOKIE) SERVINGS.

EACH SERVING *237 cal, 9 g fat (2 g sat. fat), 6 mg chol, 482 mg sodium, 34 g carbo, 3 g fiber, 6 g pro. Daily Values: 14% vit. A, 45% vit. C, 7% calcium, 9% iron.*

NO-KNEAD CHOCOLATE AND COCONUT ROLLS

PREP: 30 MIN. RISE: 1½ HRS. BAKE: 15 MIN.
COOL: 5 MIN. OVEN: 350°F

4	cups all-purpose flour
1	pkg. active dry yeast
1	cup milk
⅓	cup sugar
¼	cup butter
2	eggs
1	13-oz. jar chocolate-hazelnut spread
1	cup shredded coconut
1	recipe Icing

1. In bowl combine 2 cups of the flour and yeast. In saucepan heat and stir milk, sugar, butter, and ½ teaspoon *salt* until warm (120°F to 130°F). Add milk mixture and eggs to flour mixture. Beat with electric mixer on low to medium for 30 seconds. Beat on medium speed for 3 minutes. Stir in remaining flour. Cover; let rise in warm place until double in size (45 to 60 minutes).

2. Turn dough out onto a floured surface. Cover; let rest 10 minutes. Grease a large baking sheet; set aside. Roll dough in a 12×9-inch rectangle. Spread ⅔ cup hazelnut spread on dough, leaving 1-inch edge along one long side. Sprinkle coconut on hazelnut spread. Roll up rectangle, starting from long side with filling spread to edge. Pinch dough to seal seams. Slice in nine pieces. Arrange 2 inches apart on prepared baking sheet. Cover; let rise in warm place until double in size (45 minutes).

3. Preheat oven to 350°F. Bake 15 to 20 minutes or until golden. Cool 5 minutes; transfer to wire rack. Drizzle with Icing.

MAKES 9 SERVINGS.

ICING In small bowl stir together remaining hazelnut spread and 2 to 3 tablespoons milk until drizzling consistency.

EACH SERVING *590 cal, 24 g fat (8 g sat. fat), 64 mg chol, 272 mg sodium, 83 g carbo, 3 g fiber, 12 g pro. Daily Values: 5% vit. A, 5% calcium, 16% iron.*

Dyana Lyons, WOODLAND HILLS, CA

FRENCH TOAST CUPS
PREP: 25 MIN. BAKE: 25 MIN. COOL: 5 MIN.
OVEN: 325°F

	Nonstick spray for baking
½	an 8-oz. tub. cream cheese spread with pineapple or plain cream cheese
1	tsp. vanilla
½	tsp. salt
1	cup milk
6	eggs
½	cup butter, melted
½	cup pure maple syrup
12	oz. cinnamon-raisin bread, cut in ½-inch cubes (6 cups)
¾	cup fresh or frozen blueberries
	Pure maple syrup

1. Preheat oven to 325°F. Spray twenty 2½-inch muffin cups with nonstick spray for baking; set aside. In a large mixing bowl beat cream cheese with an electric mixer on medium to high speed for 30 seconds. Add vanilla and salt; beat until combined. Gradually beat in milk until smooth. Add eggs, butter, and ½ cup maple syrup and beat until combined. Fold in bread and blueberries until combined.
2. Spoon about ¼ cup bread mixture into each muffin cup. Bake 25 minutes or until puffed and golden. Cool 5 minutes in pans on wire rack. Remove from muffin cups. Serve warm with maple syrup.
MAKES 20 CUPS.
EACH CUP *185 cal, 9 g fat (5 g sat. fat), 84 mg chol, 205 mg sodium, 22 g carbo, 1 g fiber, 4 g pro. Daily Values: 6% vit. A, 1% vit. C, 4% calcium, 5% iron.*

CARAMEL-PECAN WAFFLES WITH PEACHES AND BRIE
PREP: 25 MIN. COOK: 4 MIN. PER BATCH
OVEN: 200°F

1	cup packed brown sugar
5	Tbsp. butter
¾	cup whipping cream
1	Tbsp. light-color corn syrup
1	cup frozen peach slices, thawed and coarsely chopped
⅔	cup pecans, toasted and coarsely chopped
4	eggs
¾	cup milk
2	tsp. vanilla
12	frozen waffles, thawed
½	an 8-oz. round Brie cheese, cut in 6 wedges

1. Preheat oven to 200°F. In a medium saucepan heat brown sugar, 2 tablespoons of the butter, whipping cream, and corn syrup over medium heat until butter is melted and sugar is dissolved. Simmer, uncovered, 5 minutes. Add peaches and pecans; cover and keep warm.
2. In a shallow dish whisk together eggs, milk, and vanilla. Dip waffles, one at a time, in egg mixture, turning to coat both sides. In a 12-inch skillet melt 1 tablespoon of the butter over medium heat. Cook waffles in batches, 2 to 3 minutes per side or until golden. Transfer to a large baking sheet and keep warm in oven while cooking remaining waffles.
3. To serve, top each waffle with peach-pecan sauce and a wedge of Brie.
MAKES 6 SERVINGS.
EACH SERVING *764 cal, 45 g fat (19 g sat. fat), 239 mg chol, 717 mg sodium, 76 g carbo, 16 g pro. Daily Values: 42% vit. A, 4% vit. C, 37% calcium, 29% iron.*

APRICOT-CHERRY CREAM CHEESE BREAD
PREP: 30 MIN. STAND: 30 MIN. BAKE: 55 MIN.
COOL: 10 MIN. CHILL: 8 HRS. OVEN: 350°F

1	cup dried apricots, cut into thin strips
½	cup dried sweet cherries, coarsely chopped
2	cups all-purpose flour
2	tsp. baking powder
½	tsp. baking soda
½	tsp. salt
¼	cup butter, softened
½	cup granulated sugar
½	cup packed brown sugar
1	egg
¾	cup orange juice
½	cup chopped pecans, toasted
½	an 8-oz. cream cheese, softened
2	Tbsp. granulated sugar
1	Tbsp. all-purpose flour
1	egg yolk
	2 tsp. finely shredded orange peel

1. In a small bowl combine apricots and cherries. Add enough boiling water to cover. Let stand 30 minutes; drain well.
2. Preheat oven to 350°F. Grease and lightly flour a 9×5×3-inch loaf pan; set aside. In a large bowl combine flour, baking powder, baking soda, and salt; set aside. In a large mixing bowl beat butter with an electric mixer on medium to high speed for 30 seconds. Add ½ cup granulated sugar and brown sugar and beat until combined. Beat in 1 egg. Alternately add flour mixture and orange juice, beating on low speed after each addition just until combined. Stir in drained apricots and cherries and ¼ cup of the pecans.
3. For filling, in a blender or food processor combine cream cheese, 2 tablespoons granulated sugar, flour, egg yolk, and orange peel. Cover and blend or process until smooth, scraping down sides.
4. Pour two-thirds of the batter into the prepared loaf pan. Spread filling evenly over batter. Top with remaining batter. Lightly swirl with a knife. Sprinkle with the remaining ¼ cup pecans. Bake for 55 to 60 minutes or until golden brown and edges just begin to pull away from sides of pan. Cool in pan on a wire rack for 10 minutes. Remove from pan and cool completely on a wire rack. Wrap and refrigerate overnight before slicing.
MAKES 1 LOAF (12 SERVINGS).
EACH SERVING *313 cal, 11 g fat (5 g sat. fat), 56 mg chol, 279 mg sodium, 51 g carbo, 2 g fiber, 5 g pro. Daily Values: 17% vit. A, 14% vit. C, 1% calcium, 1% iron.*

CHERRY COFFEE CAKE
PREP: 25 MIN. RISE: 45 MIN. BAKE: 30 MIN.
COOL: 30 MIN. OVEN: 375°F

	Nonstick cooking spray
1	pkg. 2-layer yellow cake mix
1	cup all-purpose flour
⅔	cup warm water (120°F to 130°F)
2	eggs
1	pkg. active dry yeast
⅓	cup butter, melted
⅓	cup sliced almonds
1	tsp. ground cinnamon
1	12-oz. jar cherry preserves
1	recipe Icing

1. Lightly coat a 13×9×2-inch baking pan with cooking spray; set aside. In a large mixing bowl combine 1½ cups of the cake mix, the flour, water, eggs, and yeast. Beat with an electric mixer on low speed just until combined. Beat on medium speed for 2 minutes, scraping sides of bowl occasionally (mixture will be thick).
2. Spread batter into prepared pan; cover loosely and let stand at room temperature to rise for 45 minutes.
3. Preheat oven to 375°F. For streusel, in a medium bowl stir together the remaining cake mix, butter, almonds, and cinnamon until combined. Spoon preserves in small mounds evenly over batter in pan. Crumble streusel evenly over preserves.
4. Bake 30 to 35 minutes or until top is golden brown. Remove from oven and cool in pan on a wire rack for 30 minutes. Drizzle with Icing. Serve warm.
MAKES 12 TO 16 SERVINGS.
ICING In a small bowl stir together ¾ cup powdered sugar, 2 teaspoons lemon juice, and enough water (1 to 2 teaspoons) to make drizzling consistency. Drizzle over warm cake.
EACH SERVING *389 cal, 11 g fat (5 g sat. fat), 49 mg chol, 338 mg sodium, 71 g carbo, 4 g pro. Daily Values: 4% vit. A, 5% vit. C, 1% calcium, 9% iron.*

Pork Tenderloin

Bridget M. Klusman, KALAMAZOO, MI

SOUR CREAM-FENNEL PORK TENDERLOINS

PREP: 30 MIN. ROAST: 25 MIN. OVEN: 425F

2	medium fennel bulbs
2	1- to 1½-lb. pork tenderloins
1	Tbsp. snipped fresh rosemary
1	Tbsp. fennel seeds, coarsely crushed (optional)
2	Tbsp. olive oil
1	medium onion, sliced
6	cloves garlic, minced
½	cup chicken broth
½	cup dry vermouth or chicken broth
¼	cup sour cream
	Rosemary sprigs (optional)
	Sour cream (optional)

1. Preheat oven to 425°F. Trim and core fennel, reserving some of the leafy tops. Cut each fennel bulb in thin wedges; set aside. Sprinkle pork with rosemary, fennel seeds, 1 teaspoon *salt*, and ¼ teaspoon *black pepper*. In 12-inch straight-sided oven-going skillet brown pork on all sides in hot oil. Remove pork from pan; set aside.
2. Add fennel, onion, and garlic to skillet; cook 4 minutes or until lightly browned, stirring occasionally. Remove skillet from heat; add broth, vermouth, and sour cream. Return to heat. Bring to boiling. Return pork to pan; transfer to preheated oven.
3. Roast, uncovered, 25 to 30 minutes or until slightly pink in center (155°F). Serve pork with vegetables and juices. Top with reserved fennel tops and rosemary. Pass additional sour cream sprinkled with rosemary. **MAKES 8 SERVINGS.**
EACH SERVING *212 cal, 7 g fat (2 g sat. fat), 77 mg chol, 488 mg sodium, 8 g carbo, 3 g fiber, 25 g pro. Daily Values: 3% vit. A, 32% vit. C, 6% calcium, 10% iron.*

ROASTED PORK WITH BLACKBERRY SAUCE

PREP: 20 MIN. MARINATE: 2 HRS. ROAST: 35 MIN. COOK: 5 MIN. OVEN: 425°F

1½	lb. pork tenderloin
¼	cup blackberry preserves, melted and cooled
¼	cup dry white wine or apple juice
2	Tbsp. balsamic vinegar
2	Tbsp. olive oil
2	Tbsp. Dijon-style mustard
3	cloves garlic, minced
1	tsp. soy sauce
1	tsp. finely shredded orange peel
½	tsp. snipped fresh rosemary
	Steamed green beans (optional)
	Finely shredded orange peel (optional)

1. Place tenderloin in resealable plastic bag set in shallow dish. For marinade, in bowl whisk together preserves, wine, balsamic vinegar, olive oil, mustard, garlic, soy sauce, 1 teaspoon orange peel, and rosemary. Pour marinade over pork; seal bag. Marinate, refrigerated, 2 to 5 hours, turning bag occasionally.
2. Preheat oven to 425°F. Drain pork, reserving marinade. Place meat on rack in shallow roasting pan. Roast 35 to 45 minutes or until slightly pink in center (155°F).
3. Meanwhile, for sauce, in small saucepan bring reserved marinade to boiling; reduce heat. Simmer, uncovered, 5 minutes. Slice pork; serve with sauce and green beans. Top with additional orange peel.
MAKES 6 SERVINGS.
EACH SERVING *221 cal, 7 g fat (1 g sat. fat), 74 mg chol, 244 mg sodium, 11 g carbo, 0 g fiber, 6 g pro. Daily Values: 14% vit. A, 45% vit. C, 7% calcium, 9% iron.*

Sharon Stillman, MEQUON, WI

CRUSTED FENNEL-LAVENDER PORK TENDERLOIN

PREP: 25 MIN. ROAST: 25 MIN. STAND: 10 MIN.
OVEN: 425°F

1	1 lb. pork tenderloin
1	Tbsp. fennel seed, crushed
2	tsp. dried lavender
½	tsp. salt
¼	tsp. ground black pepper
1	Tbsp. butter
1	small shallot, chopped
1	clove garlic, minced
1	14-oz. can chicken broth
¼	cup whipping cream
2	Tbsp. dry white wine (optional)
1	Tbsp. butter, softened
1	Tbsp. cornstarch
	Hot cooked rice or hot cooked wild rice

1. Preheat oven to 425°F. Trim fat from pork. In a shallow dish combine fennel seeds, lavender, salt, and pepper; remove 2 teaspoons seed mixture and set aside. Coat pork in remaining seed mixture. Place pork on a rack in a shallow roasting pan.
2. Roast meat, uncovered, for 25 to 30 minutes or until meat thermometer registers 150°F. Cover with foil and let stand while preparing sauce.
3. In a large skillet melt butter. Add shallot and garlic; cook and stir until shallot is tender. Add chicken broth, whipping cream, wine, and reserved seed mixture; bring to boiling. Boil gently, uncovered, 5 minutes. Meanwhile, combine softened butter and cornstarch; add to skillet. Cook and stir until thickened and bubbly. Cook and stir 2 minutes more. Strain sauce and serve with pork and rice.

MAKES 4 SERVINGS.

EACH SERVING *315 cal, 14 g fat (8 g sat. fat), 110 mg chol, 798 mg sodium, 18 g carbo, 1 g fiber, 26 g pro. Daily Values: 9% vit. A, 2% vit. C, 5% calcium, 14% iron.*

LOW FAT

INDIAN-SPICED PORK AND PINEAPPLE KABOBS

PREP: 30 MIN. MARINATE: 2 HRS. GRILL: 13 MIN.

1	6-oz. carton plain yogurt
2	Tbsp. honey
1	tsp. finely shredded lemon peel
2	Tbsp. lemon juice
1	Tbsp. grated fresh ginger
2	tsp. garam masala
1	tsp. minced fresh garlic
¼	tsp. cayenne pepper
1	lb. pork tenderloin, cut into 1-inch cubes
1	red sweet pepper, cut into 1-inch pieces
1	green sweet pepper, cut into 1-inch pieces
½	a medium cored, peeled pineapple, cut into 1-inch pieces
4	individual flatbreads or 10-inch flour tortillas
2	Tbsp. snipped fresh cilantro
2	Tbsp. snipped fresh mint

1. In a small bowl whisk together the yogurt, honey, lemon peel, lemon juice, ginger, garam masala, garlic, and cayenne pepper. Reserve ⅓ cup of mixture; cover and chill until serving time. Place pork in a large resealable plastic bag; pour on remaining yogurt mixture. Cover and chill 2 to 10 hours.
2. Drain pork, reserving marinade. On eight 8- to 10-inch skewers thread pork, sweet peppers, and pineapple. (If using wooden skewers, soak in water at least 30 minutes before threading with food to prevent burning when grilling.)
3. For a charcoal grill, place the kabobs on the greased rack of an uncovered grill directly over medium coals for 12 to 15 minutes or until pork is slightly pink in the center, turning once and brushing with reserved marinade halfway through grilling. (For a gas grill, preheat grill. Reduce heat to medium. Add kabobs to greased grill rack. Cover and grill as above.)
4. Remove kabobs from grill. Add flatbreads or tortillas. Grill for 1 minute per side or until lightly browned.
5. In a small bowl combine reserved lemon peel, cilantro, and mint. Sprinkle over cooked kabobs. Drizzle with reserved yogurt mixture. Serve with flatbread.

MAKES 4 SERVINGS.

EACH SERVING *477 cal, 10 g fat (5 g sat. fat), 262 mg sodium, 64 g carbo, 3 g fiber, 34 g pro. Daily Values: 3% vit. A, 164% vit. C, 18% calcium, 24% iron.*

GRILLED PORK TENDERLOIN WITH ORANGE SPICED NOODLE SALAD

PREP: 30 MIN. GRILL: 30 MIN.

8	oz. soba (buckwheat noodles)
¼	cup canola oil
2	tsp. finely shredded orange peel
¼	cup orange juice
1	Tbsp. toasted sesame oil
1	Tbsp. red wine vinegar
1	Tbsp. soy sauce
1	Tbsp. sugar
2	cloves garlic, minced
1	tsp. crushed red pepper
½	tsp. Dijon-style mustard
½	cup sliced green onions
½	cup chopped peanuts
¼	cup snipped fresh cilantro
1	lb. pork tenderloin
1	tsp. packed brown sugar
½	tsp. salt
½	tsp. ground cumin
½	tsp. chili powder

1. Cook noodles according to package directions; drain and rinse with cold water. In a screw-top jar combine canola oil, orange peel, orange juice, sesame oil, vinegar, soy sauce, sugar, garlic, crushed red pepper, and mustard; shake to combine. Transfer noodles to a bowl; stir in ½ cup of the dressing and about three-fourths of the green onions, peanuts, and cilantro. Cover and let stand at room temperature. Reserve remaining dressing.
2. Trim fat from pork. In a small bowl combine brown sugar, salt, cumin, and chili powder. Rub spice mixture on pork.
3. For a charcoal grill, arrange hot coals around a drip pan. Test for medium-high heat above pan. Place meat on grill rack over pan. Cover; grill for 30 to 35 minutes or until a meat thermometer registers 150°F, brushing with reserved dressing the last 5 to 10 minutes of grilling. (For a gas grill, preheat grill. Reduce heat to medium-high. Adjust for indirect cooking. Cover and grill as above.) Serve pork with noodle salad. Sprinkle with reserved green onions, nuts, and cilantro.

MAKES 4 SERVINGS.

EACH SERVING *615 cal, 29 g fat (4 g sat. fat), 74 mg chol, 1,079 mg sodium, 56 g carbo, 5 g fiber, 37 g pro. Daily Values: 12% vit. A, 29% vit. C, 6% calcium, 21% iron.*

Apple Desserts

Susan A. Reade, GRANTS PASS, OR

CHUTNEY-STYLE APPLE COBBLER

PREP: 35 MIN. BAKE: 25 MIN. OVEN: 400°F

1	lemon
3	lb. cooking apples, cored and thinly sliced
1¼	cups packed dark brown sugar
3	Tbsp. cornstarch
½	cup chopped dried apricots
¼	cup dried cranberries
1	small jalapeño, seeded and finely chopped (see *Note, page 301*)
1	tsp. pumpkin pie spice
2	cups all-purpose flour
¼	cup granulated sugar
1	Tbsp. baking powder
½	cup butter
1¼	cups buttermilk
	Vanilla yogurt

1. Preheat oven to 400°F. Shred 1 teaspoon peel from lemon; set aside. In bowl squeeze 2 tablespoons juice from lemon. Add apples; toss to coat.

2. In 4- to 6-quart Dutch oven stir together brown sugar and cornstarch. Stir in ⅔ cup *water*, apricots, cranberries, jalapeño, and pie spice. Cook and stir over medium heat until boiling. Cook and stir 1 minute more. Remove from heat; stir in apple mixture. Spoon evenly into a 3-quart rectangular baking dish.

3. In large bowl combine flour, granulated sugar, baking powder, 1 teaspoon *salt*, and lemon peel. Cut in butter until pieces are pea size. Stir in buttermilk just until combined. Drop mixture into 12 mounds on top of fruit.

4. Bake 25 to 30 minutes or until top is golden and filling is bubbly. Cool on rack 30 minutes. Serve warm with yogurt.
MAKES 12 SERVINGS.
EACH SERVING *393 cal, 9 g fat (6 g sat. fat), 24 mg chol, 415 mg sodium, 75 g carbo, 4 g fiber, 7 g pro. Daily Values: 11% vit. A, 12% vit. C, 25% calcium, 9% iron.*

CARAMEL APPLE UPSIDE-DOWN CORNMEAL CAKE

PREP: 35 MIN. COOK: 8 MIN. BAKE: 30 MIN.
COOL: 10 MIN. OVEN: 350°F

6	Tbsp. butter
4	medium apples, peeled, cored, and sliced
½	cup packed brown sugar
2	Tbsp. milk
½	cup chopped pecans
⅓	cup dried cranberries
¾	cup all-purpose flour
2	Tbsp. granulated sugar
1½	tsp. baking powder
¼	tsp. salt
¾	cup cornmeal
1	cup hot water
¼	cup butter, melted
2	eggs, lightly beaten
1½	tsp. vanilla

1. Preheat oven to 350°F. In a 10-inch oven-going skillet melt 2 tablespoons of the butter over medium heat. Add apples; cook and stir 5 minutes or until tender. Remove from skillet. In same skillet combine remaining butter and brown sugar. Cook and stir over medium heat until butter melts. Bring to boiling. Remove from heat. Stir in milk. Sprinkle with pecans and cranberries. Arrange apple slices on top.

2. In bowl combine flour, sugar, baking powder, and salt. In medium bowl combine cornmeal, water, and ¼ cup butter. Stir in eggs and vanilla. Stir in flour mixture. Pour over apples.

3. Bake 30 minutes or until toothpick inserted near center comes out clean. Cool in pan 10 minutes. Invert; serve warm. **MAKES 8 SERVINGS.**
EACH SERVING *396 cal, 21 g fat (10 g sat. fat), 91 mg chol, 249 mg sodium, 49 g carbo, 4 g fiber, 5 g pro. Daily Values: 14% vit. A, 45% vit. C, 7% calcium, 9% iron.*

Lynne Hagen, MAHTOMEDI, MN

APPLE PHYLLO DESSERT

PREP: 30 MIN. BAKE: 10 MIN. OVEN: 350°F

Nonstick cooking spray
3 Tbsp. sugar
1 tsp. ground cinnamon
½ tsp. ground nutmeg
¼ tsp. ground cloves
8 sheets frozen phyllo dough
(14×9-inch rectangles), thawed
⅓ cup butter, melted
3 red cooking apples, cored and
thinly sliced
2 green apples, cored and thinly sliced
¼ cup caramel-flavored ice cream
topping
½ of an 8-oz. carton (about ⅓ cup)
mascarpone cheese

1. Preheat oven to 350°F. Lightly coat a 2-quart square baking dish with nonstick cooking spray; set aside. In a small bowl combine sugar, cinnamon, nutmeg, and cloves. Place one sheet of phyllo on a clean dry surface; brush with butter and sprinkle with 1 teaspoon of the sugar/spice mixture. Place in prepared dish. Repeat with phyllo, butter, and sugar mixture, staggering edges as placed in dish.

2. Bake 10 to 12 minutes or until lightly browned.

3. Meanwhile, place any remaining butter and sugar mixture in a large nonstick skillet. Add apples and the caramel topping. Bring to boiling; reduce heat and simmer, covered, 5 minutes or just until apples are tender. With a slotted spoon, transfer apple slices to prepared crust. Bring remaining mixture in skillet to boiling. Simmer, uncovered, for 2 minutes or until slightly thickened. Place mascarpone in a small bowl; gradually whisk in thickened caramel mixture. Spoon caramel mixture over apples. Cool slightly.

4. To serve, spoon into dessert dishes.
MAKES 8 TO 9 SERVINGS.

EACH SERVING *262 cal, 14 g fat (9 g sat. fat), 38 mg chol, 135 mg sodium, 33 g carbo, 2 g fiber, 4 g pro. Daily Values: 6% vit. A, 7% vit. C, 2% calcium, 3% iron.*

KID-FRIENDLY
PERSONAL APPLE PIZZAS

PREP: 40 MIN. BAKE: 15 MIN. OVEN: 400°F

3 medium Granny Smith apples,
peeled, cored, and thinly sliced
2 Tbsp. butter
¼ cup granulated sugar
¼ cup packed brown sugar
1 Tbsp. all-purpose flour
½ tsp. ground cinnamon
⅛ tsp. ground mace
1 13.8-oz. pkg. refrigerated pizza dough
⅓ cup cherry preserves

3 Tbsp. sliced almonds, toasted
Vanilla ice cream (optional)

1. Preheat oven to 400°F. Line a large baking sheet with foil or parchment paper; set aside.

2. In a large skillet cook apples in hot butter over medium heat for 10 minutes or until tender, stirring occasionally. Cool thoroughly. Stir in ¼ cup granulated sugar, brown sugar, flour, cinnamon, and mace; set aside.

3. On a lightly floured surface, roll pizza dough to a 20×10-inch rectangle. Cut in 8 equal portions. Transfer each portion to the lined baking sheet, building up edges slightly on each portion.

4. Place preserves in a small microwave-safe bowl; heat on 100% power (high) for 20 to 30 seconds or just until melted. Spoon 1 tablespoon preserves in the center of each pizza. Spoon apples onto each portion. Sprinkle with almonds.

5. Bake for 15 minutes or until lightly browned. Cool about 10 minutes. Serve warm with a scoop of ice cream.
MAKES 8 SERVINGS.

EACH SERVING *254 cal, 6 g fat (2 g sat. fat), 8 mg chol, 183 mg sodium, 48 g carbo, 2 g fiber, 3 g pro. Daily Values: 2% vit. A, 5% vit. C, 2% calcium, 8% iron.*

POT OF GOLD BAKED APPLES

PREP: 25 MIN. BAKE: 35 MIN. OVEN: 350°F

6 large Golden Delicious apples
1 3-oz. pkg. cream cheese, softened
¼ cup peach preserves
½ tsp. ground cinnamon
¼ tsp. ground ginger
¼ tsp. ground nutmeg
¼ tsp. almond extract
⅛ tsp. salt
¾ cup crushed gingersnap cookies (12)
¼ cup butter, melted

1. Preheat oven to 350°F. Using an apple corer or sharp knife, remove cores from apples. Peel a 1-inch strip from the top of each apple. Place apples in a 3-quart rectangular baking dish. Set aside.

2. In a medium bowl beat cream cheese with an electric mixer on medium to high speed for 30 seconds. Stir in preserves, cinnamon, ginger, nutmeg, almond extract, and salt. Spoon into apple centers.

3. In a small bowl combine crushed gingersnaps and butter. Spoon crumb mixture on each apple. Cover with foil; bake 20 minutes. Uncover and bake 15 to 20 minutes more or until apples are tender. Serve warm. **MAKES 6 SERVINGS.**

EACH SERVING *309 cal, 14 g fat (8 g sat. fat), 36 mg chol, 246 mg sodium, 46 g carbo, 5 g fiber, 2 g pro. Daily Values: 1% vit. A, 16% vit. C, 4% calcium, 7% iron.*

APPLE TART WITH HAZELNUTS AND BLUE CHEESE

PREP: 35 MIN. BAKE: 38 MIN. COOL: 15 MIN.
OVEN: 450°F/400°F

½ of a 15-ounce package rolled
refrigerated unbaked piecrust
(1 crust)
½ cup packed brown sugar
¼ cup all-purpose flour
2 Tbsp. butter, softened
6 medium tart apples, peeled and
sliced (6 cups)
2 Tbsp. butter
½ cup chopped hazelnuts
½ cup soft bread crumbs (1 slice)
2 oz. blue cheese, crumbled
2 Tbsp. butter, melted

1. Preheat oven to 450°F. Unroll piecrust; let stand according to package directions. On a lightly floured surface, roll crust to a 12-inch circle. Transfer to an 11-inch tart pan with removable sides; press pastry into fluted sides; trim even with top of pan. Prick bottom and sides with a fork. Line pastry with a double thickness of foil. Bake for 8 minutes. Remove foil. Bake 5 to 6 minutes more or until lightly browned. Cool on a wire rack.

2. Reduce oven temperature to 400°F. In a small mixing bowl combine brown sugar and flour; stir in 2 tablespoons softened butter with a fork until mixture resembles coarse crumbs; set aside. In large skillet cook apples in 2 tablespoons hot butter over medium heat about 7 minutes or just until tender, stirring gently occasionally. Spoon apples in baked crust. Sprinkle with brown sugar mixture.

3. Bake, uncovered, for 15 minutes. Meanwhile, in a small bowl combine hazelnuts, bread crumbs, blue cheese, and melted butter; sprinkle evenly over tart. Return to oven and bake 10 minutes more or until topping is lightly browned.

4. Cool tart in pan on wire rack for 15 minutes. Remove sides of pan; slide tart onto serving platter. Serve warm.
MAKES 10 SERVINGS.

EACH SERVING *314 cal, 18 g fat (8 g sat. fat), 25 mg chol, 233 mg sodium, 36 g carbo, 2 g fiber, 3 g pro. Daily Values: 6% vit. A, 6% vit. C, 6% calcium, 4% iron.*

Marvelous Mashers

PRIZE TESTED RECIPES* $400 WINNER
Aysha Schurman, AMMON, ID

HONEY-WASABI MASHED PEAS

PREP: 10 MIN. COOK: 10 MIN.

1	14- to 16-oz. pkg. frozen peas
2	Tbsp. honey
2	Tbsp. lemon juice or rice vinegar
1	tsp. prepared wasabi paste
1	small clove garlic, minced
	Lemon slices (optional)
	Watercress (optional)

1. In medium saucepan combine peas with enough *water* to cover. Bring to boiling; reduce heat. Simmer, uncovered, for 7 minutes or until very tender. Drain.
2. Stir in honey, lemon juice, wasabi paste, garlic, ¼ teaspoon *salt,* and ¼ teaspoon *black pepper.* Cook for 3 minutes. Mash slightly with a potato masher or fork until coarsely mashed. Top with lemon slices and watercress.
MAKES 6 (⅓-CUP) SERVINGS.
EACH SERVING *76 cal, 0 g fat, 0 mg chol, 178 mg sodium, 15 g carbo, 3 g fiber, 4 g pro. Daily Values: 4% vit. A, 16% vit. C, 3% iron.*

BOUNTIFUL BLUE CHEESE MASHERS

PREP: 25 MIN. COOK: 20 MIN.

2½	lb. Yukon gold potatoes, peeled and quartered
½	cup chopped sweet onion
2	Tbsp. minced garlic
2	Tbsp. butter
¼	cup dry white wine or reduced-sodium chicken broth
½	cup whipping cream
4	oz. blue cheese, crumbled
	Sliced green onion (optional)

1. In a 4-quart Dutch oven cook potatoes with ½ teaspoon *salt,* covered, in enough boiling water to cover for 20 minutes or until tender.
2. Meanwhile, in a small saucepan cook onion and garlic in hot butter until onion is tender. Stir in wine. Bring mixture to boiling; reduce heat. Simmer, uncovered, for 3 to 4 minutes or until reduced to ½ cup.
3. Drain potatoes. Mash with a potato masher or beat with an electric mixer on low speed. Add wine mixture, ½ teaspoon *salt,* and ¼ teaspoon *black pepper.* Gradually beat in whipping cream to make potato mixture light and fluffy. Fold in blue cheese. Top with green onion.
MAKES 10 (⅓-CUP) SERVINGS.
EACH SERVING *210 cal, 10 g fat (6 g sat. fat), 31 mg chol, 418 mg sodium, 25 g carbo, 2 g fiber, 5 g pro. Daily Values: 7% vit. A, 16% vit. C, 8% calcium, 3% iron.*

PRIZE TESTED RECIPES* $200 WINNER
Shannon Stephenson, FARNHAMVILLE, IA

SPICED PARSNIPS WITH TOASTED COCONUT

PREP: 25 MIN. COOK: 12 MIN.

2   lb. parsnips (about 8 medium), peeled and sliced ½ inch thick
1   lb. sweet potatoes (about 2 medium), peeled and sliced ½ inch thick
⅔ cup whipping cream
¼ cup butter, softened
1   Tbsp. mild-flavored molasses
½ tsp. salt
½ tsp. ground cinnamon
¼ tsp. ground ginger
¼ tsp. ground black pepper
½ cup shredded coconut, toasted

1. In a Dutch oven cook parsnips and sweet potatoes, covered, in a small amount of boiling water for 12 to 15 minutes or until very tender; drain and return to Dutch oven. Add whipping cream, butter, molasses, salt, cinnamon, ginger, and pepper. Mash with a potato masher or beat with an electric mixer on low speed. Reheat, if needed. To serve, sprinkle with toasted coconut. **MAKES 10 SERVINGS.**

EACH SERVING *216 cal, 13 g fat (8 g sat. fat), 34 mg chol, 197 mg sodium, 25 g carbo, 5 g fiber, 2 g pro. Daily Values: 1% vit. A, 23% vit. C, 5% calcium, 4% iron.*

CARIBBEAN MASHED SWEET POTATOES

PREP: 20 MIN. COOK: 25 MIN.

2   lb. sweet potatoes
2   medium bananas, peeled and mashed
¼ cup packed brown sugar
¼ cup butter
1   tsp. finely shredded lime peel
2   Tbsp. lime juice
½ tsp. dried thyme, crushed
½ tsp. ground allspice
1   clove garlic, minced
¼ tsp. salt
⅛ to ¼ tsp. crushed red pepper

1. Wash, peel, cut off any woody portions and ends and quarter sweet potatoes. Cook, covered, in enough boiling salted water to cover for 25 to 30 minutes or until tender. Drain and return to pan.
2. Meanwhile, in a small saucepan combine bananas, brown sugar, butter, lime peel, lime juice, thyme, allspice, garlic, salt, and crushed red pepper. Bring to boiling over medium heat, stirring occasionally. Reduce heat. Simmer, uncovered, 5 minutes, stirring frequently.
3. Add banana mixture to sweet potatoes; mash until nearly smooth.

MAKES 8 SERVINGS.

EACH SERVING *176 cal, 6 g fat (4 g sat. fat), 15 mg chol, 161 mg sodium, 31 g carbo, 2 g pro. Daily Values: 236% vit. A, 10% vit. C, 4% calcium, 4% iron.*

APPLES WITH RUTABAGA MASH

PREP: 25 MIN. COOK: 20 MIN.

1   large rutabaga (2 pounds), peeled and cut in 1-inch pieces
2   Tbsp. butter
2   Tbsp. packed brown sugar
½ tsp. salt
¼ tsp. ground black pepper
½ tsp. finely shredded lemon peel
¼ tsp. ground cinnamon
2   medium tart cooking apples (such as McIntosh or Granny Smith), peeled, cored, and chopped

1. In a large saucepan cook rutabaga, covered, in lightly salted boiling water for 20 to 25 minutes or until very tender; drain. Return to pan.
2. Meanwhile, in a large skillet melt 1 tablespoon butter over medium heat. Add 1 tablespoon of the brown sugar, ¼ teaspoon of the salt, ⅛ teaspoon of the pepper, the lemon peel, and cinnamon. Cook and stir until sugar melts. Add apples; cook and stir 4 to 5 minutes or until tender.
3. Beat rutabaga with an electric mixer on low speed. Add remaining butter, brown sugar, salt, and pepper to rutabaga. Beat until combined. Transfer to a serving bowl. Spoon apples over mashed rutabaga. **MAKES 8 SERVINGS.**

EACH SERVING *92 cal, 3 g fat (2 g sat. fat), 8 mg chol, 186 mg sodium, 16 g carbo, 3 g fiber, 1 g pro. Daily Values: 2% vit. A, 43% vit. C, 5% calcium, 3% iron.*

CREAMY CAULIFLOWER AND CELERY ROOT

PREP: 25 MIN. COOK: 25 MIN.

1   large head (2½ lb.) cauliflower, cut in florets
1   medium (1 lb.) celery root, peeled and cut into 1-inch pieces
2   cloves garlic, minced
2   Tbsp. butter
2   Tbsp. olive oil
1   Tbsp. coarse-grain brown mustard
1   Tbsp. garam masala
1   tsp. salt
½ cup ricotta cheese
1   tsp. cumin seeds, toasted* (optional)

1. In a 4-quart Dutch oven cook cauliflower, celery root, and garlic, covered, in enough boiling salted water for 25 minutes or until tender. Drain.
2. In a large bowl combine butter, olive oil, mustard, garam masala, and salt. Stir in ricotta cheese and cauliflower mixture. In a food processor bowl process the mixture, half at a time, until smooth. Sprinkle with toasted cumin seeds.

MAKES 10 (½ CUP) SERVINGS.

*TOASTING CUMIN SEEDS Place seeds in a small skillet. Cook, shaking pan occasionally, for 4 to 5 minutes over medium heat until fragrant.

EACH SERVING *93 cal, 7 g fat (3 g sat. fat), 12 mg chol, 322 mg sodium, 6 g carbo, 2 g fiber, 3 g pro. Daily Values: 3% vit. A, 37% vit. C, 5% calcium, 4% iron.*

CHEESY CHIPOTLE-MASHED POTATOES

PREP: 20 MIN. COOK: 20 MIN.

3   lb. baking potatoes (such as russet or Yukon gold), peeled and chopped
1   tsp. salt
½ cup sour cream
1   cup shredded Mexican-style four-cheese blend (4 oz.)
1   chipotle chile pepper in adobo sauce, chopped
¼ tsp. ground black pepper
2   Tbsp. snipped fresh cilantro
    Shredded Mexican-style four-cheese blend (optional)

1. In a 4-quart Dutch oven cook potatoes with and ½ teaspoon of the salt, covered, in enough boiling water to cover for 20 minutes or until tender; drain. Return to hot saucepan.
2. Mash with a potato masher or beat with an electric mixer on low speed. Add the sour cream, 1 cup cheese, chile pepper, remaining salt, pepper, and cilantro; stir well. Top with additional cheese.

MAKES 8 SERVINGS.

EACH SERVING *211 cal, 7 g fat (4 g sat. fat), 19 mg chol, 439 mg sodium, 32 g carbo, 2 g fiber, 6 g pro. Daily Values: 3% vit. A, 35% vit. C, 10% calcium, 4% iron.*

Hot Drinks

FAST

COCONUT TRES LECHES HOT CHOCOLATE

START TO FINISH: 10 MIN.

- 3 cups fat-free milk
- 1 14-oz. can unsweetened coconut milk
- ½ a 14-oz. can sweetened condensed milk (⅔ cup)
- 2 Tbsp. unsweetened cocoa powder
- ½ tsp. vanilla
  Sweetened whipped cream (optional)
- ¼ cup chocolate shavings (optional)

1. In medium saucepan combine fat-free milk, coconut milk, and sweetened condensed milk. Bring to a simmer over medium-low heat, stirring occasionally. Whisk in cocoa powder until combined.
2. Remove from heat; stir in vanilla. Serve in mugs topped with whipped cream and chocolate shavings.
MAKES 5 (8-OZ.) SERVINGS.
EACH SERVING *445 cal, 26 g fat (20 g sat. fat), 33 mg chol, 137 mg sodium, 43 g carbo, 0 g fiber, 11 g pro. Daily Values: 12% vit. A, 2% vit. C, 33% calcium, 8% iron.*

FAST

SPICED TEA

PREP: 10 MIN. STAND: 10 MIN.

- 7 cups water
- 1 cup sugar
- 1 1-inch piece peeled fresh ginger
- 3 whole cloves
- 1 3-inch stick cinnamon
- 1 star anise (optional)
- 4 black tea bags
- 1 cup pomegranate juice
- ¼ cup lemon juice
  Lemon slices (optional)
  Cinnamon sticks (optional)

1. In large saucepan combine water, sugar, ginger, cloves, cinnamon, and star anise. Bring to boiling, stirring to dissolve sugar. Boil for 1 minute. Remove from heat and strain. Return mixture to saucepan.
2. Add tea bags. Steep 10 minutes. Remove tea bags. Stir in pomegranate juice and lemon juice. Return to heat; heat through. Serve with lemon slices and cinnamon sticks.
MAKES 8 (8-OZ.) SERVINGS.
EACH SERVING *122 cal, 0 g fat, 0 mg chol, 11 mg sodium, 32 g carbo, 0 g fiber, 0 g pro. Daily Values: 6% vit. C, 1% calcium.*

FAST
ESPRESSO CLOUD WITH VANILLA CREAM
START TO FINISH: 20 MIN.

- 1¼ cups whole milk
- 1¼ cups brewed espresso
- ¾ cup whipping cream
- 1 Tbsp. powdered sugar
- ½ tsp. vanilla

1. In a medium saucepan stir together milk, espresso, and ½ cup of the cream. Heat over low heat (do not boil).
2. In a medium bowl beat remaining ¼ cup cream, powdered sugar, and vanilla with an electric mixer or wire whisk until soft peaks form.
3. To serve, pour coffee mixture into mugs; top each with whipped cream.
MAKES 4 (6-OZ.) SERVINGS.

EACH SERVING *211 cal, 19 g fat (12 g sat. fat), 69 mg chol, 58 mg sodium, 7 g carbo, 0 g fiber, 3 g pro. Daily Values: 15% vit. A, 1% vit. C, 12% calcium, 1% iron.*

FAST LOW FAT
HOT POMEGRANATE GROG
PREP: 15 MIN. COOK: 5 MIN. COOL: 5 MIN.

- 4 cups pomegranate juice (two 15.2-oz. bottles)
- 1 cup water
- ¾ cup orange juice
- ½ cup lemon juice
- ½ cup sugar
- 3 tablespoons rum
  Orange peel curls

1. In large saucepan combine pomegranate juice, water, orange juice, lemon juice, and sugar. Bring mixture just to boiling. Remove from heat; let stand for 5 minutes. Stir in rum. Garnish with orange peel curls.
MAKES 6 (8-OZ.) SERVINGS.

EACH SERVING *213 cal, 0 g fat 0 mg chol, 9 mg sodium, 50 g carbo, 0 g fiber, 0 g pro. Daily Values: 1% vit. A, 42% vit. C, 1% calcium.*

FAST
WARM CARIBBEAN SIPPER
START TO FINISH: 10 MIN.

- 3 cups unsweetened pineapple juice
- ¾ cup orange juice
- ½ cup cream of coconut
- ¼ cup lemon juice
- 1 3-inch stick cinnamon
- 1½ to 2 oz. (3 to 4 Tbsp.) coconut-flavored rum or rum
  Cinnamon sticks (optional)

1. In a medium saucepan combine pineapple juice, orange juice, cream of coconut, lemon juice, and cinnamon stick. Cook and stir over medium heat just until warm. Remove cinnamon stick. Stir in rum.
2. Divide mixture among mugs. Serve with a cinnamon stick stirrer.
MAKES 6 SERVINGS.

EACH SERVING *165 cal, 7 g fat (6 g sat. fat), 0 mg chol, 4 mg sodium, 22 g carbo, 1 g fiber, 1 g pro. Daily Values: 1% vit. A, 55% vit. C, 2% calcium, 5% iron.*

FAST KID-FRIENDLY
ICE-CREAMY ROOT BEER
START TO FINISH: 10 MIN.

- 1 pint cinnamon-flavored ice cream*
- 1 12-oz. can root beer
- 1 tsp. vanilla

1. In a medium saucepan combine 1 cup of the ice cream, root beer, and vanilla. Cook and stir over medium-low heat just until warm and ice cream is melted. Divide mixture among four mugs. Place a scoop of the remaining ice cream in each mug. Serve immediately.
MAKES 4 SERVINGS.

*If you can't find cinnamon-flavored ice cream, use vanilla ice cream and add ¼ teaspoon ground cinnamon.

EACH SERVING *187 cal, 8 g fat (5 g sat. fat), 32 mg chol, 69 mg sodium, 26 g carbo, 1 g fiber, 3 g pro. Daily Values: 6% vit. A, 1% vit. C, 10% calcium, 1% iron.*

FAST
DOUBLE CHOCOLATE HAZELNUT COCOA WITH ALMOND CREAM
START TO FINISH: 15 MIN.

- 3 cups milk
- ½ cup chocolate-hazelnut spread
- ½ cup semisweet chocolate pieces
- 1 tsp. instant coffee crystals
- ½ cup whipping cream
- ¼ tsp. almond extract
- 1 tbsp. very finely chopped toasted hazelnuts

1. In a medium saucepan combine milk, chocolate-hazelnut spread, chocolate pieces, and coffee crystals. Cook and stir over medium heat until chocolate is melted and mixture is heated through.
2. In a medium mixing bowl combine whipping cream and almond extract. Beat with a whisk or electric mixer until soft peaks form.
3. Divide cocoa among four mugs. Top with cream mixture and sprinkle with hazelnuts.
MAKES 4 (8-OZ.) SERVINGS.

EACH SERVING *474 cal, 31 g fat (13 g sat. fat), 57 mg chol, 119 mg sodium, 43 g carbo, 1 g fiber, 10 g pro. Daily Values: 16% vit. A, 1% vit. C, 24% calcium, 5% iron.*

One-Bite Hors d'Oeuvres

Judy Castranova, NEW BERN, NC

LOW FAT

AVOCADO PESTO-STUFFED TOMATOES

START TO FINISH: 45 MIN.

30	cherry tomatoes (about 1¼ pints)
½	medium avocado, pitted, peeled, and cut up
2	oz. cream cheese, softened
2	Tbsp. homemade or purchased basil pesto
1	tsp. lemon juice
	Snipped fresh basil (optional)

1. Cut a thin slice from the top of each tomato. (If desired, cut a thin slice from bottoms of tomatoes so they stand upright.) With a small spoon or small melon baller carefully hollow out the tomatoes. Line a baking sheet with paper towels. Invert tomatoes on the towels. Let stand about 30 minutes to drain.

2. Meanwhile, for filling, in a food processor bowl combine avocado, cream cheese, pesto, and lemon juice. Cover; process until smooth. Spoon filling into a pastry bag fitted with a large plain round or open star tip.

3. Place tomatoes, open sides up, on a serving platter. Pipe filling into the tomato cups. Serve immediately or cover loosely and refrigerate up to 4 hours before serving. Sprinkle with snipped basil before serving. **MAKES 30 APPETIZERS.**

EACH APPETIZER *18 cal, 1 g fat (1 g sat. fat), 2 mg chol, 16 mg sodium, 1 g carbo, 0 g fiber, 0 g pro. Daily Values: 3% vit. A, 4% vit. C, 1% calcium, 1% iron.*

BACON-PEACH PINWHEELS

PREP: 30 MIN. BAKE: 15 MIN. OVEN: 375°F

4	oz. blue cheese, crumbled
1	3-oz. pkg. cream cheese, softened
4	slices bacon
⅓	cup finely chopped onion
⅓	cup peach preserves
1	Tbsp. balsamic vinegar
1	8-oz. pkg. refrigerated crescent dough for recipes
⅓	cup pecans, toasted and finely chopped
½	tsp. dried basil
	Crumbled blue cheese (optional)
	Thinly sliced green onions (optional)

1. Heat oven to 375°F. In a small mixing bowl beat cheeses on medium to high speed until fluffy. In large skillet cook bacon until crisp; drain and crumble. Reserve 1 tablespoon drippings in skillet; cook and stir onion in drippings over medium heat until tender. Remove from heat; stir in preserves and vinegar.

2. Unroll dough. Cut in half to two approximately 3×10-inch rectangles. On each rectangle spread half the cheese mixture to within ¼ inch of one long edge. Top cheese with bacon, pecans, and basil. Beginning at a long edge, roll up each rectangle. Press seams to seal. Cut each roll in 10 slices. Place, cut sides down, on ungreased baking sheet. Bake 15 to 18 minutes or until golden brown. Spoon onion mixture on rolls. Remove from baking sheet. Serve warm. Sprinkle additional cheese and top with green onions. **MAKES 20 APPETIZERS.**

EACH APPETIZER *124 cal, 8 g fat (3 g sat. fat), 11 mg chol, 221 mg sodium, 9 g carbo, 0 g fiber, 3 g pro. Daily Values: 6% vit. A, 14% vit. C, 4% calcium, 3% iron.*

Tulie Trejo, CHULA VISTA, CA

MINI TORTILLA STACKS

PREP: 40 MIN. BAKE: 7 MIN. OVEN: 350°F

6	oz. uncooked chorizo sausage
1	medium onion, finely chopped
1	clove garlic, minced
1	Tbsp. dried oregano, crushed
½	tsp. crushed red pepper or 1 fresh serrano chile pepper finely chopped*
¼	tsp. salt
1	16-oz. can refried beans
1	Tbsp. chopped fresh cilantro
	Nonstick cooking spray
1	13- to 16-oz. bag bite-size round tortilla chips
	Refrigerated avocado dip (guacamole), bottled sliced pickled jalapeño peppers, dairy sour cream, and/or bottled salsa

1. Preheat oven to 350°F. In a large skillet cook chorizo, onion, garlic, oregano, crushed red pepper, and salt until chorizo is browned and onion is tender. Stir in refried beans and cilantro. Heat through.
2. Lightly coat two 15×10×1-inch baking pans with nonstick cooking spray. Arrange tortilla chips in a single layer in the pans. Lightly coat chips with nonstick cooking spray. Top each chip with about 1½ teaspoons of the bean mixture. Top with a second chip, sandwich style. Lightly coat top chips with nonstick cooking spray. Bake 7 minutes or until lightly browned.
3. Top each appetizer with guacamole, jalapeño slices, sour cream, and/or salsa.
MAKES ABOUT 80 APPETIZERS.
*NOTE Hot chile peppers contain oils that can burn skin and eyes. When working with them, wear plastic or rubber gloves.
EACH APPETIZER *36 cal, 1 g fat (0 g sat. fat), 2 mg chol, 94 mg sodium, 5 g carbo, 1 g fiber, 1 g pro. Daily Values: 1% vit. C, 1% calcium, 1% iron.*

SHRIMP BROCHETTE WITH CHIPOTLE LIME CREAM

START TO FINISH: 45 MIN.

1	8-oz. pkg. cream cheese, softened
1	avocado, halved, seeded, peeled, and cut up
1	small fresh jalapeño pepper, seeded and finely chopped*
1	Tbsp. snipped fresh cilantro
1	Tbsp. lime juice
¼	tsp. ground chipotle chile pepper
40	toasted baguette slices
1	7-oz. pkg. frozen peeled, cooked salad shrimp, thawed and well drained
2	green onions, very finely chopped
1	Tbsp. cilantro, very finely chopped

1. In a large mixing bowl beat cream cheese with an electric mixer on medium speed until smooth. Add avocado, jalapeño pepper, 1 tablespoon snipped cilantro, lime juice, and the chipotle chile pepper. Beat until smooth and fluffy. Place in a large resealable plastic bag. Snip off one corner of the bag.
2. Pipe avocado mixture on baguette slices. Top with shrimp. Combine the green onion and finely chopped cilantro; sprinkle. MAKES 40 APPETIZERS.
*NOTE Hot chile peppers contain oils that can burn skin and eyes. When working with them, wear plastic or rubber gloves.
EACH APPETIZER *67 cal, 3 g fat (1 g sat. fat), 16 mg chol, 115 mg sodium, 8 g carbo, 1 g fiber, 3 g pro. Daily Values: 2% vit. A, 1% vit. C, 1% calcium, 4% iron.*

TUSCAN CHEESECAKE BITES

PREP: 25 MIN. BAKE: 12 MIN. COOL: 10 MIN. OVEN: 350°F

⅓	cup panko (Japanese-style bread crumbs)
⅓	cup ground walnuts
½	tsp. dried basil, crushed
2	Tbsp. butter, melted
1	8-oz. pkg. reduced-fat cream cheese (Neufchâtel), softened
½	of an 8-oz. pkg. feta cheese with basil and tomato, crumbled
1	egg
2	Tbsp. sour cream
2	Tbsp. chopped pitted ripe olives
2	Tbsp. snipped fresh basil

1. Preheat oven to 350°F. Line twenty-four 1¾-inch muffin cups with paper liners; set aside. In a small bowl combine panko, walnuts, and dried basil. Stir in butter. Spoon a slightly rounded teaspoon of panko mixture in each lined cup. Press into bottoms using the rounded side of a measuring teaspoon; set aside.
2. For filling, in a medium bowl beat cream cheese with an electric mixer on medium speed until light and fluffy. Add feta and egg. Beat until combined. Stir in sour cream. Spoon about 1 tablespoon filling into each crust-lined muffin cup.
3. Bake for 12 to 15 minutes or until filling appears set. Cool in pan on a wire rack for 10 minutes. Carefully remove to a serving platter. Serve warm topped with olives and basil. MAKES 24 TARTS.
EACH TART *64 cal, 6 g fat (3 g sat. fat), 103 mg sodium, 1 g carbo, 2 g pro. Daily Values: 4% vit. A, 3% calcium, 1% iron.*

PEANUT-HONEY-BACON CRUNCHIES

PREP: 25 MIN. BAKE: 12 MIN. OVEN: 425°F

1	lb. thick-sliced bacon, halved crosswise
2	Tbsp. honey
⅓	cup honey roasted-peanuts, finely chopped
1	tsp. ground ancho chile pepper
1	8-oz. can whole water chestnuts, drained and halved

1. Preheat oven to 425°F. Line two large baking sheets with foil. Arrange bacon on sheets. Bake for 7 to 9 minutes or just until bacon is just browned and pliable. Drain bacon slices on paper towels. Discard the foil and line the baking sheets with clean foil. Place drained bacon slices on the clean foil.
2. Meanwhile, in a small bowl combine honey, peanuts, and chile pepper. Spoon a small amount (½ teaspoon) of peanut mixture in the center of each bacon slice. Place a water chestnut half over the peanut mixture. Fold ends of bacon slices over water chestnut pieces, overlapping in the center. Push a wooden toothpick through the bacon into water chestnuts.
3. Bake about 5 minutes more or until bacon is golden brown and chestnuts are heated through. Serve warm.
MAKES ABOUT 24 APPETIZERS.
EACH APPETIZER *85 cal, 5 g fat (2 g sat. fat), 10 mg chol, 148 mg sodium, 3 g carbo, 0 g fiber, 3 g pro. Daily Values: 1% vit. A, 1% vit. C, 1% iron.*

Childhood Sweets

Torie Christensen, STEAMBOAT SPRINGS, CO

GINGERBREAD CINNAMON ROLLS

PREP: 30 MIN. RISE: 1 HR. 45 MIN. BAKE: 22 MIN.
STAND: 15 MIN. OVEN: 350°F

2	pkg. active dry yeast
½	cup evaporated milk
⅓	cup molasses
¼	cup packed brown sugar
1	egg, lightly beaten
2	Tbsp. vegetable oil
4	cups all-purpose flour
¼	cup packed brown sugar
2	Tbsp. granulated sugar
1	tsp. ground cinnamon
½	tsp. ground ginger
2	Tbsp. butter, softened
1	recipe Glaze
	Sugared cranberries*

1. In a bowl combine yeast and ¼ cup *warm water* (about 115°F). Let stand 5 minutes. Stir in milk, molasses, ¼ cup brown sugar, the egg, oil, and ½ teaspoon *salt.* Stir in as much flour as you can. Turn dough out onto floured surface. Knead in enough remaining flour for moderately soft, smooth, elastic dough (about 5 minutes). Shape in ball. Place in greased bowl; turn once. Cover; let rise until double (about 1 hour). Punch down. Turn onto lightly floured surface. Cover; let rest 10 minutes.

2. Grease a 13×9×2-inch pan. For filling, in bowl combine ¼ cup brown sugar, granulated sugar, cinnamon, and ginger. Roll dough to 12×8-inch rectangle. Spread butter on dough. Sprinkle filling to within 1 inch along one long side. Roll up, beginning at long side of filling. Pinch to seal. Cut 12 slices. Place in pan. Cover; let rise until nearly double (45 minutes).

3. Heat oven to 350°F. Bake 22 to 25 minutes or until golden and set. Let stand 5 minutes; invert onto platter. Drizzle with Glaze. To serve, top with sugared cranberries.

MAKES 12 ROLLS.

GLAZE Combine 1½ cups powdered sugar, ½ teaspoon cinnamon, and ½ teaspoon vanilla. Whisk in enough milk (4 to 5 teaspoons) for drizzling consistency.

*NOTE For sugared cranberries, roll frozen cranberries in sugar.

EACH ROLL *332 cal, 6 g fat (2 g sat. fat), 26 mg chol, 136 mg sodium, 64 g carbo, 1 g fiber, 6 g pro. Daily Values: 2% vit. A, 7% calcium, 15% iron.*

CHOCOLATE-PEANUT BUTTER BARS

PREP: 25 MIN. BAKE: 20 MIN. OVEN: 350°F

¾	cup butter, softened
1	cup packed brown sugar
1	egg
2	tsp. vanilla
½	tsp. salt
2	cups all-purpose flour
1	12-oz. pkg. semisweet chocolate pieces
3	Tbsp. butter
¼	cup hot strong coffee
¼	cup peanut butter
1	cup powdered sugar

1. Heat oven to 350°F. Lightly grease a 15×10×1-inch baking pan or line the pan with foil or parchment; set aside. For cookie base, in large mixing bowl beat the ¾ cup butter on medium to high for 30 seconds. Add brown sugar; beat until combined, occasionally scraping sides of bowl. Beat in egg, vanilla, and salt until combined. Beat in as much flour as you can with mixer. Stir in any remaining flour. Evenly spread dough in prepared pan. Bake for 20 to 22 minutes or until edges are golden brown. Cool completely on wire rack.

2. For frosting, in small saucepan combine chocolate and 3 tablespoons butter. Stir over low heat until melted and smooth. Remove from heat. Transfer chocolate mixture to a medium bowl. Whisk in coffee and peanut butter until combined. Whisk in powdered sugar until smooth. Spread on cookie base. Let stand until frosting is set. Cut in bars. **MAKES 36 BARS.**

EACH BAR *164 cal, 9 g fat (5 g sat. fat), 19 mg chol, 78 mg sodium, 18 g carbo, 2 g fiber, 1 g pro. Daily Values: 3% vit. A, 1% calcium, 2% iron.*

Ilona Wagner, DEWEY, AZ

SWEET POTATO FIG PRALINE CHEESECAKE

PREP: 45 MIN. BAKE: 1 HR. COOK: 10 MIN.
COOL: 45 MIN. CHILL: 8 HRS. OVEN: 350°F

- 1½ cups graham cracker crumbs
- ¼ cup granulated sugar
- 2 Tbsp. all-purpose flour
- ⅓ cup butter, melted
- 3 8-oz. pkg. cream cheese
- ¾ cup packed brown sugar
- 1 cup pureed cooked sweet potatoes
- ½ cup fig jam
- 2 tsp. pumpkin pie spice
- 3 eggs
- ⅔ cup whipping cream
- ⅔ cup packed brown sugar
- ¾ cup chopped pecans
- 1 tsp. vanilla

1. Preheat oven to 350°F. For crust, in a medium bowl combine graham cracker crumbs, granulated sugar, and flour. Stir in melted butter. Press the crumb mixture onto the bottom and 1½ inches up the sides of a 9-inch springform pan. Bake for 10 minutes. Cool on a wire rack.
2. In a large mixing bowl beat cream cheese and ¾ cup packed brown sugar with an electric mixer on medium speed until smooth. Beat in sweet potatoes, fig jam, and pumpkin pie spice. Add eggs; beat just until combined.
3. Pour filling into crust in pan. Bake for 50 to 60 minutes or until center appears nearly set when gently shaken.
4. Cool in pan on a wire rack for 15 minutes. Using a small sharp knife, loosen the cheesecake from pan sides; cool for 30 minutes.
5. Meanwhile, in a small saucepan combine whipping cream and ⅔ cup brown sugar; cook and stir until mixture comes to a boil. Reduce heat and simmer, uncovered, 10 minutes. Remove from heat; stir in chopped pecans and vanilla. Cool completely. Spread evenly over cheesecake. Cover and refrigerate cheesecake overnight. Before serving, remove sides of pan.

MAKES 12 SERVINGS.

EACH SERVING 572 cal, 36 g fat (18 g sat. fat), 147 mg chol, 316 mg sodium, 56 g carbo, 2 g fiber, 7 g pro. Daily Values: 87% vit. A, 8% vit. C, 12% calcium, 9% iron.

FINNISH BERRY BARS

PREP: 30 MIN. BAKE: 40 MIN. OVEN: 350°F

- 1 cup all-purpose flour
- 1 cup quick cooking oats
- 1 tsp. ground cardamom
- ⅔ cup packed brown sugar
- ¼ tsp. baking soda
- ½ cup butter
- ¾ cup fresh blueberries
- ¾ cup seedless raspberry preserves
- 1 tsp. finely shredded lemon peel
- 1 Tbsp. lemon juice
- ¼ tsp. ground cardamom

1. Preheat oven to 350°F. Grease a 9×2-inch square baking pan; set aside. In a large bowl combine flour, oats, 1 teaspoon ground cardamom, brown sugar, and baking soda. Using a pastry blender, cut in butter until the mixture resembles coarse crumbs. Measure ½ cup of the crumb mixture; set aside for topper. Press remaining crumb mixture into the bottom of prepared baking pan. Bake crust in preheated oven for 10 minutes.
2. In a medium bowl combine blueberries, preserves, lemon peel, lemon juice, and ¼ teaspoon cardamom. Carefully spoon over partially baked crust. Sprinkle with reserved crumb mixture. Bake for 30 to 35 minutes or until top is golden. Cool in pan on a wire rack. Cut into bars.

MAKES 25 BARS.

EACH BAR 115 cal, 4 g fat (2 g sat. fat), 10 mg chol, 44 mg sodium, 19 g carbo, 1 g fiber, 1 g pro. Daily Values: 2% vit. A, 3% vit. C, 1% calcium, 3% iron.

RASPBERRY PECAN TEA CAKES

PREP: 1 HR. BAKE: 12 MIN. OVEN: 375°F

- 1 cup butter, softened
- ⅔ cup sugar
- ½ tsp. vanilla
- ⅛ tsp. salt
- ¼ cup whipping cream
- ¼ cup ground toasted pecans or walnuts
- 2¾ cups all-purpose flour
- ½ cup seedless raspberry jam
- 2 egg whites
- ⅔ cup sugar

1. Preheat oven to 375°F. In a large mixing bowl beat butter with an electric mixer on medium to high speed for 30 seconds. Add the first ⅔ cup sugar, ½ teaspoon vanilla, and salt. Beat until combined, scraping sides of bowl. Beat in cream, ground nuts, and about half of the flour. Stir in remaining flour.
2. Shape dough in 1-inch balls. Place balls 1 inch apart on parchment-lined baking sheets. Using your thumb, make an indentation in the center of each ball. Fill each indentation with about ½ teaspoon jam; set aside.
3. For meringues, in a medium bowl beat egg whites with an electric mixer on high speed until soft peaks form. Gradually add remaining ⅔ cup sugar, about 1 tablespoon at a time, beating until stiff peaks form. Spoon mixture on filled balls, spreading to cover the jam.
4. Bake 12 to 14 minutes or until meringue is golden and set. Transfer to a wire rack and let cool completely.

MAKES ABOUT 50 COOKIES.

EACH COOKIE 96 cal, 5 g fat (3 g sat. fat), 11 mg chol, 36 mg sodium, 13 g carbo, 0 g fiber, 1 g pro. Daily Values: 3% vit. A, 2% iron.

RED WINE CAKE

PREP: 25 MIN. BAKE: 60 MIN. COOL: 20 MIN.
OVEN: 325°F

- 1 pkg. two-layer red velvet cake mix
- 1 4-serving size pkg. vanilla instant pudding and pie filling mix
- 4 eggs
- 1 cup water
- ½ cup cooking oil
- ¼ cup fruity red wine or cranberry juice
- 1 cup chopped pecans or walnuts
- 1½ cups powdered sugar
- 2 Tbsp. fruity red wine or cranberry juice

1. Preheat oven to 325°F. Grease and flour a 10-inch fluted tube pan; set aside.
2. In a large mixing bowl combine cake mix, pudding mix, eggs, water, oil, and ¼ cup wine. Beat with an electric mixer on low speed 30 seconds. Beat on medium speed 2 minutes (batter will be thick).
3. Sprinkle nuts in prepared pan. Spoon cake batter over nuts; spread evenly. Bake 60 to 70 minutes or until a toothpick inserted into the center comes out clean. Cool on a wire rack 20 minutes. Invert onto a serving platter.
4. In a medium bowl combine powdered sugar and wine or cranberry juice to make a glaze; spoon over cake.

MAKES 12 SERVINGS.

EACH SERVING 428 cal, 21 g fat (4 g sat. fat), 71 mg chol, 422 mg sodium, 59 g carbo, 1 g fiber, 4 g pro. Daily Values: 2% vit. A, 10% calcium, 7% iron.

recipe index

A

All-American Cheeseburger Soup, 28
ALMONDS
  Almond-Crusted Chicken, 109
  Blood Orange and Toasted Almond
    Couscous, 273
  health benefits, 106
Alphabet Cookies, 33
Alphabet Cupcakes, 33
Antipasto Pinwheels, 274
APPETIZERS. *See also* **DIPS AND**
SPREADS
  Antipasto Pinwheels, 274
  Avocado-Pesto Stuffed Tomatoes, 316
  Bacon-Peach Pinwheels, 316
  Blue Cheese and Bacon Mini Corn Dogs, 118
  Endive Satay Bites, 275
  Fontina-Stuffed Meatball Kabobs, 288
  Garden Sliders, 120
  Mini Tortilla Stacks, 317
  Peanut-Honey-Bacon Crunchies, 317
  Pecan-Bacon-Peach Appetizers, 316
  Shrimp Brochette with Chipotle Lime
    Cream, 317
  Smoked Salmon Toasts, 275
  Strawberry Fritters, 96
  Strawberry-Goat Cheese Bruschetta, 91
  Turkey Meatballs in Peach Sauce, 289
  Tuscan Cheesecake Bites, 317
Apple Cider Brine Pork Chops, 146
APPLES
  Apple-Glazed Pork Loaf, 217
  Apple Phyllo Dessert, 311
  Apples with Rutabaga Mash, 313
  Apple Tart with Hazelnuts and Blue
    Cheese, 311
  Beet and Apple Soup with Horseradish
    Cream, 30
  Caramel Apple Upside-Down Cornmeal
    Cake, 310
  Chutney-Style Apple Cobbler, 310
  Cinnamon-Apple Spice Cake, 240
  Personal Apple Pizzas, 311
  Pot of Gold Baked Apples, 311
  Steak with Blue Cheese and Apples, 305
APRICOTS
  Apricot-Cherry Cream Cheese Bread, 307
  Apricot Pork with Garlic Green Beans, 126
  Golden Grilled Chicken Thighs with
    Apricots, 296
  Passover Apricot Squares, 69
  Roast Loin of Pork Stuffed with Dried
    Apricots and Plums, 263
  Zesty Apricot Beef Stew, 281

ARTICHOKES
  Greek Lamb with Spinach and
    Artichokes, 278
  Strip Steak with Cheesy Artichoke
    Topper, 305
ARUGULA
  Olive and Arugula Flatbread Pizza Salad, 185
  Pear and Arugula Salad, 232
  Smoked Turkey Salad with Oranges, 272
Asian-Style Barbecue Ribs, 279
ASPARAGUS
  Green Green Spring Vegetables, 50
  Orange, Mint, and Asparagus Pasta
    Salad, 272
  Spring Green Risotto, 55
  Tender-Crisp Spring Braise, 73
Autumn Sangria, 204
AVOCADOS
  Avocado-Pesto Stuffed Tomatoes, 316
  Pepper-Avocado Omelet, 15
  Shrimp Brochette with Chipotle Lime
    Cream, 317

B

BACON
  Bacon, Egg, Spinach, and Tuna Salad, 191
  Bacon and Egg Pasta, 99
  Bacon-Peach Pinwheels, 316
  BLT Salad with Warm Vinaigrette, 126
  Blue Cheese and Bacon Mini Corn Dogs, 118
  Bread Pudding Quiche with Berries and
    Bacon, 78
  Corn Bread with Tomato-Bacon
    Ribbon, 291
  Peanut-Honey-Bacon Crunchies, 317
  Roasted Pumpkins with Bacon and Brown
    Sugar, 211
Baked Mozzarella and Tomato-Basil
  Antipasti, 186
Baking Powder, Homemade, 44
BANANAS
  Banana-Berry Jam, 95
  Bananas Foster Gelato, 302
  Caribbean Mashed Sweet Potatoes, 313
Barbecue Chicken with Raspberry Glaze, 297
Bar cookies. *See* Cookies and bars
Barley Salad and Tomato Vinaigrette, Lamb
  Chops with, 157
Basic Beef Bolognese, 20
BASIL
  Antipasto Pinwheels, 274
  Baked Mozzarella and Tomato-Basil
    Antipasti, 186

Basil Lemonade, 118
  Basil-Tomato Salad, 123
  Lemon Gremolata, 162
  Open-Face Pesto-Chicken Burgers, 296
  Spaghetti with Fresh Pesto, 182
Bass, Grilled, with Lemon and Herbs, 130
BEANS. *See also* **BLACK BEANS;**
GREEN BEANS; WHITE BEANS
  Chilled Cucumber-Chickpea Soup, 161
  Classic Succotash, 134
  Easy Succotash, 101
  Herbed Frittata with Edamame, 102
  Mediterranean Eggplant Dip, 186
  Mini Tortilla Stacks, 317
  Pork and Potato Stack, 99
  Shrimp, Chickpea, and Feta Cheese
    Nests, 181
  Southern Cobb Salad, 124
  Spicy Green Stir-Fry with Peanuts, 109
  Sweet and Tangy Four-Bean Salad, 115
BEEF
  All-American Cheeseburger Soup, 28
  Basic Beef Bolognese, 20
  Beef and Tapenade Open-Face
    Sandwiches, 65
  Beer-Braised Meatballs, 289
  Blue Cheese and Bacon Mini Corn Dogs, 118
  Braciole, 279
  Classic Meat Loaf, 66
  Corned Beef, Cabbage, Carrots, and New
    Potatoes, 247
  Cowboy Chuck Roast with Onion Gravy, 18
  Cowboy Steak Tacos, 269
  Easy Chili, 101
  Espresso-Rubbed Steak with Green Chile
    Pesto, 304
  Fireside Chili, 203
  Flank Steak with Mushrooms, 305
  Fontina-Stuffed Meatball Kabobs, 288
  Ginger-Beef Lettuce Wraps, 43
  Gingered Beef and Broccoli Salad Bowl, 105
  Grilled Steak, Cucumber, and Radish
    Salad, 305
  Grilled Steak and Onion Salad with Blue
    Cheese Toast, 151
  Italian Beef Sandwiches, 279
  Mini Meat Loaves with Green Beans, 36
  Nuevo Latino Short Ribs, 279
  Pan-Fried Garlic Steak and Potatoes, 188
  Peach-Horseradish Sauced Ribeyes, 304
  Pumpkin Black Bean Bake, 213
  Ranchero Beef Hash, 19
  Skillet Beef Tenderloin, 11
  Skillet Meat Loaf, 281
  Smoky Calzone, 21

D

G

H

M

N

Q

QUESADILLAS

R

S

SALAD DRESSINGS

SALADS